Post to Post:

Collecting Gems Along the Way

Book 5

By

Raydia Kelley & Jeannette Haley

Hidden Manna Publications

Post to Post 5: Collecting Gems Along the Way

GENTLE SHEPHERD MINISTRIES

www.gentleshepherd.com

ISBN: 979-8-9994555-2-9

Except where otherwise indicated, all Scripture quotations in this book are taken from the King James Version of the Bible.

Hidden Manna Publications

P.O. Box 3572

Oldtown, ID 83822

www.gentleshepherd.com

Facebook:

https://www.facebook.com/HiddenMannaPublications/

Contents

Introduction

This is the fifth book of the combined Facebook posts of authors Rayola Kelley and Jeannette Haley. These two authors are diverse in their writings, while providing interesting presentations that uncover various gems that include personal experiences and insights comprised of lessons learned through trials, wisdom gained in experiences, and spiritual truths unveiled in practical ways.

As believers we are on a journey through a challenging world, but we can take heart. The Lord has provided the necessary gems of truth and wisdom in His Word, His creation, and examples that enriches the pilgrim's travels regardless of how dark the way or how lean and barren the times may be when there is no hope in sight.

The purpose of these devotions is to uncover Scriptural gems that are obscured by shadows and darkness due to man's limited understanding as well as the world's propensity for perverting what is pure, true, and righteous. These devotions are simple, yet they reveal heavenly-inspired, profound wisdom that is life-changing to those who assimilate and walk out their truths.

The prayers of the authors are that the reader will begin to collect gems along the way for themselves that will give them glimpses into their heavenly inheritance, enrich their testimonies, and prepare them to enter into the eternal bliss of all of God's promises.

January

January 1

"And the hope maketh not ashamed; because the love of God is shed abroad in our hearts by the Holy Ghost which is given unto us" (Romans 5:5) I was thinking of salvation. We have entered another year. Perhaps some are looking back at last year to evaluate the significance of it when it comes to their lives. It is easy to overlook the pressing issues of today in lieu of another new year, but where are we spiritually?

As you consider the great plight of humanity in a world that is becoming darker with the most insane, abominable practices that are being literally flaunted in our faces, you realize that something has gone terribly awry with the powerful message of the cross. There seems to be a mishmash of religious nonsense that is worldly, unscriptural and clearly missing the mark of the high calling a believer has in Christ Jesus.

To me the real test comes down to the type of burden one has for those who are lost. It seems there are few who know of, or speak of justification, because all sin has been and is being properly addressed in their lives according to Scriptures. Meanwhile the work of sanctification is totally absent from preaching in many pulpits where the preacher is stressing that the life of Christ in us is being set apart by an inner work of the Spirit to reflect the glory of heaven. As a result, the revelation of redemption seems far from many who claim they belong to the kingdom of God.

We can talk about the love of God without really knowing and experiencing His love. It is the love of God that compels us to carry out our commission to reach the lost with the true Gospel because it has put an incredible spotlight on the redemption that was paid by the sacrifice of Jesus Christ. It is the love of God that is eternal and far reaching, capable of reaching high enough to meet us in our search and go far enough to find us. We must never be content to settle for just barely enough so that we fail to strive for what is excellent according to the righteousness of God.

Prayer: Lord, we miss much because we do not expect much when it comes to our Christian life. There is no anticipation in hope that is waning because God's love is missing, the heavenly vision dimmed by disillusionment of the world, and love is rendered ineffective because it has become caught up with the nonsense of this life. Oh Lord, how we often need to be revived by Your Spirit. Amen.

January 2

"For though I preach the gospel, I have nothing to glory of: for necessity is laid upon me; yea, woe is unto me, if I preach not the gospel" (1 Corinthians 9:16). If our presence here is all about us being saved, then why not take us home so we can bypass the terrible "Ts" of this world: Temptations, tribulations, troubles, and grave testing of our faith?

The answer comes down to the "Cs" of our spiritual life: Commission, calling, and consecration. We have a commission to preach the Gospel so others can be saved. We have a calling to ensure that God's plan of bringing forth the kingdom of heaven on earth in the hearts of others is established through the message of redemption and discipleship. To accomplish this we must consecrate our lives to the call to make sure that we bring glory to Him. Anything outside of these three "Cs" will prove to be a vain exercise of nothing.

The truth is that if one's past fails to lead to the cross of Christ and His redemption, it will be used as an indictment against them because their sins have not been dealt with before a holy God who can't look upon such offense without judging it. We can look to the future but unless our life in Christ overshadows it with His great light and promise of a real place that is full of worship of, and service to, a holy deserving God, who is our creator, we have no real hope.

We can ignore the present as we operate in wishful thinking that all is well for those who have gone on before us. It must also be well for us because there is a consensus that there is a God and some type of heaven that has been made for man's pleasure so that man, regardless of how he lived here on earth, without any real consideration of God can fulfill his deepest desire.

Heaven is not about man but God. It is not what man has been promised, but the environment in which God resides in His untarnished glory. It is a place of worship, not pleasure, a place of adoration for the holy and not exaltation of the unholy, a place where man's soul is truly at peace with God and is in harmony with His Spirit, plan, and will.

True salvation is all about man being pulled from the grasp, claims, and power sin has over his life. Redemption is about man's destiny, and the cross about man's hope, but heaven is about man fulfilling his highest of all callings, to truly worship and serve his wonderful Creator in Spirit and in truth.

Prayer: Lord, it is natural to try to make paradise down here, but the truth is without You there is no paradise to be found. It is Your presence that makes everything right for those who are Your people. Amen.

January 3

"For he saith, I have heard thee in a time accepted, and in the day of salvation that I succoured thee: behold, now is the accepted time; behold, now is the day of salvation" (2 Corinthians 6:2). Paul's great concern for every soul is that they realize the seriousness of their

journey here. It is appointed unto man to die once then judgment, a judgment that can't be reversed past the physical stage of this life on earth. The truth is every soul needs to be saved from spiritual death or separation from God due to their sins. Although heaven clearly marks the destination of the saint, it is the presence, majesty and glory of God that makes heaven, heaven.

Paul makes it clear that today is the day of salvation. Salvation of the soul is one of the most urgent calls of not only our time, but in each passing and new generation. We as believers can get caught up with so many biblical debates but when it comes right down to the real crux of a matter it will always come back to the same reality, and that is we are constantly contending for the well-being of souls.

Whether we are trying to pull some poor soul out the clutches of hell with warnings, challenge the struggling soul to come out and be separate from that which is destructive to their soul with truth, or trying to awake or alert an unsuspecting soul as to the dangers ahead with great urgency, it all comes back to the condition of one's soul as to how they meet and stand before their Creator and Judge of us all.

It is not God's will that any perish in their sins, but all come to repentance. Repentance is truly turning from sins to face our God. It is the Lord who wants to, and is able to reason, address, cleanse and redeem each of us from sin's claims, hold, and judgments made on and towards our souls.

Prayer: Lord, there is so much that we Christians can get caught up with when it comes to the world, but the real test is how much am I caught up with You, how much concern do I have for the lost souls of the world and the struggling souls of the household of faith? Give me a heart for the lost, as well as loving, caring ways for those struggling in their spiritual lives. Amen.

January 4

In the longest part of winter, I often look at what is coming by considering what continues to live in spite of the cold of winter taking hold of the landscape. Once I do, a warm glow of happiness rises up in my heart that proves to be pleasantly surprising. After all, it is still overcast and cold, but those two little potted rosemary plants I found and purchased in a local grocery store somehow exuded the amazing miracle of life and hope that accompanies spring.

At the same time, in spite of a bitterly cold winter that always seemed to last far too long, bright green shoots in a flowerbed will soon enough produce a few crocuses, while the promise of nearby tulips will make their appearance as they grow by the day. Two lilac bushes that looked hopelessly dead will be producing leaf buds, and other bushes as well.

All of this serves to remind me that no matter how unspeakably horrific the works of the "god of this world" are in these latter days, God is still in control, His eternal Word still stands as truth, and His promises never fail. Therefore, those of us who belong to the LORD Jesus Christ have sure and everlasting promises such as *Psalm 30:5, "For his anger endureth but a moment; in his favour is life; weeping may endure for a night, but joy cometh in the morning,"* and *Revelation 21:4, "And God shall wipe away all tears from their eyes; and there shall be no more death, neither sorrow, nor crying, neither shall there be any more pain: for the former things are passed away."* Hallelujah! – J. Haley

Prayer: Lord, the winter may seem long, but life around me reminds me that it will not last forever. This is true for our Christian walk. The cold may cause my life in You to feel dormant, but Your Spirit reminds me that Your work of regeneration never ceases. Amen.

January 5

"Rejoiceth not in iniquity, but rejoiceth in the truth (1 Corinthians 13:6)." What is your greatest concern about the religious environment of today? We could point out various aspects of it such as the great darkness of wickedness and the vexation caused by the unspeakable evil that has been perpetrated against humanity behind the guises of various philosophies such as "political correctness", "tolerance" and

the latest being "Woke." We could talk about how much the world has encroached into churches and how the leaven is leavening the whole lump in ways that we would have never imagined, and yet if we are living in the days of Noah, what can we expect when we are told that the imagination in that day was continually evil.

It is all overwhelming. When we think it can't get any worse, greater abominations are being flaunted even in "so-called" Christian denominations, and sadly much of it is done in the name of "love." Such love is not a godly love for it will never rejoice in iniquity. Godly love is honorable and will not sit idly by when one is on the path of destruction. It prefers the well-being of others over itself and will not lower itself to get along with those who are walking the broad path to hell. Godly love demands excellence in attitude towards others, in conduct before others, and in lieu of it being shed abroad in our hearts by the Holy Spirit so we can walk in it.

To most the opposite of love is hatred when it is not the case. To hate someone, you had to have some type of emotion aroused to even rise up in such opposition. Hatred comes out of fear that can be founded on conditioned prejudices of others, the ignorance of the unknown, the unusual, or rejection, as well as unabated jealousies and insecurities.

However, another sign of hatred is indifference. Godly love can't help but to genuinely care, but indifference is a demonic passivity where emotions are closed to avoid acting on a matter. It can't afford to be aroused and take a definite stand for truth against sin or a wrong committed or feeling any righteous indignation against unrighteousness. Behind indifference is a cold heart towards the matters of God. If there is any façade of religion where a cold heart exists, it is simply hiding the sin of unbelief, while often becoming a form of deception to the person wearing the mask.

Prayer: Lord my heart can grow cold because I do not believe You or Your Word; instead, I choose to believe what I see, feel, and think. I know that if I let the old man run amuck in me without the application of the cross and godly discipline of Your truth, others will see that I am not all that religious and I will lose face. Lord, I'd rather lose the religious mask and turn in true repentance to face my cold heart in lieu of Your warm, embracing love of forgiveness and grace to avoid missing You in the end. Amen.

January 6

"And because iniquity shall abound, the love of many shall wax cold" (Matthew 24:12). It seems lately I have been waking up when I have been speaking some type of truth or exhortation to some faceless individual. I always must consider if what I am speaking is for my personal edification or am I to share it or both? One morning, I woke up with a question. It goes like this, "What will you lose when compromising in small ways?"

It is easy to slowly compromise with the things of the world. We always think we can handle it. After all, we are intelligent and are wise enough to know how to handle such matters without being taken in by lies. However, the truth is that those small compromises are conditioning us to accept greater compromise.

Compromise is like a little seed that once it is given some type of infusion, it begins to develop roots here and there. Although it may seem harmless enough in the landscape of our thinking, it is like a weed that will choke out the truth as to the dangerous hold it can take on our lives. It may even have some beautiful looking bloom on the top of it, but it is still a noxious weed to our spiritual lives and must be confronted before it overtakes the garden of our heart.

The question is what will we lose when compromising in small ways? The answer is our integrity. For the Christian that integrity is tied to their faith. Job had integrity and refused to compromise his faith because he knew what he knew about God, and regardless of what was thrown at him, everything outside of his faith towards God was a lie that would eventually be exposed as such.

Compromise is a choice and regardless of how small a seed it is, it will ultimately defile what is true, pure, and acceptable to God.

Prayer: Lord, I would like to think I am smart enough, wise enough, and intelligent enough to not let compromise be a weed that overtakes me. But if I am so wise about such matters, why am I planting this noxious seed in my spiritual life in the first place knowing that it will only produce tares that take up valuable space, defile what is pure, and choke out what is true? Forgive me for my high-minded arrogance. Amen.

January 7

"But the word of the Lord endureth for ever. And this is the word which by the gospel is preached unto you" (1 Peter 1:25). I became a Christian in 1976. At the time of being newly saved, I attended churches that had church pews, hymnals, pianos, and organs, and people brought their Bibles because they were encouraged to open them and learned what was in them and how to handle the Word properly. Even though I initially grew up in a cult, there was a time when my mother was in search of what was real and true, and we all attended a small community church. At the time, I had a certain incentive to attend Sunday School so I could receive a Bible.

I remember the day I did receive that Bible at age 11 almost 60 years ago. Since I was a girl, I was given a white covered KJV of the Bible. I still have that Bible to this day and I can tell you the name of my Sunday School teacher who has gone on to glory, his name was Horace Patterson.

To me that Bible is more precious than ever. It reminds me of the seeds from others that God used to plant in my life. When I was saved, I returned to that small community church and received valuable foundational teaching.

That small church which sat on the hill that housed so much history for me and the community has been turned into a house, along with another church I also attended in the same area. Granted one church was replaced with a better facility, but the other one closed for good.

We are not to worship a building, we call a "church." After all, many attend a building because it is referred to as a "church" regardless of what they teach. Such buildings often proved to be auditoriums and not sanctuaries of prayer and worship. However, in my years of being a Christian I have been in buildings that truly proved to be a place of worship that showed me how a true sanctuary functioned, and that what made it as such were the people in it.

There are church bodies, and then there is the Church who is the body of Christ. The church body can be an organized group of people who hold to a certain tradition and way, but the body of Christ is universal, and its goal is to ensure that it is lining up to the head, Jesus Christ, by loving the purity and absolute authority of God's Word.

Prayer: Lord, we have accepted many substitutes in our lives, and as a result we struggle with what is real and lasting. I am so thankful that your real Church is not a lifeless building, but a living organism that houses Your Spirit and reflects the life and glory of its true Head. Thank You for being the head, putting in me a new Spirit and heart to know You and the means to follow You into a new life. Amen.

January 8

"That he might present it to himself a glorious church, not having spot, or wrinkle, or any such thing; but that it should be holy and without blemish" (Ephesians 5:27). How many of us long for the "old days." We sometimes sit and reminisce on fond memories and then we begin to lament over what is clearly missing. When I think of the newness of the Christian life, I do sometimes wish for that initial naiveness that caused me to look at the Christian walk through fanciful lens, but then I remember what God had to do to "grow me up" into the Head of the Body, Jesus Christ. I must admit, I love the result, but I could live without having to experience all of the growing pains.

It is as I study the life of the saints that have gone on before me and read about the ones who are presently suffering persecution because of their faith, I realize that in this world Christians can expect to meet with trouble and challenges. As I consider the Church, we are told it will be presented without spot and wrinkle, and that points to a process of cleansing which can be intense. It involves hanging it out to dry which makes it subject to the elements and ironing out the wrinkles that involves heat.

When we consider those who came before us, they came to the sanctuary for one purpose. I referred to this because many in Christendom in America come to a building to be entertained and made to be left feeling good about a substandard Christianity that simply gets them by with some surface religious encounter. The saints refined in fire came for one purpose and that was to meet with God, exalt Him with praise, worship Him with their heart, and honor Him with their devotion.

A meeting place with God was to be sacred, a time of worship. It was to produce reverence, while anointed preaching was to bring about repentance from the sinner, rededication from half-hearted Christians, a renewed vision for the weary Christians, and growth for struggling Christians.

Perhaps some would refer to such a time as "that Old Time Religion" that would seem outdated, obsolete, or foolish to the trend of modern-day Christianity, but for me I am so thankful I have witnessed such religion. I know that when I think of that church on the hill that I mentioned in my last post, it was not the building itself that is dear to me, but the work God did in me during my time there. It was not old but new. It was not obsolete but exciting and fresh. It was not outdated; rather it was much needed.

There is something else about that "Old Time Religion" and that it continues to serve as a living, viable witness of what has always been true and continues to be true. It will also remain as so when all the religious trends that were adjusted to attract the worldly masses instead of hungry, thirsty souls will fall and become part of the dust of vanity that will be taken away with the winds of judgment. As the song goes, you can "Give me that Old-time Religion" every time over the religious trends of today.

Prayer: Lord, it is natural to get caught up with the shiny new things and methods of the world, but what You have provided through redemption is new every day to a soul that needs to be revived by Your life, refreshed by Your Spirit, and inspired with a greater revelation of You. Lord, I choose what is real, sure, and promised because it meets me where I am each day and prepares me to come face to face with You in eternity. Amen.

January 9

Your glorying is not good. Know ye not that a little leaven leaveneth the whole lump? (1 Corinthains 5:6). What has happened to the Church? In a recent post, I talked about individual compromise, but has the visible church made any compromise and if so, how has it affected it?

Congregations are now called audiences. Instead of the distinction that one has come into a place of worship and prayer, it appears that many are coming to a place of entertainment with the best sound system, lighting system, and the latest chorus songs that they can swing and jump to. Don't get me wrong the true worshippers know how to become closed in with God to truly bring Him honor and glory in sweet communion, but my concern is what attitude is being established in those who have never been exposed to that "Old Time Religion?"

Regardless of the times we live in, God has not changed and neither has His truth, His method, or His ways. His truth can't be adjusted to the philosophies of the times to embrace every type of abomination because He will never cease to be holy. It is important to point out that we can't see the Lord without holiness and that His holiness is the type of transparency that is a consuming fire when it comes to that which is not holy. All I have to do to confirm this simple fact is to mention two names: Nadab and Abihu, the two sons of

Aaron that offered strange fire before the Lord in *Leviticus 10:1-3* and were struck down.

It has been clear for a while that the visible church has greatly compromised with the world. It has adopted methods in which to attract numbers. It has developed schemes in which to appear successful to the world. It has instituted worldly practices to entertain the crowd. The Bible is clear that we are to come out and be separate from that which is profane. It has also made it clear that the world is the enemy of God, and that if the love of the world is in us, the love of the Father will not be in us.

What will a church lose by compromising with the world's ways and means? It will lose its soul, its ability to interact with God, stand in the storms and in the gap. It will not reach the heart of the seeking soul with truth, serve as a conduit of healing to the wounded, and present the keys that will set the captive free. Ultimately, it will fail to be part of the great move of God in the harvest field to bring in the sheep of His fold into a place of salvation, safety, and rest.

We must remember that God's only method are people who are open to His Spirit. They are willing to be used in whatever manner or way He chooses and will adhere to their heavenly calling no matter the obstacle. It is the saints that make up the real church. These saints are believers that comprise the living Body of Christ, and we know that when it comes to this church, the true assembly that has been called out of this world and this age, that the gates of hell will not prevail against it.

Prayer: Lord, Your Church is to stand distinct from the world and not be marked as a successful corporation, trend, or movement. Such a miserable combination speaks of surface religion that hides hypocrisy, dead-letter doctrine, self-righteous garments, and a lifeless tomb. Amen.

January 10

"And Jesus stood..." (Luke 18:40). In the posts where I talked about missing that "Old Time Religion," my friend, Jeannette, made a

comment about the presence of God that I summarized in the following sentence. The 'Old Time Religion' included reverence before God, sound doctrinal hymns that caused the mind to reach beyond the present, the soul to take flight in the Spirit in praise towards God, and the spirit to be uncapped with His purifying and refreshing Living Waters. It is His presence among us that allows Him to honor His people. It clearly identifies His distinction and glory as God.

God's presence is what was necessary to ensure real ministry, praise, and worship. He must stand in our presence to ensure humble, adoring worship. Without God's presence there is no place of agreement with Him. And if it is missing, God's people might as well go home because they can't do business with God and God can't do business with them.

This is the main problem in most church building, few come to do business with God. They come to soothe religious conscience, to do their religious duty for the week, to please spouses, reluctantly set examples to their children, and give a pious impression to onlookers but their hearts are far from God.

A building that houses the real Church must be a place of prayer and intercession, a hospital for the wounded, a sanctuary for the lost to be found, a refuge for the weary, and the place of an altar where those seeking mercy can grab hold of it until they know all is well between them and their God. It must be a place where God can do business with His people.

Sadly, there are those like the children of Israel that assume God must honor them with His presence and blessings because they have some religious token such as their form of worship. They also have a certain take on doctrine, while taking pride in their religious deeds and rituals, and like the ark, these practices have been arrogantly put on display to verify their importance.

The Ark of the Covenant represented the presence of God in the children of Israel's midst, and they felt God would surely honor them with a victory if they would cause it to pass before their enemy. However, God does not have to honor any such token if there is a flippant attitude towards what He has deemed sacred.

Prayer: Lord, thank You for being my Ark, a place of safety, peace, and communion. Amen.

January 11

"And she named the child Ichabod saying, The glory is departed from Israel: because the ark of God was taken, and because of her father and husband" (1 Samuel 4:21). Flippancy is one of the major attitudes you can distinguish from those who are simply trying to get by as they keep demanding monsters at bay that stirs conscience, challenges the sense of righteousness, and rocks religious boats.

This flippancy was obvious in the blatant sins in the priesthood at that time. The High Priest Eli warned his sons about their wicked ways but took no action to discipline them and remove them from the priesthood because he was complacent towards God's holiness.

It is important to point out why Eli turned a blind eye to his sons' sins. It is because he benefitted from them. The sons kept the best of the meat with the fat that was to belong to the Lord and shared it with their father who enjoyed eating it.

This is the big problem with many who are part of the religious world. They pick and choose when to stand and how to stand when it comes to sin.

Sin bribes, blinds, and causes one to bow before it when they lack the integrity to stand against it in their own lives by fleeing its temptation. The more one gives way to sin in this manner, the more they lose any authority to speak into the lives of others about it and the consequences that will follow.

God cannot look on the unholy without judging it, and in many cases, He will withdraw His presence and leave those who are being foolish to their own devices to keep them from tasting the fullness of His wrath. His withdrawal is a type of judgment where the reins of grace are removed to let the troubled waters of circumstances roll in, ending in the people tasting the bitter fruit of its consequences.

Prayer: Lord we are foolish to think that we can sow the seeds of the flesh and not reap the whirlwind of consequences and judgment. Forgive us for being foolish in our thinking and ways. Set us free to soar in the liberty of Your Spirit. Amen.

January 12

Sometimes you win, and sometimes you lose when it comes to ordering stuff advertised online. Well, my last gamble didn't pay off and I should've known better than to try for an "end run" around the formidable "system."

The entrenched "system" I'm referring to is one of the tentacles of the monstrous, impersonal, "gotcha," "make-heap-big-money" medical system, and in this particular case it involved vision—that is, eyeballs. Even in the good old days when all you had to do was choose which lens you could see the clearest through as the optometrist flipped them back and forth, I still felt faint, so you can just imagine how I feel in the new way of doing things.

Nowadays, in order to get a new pair of glasses, you are forced to suffer through horrible eyedrops that dilate your pupils for at least 12 hours, along with some other goop that makes everything blurry so that when asked to read itsy bitsy letters on a wall 15 feet away, you cannot. On top of that, even though we're told to never look directly at the sun, you find yourself feeling as helpless as a trapped deer tangled up in a barbed wire fence as lights brighter than the sun penetrate into your brain and probably shine out of the back of your head.

Somehow you end up numbly stumbling out the door without ever having had the opportunity of being tested by the apparently out-of-date method of choosing which is "clearest." All you know is you need one of two things—invasive and out-of-this-world expensive surgery (according to the experts), OR a miracle from the Great Physician. Well, that is a no-brainer for me!

Since my new glasses are no better than my old ones, when an ad came along for adjustable eyeglasses that are supposed to work whether you're far-sighted, or near-sighted, I decided to give them a try. Here's the thing, when they finally arrived, the accompanying instructions were in print so small a gnat couldn't even see them, and then when we figured it out, they didn't work for me anyway.

It makes you wonder about these days—do people even think just a little? Sometimes all you can do is laugh at the whole somewhat insane situation and rejoice in the Lord because nothing is too hard or impossible for Him. Nothing is greater or more powerful than He is, and nothing can snatch us out of His hands. *"Be merciful unto me, O God, be merciful unto me: for my soul trusteth in thee: yea, in the shadow of thy wings will I make my refuge, until these calamities be overpast. I will cry unto God most high; unto God that performeth all things for me" (Psalm 57:1, 2).* – J. Haley

Prayer: Lord, we will continue to prove to be losers and failures if we do things our way in this life. It is when we line up to Your way that we will begin to taste sweet victory over the flesh, the world, and Satan. Amen.

January 13

"And it shall come to pass in that day, saith the LORD of hosts, that I will cut off the names of the idols out of the land, and they shall no more be remembered: and also I will cause the prophets and the unclean spirit to pass out of the land" (Zechariah 13:2). In one of my last posts, I talked about how the people of Israel made assumptions about the Ark of the Covenant. This ark represented the presence of God. The priests felt it would protect them regardless of being in sin, and the children of Israel felt if it led them, they would have victory, but a token means nothing if the covenant, blessings or promises attached to it are not being honored in a proper way. As a result of their assumption, the Israelites lost the ark.

The biggest reason for such a great loss was because God was not with them in the first place. It is important to know God does not have to defend His reputation when man's foolishness reigns because He will have the last word by showing Himself to be God in the judgment that often follows such foolishness.

Our tendency is to think that if we are adhering to all the religious ways, then God will be with us, when in reality if one is not honoring God in the right way, He will not be in the midst of what is being done in His name. When sin reigns, whether it is in the priesthood or leadership, God presence will be missing, as His glory departs from that which is profane to Him.

When it came to the Philistines, they presumed they had defeated and silenced the God of Israel. It is important to recognize most idols were given power based on the strength and victories of the armies that honored them. We can understand why the Philistines had no regard for the Ark of the Covenant and took it to the temple of their idol as a trophy,

What happened with these ignorant individuals who held to such assumptions and presumptions? Well, they had to learn a very hard lesson. The Philistines' god, Dagon was brought down before the ark, not once but twice, losing its hands and its head. Not only was their idol brought down, but the Philistines started to have some unpleasant physical challenges, and the ark became a hot potato as it was passed between their communities.

The reality is God will not be mocked. Idols will be brought down and flippancy will turn into sobriety. Sobriety will turn into silence even if men rage inside, and in the end the fear of the Lord will fall on all, including fools.

Prayer: Lord, we think You will tolerate and ignore idolatry and the profane practices it brings with it, but in the end it all will be judged. Forgive us for minimizing who You need to be in our life. Amen.

January 14

"And he smote the men of Bethsemesh because they had looked into the ark of the LORD…. And the men of Bethshemesh said, Who is able to stand before this holy LORD God? and to whom shall he go up from us?" (1 Samuel 6:19a, 20). It is easy to understand why the pagan idolators were casual towards the Ark of the Covenant, but we

also see flippancy on the part of the people of Israel when the ark was returned. They looked inside the forbidden ark without any regard as to the strict instructions that were given to the priests concerning the handling of it.

When it came to the men that looked inside of the Ark of the Covenant, they were struck dead and what about the priesthood who did not regard God's warnings? The rebellious sons of Eli were killed when moving the ark to lead the people in battle, and when the old priest heard of the ark being taken, Eli fell backwards and broke His neck. After giving birth to Eli's grandson, the mother died.

The result is summarized in the name of the child, "Ichabod," *"The glory is departed from Israel: for the ark of God is taken" (1 Samuel 4:22)*. The question I must ask is how many churches in America are missing the presence of God because of profane leadership, flippant attitudes, and the inroads the enemies of the cross and truth have made? God's presence in such an evil mixture can't be found because His glory has departed.

This brings us to the real question of how many in such lifeless institutions are even aware that He is missing because there is no real distinction of the holy ever being there because the unholy has been embraced, labeled as religious, assumed as being acceptable, and presumed that God is in it because there is some mere token that has long ago lost its luster in the midst of the profane, the casual, and the common practices of the flesh and the world?

Prayer: Lord, we fail to realize that for You to be in our midst the environment must be holy for if it is not, You must depart out of mercy or judgment will fall. Lord, forgive us for making that which You have entrusted to us common so that it fails to stand distinct, flippant so we can mishandle it without fear of repercussions, and become casual with it so that You must withdraw Yourself from all of it to avoid judging it. Send the fire Lord, to purge, purify, and revive your sheep once again. Amen.

January 15

"For there are certain men crept in unawares, who were before of old ordained to this condemnation, ungodly men, turning the grace of our God into lasciviousness, and denying the only Lord God, and our Lord Jesus Christ" (Jude 4). In the book of Jude, we see him contending with the sanctified who somehow let ungodly men in to operate among the congregation (*Jude 1*). These men were in it to heap upon their own lusts what they could take from the sheep regardless of what condition they left them in.

This brings me to a point of self-examination as one who knows I have been set apart by the Lord with His Spirit and life. Am I ignoring the ungodly in my midst. When it comes to God, what are we as a body willing to settle for to have our religious conscious and desire for some semblance of worship temporarily satisfied?

Are we willing to put up with the wolves by giving them open season to prey on the vulnerable in the congregations, and the hireling the opportunity to fleece the sheep some more? Will we keep open the door of lifeless churches that have become nothing more than tombs? Let's face it, there are many empty church buildings and where have all the people gone?

Meanwhile, what is happening to the true shepherds? Are they being overlooked due to being uncompromising with truth and perhaps overused because the people are complacent and have no vision outside of self. Maybe they have been out used because they will not give way to the trends, and abused because they stand for what is right which is considered outdated, unloving, and foolish?

In *Ezekiel 10:18*, we see where the glory of the Lord departed from His own temple due to the idolatrous sins of the priests and the people. Granted, the worship of idols was done in secret places, mainly the imagination of the people's minds where all idols must first be exalted. However, the worship done in the secret chambers was a stumbling block to the heart of the people and the worship of the imagination done in high places demoted the glory of God in their minds (*Ezekiel 8:11-12; 14:3-5*).

It appears as if the visible Church is under judgment as more and more leaders fall and more and more church buildings are being closed. Even though empty church buildings speak of some great breakdown within our religious institutions, it also speaks of the real church, the body of Jesus, coming out and being separate from lifeless institutions.

Although we may not see it, God is always refining His people in secret to come forth as the chaste bride of His Son. It is not only a great work, but a deeper work of preparation to ensure that the gates of hell will not prevail against it.

Prayer: Lord, we get caught up with the world's religious way of keeping people from realizing their highest calling. Thank You that You are always calling out Your people, the true church to come out and be separate from the fleshly, the worldly, and the temporary ways of this age. Amen.

January 16

"Then the glory of the LORD departed from the threshold of the house, and stood over the cherubims" (Ezekiel 10:18). In Ezekiel we see God's glory departed from the temple to hover over and distinguish that which is holy, but what about the individual?

As believers we are temples of God; We house the presence of His Holy Spirit. Will the Spirit depart from us if there is sin? King David made this statement in his prayer of repentance after his sin, *"Cast me not away from thy presence; and take not they holy spirit from me" (Psalm 51:11).* Clearly, what is holy can't maintain its integrity in the midst of sin.

Consider the likes of fleshly Samson. He was under a Nazirite vow which was mainly manifested by the outward token of uncut hair. His authority, strength, and power came from the Spirit of the Lord and were attached to the vow, but his uncut hair was the symbol that he was identified to it. However, because of his sin of fornication, his hair was cut when he was asleep.

When the enemy came to apprehend Samson, he assumed he still had the strength and power to overcome, but he did not. Sadly, he was so dumbed down by the unholy environment and put to sleep by his sin that he was unaware when the Lord withdrew from him, leaving him to taste the foolish consequences of his unrighteous ways (*Judges 16:17-20*). Like the lusts that made Samson close his eyes to his sin in the first place, causing him to become a servant to it, the enemy also destroyed his eyesight that caused him to lust after Delilah, and made him their slave.

We are warned in *Genesis 6:3* that the Spirit of God will not always strive with us. It is time for we as believers to see the seriousness of our times, be realistic about any subdued attitudes towards truth and holiness, while ignoring sin among us, and awake out of worldly, religious environments. We need to repent of any complacency towards the matters of God's kingdom, take up the sword of His Word and as true disciples follow Jesus into the overcoming, victorious life He is calling us too.

Prayer: Lord we foolishly toy with the unholy in our hearts, exalt the possibilities of it in our imaginations, and parlay with the lusts that are stirred up, while wearing a veneer of religion that the rest of the religious world can buy when it comes to the welfare of the soul. However, You see the hypocrisy of the heart, the wicked imaginations of the mind, and the lusts that are taking us captive to serve the flesh. We need to do as Your Word states: to come out and be separate from the world, crucify the lusts of the flesh, and submit all to You knowing the devil will flee. Amen.

January 17

"I am come that they might have life, and that they might have it more abundantly" (John 10:10:b). Who are you? Why are you here? What is your purpose here? How we answer these questions will determine who we become, whether we have direction or we are aimless. It will show us if we possess true hope that is founded on the eternal or

holding on to wishful thinking that swings from fanciful notions that eventually will collide with some reality.

So much of my initial identity was founded on family influences, cultural conditioning, and Hollywood. My gender determined much of my understanding about myself as family encouraged me towards certain preferences, while culture pin holed me according to it, and religion told me my place because of these preferences. I did not realize that these influences were giving the world the means to define who I needed to be to be accepted and to belong in Satan's systems. Eventually it all led me to a confusing mess that I tried to wade through, only to find myself being consumed by it all.

Who we are will come down to the life we possess. Why we are here will come down to the life we are pursuing, and what our purpose is for being here will be based on the philosophy about God and the life we adopt. I admit, I was lost in the vacuum that the world creates. It is empty of real meaning and purpose. The world presents a veneer of attractive but false promises that once you have pursued them, tasted them, and experienced them, you find yourself dissatisfied, disillusioned, and miserable because nothing makes sense.

When I met Jesus, He began to answer all of my questions about my existence. I found my life, purpose and identity in Him. It took me a few years of growing up in Him to understand that He is my all in all. It was Jesus who came to give me life and to give it abundantly.

When we receive Jesus as Savior and Lord we receive His life. As we grow in the knowledge of Jesus, we begin to walk in His life to walk it out. As we walk in His life, we begin to experience the abundance that His life will bring us, and as we walk it out, we discover the abundant fruitfulness of His life that will become sweet and satisfying to others.

Prayer: Lord, I can let everything else define me, but if I do, I will become lost in something that is void of identity. Lord, You are my Creator and You know who I am and who I can be. Have Your way Lord and be glorified in my life. Amen.

January 18

"For we can do nothing against the truth, but for the truth" (2 Corinthians 13:5). When it comes to the truth of God, there are just a few things we must remember about it.

1) Truth is eternal. When all other beliefs, philosophies, and theologies lie in utter judgment and ruin, truth will remain standing. In fact, it will judge all other realities that prove to be contrary to it as being a fallacy.
2) Truth is trustworthy. Granted, it may be sharp for it is meant to circumcise the heart. It is blunt for it is meant to awaken our spirits, and it is like a hammer that will shatter what is faulty to nail down what is right.
3) The truth is also a fire that purges, cleanses, and liberates a person's soul from bondage. But in the end, it will prove to be the only trustworthy stake or standard that one can trust.
4) Finally, truth is simple. It is summarized in two words: Jesus Christ. Truth is not an intellectual notion, a religious stance, or a philosophy; rather, it is a person. Jesus is God in the flesh. As a result, nothing can silence or do away with the truth. All one can do is stand on it, stand for it, and withstand with it.

Prayer: Lord, we are so thankful for Your unchangeable truth. We so love You because You will never be moved from who You are. You are the eternal, the unchanging manifestation of truth to this world. Amen.

January 19

"For we know that the whole creation groaneth and travaileth in pain together until now" (Romans 8:22). We live in a world that is designed for destruction. It is dying and all creation moans underneath the great weight of a curse and sin. The god of this world, Satan, uses every device to spoil what is true, pure, and righteous. We know that

he is both a liar and a murderer. He has no intention of playing fair in this world. He has clearly come to use his systems to rob us, his designs to murder any witness of God, and his means to destroy any essence of life, truth, and righteousness.

It is amazing what damage the enemy does, but he is able to bring such destruction because there are instruments in this world who are open to do his bidding that are divisive, accusing and slanderous. His great goal is to divide so he can conquer. However, there is one thing that can stop his advancements: the Word of God. There is one thing that can cause him to flee: a believer that draws near to God and humbles themself. There is one thing that can silence all accusations: God's truth and man's repentance and confession when it comes to sin.

It has become obvious to me that if people do it God's way, they avoid many pitfalls, but many Christians fail to obey what the Bible says. Some of it could be ignorance but most of it is stiff-necked rebellion. Such rebellion comes down to a person wanting the world and their way more than the Lord.

We are living in the time when Satan will wreck his havoc and revenge on the world for his time is short. We need to be watchmen over our souls, guard the entrances of our sanctuaries, and be on alert that we are called to be soldiers, not just church-goers, pew warmers, or debaters of the Word but soldiers who know how to stand by the authority of their commander, withstand with their weapon, and continue to stand because if they don't, they will never know victory.

Prayer: Lord, only Your Spirit can unveil the mystery behind Your simple truths, adding profound insights that can make the spirit soar above this world, and the soul rejoice in adoring worship. Amen.

January 20

It's not always the big miracles that bring a sense of awe into our hearts, but it's oftentimes the little things that unexpectedly take place. Not long ago, the three of us ladies of Gentle Shepherd

Ministries were blessed in a way that left no doubt whatsoever but that the LORD had arranged all the details.

You see, one situation we always have a struggle with is trying to keep our two-car garage organized and somewhat neat, at least so we can get one car parked inside. Along with two freezers, and an old refrigerator, there is a big pantry and lots of shelving for food and kitchen items because our small kitchen appears to be an afterthought.

The big items like the riding lawnmower, push mower, shop vac, water storage, and a host of assorted tools, cans of paint, garden stuff and what-have-you along with supply cabinets for the ministry take up much space. We knew that something had to be done, but the formidable cost of a garage renovation was out of the picture.

Then one day Carrie took garbage to the dump and just when she got there a man was unloading a big metal tool chest on wheels. It was in perfect shape, and just what we needed to help with our situation! Another man who works there and knows Carrie saw that she wanted it but couldn't lift it by herself so he signaled to the owner of the metal cabinet and thanks to their help, the next thing you know she was home and excitedly telling us her story.

We were all amazed and thrilled at God's timely intervention and wonderful gift. It took the girls a few days of sorting, hard work, and some easy assemblage of a purchased tall metal cabinet, but now we finally have a workable garage situation along with ideas to make it even better. Every time we see that bright orange tool storage chest sitting so securely in our garage, we smile to ourselves and thank the Lord for His intimate grace, mercy and love that not only supplies all our needs, but some of our "wants" too! *"But my God shall supply all your need by Christ Jesus" (Philippians 4:19).* – J. Haley

Prayer: Lord, we don't always know what we need until You supply it. Your blessings not only meet our needs but pleasantly show us that You are aware of our wants. Thank You for Your faithfulness and blessings. Amen.

January 21

"Thus saith the LORD, In this thou shalt know that I am the LORD: behold, I will smite with the rod that is in mine hand upon the waters which are in the river, and they shall be turned to blood" (Exodus 7:17) Are you holding something in your hand? What is it?

Aaron had the rod of God, but the magicians of Egypt had their magical rod that could no doubt be traced back to the black arts or witchcraft. The magician's rod was a counterfeit rod and was limited as to how much it could control the natural laws of God. The truth is such rods are limited but God's rod is an extension of His hand and power.

Our rod is the Bible. It is not only the revelation of God, but it is an extension of His power in the hands of His people who know how to lift it up by faith while waiting to obey the next command. It is for this reason no counterfeit will match the power and victory of the Rod of God once it is lifted up by faith at His command.

The problem is that even Christians have no idea the power they hold in their hands when they truly are holding God's Word. They don't know the power because they don't know the author who has maintained it with His power, inspired it through His Spirit, and caused it to become alive through His Son. They do not know how to properly handle it because the heart is not pure towards seeking out its truths. Their hands are defiled because they handle the lifeless things of man's religion as well as the world while mixing the unholy with the holy. Their minds are also corrupt because they have filters that adjust, change, and rearrange its truth towards personal preferences and beliefs. As a result, those who handle God's truth in unrighteousness will come under His wrath (*Romans 1:18*).

We must keep in mind that the power of Satan's rod will eventually be swallowed up by the Rod of God as all matters will eventually come into submission to the Lord's authority as Sovereign Creator.

Prayer: Lord, we get so caught up with the circumstances of this present world, we often forget to lift up Your Rod by faith, knowing that it will overpower and eventually swallow all the concerns of this age. Amen.

January 22

"But speaking the truth in love, may grow up into him in all things, which is the head, even Christ" (Ephesians 4:15). Who is your head?" That is the latest question I woke up with reverberating in my mind. There are two types of heads that are influencing our way of thinking and that is either the old Adam who sinned in the garden or the New Adam, Jesus Christ who overcame in a garden.

When it comes to the location of the present garden, we are in the garden of this world that is under a curse. It is a garden that appears to possess a variety of choices, but they all narrow down to two paths that leads to life or death.

One path leads you into the heart of the garden where the ruler is Satan, pride is the king of the hill, the flesh is the taskmaster, and the affections are the slaves. This path is quite attractive. You can partake of everything you desire, but the problem is that the fruits that line this path are poisonous.

They slowly rob you of life, as they kill your ability to detect or resist them. They destroy any energy or inspiration to pursue any real aspect of life. Ultimately, such poison fruits bring great oppression to your life as you do everything you can do to survive the great intrusion taking place in your well-being.

This garden is made up of the evil systems that Satan oversees. They invite all to freely partake of its various poisonous fruits that have no means of sustaining life; rather, they will spiritually bankrupt you and cause one to operate in a lifeless state of limbo. What you discover in this garden is a spiritual vacuum that becomes a type of black hole, and the more it sucks you into it the more empty, miserable and dissatisfied you become with your existence. However, since it is all you know, you will cling to it and wish for the best as your soul becomes a barren wilderness void of life and hope.

Prayer: Lord, we are warned about the fruit that comes from the world's tree of knowledge of good and evil, but we have a hard time taking it seriously because we perceive that we can handle taking bits of poison here and there without being affected. But, when we consider what it did to Adam and Eve, such a conclusion is deceptive and destructive. Lord, we need to be saved from our limited, inept, and foolish conclusions. Amen.

January 23

"For if by one man's offence death reigned by one; much more they which receive abundance of grace and of the gift of righteousness shall reign in life by one, Jesus Christ" (Romans 5:17). In the previous post, I talked about one of two paths people walk according to the head that influences them: Satan or Jesus. The path Satan presents is one that is very attractive to the flesh, appeals to the pride, and entices the eyes. Sadly, many naturally will choose this particular path, even though they might hedge themselves in with certain rules.

The other path is not attractive. It begins with an old rugged cross, an instrument of death. You know that this cross marks the entrance of redemption, but it also marks death to the old way that you are used too and believe that you have control over. For this reason, some hide in the shadows of the cross and never really enter it. After all, the lure to taste the deadly fruit of the world to tempt death to experience temporary satisfaction that leaves one disillusioned and empty every time, is so great that one is willing to sell their soul to partake of it.

Those that enter by way of the redemption of Christ find a hard, narrow way, but it is the only path that leads you through the barren, deadly garden of the world to that which is beyond its influences and claims on you, that which is eternal and glorious. Along the way the beauty of creation will remind you there is a Creator. The challenges of this world will remind you that life here is a struggle even with God, but a grave tragedy without Him.

Life in the garden of the world makes you part of an unpredictable current that leads you into tumultuous waters of tribulation, but if you, by faith, grab hold of the Savior, Jesus Christ. He will bring you into the Rivers of Living Water of the Spirit that will lead you to fountains of life and springs of refreshment that ultimately ends at the headwaters of the fullness of salvation, peace, and promises.

This brings us back to the head. Is Satan influencing your thinking and way or are you being brought daily into the headwaters of eternal life because Jesus Christ is your head?

Prayer: Lord, You are the only true head, but Satan has dominance in this world due to man's rebellion and sin. Lord, I choose You to be my head, and my desire is to walk in the ways of righteousness that will ensure me that I will grow up in You as the only source of influence in my life. Amen.

January 24

"Thus saith the LORD, Keep ye judgment, and do justice: for my salvation is near to come, and my righteousness to be revealed" (Isaiah 56:1). The other day I asked a friend if there is a difference between fairness and being right. What would your answer be to such a question? Recently, I put a post on that stated there is no fairness in the world, but what do we seek the most when it comes to that which might challenge our life, our sense of justice? Do we seek fairness for our lives or righteousness in the matter?

Consider the prospect of fairness. There is no one standard as to what is fair. We all have our standards of fairness and it is often based on how we perceive how we should be treated or regarded in a matter. When you delve into rights it often is not a matter of justice but pride. In other words, one's sense of justice is often tied up in one's idea of self and how it affects them. If those "so-called" rights are violated or disrespected in some way because pride has been offended, we declare it is "unfair."

It is true, some have an unbiased idea of fairness, but how many people out there are in the quagmire of anger, bitterness, and misery because life has been unfair to them? Someone has not treated them right, life has dealt nothing but wrong cards, and no matter what one does, they can never get ahead. Again, you will not find any fairness or justice in this world where lies are the foundation, rebellion is the spirit, and just laws become a sick game for those who are always trying to get around them to show contempt to their authority or beat the system they are attached to.

As believers, we are not about fairness in this world, but righteousness when it comes to the next world. Righteousness is about justice that is pure and will stand in the end. Fairness may be based on my idea of justice but righteousness is based on what is Scripturally true, morally right, and that which will display the high road of excellence. We have one standard to abide by: the Word, one example to align ourselves to: Jesus Christ, and one way of excellence: that of love.

Since godly love is shed abroad in our hearts by the Holy Spirit, it will become a sacrifice when the world cries foul because of some unwarranted offense. It will become a form of mercy that will turn the other cheek when it strikes out at us, a sure faith that remains silent when falsely accused, and grace that will turn around and if possible, to ultimately minister to the accuser. The mark of true righteousness is that in the end it leaves a witness of what is unmistakably the right thing to do to avoid bringing a reproach on our testimony of Christ, and insure all is for the glory of God.

Prayer: Lord, the world is always crying foul, the flesh is constantly whining about how unfair life is and pride is easily offended when the ego is hurt, and its vanity is not placated. Lord, they are all traps we fall into that can make us bitter, cause any waning or immature faith to shipwreck, and will ultimately cause us to become smaller before the world as we use its measures to rectify the unfairness of it all. I choose Your way of righteousness because in the end it is the only thing that produces acceptable fruit. Amen.

January 25

We were laughing again, the other day, Rayola and I, about the time we were helplessly locked inside of Carrie's car, sitting in our driveway, in the dark. Here's what happened: The three of us had been invited by friends, who lived a few miles from us, for dinner. Their home is located up a shared, one-lane "country driveway" that winds and climbs for at least a mile up a woodsy hill.

We enjoyed a great dinner and fellowship, but while Carrie was beautifully singing some Christian songs for us all, I noticed she seemed to be in distress. So, skipping over the details, she made us hurry out and into her recently purchased used car which has way too much technology in it for the "average bear" (me), and insisted I drive home. That's when the "fun" began.

She's tall, and I'm short, and the urgency of our flight home gave me no time to figure out how to adjust anything, it was pitch black out except for the headlights, and on top of that I felt like a stagecoach horse as she, in her misery, kept yelling, "Hurry! Faster! Go faster!" And, my response went like this, "I can't! I can't see, and there are deer, elk, mountain lions, and other wild animals you know... and maybe a cop." It was a "praise the Lord" moment when I pulled into the driveway.

Carrie grabbed her keys, jumped out of the car, shutting the car door behind her, and dashed into the house. The thing is, the engine was still running and there were no keys in the ignition so I could turn it off. Rayola finally spoke up from the back seat, "Turn off the car!" To which I replied, "I would if I could, but I don't know how!"

She said, "Hit the button."

And I said, "Which button? There's lots of buttons and I can't see." In an effort to do something—anything, I began pushing buttons and managed to get the windshield wipers going. The problem was, it was summertime, hot and dry, and I couldn't find a way to turn them off.

"Well," Rayola says, "I'll just get out and go find Carrie." That's when we found that the car was solidly locked and so we both began hitting buttons to try and extricate ourselves from the car. No success with that, either, although, I think we did manage to get some of the windows to go up and down.

Then it suddenly hit us that if our neighbor happened to see us sitting out there in the dark, in a hot car with Rayola in the backseat, and me in the front, with the windshield wipers going back and forth, the headlights on, the engine running, and the windows going up and down, he'd know for a sure thing we were all nuts.

The lessons learned here are three-fold: never eat a whole bag of stevia-sweetened candy before a meal; memorize where the big round button is on a techie car that will turn off the engine without an ignition key; and, (here's the big one) by all means, learn how to laugh at yourself!

"You will show me the path of life: in Your presence is fullness of joy; at Your right hand there are pleasures forever more." (Psalm 16:11). "For the kingdom of God is not meat and drink: but righteousness, and peace, and joy in the Holy Ghost." (Romans 14:17). – J. Haley

Prayer: Lord, thank You for laughter. Whether it is laughing at silly circumstances or ourselves, You have given it to us as a gift to lift the heart, lighten the soul, and set our spirit free with a sense of joy. Amen.

January 26

"Then said Jesus, Father, forgive them for they know not what they do. And they parted his raiment, and cast lots" (Luke 23:34). What truly distinguishes our ideas of fairness from righteousness? The answer is the fruits. Unfairness often leaves one bitter, skeptical, and depressed, while righteousness leaves one at peace with God and in their life.

The reason unfairness leaves people in such a state is because there is no way of rectifying what people consider to be unfair that proved to be a personal affront against them. In most cases the so-called "culprit" doesn't even know about the offense and continues on while those offended seethe in the toxic juices of hurt feelings and a sense of betrayal as they run the event (or feelings) over and over in the courtroom of their imagination. This is where the matter becomes even more magnified as they seek personal justification for their own wrong attitudes and actions.

Ultimately, unfairness must seek out those who would agree with its summation of the events. This is where all kinds of other offenses occur such as division, conflict, slander, and revenge. These fruits are of the devil, and it becomes clear that Satan is trying to rob people of any peace, kill the Christian testimony, and destroy relationships.

People need to keep in mind bitterness is a root that will defile all things, skepticism is a matter of unbelief and judgmentalism. Depression in this situation is anger that has turned inward and is coming to a dangerous boiling point.

It is important to note that in most cases the people can't remember what started the present tumultuous wave that is raging in their soul. The incident may have been small, but the person decided to take offense because of the present state they were in. That choice opened the door to the grave darkness of hell itself that proves to be a slide for that person as they find themselves falling deeper into a formidable endless pit. Sadly, they often take others with them.

The Bible is clear as to how to handle all matters. As believers, it requires us to choose the excellent way of righteousness. For a Christian, doing the right thing should be a natural response, but the problem is Christians do not know the Word and have no idea how they are to handle a matter. They often react according to their flesh and limited, worldly understanding and their idea of fairness, instead of pausing, humbling themselves before God. They must also remember what His Word says as to what it means to walk in its ways and truth, or if uncertain, seeking the Lord's wisdom in the matter.

I know for myself I have this great desire at times to give in to my flesh and, as we would say, set "the record straight." However, I have learned that everyone has their own record and recording about matters. As a believer it is not my job to set the record straight, but it is my calling to seek the right means to encourage reconciliation and restoration of hearts, souls, and relationships.

Prayer: Lord, our idea of fairness rarely changes the scales of Your justice because it has nothing to do with Your righteousness. When are we going to learn that the matters of life serve as a test to us as a means of preparing us to pass the test according to Your Spirit and truth if we will only major in Your ways. Meanwhile we must deny ourselves of our right to demand fairness for ourselves, crucify our way to thinking and truly follow You into the life You have for us. Have Your Way! Amen.

January 27

"For consider him that endured such contradiction of sinners against himself, least ye be wearied and faint in your minds" (Hebrews 12:3). For the last couple of posts, I have been talking about the concept of unfairness. When I come to the subject of fairness, I am reminded of a situation that happened over two decades ago. Before praying for Jeannette and myself, a pastor looked at us and stated, "We must declare that God is not unfair."

At the time everything seemed against us and we were struggling with endless formidable waves that were taking everything from our health and finances to the ministry out into the ocean to be consumed and plunged into the depths of uncertainty. We had clearly run out of steam (strength), gas (attempts) and methods (options).

At such times you have a couple of choices, go into the depths of self-pity or consider Jesus and choose to trust Him no matter how irrational, how dark, and how ominous the situation appears. You must walk through the darkness where you choose to look up and remind yourself that Jesus suffered the greatest injustice ever and He did it for our sakes. We must remember He took our sin on Himself as He interceded on behalf of those who were being used by both the religious and political systems to carry out the injustice.

I know of people who call themselves Christians that are bitter towards God because their life has been unfair to them. Perhaps they made an assumption about their calling or a presumption about how God was always going to have their backside if they became a crusader for some noble cause. However, if God has not called them to that particular mission or ordained their cause, it will all prove to be useless in the end.

Sometimes the Lord must allow the waves of this world to come in like a tsunami to shake foundations, expose idols, reveal our spiritual poverty, and show us the direction we are heading. Such shaking is never fun, but it is rewarding in the end because those who allow God to refine their faith in darkness come out with greater spiritual depth and maturity.

Being on the right side of a matter does not allow a believer to regard a matter in light of fairness. We must up front deny ourselves the right to consider if any matter is fair, while picking up our cross that will not only crucify the old life but discipline our walk so we can follow Jesus into the life that we are called to. It is for this reason that I have learned righteousness sees a wrong as an opportunity to do what is right and to either avoid, or stop others from falling into the trap that the selfish standards of the flesh and the self-serving standards of the ways of the world refer to as being "fair."

Prayer: Lord, we like to think we are fair minded about all things but most of the time that fairness is pointing to how something affects us. It becomes obvious we are not at all interested as to whether that "fairness" can clearly apply to everyone else, or if it will prove to be hypocritical. Lord, I don't want to fall into the trap of "fairness;" rather, I want to walk in the ways of Your righteousness. Amen.

January 28

Besides living in a time of "techie cars" full of "buttons" that require a "techie genius" to completely understand and operate all the techie stuff in them, we also have touchy "techie" TV's, washing machines and other appliances that don't work well or last long; phones, computers, music electronics, as well as an endless array of other stuff. Everything that we've been told is for our "convenience" or to make life "better" and help us "save time and energy" is anything but.

Let's face it, it's all a huge distraction from what is really important while we waste great gobs of precious time (because God only grants each of us a certain amount of time, as you know) trying to either figure out how it works, or trying to fix it so it works. And, when it does work, we often use it to project ourselves into some sort of zombie land that gobbles up (you guessed it) both our time and energy.

Other than taking advantage of some of these inventions to thankfully further the Gospel while the opportunity remains, one can ask if all if this is really the way God intended for mankind to live? (After all, most of it contains "spyware" for the antichrist system.) I don't expect everyone to agree with my overview of our "plastic planet," but hopefully there will be some agreement to this analogy—and that is this: I fear that far too many Christians approach the Word of God in a "techie manner" as if a little "tap" here, a little "push" there, or a little "quick scan" over a few verses is going to keep their boat afloat when the coming tsunami overtakes them.

The thick, dark, foreboding darkness I saw decades ago in more than one vision rolling over the western sea towards this nation has hit the shoreline and is rapidly descending. Do you know your God, know His Son, Jesus Christ, know the Spirit, and know the Word well enough to stand, and when all else around you is gone, remain standing? Paul wrote, *"And that, knowing the time, that now it is high time to awake out of sleep: for now is our salvation nearer than when we believed. The night is far spent, the day is at hand: let us therefore cast off the works of darkness, and let us put on the armour of light . . . put you on the Lord Jesus Christ, and make not provision for the flesh, to fulfil the lusts thereof." (Romans 11, 12, 14.)* – J. Haley

Prayer: Lord, we find ourselves at the mercy of technology that keeps moving forward at lightning speed. It runs our life and creates insanity because it is divorced from reality. Even though it catches me off balance, nothing catches You off guard. I am looking forward to leaving lifeless technology behind, knowing that when I see You face to face, I will be made complete to enjoy Your glory forever. Amen.

January 29

"...he began to say unto his disciples first of all Beware ye of the leaven of the Pharisees, which is hypocrisy" (Luke 12:1c). The disciples realized that the leaven Jesus was referring to was the religious leaders' doctrine (*Matthew 16:6, 12*). The other morning, I woke up thinking about doctrine.

People sometimes misconstrue doctrine to simply mean theology. Granted, doctrine is based on what a person believes, but such belief will turn into action because it is considered true and right.

The reason I point this fact out is because you are considered a hypocrite if you do not practice what you believe or preach. The other aspect of doctrine that Jesus brings out in His sermon on the mount is that pure doctrine will also produce a right attitude in you that will maintain the integrity or motive behind your action. (See *Matthew 7:28-29.*)

It is easy to become a Pharisee or Sadducee. All you must do is make a doctrine a matter of theology or a man-made religious tradition of rigid unrealistic practices that applies to everyone but yourself. Theology often remains an intellectual understanding that can allow one to divorce themselves from living it or acting on it. They think if they know a matter is true then they are okay, but the truth is a matter is not so until it has been walked out and tested as being so in our lives. In other words, truth is practiced to establish, confirm, or uphold a witness as to the validity of one's doctrine.

Through the years I have discovered that the main fruit of unleavened doctrine is the lack of love. Such people do not love God, love the truth, or love others who fail to live up to their hypocritical doctrine. They will unmercifully judge while exalting themselves in their mind to also become the jury while justifying the noxious attitude that they adopt toward those who now prove to be their inferiors and would dare question their doctrine.

It is the natural tendency of the various schools of thought to major in theology and not pure doctrine. In fact, one's particular theology becomes the filter by which they interpret, judge, and traditionalize what they consider to be their doctrine. It may sound right, reasonable, and realistic, but it eventually becomes obvious it is nothing more than a veneer like the garments of the Pharisees and Sadducees to make them appear religious to hide the fact they possess a lifeless religion that hides their hypocrisy.

Prayer: Lord, I have been like the Pharisees with my theology, but You helped me see that it lacked life and love, exposing me as a bona-fide hypocrite. Lord, forgive me for my hypocrisy, disobedience, and indifference towards my fruit. Enable me to walk in Your pure doctrine to establish the life and witness that will bring You glory. Amen.

January 30

"For I bear them record that they have a zeal of God, but not according to knowledge" (Romans 10:2). Many new believers start out with zeal, while being ignorant of what constitutes righteousness. They often think what they may religiously know is enough, but they have not been established in sound doctrine. Doctrine is often nothing more than a creed to some. Their creed may be correct, but it is lifeless if it is not walked out in obedience by faith.

Christianity is about gaining the life of Christ and that can't happen unless we have been born again with the breath of His life, the Holy Spirit. This life requires us to walk by faith towards that life because it is a gift of God that is promised to all who believe. Again, Christianity is not a creed or doctrine, it is the life of Christ that has been imputed to us by God's grace and worked in us through faith.

The problem I encountered when I first became a Christian is that I tried to fit the Christian life into my religious notions and understanding which was corrupt because of the world and man's influence. We all start out our new life in Christ with untrustworthy filters and it is for this reason that our minds must be transformed so we will keep from conforming our new-found life in Christ to the world's way of thinking and doing. Keep in mind, any time man puts his two-cents worth in the pot as to how something should look or how it must work to meet his approval, he has just perverted what is true and pure and he will end up with an unhealthy mixture.

As a new Christian, I was zealous in my new-found life, thinking nothing could stop me from reaching great heights in my new faith. The problem I had was that my zeal for God lacked wisdom. Instead of being grounded on the truth, I was flying high according to my idea of what constituted righteousness and not according to the righteousness of God

I had to hit the ground hard more than once to realize that God's righteousness is far from any religious notions man may adhere to. It is not summarized by what we do; rather, it is about the life of Christ being established in us for He is the real essence of righteousness to everyone who believes and receives His life by faith.

Prayer: Lord, we start our new life in You from the peak of our own religious notions without realizing You are not in any of it. Oh, how we must often be brought down from the peaks of foolishness to discover what is acceptable to You. Amen.

January 31

"If any man will do his will, he shall know of the doctrine whether it be of God, or whether I speak of myself" (John 7:17). Many new believers start out thinking we have to get our doctrine down before we can know God's will. However, that is backwards.

God's will has been instilled into our conscience and is obvious to those who are honest about what is morally right and what is wrong. Much of this moral ruler has been hidden in darkness to avoid guilt and shame on our part as we veer off the right course to do our own thing.

God's will has also been confirmed in His Word. The Scripture above tells us that if we do the will of God based on what we know is right, we will know if the doctrine we are holding to, or that is being established, is of God.

Many people approach God's will and His doctrine from the perspective of <u>trying</u> to do it when in reality God's will require us to

DO IT! The right thing is not hard; rather, it is a choice that requires us to deny up front what is self-serving, convenient, and acceptable to us at the time.

It is time for those who claim to be Christians to realize they are not here to do their will but the will of the Father. It is time to be honest with ourselves that we instinctively do know the will of God. The flesh is always trying to justify why we don't have to do it now. On the other hand, the world is ready to offer us some method, some notion, or some religious act that there is another way of doing it that will allow us to still fit into the ways of the world without truly consecrating our life. If we do consecrate ourselves, we will be considered radical by most people and foolish to the world.

We are instructed by God's Word to come out and be separate from the world and its ways, as well as reminding us that we do not have agreement with the spirit of this world. It is time we consecrate ourselves by presenting our bodies to the Lord to prove what is His good, acceptable, and perfect will.

Prayer: Lord, we have a tendency to squeeze by the questionable by staying in the grey areas of compromise, climb over the ridiculous with our excuses, and cause the cloud of dust to hide the unacceptable with our logic, but in the end it will all give way to the truth that we were hypocrites hiding the obvious behind a mask of religion. Expose all such hypocrisy in my life Lord. Amen.

February

February 1

"So likewise, whosoever he be of you that forsaketh not all that he hath, he cannot be my disciple" (Luke 14:33). I woke up this morning thinking about the cost that a true disciple of Jesus must be willing to pay to follow Him.

For many people in what we refer to today as the Americanized version of Christianity, they associate Christianity along the lines of what they will get out of it. Every Sunday, they go to get their religious experience for the week, come out feeling happy or good about it, but have no clue that there is a cost to truly follow Jesus to gain their life in Him.

Jesus counted the cost in eternity and made a commitment to die on our behalf. As someone once said, "Where there is no loss, there is no gain." In the Christian life it is not a matter of what we lose; rather, it is a matter of realizing what we can freely give up and truly gain if we let go of the present life that we need to be delivered from to actually gain the life of Jesus.

For example, if we don't lose the world, we will lose our soul in the end. If we don't lose our sin along the way, we can't be assured of being born again and being overcomers. If we don't lose the influence of our earthy relationships, we will never know the freedom to follow Jesus without always looking back. If we don't lose our right to ourselves, we will never reach our potential in His kingdom.

For many of us we start out backwards in our relationship with Jesus. We first count the cost of the false but attractive promises of the world, along with worldly relationships which can include families, aspirations, childish dreams of grandeur, empty successes, and temporary riches. At such a time, we consider if it would be worth it to follow Jesus.

As we can see, what we must first learn to count is the great cost of our soul, well-being, and calling if we don't let go of what the past. We must count ourselves dead to the present attractions and temptations of the world and begin to follow Jesus into the glorious life we are called to.

I must admit, following Jesus means identifying with His sufferings, as well as finding ourselves on the road to Calvary where the dark night of the soul engulfs us and the ongoing demise of the old looms before us. However, beyond the work of the cross of Christ is the glorious light of His promises awaiting us.

To gain Christ is never a loss, but we must count the cost of this present world with the heart conviction that if it cost us everything of this life to gain Him, HE IS WORTH every bit of it!

Prayer: Lord, since our world is upside down, it only makes sense that we will be backward in how we perceive and approach a matter. However, the more we follow You into the life You call us to, the more You will turn our world right side up and straighten out our backward approaches to line us up to the matters of Your kingdom. Praise Your Name. Amen.

February 2

"Let this mind which is in Christ be in you" (Philippians 2:5). In my morning meditations I was considering what it means to have the mind of Christ. When you consider the mind, what you really need to examine is your attitude towards a matter. Let me ask, "What do you consider when trying to make a judgment call?"

For most of us without realizing it, we will go with whatever our own attitude is about it. If it disturbs us in some way, we may take issue with it or if it is not all that important to us, we might say what is the big deal? If we take pride in our intelligence, we will say, "I know the difference; therefore, I will take what I can out of it and leave the rest."

However, in God's kingdom it does not matter what we think or feel about a matter, or if we think we are clever enough to handle something that in all honesty is questionable when it comes to the spirit or intent of it. What matters in God's kingdom IS HIS ATTITUDE towards a matter.

I read a post that stated, "There is one thing missing in the Bible: YOUR OPINION!" How many of us realize that our conclusions for the most part are our opinions. How can we make sure that our conclusions are true and right before God, acceptable to His way, and wise in their judgments? We have to come into line with God's attitude about the matter, by agreeing with what His Word says about it. We need then to line up to it in our thinking in order for our actions or conduct, to respond accordingly.

The Bible instructs us to let the mind of Christ be in us. This means we will take on the same attitude Jesus has towards a matter. The more we come into agreement with God and line up to His Word, the more the attitude of Christ is developed in us. This is how we let the mind of Christ be in us which also points to our mind being transformed and continually renewed by the Holy Spirit.

Prayer: Lord we can always declare that we want to have Your mind, but until we face the harsh fact that until it is transformed and renewed daily by Your Spirit and Word, our attitude will prove to be contrary to Yours and we will end up reacting to it in a casual way and walk it out according to our old worldly way of thinking. Forgive us for being so high-minded and stiff-necked towards Your Word and Your Ways. Amen.

February 3

"Come now, and let us reason together, saith the LORD: though your sins be as scarlet, they shall be as white as snow; though they be red

like crimson they shall be as wool (Isaiah 1:18). This verse in *Isaiah* had always made me pause. We often approach this verse from the backside because we simply quote it without considering the text above and below it. We readily accept that the Lord wants to make our sins as white as snow, but how many of us consider the first part of the Scripture. It is an invitation, but to what? To come to the Lord so He can reason with us about our sin.

When it comes to personal sin, our flesh and pride have a big aversion to it. There are different reasons for us not wanting God to reason with us about such a matter because we would have to come into agreement with Him about how He views it. We would have to agree with Him as to why it is such an offense to that which is holy. We would have to repent or turn from showing contempt towards His righteous ways and begin to line up to what is right. We would have to admit that it is a perversion of His truth, an insult to His Spirit, and a disregard to His authority. We would have to take responsibility for the hurt, wounding, and destruction that it has caused in our relationship with Him as well as others. In the end, such reasoning may actually break us into numerous pieces at the point of our pride, while striking a possible death blow to the flesh.

The Lord has to first reason with us about our sin before He can cleanse us because there is no remission of sin without seeking His forgiveness and confessing it. The Bible is clear we can't hide sin from Him, but we sure can whitewash it when it comes to our way of thinking. We can put fig-leaves of excuses over it, cover it with religious garbs of self-righteousness, or shine a false light of personal goodness to cover up the real state of our affairs. The problem is when God looks at our whitewashed coverings, he sees the tombs of dead men's bones of religion with decaying garbs of past attempts.

The cure to our plight is to adhere to the call to real discipleship. It requires us to first deny pride any audience, nail the carnal, old man to a cross daily, and follow Jesus into the life He is calling us to. However, the problem with being a disciple is that it requires us to first consecrate our lives by offering our bodies as a sacrifice. In the end, this will allow us to prove what is the acceptable, good and perfect will of God.

Prayer: Lord we often sidestep the real problem and try to get around the matter by dressing it up in some way, but the stench remains that proves death is attached to our ways before You. Lord, forgive us for avoiding humbly coming to Your table so You can reason with us about the nature of our true spiritual plight to bring restoration to our wandering souls. Amen.

February 4

"All the ways of a man are clean in his own eyes; but the LORD weigheth the spirits. Commit thy works unto the LORD, and thy thoughts shall be established" (Proverbs 16:2-3). The one thing I have struggled with when it comes to God is having my way in a matter. It is never my intention to start out to be wrong or do wrong. After much calculation, my way seems right to my thinking, feels right to my psyche, can be considered harmless in action as far as others, and is something that I see as benefitting me in the end. Therefore, in my reasoning I can't imagine what the big deal is when I insist on or get my way in the end.

I have said this before, but it matters little what we think about an issue for it will always come down to how God perceives it. We need to remember that we do much based on selfish motives that allow us the liberty to insist on our way, while maintaining a fierce independence that will have its way. Behind all of it are prideful notions that will justify our way, and a natural ability to make it right in our own sight.

When you consider where our way leads us, it should bring some sobriety to how God views our attitude and conclusions. Our ways lead to death, spiritual ruin, and are strange to God (*Proverbs 14:12; 16:25; 21:8*). When He is considering what we are doing, it is not based on how we see it but the spirit in which we are doing it. If any part of self with its rebellious ways and its propensity to make our way right in our own mind is present, then we will find ourselves on the contrary side of God in a matter.

The truth is our ways lead to death because there is no real life, eternal purpose, or heavenly consideration in them. What is behind our way is a rebellious spirit that has no problem putting God to a foolish test and coming into agreement with the spirit of the world, Satan. In the end it will always come back to the simple fact, I WANT TO DO IT MY WAY regardless of how God views it.

Prayer: Lord, in my spiritual immaturity as a Christian, You let me get away with having my way with very few repercussions. As I grew in my knowledge of You, Your dealings with me became more obvious as You began to hedge me in Your narrow way, and now I can find no wiggle room. I must come into line with Your way or I will sense Your Spirit lifting, know leanness in my own spirit, and know the bitterness of bringing displeasure to You. Forgive me for insisting on my way when I know that the safest way is, "Not my way, but Your Way O God and not my will but Your will." Amen.

February 5

"Righteousness exalteth a nation: but sin is a reproach to any people" (Proverbs 14:34). What does it mean to line up to the center of life, truth, and eternity? I am coming to realize more and more just how narrow the way is to eternal life. When it comes to my political views, I am considered a conservative, but I realize that what I need to be, when all is said and done, is righteous.

Is there a difference between conservative and being righteous? Keep in mind I don't believe in being liberal about anything when it comes to the moral, financial, and ethical matters that greatly affect the soul of this nation and threatens the survival of countless souls, but have I taken liberty with the truth of God's Word in some way? Have I veered off a matter by getting caught up with the causes to save the country or the world instead of the great cause of God to see souls saved?

The problem for many people is that they do not think they need to be saved from that which is corrupt, or they do not want to be saved because they are fine with their views regardless of the rotten, destructive fruits that it leaves behind. In some cases, they only hear what they want to hear and are willing to die on some molehill because they stubbornly hold to their position whether it is true or false.

Some people are clearly called into the public arena to contend for the soul of this nation as mediators for those who are losing their voice to corrupt, lying, and insane politicians. God has always had such mediators, but even they must constantly line up to center to keep their moral compass and sanity in the midst of incredible corruption. We need to know such individuals and hold them up in prayer, support them at the polls, and do what part the Lord clearly outlines for us as we stand with them, but we must personally distinguish calling from causes.

As believers there is only one stand we can and must take and that has to do with righteousness. This righteousness is not based on man's best presentation, their most passionate arguments, or their intellectual and philosophical stands; rather, it is based on Jesus Christ, the Son of the Living God.

Prayer: Lord, You have told us in Your Word what is acceptable and right to You, but we do not believe we need to agree with Your Word to be right. Lord, forgive us for our arrogance and our unbelief towards You and Your Word. Amen.

February 6

"*Now then we are ambassadors for Christ, as though God did beseech you by us; we pray you in Christ's stead, be ye reconciled to God" (2 Corinthians 5:20).* It is natural for man to go his own way when it comes to his conclusions about matters. There are various means such as our understanding, feelings, and experiences, that erect peaks that make us feel infallible in our judgments. When we hit the heights of infallibility, that is when it becomes blinders to our eyes, preventing us from having any real peripheral vision as to what is really going on.

We may intellectually know what is right, but to come to the sober reality that until we do line up to the center of what is righteous and take our rightful position in Christ's kingdom, we are still wandering in some type of darkness. Whether it is assumption that come close enough to the center or a presumption that perceives that it knows a matter to be true regardless of whether there is any fruit to verify it, people will hold to it. There is also wishful thinking that some type of association, affiliation, or religious school of thought will do the trick in the end, but they are lies that are covered up by false illusions.

It is righteousness, not a certain religious, conservative philosophy that will exalt a nation. Righteousness leads us back to God where a conservative philosophy will most likely lead us back to the world's nobler notions, ways, and ideas, but will ultimately fall short of bringing us all the way back to God's perspective of a matter where we can effectively represent Him as ambassadors wherever we live and minister.

As a believer, I am a citizen of another kingdom, representing it as an ambassador in this present age according to a higher calling. I am becoming more and more a stranger in the land as I get closer to my real home. But in the meantime, I must discern between calling and causes to avoid spending out my strength in the wrong way. I must also make sure I am standing on what is true so when the storms and shaking comes I will remain standing. I must also keep my focus on the eternal because that is what will be left standing when all else is brought down by God's judgment.

Prayer: Lord, I have learned the "best" may not be excellent, the "decent" may not be what is good, the "moral" may not be in line with the holy, and that no matter how conservative I am about the world's issues it may not lead me all the way back to Your righteous standard and ways. Lord, I desire to line up to what is the center to all matters: You, Your truth, and Your ways because in the end that will be the only things that make sense in this corrupt, insane world. Amen.

February 7

A slight frown began to form on my boyfriend's brow as, with the inexperienced exuberance of youth, I happily detailed what kind of a life and future I wanted. It had been a fun date, and now that we were in a somewhat serious conversation while parked in front of my parents' house, why not just tell him my dreams? After all, what could possibly be wrong with high expectations?

In spite of the semi-darkness, I sensed his slight kneejerk reaction. Too late I realized my detailed description of a huge mansion perched above the Pacific Ocean, with miles of accessible beachfront, 40 acres of white-fenced pastureland for horses, a stable and enough hired help to take care of it all was just a bit too much. At that point, he said something that I have occasionally reminded myself of through the many years which have come and gone since then. What he said was, "You have visions of grandeur."

I suppose it goes without saying that my "visions of grandeur," fantasies and unattainable daydreams all dissipated through the years as the dawning light of reality grew brighter. *Ecclesiastes 1:2* sums it up, *"Vanity of vanities, saith the Preacher, vanity of vanities; all is vanity."*

Christians, of all people, should know this, yet how many professing Christians have embraced the lie that "whatever the mind of man can conceive and believe he can receive?" Does repeating some prayer to "accept Christ", or becoming a member of an organized church or religious group automatically guarantee you that God will grant you a trouble-free life? Do you believe that your "visions of grandeur" will become a reality if you just picture it in your mind, continually focus on it, and believe it will be yours because your concentrated "energies" are powerful enough to move the hand of God to give it to you? If so, you are practicing witchcraft.

You can try to think positive thoughts, speak positive words, and pray positive platitudes all you want, but in the end, you will discover that you have embraced "another Jesus," "another spirit," and "another gospel." (See *2 Corinthians 11:4.*) – J. Haley

Prayer: Lord, we can have unbridled imagination that will cause us to float above this world in a fantasy that does not exist, nor will it ever amount to anything without costing a person their soul. In the end they will discover it is vanity and adds nothing to their life. I want what You have ordained for my life. To know it is from You is my source of real contentment. Amen.

February 8

"And they brought it. And he saith unto them, Whose is this image and superscription? And they said unto him, Caesar's. And Jesus answering said unto them, Render to Caesar the things that are Caesar's, and to God the things that are God's. And they marvelled at him" (Mark 12:16-17). It is a known fact that the opposing sides in this world make up the same coin.

It is true that one side claims it is for that which is moral and right, while the other side rages against any such standards in the name of rights that have gone amiss. There are those who stand behind God, while others may occasionally use Him. It all seems quite diplomatic, but according to the fruits, it speaks of unbelief. Ultimately, one group appears to deny Him in their hearts, while the others put their fist up against Him as they defy Him.

As in the case of the coin that Caesar's image was on, it was identified as belonging to His kingdom. Every coin carries some type of image or identification to identify it to a particular kingdom. In this case the coin belongs to the systems of Satan and his kingdom. One may ask if it is the same coin, why the conflict? One group often causes a ruse while the other one points the finger at them as they actually carry out wicked agendas.

The truth is a kingdom divided against itself will fall. Satan can't afford for people to see the real goal behind the two headed snake that operates within his systems. His destructive goal is to make everyone global citizens who become nothing more than serfs to a few powers in high places as well as subject to a one-world government, economic and religious system where Satan will be the one sitting on a throne and receiving underserved worship and oppressive service.

It is easy to get prideful about what we think is right, judgmental towards those who don't see it our way, and downright angry at what we think is stupid, inferior, and just plain insane, but the reality is we are all in the same boat and the only one who can save us is not some party, practice, or popular person of our time, but the God-Man, Redeemer, Son of God, Jesus Christ.

I have stated, the world is like the Titanic and as believers we are on a different ship following behind to pick up those who recognize they are on a sinking ship and are looking for a way off of it and out of it. As usual Satan has lulled many to sleep with the promise of partaking of the glory of his different kingdoms, if only they will sell their soul and bow down and worship him, while ignoring the stormy waters and icebergs that are lying in the way.

As Paul stated, *"Awake thou that sleepest, and arise from the dead, and Christ shall give thee light" (Ephesians 5:14).* It is time we awake out of any slumber and take note of what ship we are truly on.

Prayer: Lord, I have been asleep on what was considered the luxury liner of this age with all of its false promises and glory, but Your Spirit caused me to hear Your invitation to come. Jumping ship in this present age has saved my soul, and my prayer and hope is that many others will wake up to the pending danger and jump ship in order to be saved before it is too late. Amen.

February 9

"And Jesus knew their thoughts, and said unto them, Every kingdom divided against itself is brought to desolation; and every city or house divided against itself shall not stand" (Matthew 12:25). When it comes to the great battle of the soul and mind we are instructed to stand. We must stand for righteousness, withstand with truth, and continue to stand in lieu of what is eternal because there is no light, hope, or purpose in this world.

We can look around and see kingdoms fall because many in leadership positions have sold their soul, leaving only a few that stand for what is right. There are societies that fall into lawlessness because there are few withstanding with truth and righteousness, while homes collapse because one of the most neglected mission fields is the home where few are able to continue to stand because of the many immoral battles that rage around us.

The different floods of wickedness continue to ebb away the soul of this nation. Societies are succumbing to the many cultural affronts undermining all righteousness, as homes which are the beating heart of any society, become the real casualties as they lose all sense as to what is sacred, important, and necessary.

The question is why have we as a nation cease to stand for the excellent principles it was founded upon? Why do we as societies quickly surrender to the deception of the age rather than continue to stand for what is right? Why do we allow our homes to be taken away by the floods of decadence and depravity without barring the doors of truth against it?

The reason we can't stand is because we are divided in our hearts. Our heart is not single in vision, purpose, or devotion. Our foundation is often a mixture of selfishness, a worldly attitude and a wrong spirit. There is also a matter of lining up to the cornerstone as one sure truth. We must keep in mind that our reality is fickle because it is based on sentiment, worldly philosophies, and carnal conclusions. Finally, the influence we give in to must be the one true Head, Jesus Christ. He is also the only sure foundation and the right cornerstone to a believer. As a result, what lacks the right spirit and truth misses what is eternal.

Remember, we are born into an ungodly state and because of this state we are inclined towards that which is sinful, making us enemies of God. It is for this reason God has promised those who turn to Him in faith a new heart that will be inclined towards Him and a new spirit that is able to come into agreement with Him. It is only as we adhere to a new heart and line up to all truth in the right Spirit can we stand against the deception of this age, withstand with the truth of heaven, and begin to catch glimpses into the glory of the next world that will enable us to continue to stand in the midst of the tumultuous waters of this age.

Prayer: Lord, we miss it because we have not sold out to You. Our heart is not single towards You, our soul is divided about who it will serve, and our spirit feels the troubled waters of uncertainty because we are not anchored to You. Forgive us for being divided in heart, fragmented in our soul, and lean in our spirit. Amen.

February 10

Some secrets remain secrets until everyone concerned has passed from this life, except for the three-year-old who was the cause of it 79 years ago. You're right if you guessed that was me. Perhaps we can blame Canada and the British Empire because of their love for tea, tea parties, and "high noon tea" rituals.

Since my lineage on my mother's side were tea-drinking Canadians, I learned early on about such things, and even had my own little tea set. My opportunity to serve tea came about when the elderly ladies and my mother sat in the living room visiting.

Now, keep in mind, to a three-year-old anybody over thirty was "old." But I do recall that they did seem to be around Great-Grandma's age. I also remember how cute all the ladies thought I was as I went up to them with my little teapot and miniature tea cups and asked if they'd like some tea. Of course, they all graciously nodded said, "Yes" and "thank you so much" and "Ummm, it's delicious" as they sipped plain water, pretending it was the best tea ever.

I can't recall how many trips I made in and out of the living room so everyone got some "tea" but I do remember that suddenly my mother seemed to snap to attention, as she quietly asked (I think it was Grandma), "Where is she getting that water from? She can't reach the sink!" All the ladies were busy chatting, so nobody paid any attention when she jumped to her feet and followed me to my special "water source" which was, as you probably guessed, the toilet!

Horrified, she quietly said, "That's enough! You are not serving anymore tea today! Go into your room and play there."

Thankfully, nobody had any adverse effects from my special "tea," and all the tea drinkers who attend our weekly Bible studies are still being served tea by me, but I guarantee, it's the real thing!

The spiritual lesson from this story is simple yet seriously important. How do we know the true source of spiritual teaching and preaching that is being "served" to us from the many "voices" we hear from pulpits, over the airwaves, on the Internet, and from written sources? How can Christians be assured that what is being offered today as being from God is genuinely inspired by the Holy Spirit? How can we know what is real and what is not?

First, what is the source of their information? Is it from the Holy Bible or is it man's opinion, or the most recent "revelation," or from an experience that fails to coincide with biblical principles and the "Gospel once delivered to the saints?" Does it exalt Jesus Christ as Lord of lords and King of kings, God incarnate, and risen from the dead? What is the spirit behind what you are being fed? Does it exalt man or Jesus Christ?

Bottom line, are you being served a watered-down version of the Gospel, and the cost of following Christ in trust and obedience to truly live the Christian life? Or are you drinking the "toilet water" of the vain philosophies of the world where it's all about you? Hopefully, you're being served the "Living Water" of the Holy Spirit, and the Bread of Life from heaven. *"But though we, or an angel from heaven, preach any other gospel unto you than that which we have preached unto you, let him be accursed" (Galatians 1:9).* – J. Haley

Prayer: Lord, I have been fed the dregs of heresy from others, but thankfully You have given me the means to discern it. I humbly seek even greater discernment from You in these days because the deception is becoming subtle and it looks innocence enough which makes it harder to detect its source. Thank You for always answering such requests. Amen.

February 11

"And Nadab and Abihu died before the LORD, when they offered strange fire before the LORD, in the wilderness of Sinai, and they had no children" (Numbers 3:4), When I think of these two sons of Aaron, it reminds me to consider what kind of legacy am I leaving behind. Here were men who had a special calling due to their relationship with Aaron and yet they blew it. Here were individuals that were privileged in a way but squandered it. Here were two men who held positions that could make a substantial difference among many, but they did not value it. In the end these men were judged for it.

Some would think, what is the big deal? Couldn't the Lord make an exception and remember these men were human, prone to an error here and there and give them a break? However, these two men were given specific instructions about offering that which was acceptable to the Lord. They were told how to carry out their priestly duties in a proper way. Their blatant affront against God was not out of ignorance and not simply making a minor mistake, but it was because they didn't fear the Lord, and as a result were flippant about carrying out their priestly duties.

As believers we make up a royal priesthood (*1 Peter 2:9; Revelation 1:6*). It is obvious we have a high calling. Do we know our responsibilities before the Lord? We have clear instructions in His Word and if we are honest, we know what is required of us, but like Nadab and Abihu we can either perceive it as being no big deal or we might think God will accept whatever decaying crumbs, profane ashes, or unholy offering we throw at Him because He loves us and desires to show grace.

The real key to standing before the Lord in worship and service comes down to having the right attitude towards Him and our responsibility. The only healthy and right attitude is to fear Him. Does that mean we shake before Him? No, rather it means we walk in obedience to His Word, in awe of who He is, and with sobriety that we dare not displease Him because we have in some way become foolish and flippant towards Him, thereby, putting Him to a foolish test.

Prayer: Lord, we can become casual towards You in many ways. However, Your Scriptures show us that being casual is foolish and will not fare well for us. Lord, keep me in a right attitude so I do not become foolish in my thinking and ways. Amen.

February 12

"And whatsoever ye do, do it heartily, as to the Lord, and not unto men" (Colossians 3:23). It is the wrong attitude in us that will cause us to take on a casual stance in our service to the Lord. We often think that God will overlook the small lapses in our service, tolerate our half-hearted or fleshly worship, and accept whatever small crumbs we throw at Him to somehow subdue our own conscience about our inept service towards Him. However, God is noting all of it. He knows our heart, intention, and devotion towards Him, and since He is deserving of our all and our best, He will not accept our leftovers.

How can we be content to offer Him that which is strange? It is because we either do not know Him or we do not love Him. It is easy to stand behind God's love and declare He will understand. We can use His grace to believe in the end He will be the most tolerable, understanding God.

It is true God loves us, but acceptable obedience comes out of our love for Him. Love is a two-way street, and we can't properly give back what we fail to receive in humility and gratitude. God wants to show us grace, but when we lack the right attitude towards Him, we end up showing Him contempt for His righteous instructions and holy ways. Since grace reigns through righteousness, it can't abound where it is failing the test by disrespect, squandered by foolishness, and mishandled by arrogance.

For Nadab and Abihu they had no children, no legacy that would follow them, but what about you and me? The Bible talks about fruits.

As believers the type of legacy we leave will depend on the witness and fruits we leave behind. For the two sons of Aaron, they are a side note in the Bible who leave us with an example of ones who had a great calling but cheapened it by being casual towards God's instructions. For us, as believers, it will come down to whether our names are in the book of life, as well as whether we are leaving behind a faithful witness of Jesus Christ. It is that faithful witness that makes us part of the great cloud of witnesses that truly becomes more than a side note to those who follow in the footsteps of the saints who have gone before them.

Prayer: Lord, there are too many sad side notes in Your Word. I so desire to become part of the cloud of witnesses that will become the indelible testimony that has prepared the way for others through godly example, and that in the end will shine brightly in eternity. Amen.

February 13

"And they that are wise shall shine as the brightness of the firmament; and they that turn many to righteousness as the stars for ever and ever" (Daniel 12:3). It is hard to wade through the different presentations of Christianity and their influences in Christendom.

For some, Christianity has been confined to getting certain doctrines down pat and standing on them with all the tenacity they can muster up. For others, it is about going to church or doing religious activities. There are those who see Christianity as a "bless me club", a social gathering place, or a place where they can make contacts with people to promote their agenda.

However, Christianity is the life of Christ in us. The Holy Spirit is working His life in us so we can be conformed to the image of Christ. When people see us, hopefully, they are seeing Jesus and not our religious best. In a way Daniel is making reference to those who are wise about the matters of God. They will shine as the brightness of the firmament.

If the life of Jesus is in you, it means the light of the world is in you as well. The light of Jesus is what penetrates the darkness of the present world and it is His life that will shine through us. We can lift up doctrine all we want, but until Jesus is lifted up no one will get saved. We can do many good deeds but if they are not ordained by God, they will prove useless in the end. We can join whatever club there is in our churches, but Christianity is not represented by a club; rather, it is manifested in a Living Body, an established spiritual house, a holy temple, and a consecrated life.

Prayer: Lord, we imagined great things, but until we realize that all greatness is found in You, Your works, and doing, we will never know the greatness that ends in indescribable majesty. Amen.

February 14

"By a new and living way, which he hath consecrated for us, through the veil, that is to say, his flesh" (Hebrews 10:20). Jesus consecrated the way of salvation with His sacrifice on the cross. This brings us to an important point, "What does it mean for us as saints to be consecrated?" It is an act of holiness where something is being visibly set apart for God's use.

Such consecration is bound by certain criteria because it must be prepared to be set apart for God to acknowledge it is acceptable and ordain it as being His. This is when He can sanctify it to show that it now can be used for service to Him.

As a consecrated life we must wisely offer it up for God's purpose. This means offering our whole life to be used by the Lord. We must daily present our bodies as a sacrifice, but every sacrifice has an altar. For believers it is their personal cross where one dies to the self-life by denying self any rights to life on its terms. This means one is becoming crucified to the world by offering up the old man daily to once again cross out the matters of this present life with death.

As a member of the Body, we must know our place in it to discreetly fulfill our calling, while as part of the household we must know our responsibility and soberly carry it out. As a holy temple, we must preserve, uphold, or maintain the integrity of the life of Christ in us. We are also told in *Matthew 5:14-16*, we are not to hide the light of Christ life in us, but we must let it shine. Out of that light will come forth conduct and deeds that will bring honor and glory to the Father.

According to the Scripture in *Daniel 12:3*, when we reflect the brightness and glory of the Son, it will turn many to righteousness. Note, it does not say turning people to certain beliefs or doctrines. It is not talking about getting them caught up with man's best, his religious works or the world's successful methods. We are to turn people to the righteousness of Jesus and if we do, we have an incredible assurance that we will be as shining stars forever in His kingdom.

Prayer: Lord there is no greater calling than to turn people towards You, Your Word, Your righteous ways, and Your excellent examples. Lord, keep me from the detours that lead away from You into vain, foolish, and destructive ways. Lord, I want to keep my focus on You. Amen.

February 15

"But we all, with open face beholding as in a glass the glory of the Lord, are changed into the same image from glory to glory, even as by the Spirit of the Lord" (2 Corinthians 3:18). What does it mean to reflect the glory of Jesus? First it comes down to exposure. The more we expose ourselves to something the more we take on like attitude. The more we learn of something, the more we are influenced in our thinking. The more we come into agreement with something, the more we take on its glory, bringing distinction.

We are told in this Scripture that even though we are beholding Jesus' glory through some type of glass, we are being changed from glory to glory. We know that the glass is the Word of God (*James 1:22-25*). However, we must approach it with an open face.

It is natural to approach the Word with our own notions, opinions, and beliefs. These things serve as filters that will keep us from seeing the truth of Jesus, experiencing His life which is revealed in His Word, and knowing the life-changing qualities of it.

"Open" points to an open heart that approaches the Word with a child-like faith and curiosity that is receptive of what it is told. We must be open to change direction (repent) of our ways, and open to being wrong in our thinking (come into agreement with God). We must be transformed in our mind (attitude), and assured that we are being set on the right foundation of truth to line up to the right cornerstone and to grow up into the head of Jesus Christ.

We are not here to put our best religious foot forward but to reflect Jesus to others. We are not here to display the best of the old man which is nothing but vainglory, but to show forth the great masterpiece the Holy Spirit is bringing forth as He conforms us to the image of Christ. It is as we give way to the righteousness of God's Word and to the life and work of the Spirit in us, we will begin to understand what it means to be changed into the same image from glory to glory.

We must keep in mind Jesus is eternal and so is His glory. It can't be measured because it has no beginning and no end. As we learn more of Jesus, discover more about His ways, and experience more of His life, we will be graduating from one degree of His glory to the next. This graduation will continue until we step through the door of physical death and enter into the fullness of His glory.

What a glorious day that will be!

Prayer: Lord, it is natural for us to spend much time trying to bring You down to our level of understanding, but in doing so we strip You of Your glory in our minds. Forgive us for failing to realize You are the ladder that ever ascends upward, and we can only be changed from glory to glory by the great work of Your Spirit as He makes Your Word alive to us, Your life a reality in us, and Your image an emerging reflection from our open faces. Amen.

February 16

"It's a giant turtle!" I excitedly exclaimed as I slowed the car. My passenger remained silent. After all, there aren't any giant turtles in north Idaho. But, even so, it sure looked just like one to me; that is, until we drove up next to it and saw that it was only a big brown tarp somebody had lost in the middle of the road.

I sighed with relief. After all, if it was a giant turtle sitting in the road, then it must be hurt, and how could I save it, or keep some speeding vehicle from hitting it? As I got to thinking of my impulsive conclusion as to what it initially appeared to be, it brought to mind how easy it is to jump to the wrong conclusions when "surfing" through God's Word if we forget to keep each verse in context, know who it was written to and/or for, discern the principle of it, and then believe it by faith as true, followed by obedience.

We are living in the prophesied "perilous times" and need to be deeply established, rooted and grounded in God's Word in order to discern truth from error, just as a closer examination of the object on the road revealed the difference between a tarp and a turtle! *"These things have I written unto you that believe on the name of the Son of God; that ye may know that ye have eternal life, and that ye may believe on the name of the Son of God" 1 John 5:13.* – J. Haley

Prayer: Lord, it is easy to wrongly perceive things. As our mind scrambles to identify something, our emotions can cause us to imagine something that is not so. We clearly must discern first, before we jump to some conclusion that will reveal how inept we are in determining the real nature of something. Lord, keep me aware, sharp, and realistic so I can discern the depths of something before I jump into muddy waters. Amen.

February 17

"And he touched her hand and the fever left her; and she arose, and ministered unto them" (Matthew 8:15). It is natural when we think of God that we often consider His great works of parting the sea, calming the stormy waters, doing the incredible, and wowing us with the impossible. However, what changes one's life are His personal touches.

These touches are rarely noted by others, but they are what goes the deepest into a person's soul. I have seen God "part the sea, move mountains, and calm the storms" but what has done the greatest work in me are those touches that show me not only how personal and upfront He is with me, but His desire to also have an intimate relationship with me.

Sadly, many are looking for great acts of God, but not intimate touches. They have no expectation that the Lord would bother to come their way, allowing them to have their own personal encounter with Him. They may pursue after the witness of His great works but never imagine that He might want to call them out of the crowd, sensing their need to touch Him, and pause to touch them. They want to be wowed without realizing it is the simple touches of God upon our lives that reach deep into our soul that causes love to abound more, grace to be embraced with humble gratitude, and faith to be enlarged as our confidence towards Him is confirmed, our trust in Him is established, and our assurance of Him becomes more grounded in what is eternal.

In my walk with the Lord, these touches have come unexpectedly. It is as if the Lord simply came my way and gently touched me. What was left was the sweetness of simply encountering His presence and sensing His caring, abiding ways.

It is clear that we have been conditioned by much of the world to respond to sensationalism. This conditioning of the world stirs up the imaginations and lusts, but it causes us to miss the simplest gestures of love, consideration, and care that comes from those gentle touches of God and others, leaving us hollow, clueless, and often indifferent to what is sincere and pure.

Prayer: Lord, You have touched my life in many ways. Sadly, I have missed some of those touches because I was caught up with the frivolous things around me. Forgive me for being clueless at such times, and I want to thank You for all of those priceless touches that have indeed reached my soul, touched my heavy heart and revived my sagging spirit. Amen.

February 18

"Yea, and all that will live godly in Christ Jesus shall suffer persecution" (2 Timothy 3:12). I have been reading a book about

persecuted Christians. In our small religious worlds in America, we tend to think our form of Christianity is the only real standard of what Christianity looks like. We think that persecution in Christianity is a form of chastisement or punishment and not a matter of graduation.

Perhaps my statement may be a bit shocking to you. There has been and continues to be persecution against the Christian faith in this country. It has not been blatant because it has been a subtle persecution. In fact, it often comes from those who consider themselves religious or Christian. The truth is, we have been in a boiling pot that has been testing and conditioning us for a long time when it comes to our freedom to worship the Lord.

In some places in America believers have been losing their rights here and there to worship the Lord openly without censorship, penalty, imprisonment, and persecution. However, the winds that are blowing in America point to the fact that blatant persecution of believers is on the horizon and if Jesus tarries, those who call themselves Christians will find out just how deep their devotion towards their Lord really goes. Will it be founded on the Rock or is it just surface, fickle, and a mere fad they got caught up with?

In the book I was reading about persecution, the man was in China interviewing Chinese pastors. He asked who would like to be interviewed first. The youngest of the pastors zealously volunteered to be first. The author was taken aside by his host when he told him to beware of the young zealot because he could not yet be trusted. When the author questioned the host, he stated the young man would someday be a great man of God but that he had not yet been in prison.

The host went on to state that America has seminaries that try to prepare those with a calling, but China has prisons. Every pastor there except the young zealot has been in prison at least one time and the initial sentence for preaching and teaching their faith was three years.

Persecution comes in various forms that are meant to suppress any opposition, silence any contrary voices, mistreat anyone who will not go along with the agenda, and torture those who dare to stand for what would challenge the narrative. It is designed to rob the vulnerable, kill the abstainer, and destroy the strength and voice. It is clearly a fire that will test one's faith.

We would all like to think we would be willing to die for our faith, but for most Americans it comes down to choosing to live for Christ. Living for Christ brings a contrast that can be resented by those who want the recognition from others for their Christian life but fail to live it when it comes to conduct and the affairs of the age.

Prayer: Lord, we can have much zeal towards You when the fire are not testing our faith. It is only in the testing of our faith that we learn just how deep and real our commitment is. Lord, I want to endure to the end knowing that I have kept the faith. Keep the fire coming from Your altar. Amen.

February 19

"Many are the afflictions of the righteous: but the LORD delivereth him out of them all" (Psalm 34:19). It is hard for Christians that have been raised on spiritual pablum to believe that the Christian walk can be hard. However, some of the greatest casualties in Christianity are pastors and their family.

It is hard for pastors to keep up a front that all is well in their lives when their families are in turmoil, and their churches are being bombarded by power plays in leadership and schisms in the body. Some of what they are facing is because of the lack of integrity in the leadership, others because of different factions that have their own agenda, and some because there is a lack of true discipleship establishing believers in their lives in Christ. The truth is if righteousness exists in leadership and the body, there will be afflictions that often come in the form of persecution to bear along the way.

Persecution defines the Christian walk. It tests character, refines faith, establishes a testimony, and reveals that one has indeed stood for their faith and would not deny Jesus. As I consider some of the pastors I have met through the years, I can't honestly say they are trustworthy when it comes to their faith for there is no real sign they have truly graduated.

Some have become burned out, others are stagnant and barely holding on. There are those who are plain weary, but how many have tasted the sorrow of rejection due to their faith? How many have endured the fires of slander for standing for righteousness, and have tasted the bitterness of having their sincerest intentions misunderstood and profaned by those they serve the most? How many, in spite the buffeting, continue to stand?

Such individuals are not marked by degrees but by humility. Their badges of honor are not based on trophies, but on losses that often include those closest to them because they would not dishonor their Lord by compromising. Their scars are not physical but spiritual where they have indeed entered into the sufferings of their Lord, experiencing a broken heart over sin, sorrow with those wounded by life and bruised by the sin of others, and feeling the great cost of sin: the loss of souls.

Prayer: Lord we can talk the talk when all is well and present a certain face when our Christian walk becomes a bit challenging, but when we are about to lose it all, that is where we let go of what we know and go our way or we decide to cling to who You are. We do so, knowing that in the end we will be standing on the right side of eternity, regardless of how upside-down or sideways the world becomes towards You and Your truth. Amen.

February 20

"Blessed are they which are persecuted for righteousness' sake: for theirs is the kingdom of heaven" (Matthew 5:10). "Blessed" in this text points to "happy." Are we to understand that we are to be "happy" when we are persecuted for righteousness' sake? There are two reasons we can be persecuted. One is for what we think are noteworthy causes or the second one for righteousness.

The idea of persecution has to do with standing for something that may prove to be contrary to those in power. Jesus told us since the world hated Him, it will hate us as well. However, if we don't stand for what is right, the world will not give us a second thought. It is only as we run against the grain of a matter that anyone takes notice of us. We don't even have to be different, obnoxious, or rebellious, we just have to stand for what is right and true, the world will take notice. Righteousness is contrary and convicting in a world that is wrong and becoming worse. This world continues to slide into greater madness in its perversion, and the result is that righteousness will create some type of reaction, and for the most part, it will not be pleasant for the one standing upright.

Jesus told us to count the cost, and the cost is any compromise with the world to be at peace with it. The world has no real peace and the only true peace we will find in it is when we are at peace with God. This peace only comes when Jesus is sitting in His rightful place on the throne of our heart as the Prince of Peace.

It is easy to want to avoid persecution in this world, but we are told to stand, and if we are obedient to do so, persecution will come in one form or the other and it will cost us relationships. We will be misunderstood, be falsely accused, and sometime hung out to dry in the bitter winds of rejection and betrayal, but at the same time we need to remember we are becoming identified with Jesus in His sufferings.

Jesus embraced mankind's greatest affront for our sake, and for His sake we must be willing to stand as a light in a world that hates Him. We not only do it for His `sake, but the sake of others who are desperately searching for some light of hope and purpose.

Prayer: Lord we would like to think that the Christian life will be void of storms, dangerous curves, contrary, challenging winds, and earthquakes but all are necessary to prepare us to stand in times of persecution. Thank You Lord for being faithful to prepare me to endure to the end. Amen.

February 21

"Confirming the souls of the disciples, and exhorting them to continue in the faith, and that we must through much tribulation enter into the kingdom of God" (Acts 14:22). One of the impressions of Christianity that has been given in America is that it is a walk through the park. Supposedly, if you are a Christian, you are immune from the challenges, struggles, and sorrows of life.

I remember a time when I was wrestling with some of the challenges life was bringing me. I was in full-time ministry and it seemed that I was being challenged on every front. I became confused because my thinking was if you are serving God, surely everything should fall into place allowing you smooth sailing through the oceans of the world. I could not understand how God could let high waves and storms rock my boat, bringing it close to the abyss of destruction. I even complained to Him about it. His answer was *Matthew 5:45, "That ye may be the children of your Father which is in heaven: for he maketh his sun to rise on the evil and on the good, and sendeth rain on the just and on the unjust."*

I began to realize Christianity does not spare anyone from the challenges of life; rather, believers are imbued with a new life that enables them to walk through the present age by wisely choosing to get in the current of His Spirit. This requires them to follow the compass of His Word, and trust that they are indeed hidden in the ark of Jesus' life. I also recognize that it is the storms of this world that prepare believers for the next, and it is for this reason each of us must accept that it is through tribulation of the present world that we will enter into the kingdom of God.

Prayer: Lord, I realize that some are attracted to You based on the idea of Eden on earth, but due to sin Eden is nowhere to be found. Eden existed because of Your relationship with Adam. You walked with him in the garden in sweet communion but without such a relationship with You, all that lies before us is the barren wilderness of a dying world. Lord, forgive us for looking to, in, and through this world for Eden, instead up looking up with a repentant heart, contrite spirit, and seeking You with everything in us to be reconciled back to You in that sweet place of fellowship with You. Amen.

February 22

It was a cold, wet, tough “tug o’ war” between me and the clam. Not just any clam, mind you, like a mussel, littleneck, horse clam, butter clam or geoduck, (among others) that thrive (or used to) on the coastal beaches of the Pacific Northwest, but a razor clam.

As I write this, I have to admit that I do miss those low-tide, early morning “hunting” escapades on Copalis Beach in Washington state back in the 1950’s when I was a kid. It wasn’t always initially fun though, crawling out of a sleeping bag at 3:00 in the morning when there was an ebb tide.

At my parents’ urging, the scramble was on to hurriedly find my clothes, bundle up, shove my feet into rubber boots, zip up a jacket, grab a clam gun (a type of short-handled, curved shovel) along with a gunny sack, exit the tent that always felt and smelled wet, and start the long trek over sand dunes before heading straight for the retreating water’s edge. Once there, the hunt began, often with the help of flashlights, for the telltale signs of razor clams by looking for small round holes in the sand. If squirts of water are spotted coming out of the hole, all the better, but you had to be quick about it.

I was taught to stand about a foot from the hole with my back to the roaring ocean and then begin digging a few inches from the clam hole so the shovel wouldn’t crush the clam’s shell. As soon as the razor clam senses your presence, it uses its “digger” (some call it a “foot”) and down it goes, deeper and deeper. Once you see the tip of its neck going down, you drop your shovel, get on your knees, shove your arm into the hole, and start “digging” with your fingers. Since the wet sand quickly fills in around your arm, all you can do is keep going until the sand is up to your armpit.

Anyway, if you manage to grab the clam by its neck before it gets away, you have to squeeze hard and keep trying to pull it up while it tries to dig itself deeper. In the meantime, the whole Pacific Ocean is at your back like an unpredictable wild thing watching for an opportunity to send an unusually big breaker towards your backside, especially when the "tug-o'-war" is at its most intense moment. That would be when you're practically lying on the wet sand with your arm buried as far as it can go. In my mind I can still hear the ominous "boom-crack-swish" that announces the rush of an incoming wave. How did that end?

Well, so far, I'm still here to tell how it once was. But this story wasn't written to be a lesson in razor clam digging, but rather to serve as a type of illustration to challenge both myself and other Christians in this unpredictable, often frightening, and turbulent world. We need to remind ourselves of why we are here in such a time as this, what our calling and commission is, how to prepare for it, what our true, God-given goal is, and then, no matter how inconvenient, uncomfortable, unpredictable, or even unsuccessful it may seem to be, to keep going, keep fighting evil, keep pressing in, keep hanging on, keep following Jesus, keep obeying the Word, keep believing God, and *"contend for the faith which was once delivered unto the saints" Jude 3b.*

"Wherefore seeing we also are compassed about with so great a cloud of witnesses, let us lay aside every weight, and the sin which doth so easily beset us, and let us run with patience the race that is set before us, Looking unto Jesus the author and finisher of our faith; who for the joy that was set before him endured the cross, despising the shame, and is set down at the right hand of the throne of God." (Hebrews 12:1, 2.) "And let us not be weary in well doing: for in due season we shall reap, if we faint not." (Galatians 6:9.) – J. Haley

Prayer: Lord, it is amazing what we will endure to taste the things of the world, but how many of us get up early to meet with You, dig deep in Your Word to glean nuggets, and allow ourselves to be filled up with Your Spirit? Amen.

February 23

"And Jesus answered and said, Suffer ye thus far. And he touched his ear, and healed him" (Luke 22:51). In a recent post I talked about the personal touch of God. On the night Jesus was arrested, zealous Peter cut off the ear of the servant of the High Priest. Jesus commented that Peter has come thus far with Him without raising the sword, why now when what was prophesied was about to occur?

We often look for greatness of deliverances, seek some miraculous sign and sensational acts in Scripture. But how many of us take note of Jesus touching the servant of His enemy and healing his ear? Sadly, some want to be entertained like Herod when Jesus stood before him on His way to Calvary, others want an explanation or defense like Pilate when he questioned Jesus, or some want proof that He is God like those who taunted Him to come down from the cross and save Himself.

The truth is Jesus did not come to perform or entertain but to die on a cross to ransom mankind. He will never explain Himself for He is who He is, but He will leave behind impressions or revelations that will not recede into the background of nothingness. He also has no need to prove who He is because the witness He leaves behind confirms His identity, and all one needs to do is believe.

However, the Lord does not want to simply leave impressions behind that can haunt us, revelations behind that will be used to judge us for our unbelief, or silence behind to let man's mocking stand until darkness engulfs him. He wants to touch us personally in such a way that we will be forever changed.

Prayer: Lord, You came to heal and save mankind the first time and sadly man's attitude towards You for the most part has not changed. There are those zealous like Peter that are out of touch of what You are doing, and the Pilates that want You to explain Yourself and give a defense as why they should believe You. There are always those like Herod that are running around seeking sensationalism in Your works and wonders in Your miracles for entertainment purposes.

Lord, I come to You seeking to know You as my Lord, Savior, King, and God. Amen.

February 24

"And when Jesus was come into Peter's house, he saw his wife's mother laid, and sick of a fever, And he touched her hand, and the fever left her: and she arose, and ministered unto them" (Matthew 8:14-15). The question is why is a personal touch from God a bit unnerving to some? I remember holding an orphaned baby from Romania. The child actually fought me as I was attempting to bring him close to me because he did not trust human touch. He had been neglected and was bracing against any future indifference and rejection. However, since I was somewhat watching over him at the house of a friend, I persisted and after a couple of days he did allow me to hold him close to me.

Perhaps many are like that baby. The main reason that a touch is pushed away is because it will require a person to both receive and emotionally respond to it in some way. There are those who fear such a touch, others who refuse to be touched because of some type of unresolved issue, and those who will push it away because of mistrust or a hard heart. For Jesus' touch to mean something we must let it penetrate our being and then be ready to respond.

Take Peter's mother-in-law. After Jesus touched her and brought healing to her body, she arose and ministered to Him and the rest of the people with Him. If we are touched by the Lord, are we ready to rise up from our present state, whatever it may be, to minister to others around us?

A touch requires a response. How we respond will determine how we allow that touch to affect us, but we need to remember that once touched by God, we need to be willing to touch others in like manner, whether through service, or some type of comfort or consolation that can edify, encourage and even bring some type of healing with it.

Prayer: Lord, we can fear Your touch for various reasons, but the truth is You took on humanity to touch mankind in a personal way. It is not unusual for mankind's touch to be hurtful, merciless, unkind, indifferent, taunting, and destructive, but Your touch is heavenly and will bring all the gentleness and healing with it that will soothe the soul and refresh the spirit. Thank You for Your touch. Amen.

February 25

It's something I'm thankful for, but yet I hate it. If you think I'm talking about technology, you'd be really close, but in the more practical world of recent inventions it just so happens to be an ingenious thing called a "washing machine."

When my wonderful, faithful washing machine of many years (that had an agitator in it) became unusable because of someone else's confusion (long story), I had to find another one. The problem is, because of the "rulers of this world" and their "climate change" nonsense that we're all supposed to believe in instead of God and His power to keep the world spinning in its orbit while hanging on nothing, all of us citizens of the world (a/k/a the "herd") are forced to spend too much money on the newest stuff from washing machines (that barely use any water) to cars (that don't use gas) and barely work.

I suppose there are many lessons to be learned from all this, but while folding dingy laundry the other day it came to mind how easy it is for Christians to become "dingy" in their spiritual lives. Dingy isn't really "dirty" per se, but it's not really bright and clean either.

It's very possible to believe the Gospel at some point in our lives, and ask Jesus to "wash our sins away" and even get baptized and wet all over, and then eventually end up feeling and looking spiritually dingy. Sorry to say, but the Gospel being presented in these end days in the "fallen away" churches (that don't know they've "fallen away") has just enough "water" to dampen the emotions to make one feel "washed" without the deep cleansing of brokenness and true repentance; a thorough cleansing by the blood of Christ, as well as the water of the Word which, when believed and obeyed, results in "rivers of living water" flowing out of the innermost being.

Jesus said, *"He that believeth on me, as the scripture hath said, out of his belly shall flow rivers of living water." Titus 3:5* says, *"Not by works of righteousness which we have done, but according to his mercy he saved us, by the washing of regeneration, and renewing of the Holy Ghost; which he shed on us abundantly through Jesus Christ our Saviour." Notice that it takes the "washing of regenerating and renewing of the Holy Ghost" in order to avoid a lukewarm state of "dinginess!"* – J. Haley

Prayer: Lord in the compromising times of our age, we are apt to accept spiritual lukewarmness towards You and dinginess in our walk. Lord, I do not want to be spewed out or rejected due to uncleanness. Lord, reveal any unacceptable way in my life and bring me to the place of repentance where I am thoroughly cleansed. Amen.

February 26

"For whatsoever is born of God overcometh the world: and this is the victory that overcometh the world, even our faith" (1 John 5:4). As believers we must consider if we are being overcome by something in our life or are we being overcomers in this life. I admit I have not heard much about the subject of overcoming through the years and yet the Bible makes it clear it is not optional.

Consider the last Scripture on this subject in *Revelation 21:7, "He that overcometh shall inherit all things, and I will be his God, and he shall be my son."* It is easy to swing high on the branches of grace and excitedly waving the banner of God's love when it comes to Christianity, but it always amazes me the silence I sometimes "hear" when it comes to the subject of overcoming the three enemies of our soul: the world, the flesh, and the devil. Perhaps the reason we become silent about this matter is because it requires the walk of faith to be an overcomer.

It is easy to talk about faith, or hide behind words and terms such as overcoming, but it is something else altogether to live it. If you truly believe something in your heart it means there is a conviction that will manifest itself in action, whether it be a changed life or obedience to His Word. As they say, our actions speak louder than our words.

If there is no action to back what we declare we believe, it simply means we may have an intellectual understanding of it, but it has not got down to our heart; and, yet it is with the heart that we are not only saved because we are persuaded that Jesus died for us, was buried, and was raised three days later, but we also believe unto righteousness that manifests itself in upright actions, and it is through righteousness that grace reigns (*Romans 5:21; 10:9-10*).

As I stated, overcoming is not optional. We have been given the Holy Spirit, the Word of God, and a living witness that we know that Jesus Christ is all in all, that the Holy Spirit's power sustains and His anointing enables, and that the Word stands. The only reason we fail to overcome is because we have not fully believed these truths are so in our hearts and in sincere conviction have walked them out in unfeigned faith.

Prayer: Lord, we like to take the easy way out in our faith by riding on the shirttails of wishful thinking that rests on a false hope that grace hides our lack of conviction, love overlooks our dishonorable ways, and the inaction that rides the fence is a way of keeping our divided loyalties from being exposed as being rebellious, idolatrous, and unprofitable. Forgive us for our unwillingness to consecrate all to You. Amen.

February 27

Though these three men were in it, as I live, saith the Lord GOD, they shall deliver neither sons nor daughters, they only shall be delivered, but the land shall be desolate" (Ezekiel 14:16). It is easy to preach a matter, but in many cases the hearer is left to figure out how to apply the message. Although the Bible is full of examples for our edification, we rarely are given scriptural examples that would show us what it means to walk out the instruction. In most cases the examples are ignored, cast to the side, or considered obsolete because most of them are in the Old Testament (*1 Corinthians 10:1-11*). Sadly, it is assumed by the deliverer of the message that the hearer should know what it means to properly respond.

In the last post I talked about overcoming, but what does it mean to overcome when it comes to the enemies of the soul? It sounds good, but it can become a confusing matter: a hollow echo that rings true in the soul but leaves one floundering in the great ocean of possibilities that in the end often prove to be fleshly and worldly.

There are three main enemies of the soul: the flesh, the world, and the devil. It takes different means to overcome each enemy. It takes repentance to overcome the flesh, humility before the Lord before fleeing the influence of the world, and submission to God's authority and Word to overcome the devil.

When I think of overcoming, I know of many examples of overcomers in the Bible. In fact, there are three men of faith mentioned, not only once by the prophet Ezekiel, but three times in *chapter 14*. Ezekiel made it quite clear that due to these men's righteousness that they would be delivered from the great judgment coming on Jerusalem, but their spouses and children would not be spared. That is a hard warning to consider.

It is clear that faith is an individual choice. We can't choose it for others. Each individual must believe for themselves. This is a bitter pill for saints to face when it comes to family members that have no urgency concerning the dangerous times they are living in. These members may be preparing to live as comfortably in this world as they can, but they are not preparing to stand by faith in the destructive storms that are looming on the horizon. In the end they will be rendered inept to overcome, leaving nothing behind but casualties and desolation.

Prayer: Lord we must overcome to ensure we are not left devastated by the winds of testing and judgment. Lord, I want to be able to stand when the storms come, hide in You when all of the hellish unseen forces come at me, and rest in You when the battle rages. Thank You for being my fortress. Amen.

February 28

"Though these three men were in it, as I live, saith the Lord GOD, they shall deliver neither sons nor daughters, but they only shall be delivered themselves" (Ezekiel 14:18). Even though we know the three men mentioned in Ezekiel, they are not the ones we always point to such as Abraham, Joseph, and David. God never wastes space, words, or examples and when He names certain individuals or examples, I see it on my part as a must to make a comparison.

I studied these men's lives mentioned in *Ezekiel 14* in comparison to Abraham, who lied once because of unbelief, David, who committed adultery and murder because he was in the wrong place at the wrong time, and Joseph, who was cautioned by his father, and appeared a bit arrogant in his youth concerning what God showed him. As I considered these three men with other patriarchs and saints, I realized that the secret to overcoming has been and always will be faith.

Men that choose the way of faith will prove to be overcomers in the challenges confronting them. We can never know when such challenges will arise. We may look out at the horizon to see if there is any storm, at the waters to see if there are any major waves, at the dust of the fields and the trees to see if there is any wind, but the greatest forces that will upend us are unseen.

We may have a certain amount of strength to stand in some storms, some wit to avoid the full force of the elements, and the means to escape the damage of winds, but when it comes to the unseen, we must be prepared to face it and stand in it because we have faith that is able to endure the challenges of our age.

Prayer: Lord, many of our prayers are about being spared from the challenges of our life, but the real emphasis of prayer is that we have the measure of faith to stand and endure. Lord, thank You for always giving me the faith I need to finish the course. Amen.

February 29

"Though these three men, Noah, Daniel, and Job, were in it, they should be delivered but their own souls by their righteousness, saith the Lord GOD" (Ezekiel 14:14). I have been leading up to the three men that would be the only three delivered during the great fall of Jerusalem to the Babylonian armies.

Consider Daniel, in his youth he was being tried after being taken from the palace in Jerusalem to Babylon and tested with the fleshly ways of debauchery. It was there he purposed in his heart by faith to do it God's way and the result is that he developed an excellent spirit and proved to be an overcomer of fleshly attractions and lures, even when facing the lions (*Daniel 1:8; 6:3*).

When we consider Noah, we are told that he found grace in the eyes of the Lord because he walked with Him in the midst of a wicked world. As a result, his righteousness would bring an indictment against the whole world and he, along with his family, would be delivered through the great flood. You must keep in mind that by faith, in fear of the Lord, Noah obediently built an ark. He established a witness in the midst of an unbelieving, rebellious, lawless, violent world without ever compromising with it in spite of the mocking, the deriding, and the rejection that would have come at him (*Genesis 6:8-9; Hebrews 11:7; 2 Peter 2:5*).

Then there is Job. He was a man with a target on his back because of his faith and Satan threw everything at him. He stood on what he knew about God in the darkness, clung to Him as a Rock that would never be moved regardless of the insanity around him, and chose to trust God's work because of his relationship with Him. Because Job chose to believe God, trust Him with the outcome, and rest in His abiding ways, he endured his great trial in patience and overcame Satan. In the end he saw the Lord in lieu of His great, mysterious, sovereign work in creation (*Job 1:8; 13:15: 19:25-27; 42:5: James 5:11*).

People have all kinds of excuses as to why they don't overcome the enemies of their soul. They may give in to a lie here and there and become fearful, as well as casual and find themselves in a place of grave temptation. They can also end up standing high on the pinnacle of immaturity, arrogance and personal strength, ready to be brought down by circumstances. However, the main reason many don't overcome is because of unbelief.

These unbelieving souls either refuse to believe God and His Word, ignore the troubled waters on the horizon so they can walk according to their own drumbeat, or find themselves out of step with God and His Word and ways. The result is they will fail to be a Daniel who stands against the ways of the flesh, a Noah who withstands the affronts of the world, and a Job who continues to stand regardless of what Satan is allowed to throw at him.

Prayer: Lord, we like to think we are overcomers when we are not doing what is necessary to overcome because we want life on our terms. As a result, we will be overcome by our enemies. Forgive us for our half-heartedness, shortsightedness, and our foolishness. Forgive us for not believing Your Word in confidence, believing in You because we are persuaded to do so by what is evident in our lives and creation, and believing You because YOU ARE GOD! Amen.

March

March 1

"Jesus answered them and said, Verily, verily, I say unto you, Ye seek me, not because ye saw the miracles, but because ye did eat of the loaves and were filled" (John 6:26). I recently was presented with a simple question, "Why are you following Jesus?" Probably the first thing I must examine is, am I really following Jesus or am I really doing certain things that give me a false idea that I am following Him when in fact I am really doing my own thing, within my own comfort zones, and according to my own religious notions. Perhaps I am caught up with "noble" causes instead of the commission I have been entrusted with-that of preaching the Gospel and making disciples of Jesus.

There are various reasons why people follow Jesus. 1) They are part of the popular crowd that is following Him because of what He can do in the way of signs and miracles. 2) Another reason people follow Jesus is because of what He can do for them such as in the Scripture above. 3) The third reason people might follow Jesus is to test, try, and judge as to whether He will serve their purpose or not. 4) The final reason people follow Jesus is because of who He is.

Jesus knew that those who followed Him because it was a faddish thing to do can become part of another crowd that would call for His crucifixion. Those who follow Him because of what He can do are prone to turn on Him when His Word of truth offends them as in the case of many of His disciples in *John 6:60-69*. These individuals turned from Him and went back to their old life. We have the religious people of Jesus' time who followed at a distance waiting for an opportune time to try to trip Him up after they found out He would expose their sin, oppose their ways, and judge their wicked agendas.

Jesus' call is to FOLLOW HIM. In the eastern perspective it would be like those following a guru to learn the secrets and purpose of life. Gurus did not feed the crowds with bread. Their goal was/is to build their own kingdom with personal disciples.

Jesus serves as the believer's master or teacher. We each must be enthralled with WHO He is and not WHAT He can do before us as far as the impossible. The Lord's ways prove to be extraordinary, superior and excellent.

Prayer: Lord, it is easy to get caught up with everything around us instead of with You. Give me a love for You and Your truth that I will seek for You, pant after You, and not be content until I am found by You. Amen.

March 2

My art teacher was upset and angry, my mother was not happy with her, and I was brokenhearted over the whole thing. It all began when, in Jr. High School, my art teacher proudly announced that she had acquired a small kiln in which she could fire sculptures. Everyone in the class was given clay and instruments to use in sculpting whatever we wanted to create.

I remember being overjoyed at the prospect of sculpting my favorite subject—horses! I came up with what I thought would be a unique sculpture of a mare and her colt, lying down together, touching muzzles, and configured it into one, flowing artistic creation. This project took me longer to detail and "perfect" than the rest of the class, so while their creations were being finished and fired, I kept working on mine.

Finally, the day came when I turned it over to the teacher to fire for me and excitedly told my mother that this "great sculpture" would soon be coming home to join my horse statue collection. That's when disaster ushered in devastating disappointment for me, disgust for my mother, and depression for the teacher. With a great deal of flap and fury the next day, the teacher informed me that my sculpture had "ruined her kiln." She was madder than a wet hen because my horses had somehow managed to mysteriously melt in her kiln and then harden into a mass of hard clay.

Crying my eyes out because the "greatest art creation of my life" was gone forever, and because the teacher's anger seemed to somehow be directed at me, caused my mother to fly to the forefront of the fury, confront the teacher, and comfort me. But the truth is, it doesn't matter how young or old we are, or how hard we try to "dodge bullets" and avoid disasters and disappointments in this life, we're all going to feel the sting of sorrow, suffering, sickness, and sad situations.

Where can we go, to whom can we turn to for comfort, solace, and care? His name is Jesus, He is the only One. He is the Potter and we are the clay. It is His hands that faithfully mold us and make us into vessels of His choosing—not just any vessel, but holy vessels, fit for the Master's use and for God's glory.

If He allows us to feel the intense heat of persecution, suffering and loss, it is because He is preparing us to overcome through Christ our Lord. *"But now, O Lord, thou art our father; we are the clay, and thou our potter: and we all are the work of thy hand" (Isaiah 64:8)*; "*Beloved, now are we the sons of God, and it doth not yet appear what we shall be; but we know that, when he shall appear, we shall be like him; for we shall see him as he is. And every man that hath this hope in him purifieth himself, even as he is pure" (1 John 3:2, 3)*.
– J. Haley

Prayer: Lord, life's disappointments cause us to realize that our greatest expectations in this world will come crashing down around us. You are the only One who will never let us down. Thank You for being the incredible Rock of Ages that never moves from who You are and Your promises. Amen.

March 3

"Thou shalt not sow thy vineyard with divers seeds: lest the fruit of thy seed which hast sown, and the fruit of thy vineyard, be defiled" (Deuteronomy 22:9). Our Creator laid down specific instructions so that 1) we could live healthy, productive lives, 2) so we would not sabotage ourselves with mixtures that would produce negative effects on us, and 3) so we could appreciate the gift of life we have been given.

Keep in mind we live in a cursed world. Everything is not just a matter of labor, but toil that ends with depressing results. The ground is cursed with weeds and thorns, the world is cursed with vanity, and our physical bodies are cursed with death. In fact, the world is groaning under the great weight of sin.

We are told that three aspects of this world threaten to rob, kill and destroy not only us but everything we have by rust, moth and thieves (*Matthew 6:19-20*). Rust corrupts the quality of things; moths destroy the quality of material and thieves violate the quality of life. We are being constantly challenged by all three and often brought to a state of weariness because the losses and destruction never seem to end.

However, the one thing that will do the most damage are mixtures because they end in corruption of what is pure. The holy can't change the nature of something that is unholy, but the unholy can corrupt the holy (*Haggai 2:11-14; 2 Corinthians 6:14-18*). It is a principle that you can find throughout the Bible. This is why it can be disconcerting seeing Christians try to operate in mixed spirits, allow the poison seed of heresy to be mixed with pure doctrine, and godly practices to be compromised with worldly influences and methods.

The other tragedy is that the fruit left behind is an indictment that such combinations never work and will be met with complete failure, and in some cases judgment. The Bible is clear that the only thing that can be mixed in any equation when it comes to God is faith (*Hebrews 2:4*).

Faith comes by hearing and hearing by the Word of God. It chooses to believe what the Word says as being true, and acts upon it in good faith which leads to obedience. Anything outside of unfeigned faith proves to be a corrupt mixture, a vain attempt, and a point of unbelief, and is considered sin, rebellion, and disobedience.

Prayer: Lord, we think in our conceit we can handle any unholy mixture, arrogantly keep on top of any compromised way, and come out untouched by any wrong spirit, but that is a lie. The unholy corrupts foundations, eats away at discernment, and eventually will rob us of a sure testimony. Forgive us for our vain imaginations, foolish ways, and prideful self-sufficiency that allows us to play footsies with the unholy, parlay with the devil, and compromise with the wrong spirit. Amen.

March 4

"Thou shalt not wear a garment of divers sorts, as of woolen and linen" (Deuteronomy 22:11). I learned from the study about communion that English used the word "brass" while Hebrew uses the word "copper" for the Altar of Burnt offering. All the metals that were used in the tabernacle had to be of the purest quality. However, brass is an alloy, a mixture of zinc and copper.

We Americans have a tendency of mixing things, but it is scripturally clear that such blends compromise what is real. We are now being told that mixing certain materials together robs one's body of energy, because each material gives off its own frequency that affects our energy level.

Some mixtures' frequencies represent death and not life. Although, wool and linen have the same high frequency that ensure positive results for the body, when used together they cancel each other out. The Jews were never to mix different types of material, beasts, or seeds. They were to keep things pure to ensure the integrity of all things. Yet today all we know in America are mixtures in our clothes, food, and herbs, corrupting what is pure, causing the quality of life to go downhill.

Mixtures are also found in our spiritual lives. We mix the pure Word of God with the world's methods and worldly philosophies with our Christian beliefs. We mix pure doctrines of Christ with popular interpretations instead of letting them stand as truth. It is easy to mix the things of man and the world with our Christian convictions, but eventually it will all become corrupt, causing confusion and spiritual complacency.

In America we want to mix things to make them easier to manage, bigger, or better, but when something good or pure is compromised it becomes corrupt and will prove to be contrary to its purpose in the end. I often wonder when we will finally learn that such principles found in the Bible are as valid today as when they were first given to Moses on Mount Sinai. We often think that if a principle was established back in Moses' day it is obsolete, and we will eventually prove it has no real significance.

It is clear that mankind of today in his research of the unseen, whether it be frequencies, DNA, and how energy works is not proving to be more intelligent with his mixtures and shortcuts; rather, he is discovering that God's principles stand, and now, he is just becoming wiser if he chooses to agree with God and believe that He is true. As the Bible declares, it is man who will always be found a liar and a fool if he stands contrary to what has already been established by God in His word.

Prayer: Lord, we are always about what is fast, easy and convenient, but in the end, what is fast often lacks quality, what is easy often ends in a tidal wave hitting us with all kinds of debris that was ignored along the way, and what is convenient ends up proving to be anything but convenient. Lord, forgive us for being a bit lazy, casual and self-serving, and cause us to always seek and choose the way of Your righteousness. Amen.

March 5

"And his feet like unto fine brass, as if they burned in a furnace; and his voice as the sound of many waters" (Revelation 1:15). Jesus is coming soon but when He comes back to this world it will be to judge it. Perhaps man in Jesus' first advent may have refused to hear His

first invitation to come to Him and drink of living Water that will bring life, but in the second, they will hear His voice rolling through the corridors of time and space as Judge of all.

The first time Jesus came, sin was judged in Him on the cross. Like the serpent in the wilderness, Jesus was lifted up so man could look to Him and be saved. In the last post I made reference to the Brazen Altar. Copper or bronze in Scripture represent judgment on sin. We know the cross of Jesus is our Brazen Altar where all sin was judged once and for all, but for sins to be remitted, they must be brought under the blood of Jesus as we seek His forgiveness. It is upon receiving His forgiveness that sins are taken away in order to make way for reconciliation with God.

I am so thankful my sins have been judged in Jesus, cleansed by His blood, and I have been saved out of the current of this world so the real current of life can flow through my being, bringing forth the abundance of hope, ensuring the salvation of my soul.

Prayer: Lord we either face what our sin did to You on the cross and become broken by it and truly repent and seek mercy or we will face the harsh reality that in Your second advent, You will come to judge all sin with a consuming fire that will bring all matters under Your feet. Amen.

March 6

"And all the prophets prophesied so, saying, Go up to Ramoth-gilead, and prosper: for the LORD shall deliver it unto the king's head" (1 Kings 22:12). This incident involved Ahab and his army going against the Syrian army. He invited the king of Judah, Jehoshaphat to join him in this battle. He also wanted the approval of the gods before he would venture into such dangerous waters. Like Elijah at mount Carmal, there were 400 prophets representing Baal who did nothing but encourage the king to go into battle, for the Lord, not Baal, shall deliver the army to him.

However, Jehoshaphat wanted to hear what the God of the universe had to say about it. He asked for a true prophet and like

Elijah there was only one name associated with Jehovah God in the area and that was Micaiah. When Micaiah was brought before the king, he told the king what he WANTED TO HEAR but Ahab knew differently because Micaiah never had anything good to tell him.

The king demanded that the prophet tell him the truth. The words were not of victory but of utter defeat. For telling the truth, the prophet was put in prison and fed with bread until the king's return. Micaiah stated in 1 Kings 22:28, *"If thou return at all in peace, the LORD hath not spoken by me."* We know that the king did not return.

As I read this account, I wondered why Ahab asked the false prophets, knowing that when all was said and done, they would tell him what he wanted to hear, and not the truth. He also knew that the true prophet of God would tell him what heaven had to say about the matter and that it would not be good.

It is easy to convince ourselves that we want the truth, but we need to understand we are already standing on shaky ground because we can't imagine that what we do perceive could be anything but the truth. Granted, for those who still have some realism to their thinking, there is also fear that such "truth" will not be in accordance to their idea of it.

We need to be aware that God will reveal the truth to us, but it will most likely shake us if we are not prepared to admit that we only know in part. We need to be realistic and know when it comes to the full picture of something, we are standing on a molehill that can't see much and not a mountain that could give us a more reliable perspective of the terrain and the enemy below.

Prayer: Lord, we can say we want the truth, but if we do not love it enough to cast aside what is contrary to it, we will end up on the Titanic waiting to hit the iceberg that will prove that we have been floating through life on a lie. Forgive us for not loving You and Your Word enough to reject floating off on some worldly lie. Amen.

March 7

"And there came forth a spirit, and stood before the LORD, and said, I will persuade him" (1 Kings 22:21). In the previous post I brought out Ahab and false prophets. The false prophets were preferred because they told Ahab about victory but there was something in his knower that the wicked king probably knew the truth because he was contrary to God and His Word. Such an individual creates his own reality so he never has to face the harsh reality of future judgment and even though he may hear what he wants to, doubts will keep the individual on the edge.

The truth of the matter is that behind most of mankind is they prefer to hear only what they want to hear and God will oblige them by sending lying spirits. The criterion for such lies is it must tickle ears so that people do not have to face the truth.

The truth in Ahab's day was the land was full of the sins of idolatry, fornication, perversion, pagan practices, and grave wickedness. There is no way our holy God would ever bless a king or His nation in such a state, and those who know the true God of heaven would recognize that fact. They would know that the great need is not to seek out prophets but fall on their faces in true repentance seeking His mercy rather than seeking to hear a lie.

It is important to keep in mind that in these days of great deception how many are seeking after the prophets of Baal about the tumultuous times we are living in. I would almost bet the ratio of four hundred false prophets to one true prophet probably exists today. Instead of God allowing lying spirits to fill the mouths of false prophets like He did in Ahab's case, God has sent a delusion to test the hearts of men, and we are warned that seducing spirits promoting lies and fables will be prevalent in our days.

Truth in times where evil reigns is always unpopular and that is why we must love the truth above all else so we will not be swept away with the delusion. We must never turn off our discernment towards anyone or anything. We must avoid swooning over some person while settling for empty words and prophecies that fall short of being true in every way.

Will truth at such times be popular or well received by those who only want to live in some space where they are left feeling good about sins, where lies are preferred, immorality justified, paganism celebrated, idols worshipped, and darkness is considered the light? NO! but as Christians we are called to love the truth, prefer righteousness, know justification through repentance and mercy, celebrate the life given by our Creator, worship the true God of heaven and walk towards our true destination according to the true light of the world, the Lord Jesus Christ.

Prayer: Lord, we do want the reality we can live with, but it is only Your truth and by faith that we can walk through this world towards what You have promised us. We are told that we can't even begin to imagine how wonderful and great the glory of the future world holds for us. Come quickly Lord Jesus. Amen.

March 8

"And Jehoshaphat said, Is there not here a prophet of the LORD besides, that we might enquire of him?" (1 Kings 22:7) It is easy to find a false prophet for they abound in every age. Some are seeking status in the church world, some a religious following, and some just want your money. To accomplish any of these worldly methods, you must gain man's favor. Jesus is clear in *Luke 6:26, "Woe unto you, when all men shall speak well of you! for so did their fathers to the false prophets."*

A real prophet is not caught in the snare of man's approval; rather, such an individual is seeking to please God. True prophets walk a very narrow path. They are firebrands in the sense they will create a great stir wherever they go. Many times, the stir they create is not pleasant for them as those around them will do almost anything they can to silence them.

In this case the wicked Ahab had many false prophets, but Jehoshaphat discerned they were not to be trusted because it was apparent they were telling Ahab what he wanted to hear. This is when the king of Judah asked if there was a true prophet of God they could enquire about the real mind of the Lord. This is when the true prophet Micaiah was called to appear before the king.

At first Micaiah told King Ahab what he wanted to hear, but the king knew differently, and demanded he tell the truth. The truth was that the king and his army were set up for defeat. It never ceases to amaze me that King Ahab knew that Micaiah was a true prophet of the true God, but he still chose to go along with the false prophecy.

However, Ahab had Jehoshaphat wear his kingly garments knowing that the army would chase after him, allowing him to escape death. I am sure you know the rest of the story, Ahab's cleverness never saved him, and Micaiah was once again proven to be the true prophet of God.

The question is how many are discerning among those who claim to be prophets today? I can tell you there are very few real prophets, and they are not out tooting their horns about their status because their message is not popular. Keep in mind, prophets become necessary when God's people began to fall away from Him, and sought out when tumultuous waves begin to rock the boats of nations.

We must refuse to listen to the false prophets, which will make us the odd men-out when it comes to those who are running here and there to hear any word. As saints we must demand of ourselves not to accept what is false and seek out the one who speaks what is true, while leaving in the rearview mirror the rest of the gainsayers.

Prayer: Lord, there is so much we must wade through, but we can trust You to keep us on the right path, guide us through the darkness of this age and bring us forth for Your purpose and glory. Amen.

March 9

"And when he putteth forth his own sheep, he goeth before them, and the sheep follow him: for they know his voice" (John 10:4). When I was young and growing in my faith, one of the terms that was being used was "Lone Ranger." There were even newspaper and editorial articles about it written by pastors. This was in reference to believers

who became disillusioned with church and either looked for another one or quit going.

I will not debate whether there are those who go from church to church looking for the perfect one. Like generations before, there were the grumblers who had a judgmental spirit and were looking for a church that could meet their unrealistic standards. There were the murmurers who were looking for something new and exciting. Of course, there was the saying that went like this, "Are you looking for a perfect church, and if you do and walk into it, it becomes imperfect." The reason is we are all imperfect and the true Church, the many-membered universal body, is being brought forth in perfection by the work of the Spirit.

However, not all Christians who were labeled "Lone Rangers" fell into the two categories I mentioned. Some couldn't handle petty politics, others were weary of wading through the latest heretical teachings, some were disillusioned by the lack of love in the body, and there were those who stood against some sin and were in a way crucified by leaders or from the pulpit.

I likewise was one of those "Lone Rangers." I was not church hopping looking for that "perfect church;" rather, I was seeking to come higher in my life with Christ. I was hungry. I was seeking, and I was not about to settle for mere milk and crumbs when I knew I needed the bread and meat to continue to grow.

This brings me to a harsh reality that most local churches have ceilings that can't be penetrated. These local bodies are necessary but often limited in what they can offer their sheep. Whether it is a doctrinal ceiling, a political one, or where small-minded elitism of some type keeps it together and controlled, it is hard to breach the ceiling. I have hit that ceiling many times and I remembered Jesus had to step outside of the religious kingdom to teach and minister to the lost and seeking sheep of His day.

I had to leave various churches because I hit the ceiling and knew I needed to move on. Once I left, I rarely looked back, but there are times that I miss the sweet sheep that were truly seeking green pastures and living waters.

Prayer: Lord we must always go where Your voice leads us. You may be leading us to different pastures for different reasons, but we must always listen for and adhere to Your voice to grow in our life in You. Amen.

March 10

How clean is clean? Maybe the answer to that comes down to a person's personal preferences and standards. Mine have always been if it can shine or sparkle, then it's not really clean if it's not reflecting its highest potential.

You know how that is, I'm sure—when you hold a drinking glass up to the light to make sure it's crystal clear and sparkling clean before putting it back into the cupboard. The thing is the only person who can hold myself to this standard is me. Therefore, in addition to regular cooking and cleaning, there's a lot of polishing of the glass stovetop, old copper bottom pans, kitchen appliances, faucets, furniture and anything else that should shine according to my standards (except the car because we live in North Idaho, and I gave up on it shining, years ago.)

On thinking about this "shiny obsession" of mine, I remember begging my mother for shiny "Mary Jane" black patent shoes when I was little. No doubt my parents were part of this standard because they were sticklers for fingerprints or smudges on anything, including windows in the house or the car. In fact, whenever we went for a car ride with the cocker spaniel in the backseat with me, it was my job to keep her from licking the windows which she loved to do for some strange reason, and it drove my dad nuts. They used to laugh years later when telling people that when toddlers my age came with their parents to visit, I would monitor them and not let them touch anything, especially the glass top on the coffee table.

Probably by now, if you've read this far, you're thinking you don't ever want to come for a visit, but let me assure you, it's safe. I've learned that Jesus isn't interested in how shiny and sparkly we keep our possessions—no, not at all. What He is looking for are people through whom He can brightly shine.

He tells us, *"You are the light of the world. A city that is set on an hill cannot be hid. Neither do men light a candle and put it under a bushel, but on a candlestick; and it gives light unto all that are in the house. Let your light so shine before men, that they may see your good works, and glorify your Father which is in heaven" (Matthew 5:14-16).*

May we be prepared by the Spirit and the Word to shine with the light of Jesus, holding tightly to these words of the prophet Daniel, *"And they that be wise shall shine as the brightness of the firmament; and they that turn many to righteousness as the stars for ever and ever" (Daniel 12:3).* – J. Haley

Prayer: Lord, so many times we prefer the shiny things of the world and not the glory of heaven. What we prefer we pursue. Lord, I want to see You, knowing it might cause darkness until Your light of glory breaks forth in my soul and disperses its shadows. Amen.

March 11

"And Jesus being full of the Holy Ghost returned from Jordan, and was led by the Spirit into the wilderness" (Luke 4:1). The question I ask is where do you learn the most about the Lord? In church, Bible Study, or in the times of spiritual drought, wildernesses of testing, in pits of despair, or in great need.

As man Jesus' spiritual life was hidden in obscurity for almost 30 years and when His ministry was about to break forth on the scene, He was introduced at His baptism by the Father and then led into the wilderness by the Spirit to be tempted for 40 days. His ministry on earth only lasted a mere 3½ years at the most.

What about a David? He was just a shepherd who learned to take on the predators to protect the sheep. His training was with the sheep, unseen and for the most part insignificant. Later he would be on the run for his life.

What about Elijah? He hit the scene and caused much distress for Ahab. He was in obscurity until he was called forth. There is John the Baptist who broke 400 years of silence as a voice in the wilderness. We know about events around his conception, but past that very little is known until he stepped on the scene.

I look back at my walk and am thankful for my church experiences where a foundation of the Word was established under me. I am thankful for good Bible teachers that helped me learn about how to use the Word of God. I know that we must not forsake the assembling together so we can exhort one another to live godly lives in challenging times, but the greatest fellowship I have has rarely been in a church setting.

One of my greatest times of fellowship with Christians has been sharing a meal with them, where there is a freedom to talk about the Lord. It is during meals that people are the most open to "just be," as they would say.

Jesus would often separate from the crowd to teach His disciples and come apart from His disciples to be alone in prayer with the Father. Most of the Christian life is not lived out in public but in intimate places with a few that are close to them and in secret chambers when it comes to God. The few that we share our lives with entail times of edification but our times with the Lord are where the greatest spiritual growth takes place.

Prayer: Lord, we want to live our life out on the stage where everyone is cheering us on or there are others who are taking the greatest load upon themselves so we don't have to be bothered or tested in unpleasant ways during ministry. However, Lord the burden of spiritual growth rests with each of us and we need to experience what it means to come out and be "alone" to truly seek You. Amen.

March 12

"In these days came John the Baptist, preaching in the wilderness of Judaea, And saying, Repent ye for the kingdom of heaven is at hand" (Matthew 3:1-2). In the last post I spoke about how it seems that great saints suddenly hit the scene without anyone knowing the process they went through to finally come into their calling. These saints even

make their life and calling look easy when in reality, they had to go through quite a process before they could display such grace.

It all comes back to the type of relationship we have with God and others. However, to develop a relationship with someone is not a community event. Relationships are personal, and learning about that person is also private. The reason I say this is because close, intimate relationships are developed in obscurity, away from prying eyes. A person may be a public figure, but one can never know the quality of their relationship with others.

This is true for our relationship with the Lord. So many great men and women of God came out of obscurity where they experienced spiritual drought, wildernesses, pits and great need, but that is where their life in the Lord was developed as they were prepared to fulfill their calling. To hear the Lord, they had to know His voice, to know Him meant they knew what was important to Him. To know what is important is to hit the mark, but it takes time, personal investment, and a love that desires to ever be close to Him, to seek Him, to bring pleasure to Him.

We talk a lot about relationship with God, but how many really have a close relationship with Him? Real spiritual growth came in my life when I finally discovered what it meant to sit at the table of fellowship with Jesus as His Spirit imparted the meat of His Word into my soul. The fellowship started my journey to know Him and that is when I experienced His hand of faithfulness in troubled times, His provision in the spiritual wildernesses, His comfort in loss, His abiding love in failure, and His light in great darkness.

What makes all relationships great comes down to how personal they become. There are very few you can be yourself with. There are even fewer that will walk down a dark road with you when times are the bleakest. And there is only One who can walk into the depths of utter despair with you and that is the Lord Jesus. That is why Jesus desires a friendship with us. He wants to share His heart with us and He wants us to share our lives with Him.

Prayer: Lord, we often would like knowledge about You to fall on us, but in order to learn who You are, a personal investment is required.

Give me that desire to never settle for a surface reality about You, for I desire to know You in greater ways. Amen.

March 13

"And why call ye me, Lord, Lord, and do not the things which I say?" (Luke 6:46). Obedience to the Word is not a matter of obtaining one's salvation; rather, it is about taking the opportunity to exercise your faith. Faith comes from hearing and hearing by the Word of God. Obedience accompanies active faith, and we are saved by grace through such active faith that is advancing forward.

The matter of the salvation of man's soul is the most important issue mankind must truthfully confront. However, the message has been so watered down by worldly philosophies that the very mention of the fact there is only one entrance, one door and one path that leads to salvation can create many different reactions. This includes a type of "Oh well" when it comes to Christians. After all, in our world where Universalism is held to, everyone is going to be saved, even Satan, as everyone continues as usual with their hobbies, sports, and worldly, fleshly pursuits. Meanwhile, they are thinking that what constitutes heaven in the end will be based on "their idea of happiness here."

Imagine, in the minds of such individuals, heaven is not going to be any different than the present world we now live in. And yet, how many want to be delivered from this world because at the center of it is the ongoing tragedy of losses, suffering, and death?

However, to make heaven like earth so everyone can make it there is to avoid facing the hard facts. 1) The way to heaven is narrow and few will find it. 2) Heaven or hell is a personal choice and that choice becomes obvious by how we live. We are either preparing for heaven, or we are walking towards hell in the ways of death. We will reap what we sow. 3) Heaven is a place of worship and service to a Holy God, not one of personal pleasures and useless pursuits. 4) Heaven is not about man experiencing the best of life after death but experiencing the reality of God by faith through His promises, who is all goodness.

This brings us back to what constitutes salvation. May I say up front, it is not a matter of wishful thinking. One of the most sobering realities is that not everyone who calls Jesus, "Lord" will be received into His kingdom. Many assume that if they have the language down and the right association that they will somehow make it into the kingdom of heaven, but salvation has to do with having a right relationship with the Lord.

The Scripture in Luke lays out why some people will not be received into the kingdom of heaven. Jesus posed a very interesting point: Why call Him Lord if you are not going to obey Him? If we obey the Lord, we will be assured of carrying out the will of the Father.

I realize this is a simple truth, but many people want to dress up or complicate the will of the Father, yet the Bible is very clear about what the Lord's will is and if you really love Him, you will obey Him (*John 14:15*).

Prayer: Lord, we think of salvation without any heavenly fruits. We think of grace as a free ride and not an opportunity to partake of and possess Your promises by faith. In a way, we divorce ourselves from the reality of You and Your life to create our own form of Christianity that proves convenient to the flesh without realizing we are not only going to miss the target of righteousness, but we may even miss heaven as well. Forgive us. Amen.

March 14

"Not every one that saith unto me, Lord, Lord, shall enter into the kingdom of heaven, but he that doeth the will of my Father which is in heaven" (Matthew 7:21). Many people think if the Lord is using their gifts that they must be alright, but God can use whatsoever or whosoever He will; therefore, such activities do not stipulate that one is "tight with Him." It all comes down to whether we are truly doing the will of the Father or doing our own thing according to our religious ideas.

We tend to think any good, religious work is the manifestation of salvation, but the manifestation of true salvation is obedience that comes out of believing what God says. It is not a matter of works but of doing what is scripturally established as being right and honorable for God's glory.

So many times, the works we do are what makes us feel good, look good, and earn some possible brownie points with others. But the works God asks us to do has been ordained before the foundation of the world (*Ephesians 2:10; Hebrews 4:2-3*).

Some of these works may not make sense to us because they may seem insignificant, such as giving a cup of cold water to someone, an article of clothing to one who may not even appear to need it or doing something that seems contrary to all logic. Other works may prove to be inconvenient because it has nothing to do with one's timing, but what is NEEDFUL AT THE TIME.

Many of God's works are not for public display but done in secret so that a witness can be made before heaven and earth that will give God the glory. There are those works that will prove to be sacrificial like the widow and her mites. These are the works that serve as the sweetest savor to God because He deserves not only the best, but our ALL.

Prayer: Lord, we always have our ideas about serving You, but most of the time they are not about You being lifted up but about us receiving certain recognition from others. Lord, we try to be noble about serving You, but we lack the necessary honor that ensures You are truly glorified in all matters that relate to You. Amen.

March 15

"And Samuel said, Hath the LORD as great delight in burnt offerings and sacrifices, as in obeying the voice of the LORD? Behold to obey is better than sacrifice, and to hearken than the fat of rams" (1 Samuel 15:22). It took me a while to realize that God is not interested in what I can do for Him, or what I did for Him, because He NEEDS none of it. He is interested in me simply obeying Him according to His Word.

As religious people we can become quite caught up with the deeds we do in service to the Lord. We are impressed with them, and we naturally think He should be impressed as well. After all, we did it for Him in His name.

However, the issue of obedience is not a matter of simply doing a religious deed, it is also an act of good faith on the part of an obedient saint towards the Lord, knowing what pleases Him. This act is also a matter of great love in light of the salvation He has allotted to every believer through redemption.

When I stand before Him, it will not be about what I have done for Him, but what I did with Him as in relationship to submitting to the leading of His Spirit, properly handling His Word, being faithful to His calling in my life, and obeying Him because I LOVE Him.

I say all of this because when I first became a Christian it was all about how others saw my Christianity. As I grew in the Lord, I wanted people to see how much I knew and what I was doing for the Lord to impress them. After being humbled in MANY ways, I just wanted to do right to establish a witness of my Lord to others. Now, in what some might consider the twilight of my years, I just want to be faithful to the Lord to the end by doing what is right towards Him IN SERVICE TO OTHERS.

Each step of faith that ends in obedience is what is leading me. It keeps my feet on the straight and narrow path and has led me in the ways of righteousness. As a result, my assurance is not in what I am doing for God; rather, my assurance is that the steps of obedient faith towards Him and His Word are leading me home where I will see Him as He is.

Prayer: Lord in our arrogance we want to do great things for You, but in humility, You show us greatness comes by being a meek servant to all. Such service often comes in practical, simple service that meets individual needs. Lord, people may have counted the numbers of the 5,000 being miraculously fed, but You were meeting a simple need of one soul at a time. Thank You for stepping out of eternity to faithfully meet my needs at that moment and for that time. Amen.

March 16

"And Gideon said unto him, Oh my Lord, if the LORD be with us, why then is all this befallen us? And where be all his miracles which our fathers told us of, saying, Did not the LORD bring us? And where be all his miracles which our fathers told us of, saying, Did not the LORD bring us up from Egypt? But now the LORD hath forsaken us, and delivered us into the hands of the Midianites" (Judges 6:13). Gideon has some pertinent questions. How many of us have lately asked similar questions of the Lord as we watch the great spiritual darkness begin to engulf the world.

Where are you Lord in all of this? Where are all the miracles, the parting of the Red Sea to enable us to walk through it, the great deliverance from evil forces that are breathing down our necks, the water from the Rock to sustain us in this time for we are weary, and the manna from heaven to strengthen us for our weakness is great? Where are Your incredible moves, Your miraculous intervention, and the extraordinary changing the landscape of the ordinary? Why are You forsaking us?

The real question is, has God changed? In other words, is He still doing today what He did yesterday? The other question is, has God forsaken His people? The answer to both questions is a big NO! If the answer was "yes" it would mean God is a liar. Consider Gideon.

He was thinking about God's past acts, but did he expect God to do anything in Israel's present state of sin, idolatry, and unbelief? Hopelessness is the opposite of faith. Faith reminds us that God is still God and that the miraculous is the normal for Him.

If the miraculous, the incredible and the extraordinary is missing, it is because man is missing the faith that moves the hand of God by trusting and allowing Him to be God. In such a situation, man has simply succumbed to the present barren state, often hiding himself in the shadows of despair instead of taking hold of God by stepping outside of the shadows of the "whys" into the light of God's promises, knowing He never changes.

It is man who must choose to believe God. He must make himself available to discover his calling, take his place as a person with a heavenly destiny, and be willing to take a stand in great darkness against the idols of the land. It is when man stands by faith that God can show Himself mighty through him.

On behalf of Gideon, God defeated an army.

Prayer: Lord, we have so many questions about this life, but there is usually only one answer to each question. YOU are the answer but to accept the only answer, we must choose to believe You and avoid letting present struggles cause us to hide in some dark corner to speculate as to why You are not stepping on the scene. We fail to seek You out, trusting that You are waiting for us to be prepared to not only see You move, but be part of it. Amen.

March 17

"For the eyes of the LORD run to and fro throughout the whole earth, to shew himself strong in the behalf of them whose heart is perfect toward him. Herein thou has done foolishly: therefore from henceforth thou shalt have wars" (2 Chronicles 16:9). In the last post I talked about Gideon and his struggles with what he knew about God's miraculous intervention on behalf of His people when they were slaves in Egypt as well as His silence when it came to the Midianites' oppression that was heavy upon him and the land. Man's great struggle in this world is not with God, but with himself. He is limited in what he can see when it comes to the challenges around him, as well as struggling with what it means to exercise faith when it comes to truly trusting God with the impossible.

It is natural to wonder where God is amid struggling with unbelief brought on by hopelessness due to circumstances. Why does He not intervene, and what does He expect from me since I am only one insignificant person?

Again, this is not about God, but man failing to understand the ways of God. God is not looking for an army to do His bidding; rather He is looking for that one person who will stand up, exercise faith and give Him permission to use them.

God has not changed, and His way of doing has not varied in any way. I have witnessed many miracles in my faith walk. He has brought many of my enemies down before me. God has not nor will He ever forsake His people. He sometimes withdraws His presence so the Gideons are put in such a position that they take hold of their high calling and become His instrument. In His hand we become part of the solution, sensing if we don't, we will perish in our miserable state.

How many Gideons are still hiding in the shadows asking God "why" in despair with no expectation, no hope, and no light of deliverance dawning on the horizon since they are looking at the circumstances and not seeking God with everything in them? In their despondent state they are not preparing to become part of the solution, whether it is simply standing for truth, challenging the idols of their time or leading a small army to reveal God's ability to defeat the great armies. It is important to realize that when one is on the front lines with God where the real battle is ongoing, that is when they witness His greatness to bring about the miraculous.

Prayer: Lord, we want to see the miraculous without standing, experience the incredible without confronting the enemy, and see great deliverance without marching according to Your instructions. Due to our lack of faith, we slide into despair and begin to major in the "whys" while questioning Your character. Lord, forgive us because we do not believe Your Word, believe Your intention of goodness towards us, and believe in Your sovereignty to bring everything about for our benefit and Your glory. Amen.

March 18

"Not that we are sufficient of ourselves to think any thing as of ourselves; but our sufficiency is of God" (2 Corinthians 3:5). In the last post I spoke of Gideon who asked "why" the Lord wasn't doing great things as He had done before. Where are the miracles, where is the deliverance, where is the Lord?

In Gideon's day there was much idolatry. Idolatry is always associated with paganism for a good reason. The problem with living in the midst of any paganism is that it becomes a snare where people are easily enough enslaved by it to not only serve the idol it promotes, but to flow with the culture that goes with it. Keep in mind, paganism becomes the sum of one's culture and practices. The children of Israel were chasing after other gods and not seeking the one true God. They eventually found themselves in bondage to the Midianites.

What can we learn from the children of Israel? Did they not need God and His intervention? If they did, why did they seek another god who could not intervene and would ensure bondage of some type? What happened to them?

For people who have just enough religion to soothe their conscience about the matters of God, the main bridge that leads into paganism is something called self-sufficiency. Self-sufficiency is an arrogant dependency based on what a person knows and a false reliance on personal strength that will eventually fail.

God is the only One who is sufficient to meet needs, push back unseen enemies, and show us a way out of the prison of selfishness. To ensure we end up on the right side, we need to bring to light the arrogance of being self-sufficient beginning with ourselves.

Prayer: Lord, our pride sets us up to feel self-sufficient, our intelligence convinces us that we have what it takes to come out on top and our high opinion of our abilities gives us a false sense of infallibility. Lord it is obvious that the falls, the failures, and false ways that lead to nowhere are what You use to reveal the foolishness behind our pride. Thank You for being faithful to let me falter in my ways, fall in my arrogance, and know the sting of embarrassment that comes from being foolish in my thinking. Amen.

March 19

"And that which fell among thorns are they, which, when they have heard, go forth, and are choked with cares and riches and pleasure of this life, and bring no fruit to perfection" (Luke 8:14). In the previous

post, I talked about self-sufficiency. When man is operating in it, he is dependent on his abilities to figure out a matter. It is upon his failure to change a matter or make it right that he will often look for a reason as to why he failed. The last thing he will admit is that such failure comes back to his inability to change anything that has to do with what is important, substantial, or significant.

The problem with Christians in America is they have become self-sufficient in their abundance and have not seen any need to depend or rely on God for anything. As a result, they fail to first seek His will about anything. God, in many cases, has become an OPTION that we will only desperately consult when we run out of personal solutions and hit a wall of desperation.

But until we are desperate enough, if we are really sick, we will first seek the medical profession. If we have some other need, we will first consider our worldly options to see what we need to do. If we can't do it, we will seek out the appropriate organization or business, take the necessary measures whether it is a loan, using a credit card, seeking out a particular individual and etc., because we can as long as there is an option on the horizon.

This brings us to one of the major idols in America, brought to us now by our dwindling abundance: the god of pleasure. There is nothing wrong with pleasure, but if you are seeking it rather than taking pleasure in what God has provided and learning contentment, it has become an idol.

People who think they are not in need become the neediest. Those who think they are on top are really down under a delusion, those who think they are rich are poor, and those who think they have earned the right to live unto themselves will find out that everything is a matter of God's grace and not their attempts. Those who seek pleasure reveal they have a spiritual vacuum because somewhere along the way in their self-sufficiency they became complacent by failing to execute active faith in first seeking God and His righteousness in all matters.

Prayer: Lord, we think we have all the answers when we fail to recognize You are the only answer. We think we know what to do when we fail to realize we know nothing outside of Your Spirit and Word. We seek what we think will work but fail to see You are the One who must inspire or do the work to ensure the right results. Forgive us for our wretched ways, pagan practices, selfish emphasis, and self-sufficient attitude. Amen.

March 20

"Traitors, heady, highminded, lovers of pleasures more than lovers of God: Having a form of godliness, but denying the power thereof: from such turn away" (2 Timothy 3:4-5). What are you searching for in this life? We must discern our agendas by considering 1) our emphasis, 2) our pursuits, and 3) our preferences.

So many times, we have good intentions, but we miss the mark in the end because we fail to see them through. We may have honorable goals, but they seem to elude us because the timing and circumstances are never right. When it comes to our preference, we fail to see that intellectually we may know the right and honorable thing to do, but at the base of almost all preference is selfishness that will naturally go with what feels good, is convenient, serves our purpose, and caters to our desires. Such a fleshly preference often far outweighs doing what would be the right thing to do, revealing the real core of our character.

In my last post I talked about how it appears that due to people's love for pleasure, many are seeking the god of pleasure, even some Christians. Pleasure comes from different sources and in different forms. It can come in certain activities such as sports, fishing or hunting, as well as hobbies, projects, and outings with family and friends. These pleasures give us a sense that if we could live in perpetual pleasure, we would be happy, but as the saying goes, too much of a good thing will end up being not "so good." However, the concept that pleasure brings happiness and meaning in life can cause it to become an idol that we will prefer and seek out.

There is nothing wrong with certain worldly pleasures, but there is nothing that is righteous and leaves an eternal impact on anyone either. God allots us pleasure so we can enjoy aspects of this life, but we must keep it in perspective, making sure fun and pleasure will never be our main pursuit.

We must keep in mind upfront, that this idol seems harmless enough because who would not like to have a bit of pleasure occasionally? Occasionally, we mark some pleasures with memories that in time will fade. However, those who seek out pleasure are the ones who must discern if it has become a god. They must consider if their heart is towards experiencing the pleasures of this age, or the pleasures of God, by how much emphasis, time, resources, and effort they put into their particular quest. They must discern if pleasure is their main priority or if they really prefer God's truth, way, and service.

Prayer: Lord, the world has been designed to take hearts and minds captive. It offers various idols to bow before and altars to worship at, but we rarely recognize them because some are subtle and seem harmless. Lord, give me the heart and discernment to identify any idols and pagan altars in my life. Amen.

March 21

"Jesus said unto him, If thou wilt be perfect, go and sell that thou hast, and give to the poor, and thou shalt have treasure in heaven; and come and follow me (Matthew 19:21). The world's idea of pleasure is not the same as God's. Pleasure in God's economy is to delight in who He is and what He has provided, while pleasure to the world can be anything from fun to fleshly pursuits, profane activities, and pagan practices. The pleasure in the latter has to do with pleasing, feeding, and catering to the desires of the flesh. You can't cater to the flesh, while pursuing the world's idea of pleasure and please God as well. The Bible is clear you can't serve two masters at a time.

Paul was adamant that in the end days men would be lovers of pleasure and not lovers of God. We seek out what we love. We are told to first seek God and His righteousness in all matters. Perhaps God has no problem with your particular pleasure, but on the other hand if it has become idolatrous, He might put His finger on it like He did the riches of the young ruler who came to Him, seeking eternal life in *Matthew 19*.

At such times He will tell you to give up your idol and follow Him. If that happened, the question is how would it leave you: feeling lost, empty, and confused because it has been your main emphasis in this life? If so, you have been pursuing that which is vanity, living for what will leave you feeling empty in the end, and knowing your preference will never leave any eternal mark behind in your life or in the lives of others.

We will all stand before the Lord and give an account. For Christians, they will give an account as to the type of steward they have been with the life God has given them, but for unbelievers they will give an account for what they have done in this life. Christians do not want to stand before God with ashes to show for a life of empty service, and unbelievers do not want to stand facing judgment for lacking eternal life that comes through Jesus Christ. One will bring shame, and the other will taste the wrath of God.

Prayer: Lord, in today's world many are riding the delusional wave of universalism where all will be saved, but Lord I choose to walk in this world by faith that comes from believing Your Word. Your Word tells me we will ALL stand before You as judge and that fire will test the works of the believer, and judgment will separate the unbeliever to a hellish existence. Thank You for the gift of faith and Your unchanging Word of truth. Amen.

March 22

Anyone who loves to garden knows the feeling of joyful hope as seeds are sown and plants are planted in the spring; and they also know the sinking feeling that leads to a certain kind of heartbreak when all the hope and joy is wiped out by unseasonal freezing, pounding hailstorms, accompanied by gophers, ground squirrels, moles, voles and hungry insects.

Such is the situation where we live in north Idaho. In spite of all the challenges we've faced last year, I remained faithful to the cause by replanting parts of the garden at least three times. All we can do in such times is pray hard and continue to tend to what is struggling to grow as best as we can despite the unpredictable elements.

Knowing how evil the days are, and keenly aware of the rising prices and ominous signs of food unavailability, many are beginning to realize that, in order to be at least somewhat prepared for lean times, it is a good idea to plant a garden if possible. But sometimes all does not go as planned, even to the most experienced farmer, or rancher. So, then what?

There is only One to whom we can turn, and that is to our Father in heaven. Therefore, in my own weakness, I remind myself how Jesus prayed in *Matthew 6:11, "Give us this day, our daily bread,"* as well as these words of faith: *"Although the fig tree shall not blossom, neither shall fruit be in the vines; the labour of the olive shall fail, and the fields shall yield no meat; the flock shall be cut off from the fold, and there shall be no herd in the stalls: Yet I will rejoice in the LORD; I will joy in the God of my salvation" (Habakkuk 3:17, 18).* – J. Haley

Prayer: Lord we can do all we can to survive this world, but the reality is You are the only One who can ensure the quality of our life, as well as the length of it. Lord You are the great Provider and preserver of Your people. Amen.

March 23

"*We grope for the wall like the blind, and we grope as if we had no eyes: we stumble at noonday as in the night, we are in desolate places as dead men" (Isaiah 59:10).* It is hard for those who are born with physical eyesight to believe we are spiritually blinded because we are in a world that lies in great darkness. We are like the fish in dark caves who have no eyes for they have no need for them in their present environment. Since we are born in this darkness and familiar with it, we think we see beyond it. Granted, our physical eyes see another type of light, but the darkness I am speaking of is the spiritual darkness that enslaves the soul and spirit of man.

When we have physical eyesight, we can't imagine that we are not seeing what is before us without realizing that our eyesight is untrustworthy even when it comes to this world. I lived for about three years in what they call the Camas Prairie. When you looked out over it, it looked flat but when you traveled around in it, you discovered your eyes were being tricked. This prairie hides rolling plains, canyons, and interesting places. I discovered that just because you see something it doesn't make it so, and it is only after you explore it that you discover what it really looks like.

Physical eyesight points to how we perceive things in the physical world and in the end, it proves very limited in its ability to perfectly interpret what we are seeing. However, when it comes to the unseen world, we are absolutely blind. We think we see the problems before us, understand the matters confronting us, and have the ability to address them, but when it comes to spiritual darkness, we do not realize that all we can do is fumble in it at best. We may have an idea of what we are looking for, but without the spiritual light we will remain blinded to the terrain in front of us. We may even see shadows passing before us, but shadows obscure the terrain and without clearly seeing it, we don't know the way in which we are to walk.

We may even tightly hold on to what we know, grope according to what we can feel, and hope we don't make a misstep because we can't see what is ahead of us, beside us, and even behind us because the darkness is always enfolding us. But, as long as we can grope, we perceive we are okay. However, it is that one step into the great vast darkness of eternity that will bring the final reality check to anyone who fails to see the true light of the world. Sadly, this is when these blind individuals will realize they indeed have been blinded all along by the spiritual darkness of this world to keep them from seeing the great abyss of judgment that awaits every sinner.

Prayer: Lord, we spend so much time assuming we are seeing properly, we never really realize how much we are missing because we fail to even look around us to see what is going on. Lord we are blinded in so many ways but thank You for opening my eyes to see the light of Your salvation. Amen.

March 24

"In whom the god of this world hath blinded the minds of them which believe not, lest the light of the glorious gospel of Christ, who is the image of God should shine unto them" (2 Corinthians 4:4). The great blindness in this world is brought on by the spiritual darkness that abounds in it. The natural world may offer the light that allows us to see the terrain, but it lacks the light that allows us to see the great danger of the unseen world.

We are told in *2 Corinthians 4* that Satan uses the darkness (understanding) of the age we live in to blind us to the true light of the world, Jesus. And what must he blind us to: Our lost spiritual state. We may be in an ungodly state but we have no contrast brought on by the light of heaven. Since this spiritual darkness is what has conditioned us, the result is it has become light to us and is all we know and prefer. We have sinned but there is no conviction; therefore, we remain ignorant to it and comfortable in it. We may be an enemy of God, but we see Him in an abstract way as the darkness of unbelief, skepticism, and logic causes some to become complacent towards really pursuing Him to ensure peace and reconciliation with their Creator.

However, God has provided a light. It can penetrate the greatest darkness, reach into the greatest depths, and will never be extinguished by any darkness. Remember light parts the darkness, causes it to dissipate and eventually overcomes all of it. Darkness does not determine the extent of the light; rather the light sets the boundaries of darkness. That light is Jesus Christ.

Jesus, the Savior to the lost, the Great Physician to the blind, the Great Redeemer to the captive, the wonderful Counselor to the hopeless, and the source of unspeakable joy to the seeker who is found by Him. The question is, has the great light of Jesus' life penetrated the spiritual darkness of your soul?

Prayer: Lord, the great darkness in this world is a lie. We think we are properly seeing, understanding, and perceiving what is going on around us, but the truth is, it takes Your grace for the Spirit to penetrate all spiritual darkness with Your light. It is then we gain the eyesight of faith to walk in it. Thank You for giving me the eyes of faith to see Your light in this dark, doomed, hopeless world. Amen.

March 25

"Where are you?" (Genesis 3:9b). This was God's call to Adam in the garden. Was Adam lost to God, or God lost to Adam? We can't really walk unless we see where we are going. In the physical world we can see where we need to step, what is before us and around us so we can get our bearings.

Another fact becomes clear when it comes to this world, and that is we may see our surroundings but still be lost because we do not know where we are. This is true for many who have no clue where they are with God or really want to admit they are hiding or running from Him and the reason for it.

Man has an inward sense that there is a God, but he is spiritually lost to God who is Spirit and truth. God can only find lost man at the point of true conviction over sin due to the truth of the Gospel and repentance.

Without the born-again experience, the spirit of man lies dormant and is dead to the spiritual realm. He can't see past his own understanding of matters let alone the great darkness that covers the gulf between him and His Creator. He can see the physical terrain around him, but the path in which to walk when it comes to the spiritual matters of God is hidden. It takes the eyes of faith to see the way.

God knows where we are, but we must still be found by Him. To be found by Him means we must see we are lost, hiding or even running in the opposite direction from His voice, calling, and invitation. We may know we are not in the right place with Him, but fear keeps us from facing Him, pride from humbling ourselves, and disillusionment or guilt from confessing it.

Like the prodigal son who became lost in sin, we need to rise up in humility and turn in repentance to finally come home to the place prepared by our Savior, Lord, and Redeemer, Jesus Christ.

Prayer: Lord, You are the light that penetrates the darkness to show those who have the heart and desire to see where they are in relationship with You. Once they cry out, Your light will penetrate the darkness of the mind and soul. Thank You for parting my darkness. Amen.

March 26

"In him was life; and the life was the light of men" (John 1:4). What does it take to see the light that parts the spiritual darkness of the soul and this world? It takes faith to open the eyes of our heart.

As believers, we walk by faith and not physical sight or personal understanding. The physical, fleshly rebellious world can't see the true light from heaven because it operates in a different dimension that is limited by its own spiritual darkness. This darkness is what prevents us from seeing into the unseen world. It causes our personal understanding to be darkened by the particular conditioning and indoctrination of the age we live in.

To see past this world takes faith. Faith is a gift from God given to receptive, seeking hearts that dare ask honest, thought-provoking questions about life, truth, and God, while seeking the answers even in darkness. These seekers will not be content until the light dawns in their soul to reveal the truth about where they are spiritually, as well as the path they must walk to have all their questions answered by that which is unseen.

The flesh seeks that which will satisfy it, the world desires that which is comfortable and fits nicely in its philosophies, and the intellect seeks knowledge to placate conceit, but lusts become insatiable to the flesh, while the world oppresses, and knowledge puffs up. It all leads to torment because the flesh and the world will never answer the real questions plaguing man. Ultimately, even their answers lead into greater darkness of bondage.

Meanwhile, man may see where he is going in this world, but he is lost to the next world. There are calls going out from God, invitations, both written and verbal being sent forth, and warnings being cast into the midst of the vast ocean of mankind, but few are prepared or even desire to hear, accept and receive such declarations. They hide in the shadows of compromise and behind fig leaves of excuses.

Today is the day of salvation of being delivered from the various bondages of the world we live in. One of the greatest bondages is our own insipid little world of me, myself, and I.

Prayer: Lord, we want You but on our terms. We don't want hell, but we are not preparing for heaven. We want most of the world and everything You can give us to avoid choosing one master. However, we will one day have to choose, and I choose You no matter what is going on around me. Amen.

March 27

"And straightway the father of the child cried out, and said with tears, Lord, I believe; help thou mine unbelief" (Mark 9:24). What is your expectation in this life and what is it directed towards? One of the questions I ask myself is, "Is my expectation towards a sure thing or something that swings from some branch of wishful thinking?" There are three types of expectations that people operate in.

The first type of expectation is really a worldly expectation that swings from the branches of fleshly lust. Such expectation stands on the shifting sands of fanciful notions, fickle sentiment, and unobtainable reality. It is self-based, self-centered, and self-serving. The end result of such expectation is disillusionment with life, anger towards those who will not get on the band wagon and a resentment towards God for not bringing it forth to ensure one's happiness and contentment.

The second type of expectation is towards the heavenly. It knows that the world has nothing of substance to offer. It believes in the unseen, trusts the character of the eternal, clings to the immovable Rock, and stands on sure promises. These promises include the blessed hope of Jesus' coming because it has been established as being so in the Word of God. The right perspective is realistic about the doomed state of the present world, stands by faith towards the future age, and will choose the narrow path of righteousness while holding on to the rope of truth.

The third type of expectation can be described as hope without faith. Expectation is that part of hope where faith stands upon what is true and takes flight on the wings of hope that if a matter has been promised by God, it is true and will prove to be so in due time. The first type of expectation operates according to vain imaginations and wishful thinking, the second expectation walks according to genuine faith towards God, and the third has been buried under circumstances that has erected an unseen wall of unbelief. In this case the person believes there is hope for everyone but self.

Prayer: Lord, forgive us for saying the right words that fall "deaf" on Your ears because the true expectation that causes one to rise up and do what is right is missing. Lord, we say a lot of "amens" without believing that if it comes from You, IT IS SO and will remain so no matter what is going on. So be it!

March 28

"But if we hope for that we see not, then do we with patience wait for it" (Romans 8:25). Real hope is founded on faith but becomes active when expectation is present. Hope that lacks faith has no real assurance to see a matter through and hope without expectation has no wings to fly above the circumstances.

In the last post, I talked about three types of expectations: the worldly expectation, the heavenly expectation, and the expectation without any hope of seeing a matter come to a fruitful and meaningful end. The first type of expectation uses false promises to try to soar, the second trusts the Holy Spirit to raise one up in His currents, and that last one is a deflated hope.

In the first type of expectation, people miss the small blessings that lead into greater blessings because they are so busy trying to make their expectations come true that they can't chill out and let

God be God. In essence, they can't trust Him to work out His goodness in a situation.

In the second type of expectation, they patiently wait for the promise to be fulfilled. As a result, they see the blessings come to fruition and experience the reality of God's faithfulness and greatness.

In the final expectation they may see others blessed, but they are in such a depressed state they fail to look up and believe God for themselves, trust His Word, and cling to His promises. Their soul is in distress, their spirit hopeless, and their mind tormented.

When it comes to the final state, a person must be delivered from it, but first they have to admit it exists, repent of unbelief, look up while choosing to believe God's Word, and hold tightly to who He is and what He has promised.

Like the man in the incident in *Mark 9*, Jesus needs to only speak one word or a simple sentence, and deliverance will happen. That is, if the person will only believe on Jesus and not let the circumstances drown out the power, blessings, promises, and hope of heaven above.

Prayer: Lord, we can allow our imagination to conjure up what we think would be wonderful and think it is faith, when in reality it is our imagination running amuck and our fleshly desires causing us to swing from a flimsy branch that will break and leave us freefalling towards great disillusionment. We can let circumstances dictate to us or we can look up and trust You. Lord, for a believer there is only one right choice and way. I choose to hope in You and walk out the unknown way before me by faith. Amen.

March 29

Her warning shout rang out in the hot desert air at the same time I saw the black pit in front of me. Two or three more steps and I would've disappeared into the blackness of an abandoned mine shaft that was so deep a stone thrown into it could barely be heard hitting the bottom. That's when I was informed that the Arizona desert is (or used to be) full of deadly, open mine pits that unsuspecting explorers, hikers, bikers or just curious people like myself could quickly perish in. Once again, the Lord had protected me physically because of my "gullible curiosity" of Indian, and ancient artifacts that lay scattered in the vast desert.

Spiritually speaking, He has always been faithful to protect or warn of the many demonic "black pits" created by heretics, false prophets, doctrines of demons, workers of iniquity and so forth who often "bait their hook" with the curious types in mind.

While curiosity should come naturally when it comes to learning about God, His Word, life, the wonders of the world, history, and so forth, all of which should bring glory to God, curiosity can also lure an unsuspecting soul into a dark pit of confusion and insatiable thirst for "deeper" knowledge within a labyrinth of mysteries, bizarre phenomena, altered states of consciousness, and hidden information from "a higher dimension."

If you're thinking that this could never happen to you, or to professing Christians in our "enlightened" church world, you are asleep on your watch. It would take more than a quick quote to explain the tsunami of demonic, occultic, doctrines of demons, satanic and antichrist "dark death pits" that a person can easily fall into.

I am amazed and saddened at the growing number of people who claim to be Christian that are also embracing the beliefs and terminology of the New Age, Hinduism, Unity, Mormonism, Buddhism, spiritism, Witchcraft, Jehovah's Witnesses, Catholicism, (and other cults) as well as the metaphysical, mind-science cults, and the philosophical beliefs and practices of ancient paganism. Beware of those peddling "higher learning," and wolves that openly display their heresies to gullible Christians who blindly believe that, just because some "theology expert" has more degrees than a freight train has cars, that their spirit doesn't have to be discerned!

Jesus didn't say we would know them by their degrees, but by their fruit. If Jesus Christ is not lifted up and His Word proclaimed as it is written, then back up and walk away lest you fall into a pit of deep darkness. If you truly believe that Jesus Christ is the only Way, the only Truth, and the only Life, then why look to tantalizing extra-biblical gnostic books for "mysteries" and "hidden" meanings?

If you become so caught up with some exotic, extra-biblical, ear-tickling "new revelation" (that apparently God somehow forgot to put into His Word) instead of looking to Jesus Christ and the Holy Bible, then you're in danger of slipping into a dark chasm of confusion, fear and unbelief. *"Ever learning, and never able to come to the knowledge of the truth" (2 Timothy 3:7); "Sanctify them through thy truth: thy word is truth" (John 17:17).*

Are you pursuing power and wisdom? If so, read *1 Corinthians 1:18-31*. Are you in a pursuit to understand all mysteries, and all knowledge? If so, remember, *"And though I have the gift of prophecy, and understand all mysteries, and all knowledge; and though I have all faith, so that I could remove mountains, and have not charity, I am nothing" 1 Corinthians 13:2.* – J. Haley

Prayer: Lord, we as Your people declare You are enough and yet it never ceases to amaze me as to how many of us seek out other things to satisfy our soul and bring peace to our spirit. Forgive us for speaking empty words that we simply deceive ourselves with in order to cover up our hypocrisy and unbelief. Amen.

March 30

"This I say therefore, and testify in the Lord, that ye henceforth walk not as other Gentiles walk, in the vanity of their mind" (Ephesians 4:17). How are we to walk as believers in and through the darkness of our age? The Apostle Paul is very clear that Gentiles walk in the vanity of their minds. It is clear their thinking is wrong, their conclusions miss the mark, and their imagination is awry. He goes onto say in the next verse that the Gentiles' understanding had been darkened and as a result they were alienated from the life of God through the ignorance that is in them because of the blindness of the heart.

If you are not a biological Jew, then you are a Gentile. I am a Gentile but because of my faith in God's work of redemption,

Abraham is my father as well, but the connection is a spiritual one established by faith and not a biological one. I can tell you as a Gentile saved by grace, Paul has a perfect description of how we think and walk. But as a believer, that all changed. I no longer think as a Gentile but as a saint, and the reason for this is because I have continued to put off the old ways of the former corrupt old self and life to put on the new. Since I am now in Christ I am being renewed daily in my mind, allowing me to put on His mind day by day to walk out the new life in me.

I hear different people talk about being a Christian, but I do not see any change in their walk, attitude, or way of doing things. They continue to walk as a Gentile. I remember hearing this question, "Why is it so many people are religious but are not being Christian in their ways?"

Christianity is not some doctrine and church affiliation; rather, it is walking out Jesus' life. What influenced Jesus' walk was His attitude. To Him prayer was the heartbeat of His relationship with the Father, the Father's will His meat, the way of righteousness was the norm, and the application of the cross His victorious cry.

If you truly are a child of God, your life will change. It may not be noticeable at first, but if you are taking on the mind of Christ, there will be change. You will find yourself becoming disgusted with the old and casting it aside so you can have the freedom to victoriously walk in your new life in Christ.

Prayer: Lord, I have matured in my walk before You. I started out religious in my notions and with enthusiasm. I walked in this carnality for more years than I want to admit, while tacking You on to fleshly activities, but then came that day when I stepped across the threshold into the consecrated life, thinking I have nothing to lose and everything to gain. That is when my spiritual maturity escalated. Thank You for Your longsuffering. Amen.

March 31

"Strive to enter in at the strait gate: for many, I say unto you, will seek to enter in, and shall not be able" (Luke 13:24). There are a couple of ways in which man walks. We like to think there are many ways in which we can walk, but as the Bible declares, there are only two paths man can walk on, and that is the narrow path of righteousness and the broad path of destruction. We have to remember crossroads are choices or decisions that must be made, reminding us we do have choices as to what path we walk on. What way are you going to walk in—the way of the old man (Gentile) or the way of the new man--that of Christ Jesus whose life is in us?

What mankind does on the broad path to convince themselves that they are on the narrow road is that they hedge themselves in with religious beliefs, a certain moral conduct, and even a bit of integrity that puts them somewhat on a higher ascent. This simply means that they may put others outside of the path they have made for themselves, but they are still on the broad path. They are still doing it their way and according to their terms in light of what serves their purpose. In their mind this distinction means they are on the right path that lifts them above the rest of the world.

In this case man, in his delusion, fails to realize his mind is still darkened by his old way; he is under the wrong spirit, and is walking on the path of destruction. Since his mind is darkened, he can't see the abyss, and due to a wrong spirit, he will not be able to discern the danger that is around him. He thinks he sees when in fact he is not really seeing. He can't discern the spiritual darkness behind the shadows, recognize the false light of deception before him, and realizes he is on the same path as everyone else heading headlong into destruction.

The Bible is clear that the way to everlasting life is straight and hard. It is a choice as to the way we walk in and as a believer, I choose to walk in the way of the cross. The straightway serves as a point of discipline, and the hard way is the means to prepare us to endure the harsh rigors of ever ascending to excellent heights of righteousness. Would I like an easy way? My flesh would. Would I like a glorious way? My pride would. However, I want to be identified with Christ, and to do that, I must become identified with His death on a cross and His burial in an empty grave so that I can be resurrected with Him in everlasting life.

Prayer: Lord, Your way may be hard, leading to suffering, but this is how we will be glorified with You. It may lead to death, but it is a way to life. It may lead to an empty grave, but that grave leads to Your glory. Amen.

April

April 1

What does a bag of Costco chicken dog treats and Scriptures from the Bible have in common? Give up? The answer is simple—they both have to be thoroughly chewed in order to be properly assimilated.

Our cute Yorkipoo gave us a rather unsettling demonstration of that a couple of weeks ago. You see, these particular Costco "chickie treats" are his very favorite treat in his whole world. We even limited them to one a week. The problem is, after he talks, dances, twirls, chases his tail and does just about everything except balance on one ear to get one, he instantly gulps and chokes it down.

The last episode with him turned into a frightening situation and we ended up with one miserable, bloated, constipated little guy moping around the house. We prayed for him, and all sensed that in about three days he would begin to feel better, which he did, and in a week, he was his happy self again.

As for the world we live in, let's face it—the "new norm" is dash and duck, push and pull, grab, gulp and go. In other words, hurriedly find a promise in the Word that will "work for you" while "ducking" all the warnings and conditions; "pushing" yourself to "pull" a "positive feeling" out of thin air which you try to "grab," "gulp" and "go" with for the day.

If this describes your life, how is that working for you? My guess is you spiritually feel as miserable as our fur-baby did physically. Far too many in these uncertain times are ignoring the warnings and the woes in God's Word, while still musing on what the little paper in their fortune cookie said. Of course, you can always find a "prophet" that suits your sensitive psyche on the Internet that will even offer you (for a donation, of course) a dump truck full of sand to add to the foundation of your spiritual house. Instead, let us make God and His Word our priority. "*My meditation of him shall be sweet: I will be glad in the LORD*" (*Psalm 104:34*); *"Let the words of my mouth, and the meditation of my heart, be acceptable in thy sight, O LORD, my strength and my redeemer" (Psalm 19:14); "In the multitude of my thoughts within me thy comforts delight my soul" (Psalm 94:19).* – J. Haley

Prayer: Lord, so often we want to settle for bits of Your Word that will not challenge our present notions, pieces of Your promises that allow us to ignore the conditions, and lots of platitudes that sound wise, but lack any real substance. Forgive us for being irresponsible towards Your Word. Amen.

April 2

"Multitudes, multitudes in the valley of decision: for the day of the LORD is near in the valley of decision" (Joel 3:14). Before I met Christ, I traveled the broad path mentioned in *Matthew 7:13-14*. It leads you to, in, and through the world. I discovered that the world's light is false, its promises empty, and it ends in places of utter filth and spiritual ruin, but it is the only path I knew.

The broad path was leading me to the same place as those who were also falling into the different traps of the world, traps that sucked them down into some pit. Some individuals are not all falling into the same traps and pits, which makes them think they are on a different route, or on a path of their own making, but those are the great lies of Satan.

For me, I hit the crossroad of utter failure. My dreams were gone, taking away the false illusions of the world, and what lay before me was a dark depressing reality that there was no hope for a different life. This was my lot in life at age 21, barely surviving, just getting by, and if fortunate, I could grab a bit of fading happiness, know glimpses of joy that would later mock me, and find a temporary moment where I could escape the harsh reality of my small, insipid world of nothingness.

If you had not guessed it by now, at age 21, during different personal crisis, I came face to face with the hardest reality of all—myself, lost to hope, inept to change anything, definitely not in control of my life, and miserable in my lot. It is at such a stage you either must cry out to find true hope or go deeper and eventually perish amid the cesspool of despondency.

It was there Jesus found me, and I discovered the life He had for me. At that time, I decided to follow Him and that is when my journey on the narrow path began. Don't get me wrong, I took detours back to the broad path, but each time I did I realized it led me into a state that ended nowhere other than greater frustration, failure, and despair. Each time my resolve to stay on the narrow path, no matter the temptation and attraction along the way, led me to deeper spiritual riches in my faith walk.

If you are on that broad path now, you can stop and decide to make a U-turn to face your Creator. At that point you need to repent of walking in the wrong way, your way, and turn to face the right way, choose life by choosing the Lord. It is then you need to flee the empty, useless, and destructive way that currently lies before you.

Prayer: Lord, we like to think we are on the right path when we have failed to enter in the only way provided by Your redemption. The entrance begins with the cross and the way is depicted by Calvary, but at the end of it is Your large place of promise, beauty, and glory. Amen.

April 3

"For the law was given by Moses, but grace and truth came by Jesus Christ" (John 1:17). One of the great points of consolation to the seeking soul is the revelation of God's grace. A seeking soul is one who realizes that their spiritual situation is desperate, and they have

need of something more substantial and stable. Their world is folding in on them as it seems to be collapsing into some hole that is ominous and speaks of such darkness that it causes the mind to fear, the soul to become frantic, and the spirit to despair.

The seeking soul is a seeking heart. The heart knows that things are not right. No matter what stands before the person, it is only shadows. The twilight has long passed, and what is before that person is the reality that nothing makes sense. It is not only a confusing mess, but there is a type of insanity that is beginning to reign.

There used to be dreams but they have long ago faded away. There used to be expectations, but they have disappeared into some dark murky cesspool. There used to be even a bit of religion to soothe a tormenting conscience but eventually guilt and shame begin to knock at the door to remind the person that not all is well with the soul. There used to be strength, but the bones are now dried up by the harsh purging of the heat. This heat has settled and is so stifling it weighs heavily on the chest, causing one to grasp for some fresh wind that will set the soul free and bring some relief to the sagging of a spirit that is struggling with the bitter taste the world leaves behind.

It is only as you come to this bleak reality that you can throw up your hands and realize that if God does not do something, it will all be lost in a vast of nothingness. It is at the point that you realize that you deserve nothing but hell, and what God bestows on you is indeed a matter of grace.

The beauty of grace is that it is an endless flowing river. As grace flows from above, it begins to surround you, and once it starts to enfold you, you begin to realize that there is no end to it. *John 1:16* tells us this about the grace that was revealed in Jesus, *"And of his fulness have all we received, and grace for grace."*

Prayer: Lord, all the blessings we receive from you are undeserved. Thank You for wanting to show me grace instead of what I rightfully deserve in my failing state of humanity. Amen.

April 4

"That in the ages to come he might shew the exceeding riches of his grace in his kindness towards us through Christ Jesus" (Ephesians 2:7). How far will one travel to seek what is true and eternal with all their heart, mind, soul, and might? For such a restless soul, it will not stop until the seeker finds that which can bring satisfaction to their soul.

It all comes down to how despairing they are about a matter. For one who is desperate and has nothing to lose, they will travel to the end of the earth if necessary. To the one who is weary, they often go as far as they can go and then they will collapse as they cry out in utter despair in hopes someone will hear them. And, for those who simply want relief, they will travel as long as their emotions are at the right height. Once they finally land and see they are still here, they tend to forget it and return to their former state.

The seeking soul's main search is to find lasting hope that will part the great depressing curtain that rests upon it. Where to look is the question, but the seeking soul's great desperation is not hovering over the question but is pushed on with the urgency that it must find the answer or perish. It must risk being brought to the abyss of destruction to seek mercy in the hope of being lifted up by unseen wings that will cause it to soar above its state with great expectation.

The seeking soul will eventually encounter a fountain that promises rivers of Living Water. The fountain is a Person who stands in the barren wilderness, a Voice that cries out, ever inviting lost, desperate man to drink so he can live. He offers life that is eternal, and will make sense of the present journey, but man must accept the invitation to drink from the fountain to receive the promise of eternal life. And, it is all a matter of His grace, unworthy of it but by faith a recipient of its unending availability to whosoever believes, flowing downward to whosoever is open, and reigns through the life of those who walk by faith towards the glorious reality and promises of God

The fountain is Jesus Christ. It is said of Him that of His fulness we have received, and it comes down to grace for grace. Grace is ongoing, meeting us in mercy, lifting up the downtrodden, comforting the hurting, and touching us with compassion. Christ is the glorious manifestation of grace. In love He offered His life in the place of our life. In His resurrection, our faith has been confirmed, and our hope has been established. In intercession He reminds the courts of heaven that His grace is sufficient for all our weaknesses, our ailments, and our failures. In fact, His grace is as eternal as He is and we will be learning about its ways, works, and blessings for ages to come.

Prayer: Lord it is our tendency to hide behind grace in uncertainty, try to cling to our notions about it in failures, claim it when confused, and use it when we want to justify our own way. But to grow in the knowledge of Your unfathomable grace, we sometimes must become desperate in our plight as we truly begin to understand there is nothing of worth in our present state, nothing of value in our ways, and nothing salvageable outside of You. It is that revelation that causes us to get glimpses into the wonderous, unending work of Your grace. Amen.

April 5

"Which in other ages was not made known unto the sons of men, as it is now revealed unto his holy Apostles and prophets by the Spirit" (Ephesians 3:5). My computer is telling me we are entering a different era: the new AI (artificial intelligence) era. Should we be excited about this new era? We have been informed about its capabilities to control the world through media outlets. However, how many of us thought it to be science fiction in the past but we are now coming face to face with it?

Does this technological advancement mean we are now entering the age of utopia or perfection since man is methodically being moved out of the way? Some believe we are but is it something we can bet our eternal well-being on?

It is true, where man is there is anything but utopia. Man can prove to be a bit annoying and inconvenient when he dares to have an opposing opinion, while refusing to not go along with the crowd, ever challenging the narrative of this age. Such disturbances can prove to be irresponsible towards what is right, unmotivated in doing right, ignorant in avoiding being right, and foolish in being contrary to it, while some just become silent to get along in the world. At this time, I want to remind those excited about the advancement of the latest technology that the world was created by God for man, not machines.

Without man there would be no advancement in any arena. Technology may advance our lifestyle, but it is void of creating anything. Dominion over the earth was first entrusted to the first man, Adam, and was so until he rebelled at which time it was turned over to Satan in the garden.

Naturally man's attempt to control and create a perfect world has ended up with what is void of humanity. Man is not imperfect because he refuses to be, he is imperfect because of ungodly state that serves as a motivation behind sin. Man in his humanity may reach points of excellency, but never the perfection he seeks. Supposedly, AI will get it right and will be void of being abrasive and having imperfections—right? (just glitches)? It will have all the answers. Just ask Alexia anything, and the pleasant voice will tell you what you seek to know.

I have been around people who have Alexa and these lifeless devices do answer the person or comply with their requests if everything is on the same frequency. However, as Christians we must be aware of how much we expose ourselves to modern technology. We must never seek the answers to life and eternal matters from any other source than the Word of God and we must keep in mind that technology is limited by man programing his own bias, prejudices and understanding into these gadgets. In essence, we can't trust them to give the right answer, and they certainly have no power to make anything new, right, and eternal.

Prayer: Lord, these modern conveniences cause man to think he has matters under control when everything is out of order and standing on the abyss of self-destruction. Lord, I seek You out, knowing You are eternal and can't be moved from who You are and the plan of redemption for those who seek it. Amen.

April 6

"So he drove out the man and he placed at the east of the garden of Eden Cherubims, and a flaming sword which turned every way, to keep the way of the tree of life" (Genesis 3:24). In the previous post, I talked about the new era of AI. On one hand the technology of it is incredible, but on the other hand it is frightening because it will most likely become the means by which the anti-Christ system will be used to bring all mankind into a tyrannical world-wide system.

The concept of AI is not new. We have been given insight into it through the media for years. As predicted in the famous book "1984," this AI can control the function of your household so you can sit on the couch and give commands to have it turn on and off lights and other devices. Once again, we must remind ourselves, imperfect man with his agendas and narratives are the ones programing these devices.

Man has a way of twisting, inserting, rearranging, and ignoring important facts and realities. And, we must remember, any breakdown of such devices will end in some type of ruin, and you can bank on there being a breakdown because EVERYTHING in this world is temporary. Rust, moth, and thieves (this includes our government which robs through heavy taxation) will somehow win in the end when it comes to the things and systems of this age.

The frightening reality is the fact that man has been seeking paradise or a utopia for himself since Adam and Eve were put out of the garden. He desires perfection where there are no glitches or challenges to disrupt whatever reality he desires. However, such self-centeredness fails to see that to have such a world, man must be done away with.

I am so thankful that I have long ago discovered that man may be the problem, but AI is NOT the solution. What made the first Eden complete and perfect was the presence of God.

I am quite aware of my imperfection, but I have discovered Eden is right here in this world. It is indeed a "small garden," but it is where I have found the love of God, joy in my heart, peace of mind, grace flowing like a river, and where I am prepared for a glorious, perfect world without end. Granted, it begins with an old rugged cross, but that cross lifted up the solution, hope, and source of life: the Lord Jesus Christ. It is because of Him, believing His promise of life and receiving Him into my heart, I now hide and abide in Him. He is my Eden in this world, and one day I will be brought into the fullness of His glory to worship and walk with Him through the unending beauty of His kingdom.

Prayer: Lord, we want to put stock in what we see, but our hope is in what is unseen. Lord, I put my faith, life, and hope in You because this world has nothing to offer, but in You I have everything to gain in light of eternity. Amen.

April 7

"And except those days should be shortened, there should no flesh be saved: but for the elect's sake those days shall be shortened" (Matthew 24:22). I used to ponder this Scripture. How could man be brought to such a brink of destruction? The Bible warns of wars, pestilences, and beasts.

Like many I thought of wars which included atomic bombs that could bring mass destruction, but with all the information coming out about AI controlling the world's systems, I am beginning to see how humanity will be brought to the abyss of destruction. Along with technological advancements there is also DEW (Direct Energy Weaponry) that can disintegrate objects and people, as well as transhumanism where man is now made half machine through nano particles inserted into his body through shots and chips. We must not forget weather manipulation that can be used to blackmail countries into submission to carry out evil agendas against its people, and 5G that can be used to control and destroy people, if becomes clearer how man will be brought to the abyss of annihilation.

Clearly, man is being done away with in every arena. We have machines that now can do the work of man, even in assembly lines. Does this mean man will not have to work, but if man does not work, what will he be doing? Even Adam was to dress and keep the garden in a perfect environment. Will man become like the machines of the past, cast aside to simply die, his body rotting away in some gutter of hopelessness to become compost because he has no real purpose or aim? I know man will return to dust or ashes, but compost is a bit much to take.

We have robots that act on command like a dog. It may be good in certain arenas such as police work when facing an armed criminal, but the thought of petting or hugging a machine does not attract me one bit. When you take the personality of warmth out of anything, it will become clear you do not have a living being that can comfort or enter in with your plight. This also brings up a question, "Did anyone see the movie "Westworld?" In that movie all the robots took on their own identity and began to kill people. Reports have it that this has already happened in Japan.

Mankind has no hope unless there is something greater than all of these demonically inspired methods that can bring a complete stop to their destruction. As Christians we not only know who will stop it, but we have confidence that He is our ark and that He will deliver us from spiritual destruction, regardless of the storms on the horizon.

Prayer: Lord, we have been warned about the days we live in, but how many believe Your warnings are discerning the signs, and preparing spiritually for when the night is so great, none of us will be able to work in it. Thank You for being my Ark. The waves are gaining momentum on the outside, but my soul knows how to rest in You. Amen.

April 8

"But the heavens and the earth, which are now, by the same word are kept in store, reserved unto fire against the day of judgment and perdition of ungodly men" (2 Peter 3:7). The Bible tells us we will be living in perilous times. We have been conditioned to believe the world without man's footprint (for that matter any living thing) will solve the problem of the world, and yet we can't imagine our world

being without us. It is true, man is at the core of the problem, but the problem with man is that he is out of order, out of sync with his Creator. This disruption is a result of sin, man's rebellion against his Creator. In unbelief he mocks His existence, puts a fist up to test His authority, and flings off moral disciplines in complete disdain.

We must now consider whether all this technology is a form of judgment leveled against mankind since it seems people are becoming more godless, lacking any real conviction and possessing a seared conscience. When man becomes so lost in wickedness, he becomes completely aimless in purpose, leaving him with no reason, challenge, or initiative.

This technology is not only doing away with the need for man, it is programming out all reality of God who is the ONLY hope and savior of mankind. It lacks personality, as well as a soul and it has no conscience, no sense of justice or feelings as to the destruction it might bring to the vulnerable, the innocent, and those already victimized by an indifferent world. It clearly will be part of the anti-Christ system that is meant to usher in a one-world government, but how much of a part do we dare play in it or promote it, knowing that behind the plans is Satan, the god of this world?

Jesus is clear that He will come back before His creation is wiped out. Meanwhile, it is hard to watch mankind slide into this pit, while being taken out by the tumultuous waves of this time. This is why we are told to be watchmen, ready, and prepared to be saved from a culture of death where the world is being controlled and methodically driven mad while being prepared by lifeless technology to walk into the abyss of destruction.

Prayer: Lord, we have been told that all this technology is about our convenience, when it is designed to control and ultimately wipe out any trace of You and Your people. Yes Lord, it can be used for good or bad, but the bad guys eventually take control of it because this is Satan's world, and it will be so until You come back as the King of kings and Lord of lords. Quickly come, Lord Jesus. Amen.

April 9

Once your dog learns to talk (not growl, bark, whine, woof, yip, yap or howl), but "talk," you are the one who has to learn, as quickly as possible, how to talk back. My little black and white Chihuahua, Tucker, didn't "talk" like RayRay, our Yorkipoo, does, but he did sing.

He would sing with his whole heart the entire first stanza of any hymn I played on the piano, and he also had his favorite worship songs. Therefore, concerning those Chicken chew treats I wrote about in my last post (April 1), there have been some "conversations" between fur-baby RayRay and myself about that, and why they are "all gone".

This takes place in my office because that is where most of his treats are, and then he begins to tell me what he wants. One day he was getting so long-winded and mouthy to my face about it that I finally swiveled my desk chair around and sat with my back to him. Did that detour him? No, not for one minute! It was apparent that if I wanted to get any work done, I was going to have to give him something. So, you guessed it—he got a small treat that silenced him, at least for a few hours.

This may all be cute and funny, but I wonder just how "cute" and "funny" God thinks His children are when they won't take "No" for an answer, even though what they are lusting after is not in agreement with His Word or His will for their life. I can remember back many years ago to certain times when I'd beg for something I thought I needed, or wanted, from the Lord with the pathetic tones of a desperate little kid crying, "Please, please, please" and getting no answer from the Lord.

God knows what we truly need from that which we definitely don't need. It's not His perfect will to give in to us, but if we insist on it, He may give it to us out of His permissive will, and if so, we will end up reaping the consequences. You know the wise old saying, "Beware what you ask for, because you might just get it!"

"And he [Jesus] said unto them, Take heed, and beware of covetousness: for a man's life consisteth not in the abundance of the things which he possesseth" (Luke 12:15); "If ye abide in me, and my

words abide in you, ye shall ask what ye will, and it shall be done unto you" (John 15:7). (Note the conditions!) – J. Haley

Prayer: Lord, it is hard to let go of what we calculate is important and necessary, but if we care to hear Your response, we might find out it is neither important nor necessary. Lord we are so earthbound, we often fail to consider what is heavenly and acceptable to You. Forgive us. Amen.

April 10

"And she said, Nay, my lord, thou man of God, do not lie unto thine handmaiden" (2 Kings 4:16). This story is about the Shunammite woman in *2 Kings 4*. She recognized Elisha's calling as a man of God and fed him and provided a chamber for him to stay in when he was in the vicinity. To bless her, Elisha told her she would have the desire of her heart, a child, a son.

We know that this son when he was older died. His mother laid him on the prophet's bed and immediately went to Elisha, but neither the Lord, nor the messenger that was sent before her, told the prophet what had happened. It was only when she encountered Elisha that she reminded him that she did not come to him seeking the miracle of bearing a child; rather she asked to not be deceived with false promises.

This woman's story reminds me of the promises of God. He has promised us much and yet how many of us feel that He has been lying to us? He entrusts us with certain giftings, but how many of us feel that they lie dormant and in a sense dead because there is no place to operate or walk in them? How many believers' faith has been shaken or is shaking because it seems that the dealings of God are unfair, cruel, unloving, and indifferent at times?

This woman showed genuine faith amid all the testings that went on in her life. Her faith was active because she prepared a place for Elisha. Her faith was sustained because she held on to the fact that her promised son would be raised from the dead. She had obedient faith because she obeyed the instruction to leave her home during a famine, and she had enduring faith to believe that God would hold her home for her until she returned. In the end, she was not disappointed in the source of her faith or let down in any way by the One she believed in.

Prayer: Lord, we desire great faith without realizing such faith comes out of grave testing. Lord, I want sustaining faith, and I must trust You to take me through the strong storms that will establish such faith in my life. Amen.

April 11

"...And the man of God said, Let her alone, for her soul is vexed within her: and the LORD hath hid it from me, and hath not told me" (2 Kings 4:27c). To me there are different applications in this incident with the Shunammite woman. This woman was godly and recognized who was of God and took opportunities to bless the prophet. For her ministry to the prophet, she was rewarded with a blessing that she had been denied all her married life, a son. But then came the day that it seemed God required her blessing back from her, yet she would not accept it. After all, God would not lie to her.

She was given a son and why would He take him at that time? Notice that she did not run to her husband or her servants. She did not send another with the message to Elisha as to the devastation because she was the one who needed to remind the prophet of their past interaction.

This is true for our life in Christ. If we have received Him in the chamber of our heart as Lord and Savior, He gives us promises such as eternal life. We may start out walking in the newness of life, but the world, losses, or challenges may make the promises of God seem lifeless or dead to us. The question is how do we handle it? Do we run to our family, friends, and leaders to cry and complain? Do we sit down in utter despair and hopelessness, or do we seek the one who made the promise to us?

Do we remind Him of the promise, or do we whine and complain that He did not keep His Word? This woman was a woman of faith, and her faith would not accept that her promise would end or be taken away in such a manner. The great loss caused a crisis to come to her faith, but she would not give in to the hopelessness of the situation, and she sought the one who promised. When in Elisha's presence, she caught him by the feet and would not let him go. The promise was given back to her after her son was raised from the dead.

Our Lord does not lie and what He promises, He will bring about. You must remember that the disciples lost sight of their promise for three days and nights, at which time their faith was greatly tested by the darkness of death and harshly refined by the silence of the grave, but later confirmed by Jesus' resurrection.

All faith will go through some crisis, but it will always come back to the character of one's faith. Faith begins as a gift from God, a mustard seed but it must be nourished by right living and cultivated by obedience for it to grow, but for it to be established it must be tested.

It is through the testing that faith will be enlarged to endure the test. It will grab a hold of the One who promises, and it will not let go until that part of our life in Christ which has become lifeless for one reason or the other, once again experiences that resurrection power. It is the resurrection power that raises up the glorious life of Christ in us with new revelations. Faith seeks, endures and clings because it knows it will never be ashamed for putting complete trust in God, for HE DOES NOT LIE, and WILL ALWAYS KEEP HIS WORD!

Prayer: Lord, thank You for the gift of faith. You have been faithful to bring me to crises so You can enlarge it, establish it, and ultimately show Yourself mighty on my behalf to affirm the type of faith I have put in You. Amen.

April 12

"I am he that liveth, and was dead: and, behold, I am alive for evermore, Amen; and have the keys of hell and of death." (Revelation 1:18). What would you miss the most in your life if you didn't have it or it was not available for you to obtain? How many of us would naturally think of something of a physical or earthly nature. We know the things of earth are inanimate and temporary so why would we really miss them in the long run? To me, the only right answer to the above question is Jesus Christ.

We can have religion, theology, decent living, and the right terms, but still be missing Jesus. Without Jesus we are like the empty tomb on Resurrection Sunday leaving people still searching for Him because they can't find His life in our midst. We may be like the two men on the way to Emmaus in *Luke 24* who might be talking and reasoning among ourselves at this time of the year about the events of Calvary because we are slow of heart to believe that He has indeed risen and is alive today.

We may be like others who never can imagine an empty cross along with an empty tomb. They lament the injustice of His death but fail to recognize the purpose for His great sacrifice. Yes, Jesus died a tragic death, but His death was not final. His death was not a martyr's death for He came into this world to be the Lamb of God, to be the Savior of the world. He came to die for us in light of the promise of rising three days later. His great triumphal entry was not on a colt where people prophetically acknowledged He was King; rather, it was from death itself as Lord who held the keys of hell and of death.

In all our religious stuff, and sentimentality and our emotional "walk on the road of Calvary" in this spring season, are we still missing Jesus? The great tragedy is not that Jesus died on a cross on our behalf for sin; rather, it is man remaining an empty, lifeless tomb that will never know the light that can penetrate the death that lingers upon his soul due to sin, the darkness that remains upon his mind due to the profane, and the lifeless decay of personal attempts that are like silent graveclothes.

I love the message of the angel to Mary, *"Why seek ye the living among the dead? He is not here, but is risen."* When people come to you, will they have to search elsewhere for Jesus, because you are a lifeless tomb, for He is clearly missing from your life?

The great message of this day of celebration should be clear: HE LIVES, and He LIVES in me through the presence of His Holy Spirit! The message for this season is Happy Resurrection Day!

Prayer: Lord, we have such confidence about our life and our future in You because You Live. You died on the cross but rose from the grave during this time of celebrating. Your resurrection cast the shadow and promise of a new life, pointing to a new body, and living in Your glory for evermore. Amen.

April 13

"For consider him that endured such contradiction of sinners against himself, lest ye be wearied and faint in your minds" (Hebrews 12:3). During the spring, we celebrate Resurrection Sunday. We rejoice because Jesus' death paid the price of redemption but the real victory over the wages of sin, which is death, was His resurrection.

Resurrection points to the quickening of that which is dead. In sin, man is the walking dead, under a death sentence, doomed in a world that has already been cursed by sin. This great darkness of evil was exposed by Jesus' cross, making it obvious that this world and all that is of it has been judged and condemned by God's holy Law.

We often make a big deal out of Jesus' death. Granted, when I read about His journey to Calvary, it breaks my heart that He had to endure what proved then and now to be such great contradictions for all who dare to consider what happened over 20 centuries ago. It is also true His sacrifice was great, but it was also required by the Law when it came to redemption. It was unfair, but necessary if He was to satisfy the Law as our advocate and substitute. Jesus didn't shy away from it; rather, He embraced the way of the cross because it was for the reason of redemption He came. He looked beyond the grave judgment of the cross to the promises and glory established before the foundation of the world to know the great victory that awaited Him.

This brings us back to Resurrection Sunday. What makes the work of the cross of Jesus so wondrous was not His death on the cross. Granted the fact the cross now stands empty due to His payment for redemption being sufficient is powerful assurance to every believer. However, this journey can't and must not end with just the payment being made that ended in His death. His body was also taken to a tomb and left there, but three days and nights later the tomb was empty as well.

As believers, we must follow Jesus' footprints in His Word to the cross. He declared He was the resurrection and the life. Note, resurrection comes before life because there is no life until there is the power of resurrection available to raise up the life that is dead in sin. We must recognize that it was our sin that put our Lord on that cross. His substitutionary death should cause the darkness to temporarily rest heavy on our soul as our heart is once again broken over the great suffering our Lord undertook as Man on our behalf. We should pause and mourn His death, acknowledging all sins have been laid upon Him. We must at that time repent of them, allowing them to roll off so we can look up into His loving face without shame for what our sin cost Him.

Every time I take this journey of Calvary, His suffering is heavy on my heart and soul, but I know the morning is coming when the new light will part the darkness and shadows to expose an empty tomb. Each time I come to that empty tomb I can hardly wait to read the incident where the angelic figure told Mary that Jesus was not in the tomb for HE IS RISEN.

Revelation 1:18 summarizes Jesus' victory in this way, *"I am he that liveth, and was dead; and behold I am alive for evermore, Amen; and have the keys of hell and of death."*

Prayer: Lord, we have the tendency to emphasize that which touches our sentimental side, but victory does not rest in the roller coaster of up and downs of emotions; rather, it rests when the darkness has subsided, the light has dawned and we can see for ourselves that You are once again victorious over the darkness of this age. Amen.

April 14

"And they said among themselves, Who shall roll us away the stone from the door of the sepulchre? (Mark 16:3). What are you looking for when it comes to Jesus? The last time (before that Sunday morning) when Mary Magdalene and the others saw Jesus, was when they took Him from the cross to the tomb. He had given up His spirit, and His body was lifeless. They came to anoint His lifeless body, but they had no clue how they were going to roll away the stone. They came to see a dead Savior who seemed as if He had been martyred by evil men, and not a risen Lord who would prove victorious over all the enemies of man's soul.

Today there are many looking for Jesus. They may be disappointed with man's dead religion that acts as if the Lord Jesus is not living and is not involved in the affairs of His church. He is simply some figurehead or name they use to give them creditability for their dead religious creeds and practices.

There are some who are barely holding onto some small shred of religious hope that the risen Lord is real, but they have had no real personal experience with Him. They have a mixture that has left them wanting as they realize they hold empty assumptions of others that no longer inspire or comfort them in their present state. And there are those like the women who came to the tomb early with a heavy heart to anoint Jesus' body for His burial. Clearly, they were void of any hope or expectation to see Him alive even though He had told those who followed Him that He would rise again three days later after His death and burial.

Many people are either wading through a labyrinth of religion that seems to end in dead ends leaving them in despair, or they are drowning in a quagmire of hopelessness and depression because life does not make sense. They may know in their mind that God is the answer and Jesus is the way, but when they come to such matters there is a bitterness that consumes them because no matter how much religion they have been involved in, they do not expect their lot to change.

For those who seek Jesus, but do not expect to see Him are like those ladies who came to anoint a dead body. Instead of expecting to see a living Lord, they are anxious about how to roll away a stone too great for them to handle.

The world has always resisted the light of God and created great spiritual darkness to come upon the souls of man, resulting in a crisis of faith. The great stone of unbelief can be simply rolled away by faith, but when one is being buried by the lies, drowning in muddy waters of compromise, while sinking in the quagmire of sin, and walking in hopelessness, they need someone to roll away the stone so they can see the empty tomb.

The question to the living church is are we presenting the light to those in despair, and encouraging them to believe so they can see the empty tomb? Once they see the empty tomb, we can pray they will embrace the message of hope by faith, bringing them to a place of sharing that incredible message with others about the gift of eternal life that came by grace through the work of an old rugged cross.

Prayer: Lord, we can talk the talk but how are we walking? Are we walking in faith and expectation of what You, as our Living Lord, desires to do on our behalf, or are we walking in despair towards the obstacles that keep us from seeing that You live and have risen? Open my eyes so I can see You lifted up and glorified. Amen.

April 15

Have you ever driven a car from the backseat? I doubt that you have, and neither have I, but nevertheless the other day I was called a "backseat driver." In spite of major voice loss, when it comes to my verbal exclamations, instructions and fearful quips, the driver (in this case our co-laborer Carrie) can hear me quite well.

The other day it went like this: "Slow down," "Stay in your own lane," "You're too close to the edge," "You're scaring oncoming drivers," "Didn't you see that speed limit sign?" "You'll get a ticket and your insurance will go up," and the proverbial, "Watch out!!!" We weren't on a long trip (thank God), but on just a 7-minute trip to the grocery store. So, in seven to ten minutes flat, I became the epitome of an accomplished back-seat driver.

But then, oh joy, our roles switched places once we got into the store. That is when she becomes the hovering overseer of me, the cart, the pace we set, the groceries on my list, the adventure of loading them onto the conveyor belt, and worst of all, rushing me through the button pushing process when making the purchase. By the time we get back home, unload it all, and I get everything where it should go, I'm beyond ready to reward myself (and rewire my nerves) for surviving the whole thing with a cup of tea and some of the chocolate I've hidden that nobody else knows about--not even the dog who can't have chocolate anyway.

Oh, the joy of aging! But the Lord truly knows everything about us. He knows our fears, our need to control (even if from the "backseat") and our innermost thoughts and frustrations. Regardless of whether our daily challenges are small or great, Jesus' promises to His disciples are also for those of us who love and trust Him to carry us through every situation. He said, *"Peace I leave with you, my peace I give unto you: not as the world gives give I unto you. Let not your heart be troubled, neither let it be afraid" (John 14:27).* – J. Haley

Prayer: Lord, it is easy to become a back-seat driver, but we forget we can't see it all or know it all. I am so thankful You are in the driver's seat when it comes to our lives as believers. I have sensed in the past when I have tried to tell You what to do with my life, You just smile at me and keep on moving forward. Thanks for the smile and the grace. Amen.

April 16

"Let the proud be ashamed; for they dealt perversely with me without a cause: but I will meditate in thy precepts" (Psalm 119:78). Jesus told us offense will come. There are three ways in which offense will

raise up in protest. 1) Truth will offend those who insist on their own reality. They will become threatened, insulted, or fearful about it. 2) Pride will be offended when exposed, embarrassed, and challenged. It will always make for a fragile and insecure reality that is touchy when challenged, judgmental when not properly honored, and critical and cruel when embarrassed. 3) Offense occurs when one takes up a cause which will cause them to stand and fight against what they perceive to be wrong, unfair, or improper.

There are worthwhile causes, but for the believer the main cause that will keep us on the straight and narrow path is Christ and Him crucified, otherwise any cause outside of that might find us on the outside of God's will and plan. We must remember that to get caught up with a cause, personal convictions, and ideas of justice, something of nobility must be attached to it such as patriotism. We must remind ourselves we would not give the cause much consideration unless our sentimentality and sense of fair play have been stirred up in some way to take note of it. In that case our cause often proves to be fleshly and not spiritual.

The part that confuses Christians comes down to the difference between noble causes and righteous indignation. Righteous indignation is anger that is aimed at unrighteousness that is so grievous to God's holiness and heart that His anger burns towards it. It is important to keep in mind that for the saint that possesses true righteousness, such indignation is not expressed in anger or vengeance, but in great vexation of the spirit.

Vexation of the spirit is when the spirit is broken over the offense, and the individual becomes sober about the outcome, and humbled by the sense of identification with the Lord because it is not God's will that any perish but all come to repentance. Such vexation not only means we are becoming identified with the Lord in such a way that we either become intercessors in the matter, or when given the opportunity, we take a strong stand against such egregious offense with truth, warnings, and admonitions.

Prayer: Lord there is so much in this world that can cause our spirits to be vexed, but as believers we must not remain focused on what vexes our spirits, but what will lift our spirits up to great heights of expectations to seek You, remind us of Your promises, and that such vexation is temporary in light of eternity. Amen.

April 17

"And when he had made a scourge of small cords, he drove them all out of the temple, and the sheep, and the oxen; and poured out the changers money, and overthrew the tables" (John 2:15). The preacher in Ecclesiastes talked much about vexation of spirit. As you follow him, you will see that most vexation of spirit is due to the fact that what man does in the flesh and world is vanity. Such a revelation causes much despair, confusion, and feelings of robbery, betrayal, and disdain for life. In the end, it causes offense and indignation towards everything including God.

Take, for example, Jesus' indignation that man had made His Father's house of prayer into a den of thieves that robs, rather than offer nothing of eternal significance. It is said of Jesus' response towards the moneychangers in the temple that the zeal of His house hath eaten Him up (*John 2:17*). This always causes me to consider how God is looking at the activities of churches.

How many is He taking offense towards because He is in none of their worship and service, and all such religious activities in the end will prove to be vain or useless before Him? However, His name is being used to give those in leadership within the congregation some credibility to the merchandising of souls, while they display a form of godliness but are denying the power of the Holy Spirit. In such cases, His name is being used in vain, worship is profane, and presentations lacking the authority and anointing of the Spirit, as well as the sharpness of truth.

What other things will God's anger burn towards? What about what is happening to our children? If you offend one of them, it is better that a millstone be put around your neck and cast into the deepest sea.

How about the widows and fatherless? If you oppress them and they cry out to their Creator, God will kill you. We are told that God is angry at the wicked every day. I have personally noted how it is fearful to fall into the hands of an angry God because God will recompence, but God's anger continually burns towards the dark, conniving, destructive ways of the wicked (*Exodus 22:22-24; Psalm 7:11; Matthew 18:6,10; Hebrews 10:30-31; James 1:27*).

This brings me back to causes. Personal causes are just that, but righteous indignation brings us into line with God's attitude towards a matter. David was persecuted without a cause. In other words, those who came against him had no real cause to do so. It could have been a matter of jealousy, personality conflict, or political differences. I have seen this at different times.

The problem is that if you take up a personal cause against someone because others have been offended, you could find yourself coming under a judgment because God could be their defense (*Psalm 7*). This is why when a Christian shows some type of vitriol against someone they really don't know, I asked them what has that person done against them personally?

We need to discern our causes and make sure they line up to God's plan, His calling on our life, and His way of doing.

Prayer: Lord, we can easily get caught up with fleshly causes and worldly influences and pursuits, but Lord, I want my focus to remain on You to avoid vain causes and worldly detours, so that I can be assured of ending up on Your side in the end. Amen.

April 18

"So shall they fear the name of the LORD from the west, and his glory from the rising of the sun. When the enemy shall come in like a flood, the Spirit of the LORD shall lift up a standard against him" (Isaiah 59:19). Is it important that we as believers somewhat know what is going on around us? Ignorance is wonderful in so many ways, but God is not winking at ignorance towards Him and His righteous ways according to *Acts 17:30-31*.

In spiritual ignorance, we can ride the wave of opinions, stand on dogmatic rhetoric, hold to our idea of righteousness while using it as a standard of judgment against others, and feel noble in being the odd man out when standing against what we consider to be substandard religion. However, we need to make sure our standard is not our idea of righteousness and is truly the righteousness of God.

Spiritual ignorance towards God and righteousness will not be tolerated because we have God's Word. We are told to first seek God and His righteousness in *Matthew 6:33*. In many cases God's revelation of Himself is left on shelves to collect dust and on a few coffee tables to give the impression that those present are associated with God and religion. However, Bibles that collect dust will reveal the waste taking place in a person's soul and the one on the coffee table often will reveal that whatever religion they may be holding to is surface and will not withstand the storms that will try men's souls.

The Bible speaks of God lifting up a righteous standard against those who fail to fear Him and oppose Him. This standard will cause those who have ignored, refuted, refused, mocked, and shook their angry fist at Him, to become silent, fearful, shaken, and feeling great terror in meeting the righteous Judge of their souls.

This brings us to the difference between the flimsy standard we uphold and God's standard. Our standard is one-dimensional, judgmental and unloving, while God's standard is eternal and upheld by the Holy Spirit who reveals that all righteousness is of and found in Christ. We stand upright because we are hidden in Christ's righteousness, we stand right before God because Christ's life is in us, and we do right by others because the love of God is being shed abroad in our hearts by the Holy Spirit.

Prayer: Lord our standard is right in our own eyes, and we can't imagine Your standard is even higher. Lord, help me to cast aside my standard and walk in Your standard. Amen.

April 19

"For I bear them record that they have a zeal of God but not according to knowledge. (Romans 10:2). It is natural for those who are first saved to have great zeal about their new-found life in Christ. They

can't imagine others not being excited about the great change in their heart that had taken place. As we all know that initial zeal is quickly doused by those who are either blind towards the Gospel or who have become lukewarm to it.

Even though your faith is new and you have not begun to walk in faith, let along crawl in light of who God really is, zeal can make you think you understand Him and what is right to Him. After falling down on your face in humility many times, ending up with black eyes, cuts, scathes, and bruises, you realize Your zeal does not have the means to convert the whole world and it sets you up to discover that all you have is a good testimony, but you know very little about God.

In my fleshly zeal, I have fallen into various traps thinking that I was standing on the right side of truth. I perceived there was no way I could be wrong, and it made me feel as if I was almost infallible about what I perceived to be right. However, eventually the Lord showed me I may have been standing on something, but it was my own definition of righteousness. And when people are standing on their own self-righteousness and raising up their own standard of it, they come across as obnoxious, foolish, and out of sync with reality.

In fleshly zeal you can't see, in self-sufficiency you see no need to see, and in your high-minded perception of self, you may be standing alone, but that is okay because you see yourself as a suffering martyr for the truth. It is easy to forget that the truth that separated many of Jesus' followers from Him involved the subject of the cross and not righteousness. The disciples scattered when Jesus was about to be taken to the cross, not when He was standing for what was right.

The reality is in my foolish zeal I was standing pretty much on a mound I had created according to my religious notions and conclusions about Biblical doctrines without the inspiration and revelation of the Holy Spirit who leads each of us into all truth about Jesus Christ.

Prayer: Lord, I shake my head at what I have done in the past. It is then I realize that when I was foolish, You still held the reins on how far You would let me go. When I was being unfaithful, You remained faithful, and when I was doing my thing, You remained committed to me and longsuffering with me until I regained my sanity and repented. All I can say is forgive me and thank You for never letting me go. Amen.

April 20

Once upon a time, far away and long ago, energy, passion and fiery zeal to be one of the world's greatest evangelists for Christ gripped my soul. I've always been one of those "all or nothing" types of people, and I longed to be a great success in the harvest field of the world, preaching Christ to the multitudes.

Now, a few decades later, (as I sit with an ice pack on a painfully dislocated kneecap) I look back at the long, narrow, hard path winding through a deep and dark valley that the Lord, in His infinite wisdom, mercy and grace ordained for me. This journey of many years has been a place of trials, temptations, troubles, tribulations and testing. Thankfully, my youthful notions about being another "great name" in Christendom were all "de-glittered" and dropped into the dust along the way.

Such notions are usually made up of vanity and pride, foolish fantasies, self-importance, and swelling emotional ambition rather than the Spirit's call and commission. A host of other ideas and conclusions had to be exchanged for God's wisdom and ways, which is merely a taste of what the redeemed will be learning for all eternity. Were there blessings, miracles, and victories along the way? Yes, there were, but the bottom line is, God isn't interested, as we can be, in our "greatness" or in numbers.

Millions of "converts," or hundreds of thousands of church attendees, or millions of viewers on TV doesn't make any "celebrity" a "better" Christian, or a more "holy," or a greater "anointed" or "successful" man or woman for Jesus than a solitary, unnoticed, often disregarded servant who has tirelessly and faithfully toiled in the harvest field in obedience to the Great Commission of our LORD Jesus Christ to go and make—(not "converts" to our way of thinking),—but to make disciples of the Lord Jesus Christ. (See *Matthew 28:19, 20.*)

Of a truth, *"Thine, O LORD, is the greatness, and the power, and the glory, and the victory, and the majesty: for all that is in heaven and in the earth is thine: thine is the kingdom, O LORD, and thou art exalted as head above all. Both riches and honour come of thee, and thou reignest over all; and in thine hand is power and might; and in thine hand it is to make great, and to give strength unto all" (1 Chronicles 29:11, 12).* – J. Haley

Prayer: Lord, because of earthly influences we often associate success in Your kingdom to the world's concept of it. To the world, it is about outward numbers and not transformed souls. Greatness in Your kingdom is always measured by humility and how low it will go to make sure Your glory, Word, and ways are upheld at all times. Amen.

April 21

"For they being ignorant of God's righteousness, and going about to establish their own righteousness, have not submitted themselves unto the righteousness of God. For Christ is the end of the law for righteousness to everyone that believed" (Romans 10:3-4). When I became a Christian, I assumed I had enough understanding of right and wrong and religious affiliation that I understood what it meant to be a Christian. However, my consensus of Christianity was based on notions of what it meant to be a "good person." However, the Bible makes it clear that only God is good and there is no one good, not one.

It took a while for me to realize that there was no good in me and that Christianity was not some religious cloak that put my best and my most righteous self on display. It was not a religion of good works, a presentation of some stoic life that endured much, or a rigid lifestyle of dos and don'ts. In my infancy as a Christian, I somewhat understood that there was much more to the Christian walk than such notions and outward presentations. However, confusion hit the scene because of my zeal about my new-found life of forgiveness, grace, and liberty gave me a false idea as well.

I had a zeal about my way of thinking about religious matters, but it did not have anything to do with the righteousness of God. I was not becoming identified with Jesus' righteousness by standing on my concept of personal righteousness, but it was when I began to enter into the real sufferings with Jesus FOR THE SAKE OF RIGHTEOUSNESS that I realized that if my concept of righteousness was being held up as the standard, then Jesus was not being glorified, deeming my standard as vain. After all, we are told there is a difference between suffering for the sake of what is right and being persecuted because of being on the wrong side of spirit, truth, and real righteousness.

When I see such zeal, I want to warn people that it will eventually lead them down a dead end, but they are either flying so high any warning is a bit late because of their momentum, or they are so sure they are right, they're not prepared to hear any challenge that will not cause them to dig in even farther into their self-righteousness, thinking they are actually being persecuted for it.

I can't fault such people for their enthusiasm for Jesus saving them, being critical towards those who shy away or remain silent towards their fleshly zeal, or judgmental towards those who ignore them. I can stand assured that if they are sincere in their heart towards the Lord, really love His truth, and want to know Him, that God will cause them to realize that at the end of all righteousness is not what they may know or feel about religious matters, but rather the person and work of Jesus Christ.

Prayer: Lord, we tend to make Your truths about what we know instead of seeking to know You so we can know the truth. Lord, forgive us for always getting the "cart before the horse." Amen.

April 22

"And he said unto him, Why callest me good? There is none good but one, that is, God: but if thou wilt enter into life, keep the

commandments" (Matthew19:17). In my last post I referred to the fact God is good and there is no such goodness in us. We all have our idea of "goodness."

We use the phrase, "he or she is a good person." Since we have our own ideas of goodness, we must conclude if it does not line up to God's goodness, it is not really goodness. Perhaps the person is decent enough, nice enough, moral enough, kind enough etc., to be called a "good" person according to the world, but not one is able to ever measure up to the goodness of God.

When "good" is use Scripturally in relationship to man it points to moral uprightness. We are told that God takes pleasure in our faith towards Him, but He delights in that which is pure and upright in motive, attitude, and conduct towards Him. However, when it comes to God, the word "good" is different because for God, He not only is good, but He shows goodness towards His creation.

What does it mean for God to be "good." It points to all that He does is beneficial to everyone. It will bring glory to Him, prove to be beneficial to our well-being, ensure the integrity of His plan, will line up to His righteous ways regardless of the circumstances, and will produce the correct results. This brings us back to the reality that man can't, is unable, and will never be able to prove to be beneficial on all fronts, 24/7 no matter how much he tries.

It is hard for man to not believe there is some "good" in everyone no matter how bad they are. However, the only way we are truly going to come to terms with how "good" God is and develop the proper attitude towards Him and His blessings, is to realize there is nothing in us that could ever qualify, measure up, be lasting, or could be considered as being "good" when it comes to the kingdom of God.

Once again, we must acknowledge that God shows His goodness to us because of His incredible grace.

Prayer: Lord, we want to think more highly of ourselves than we should, while making You more like us as to how You perceive matters. The problem with making ourselves big in our eyes is that we must minimize what You say about the depraved state of man in hopes of balancing the scales out so in the end we aren't so bad after all. Lord, forgive us for accepting the low ways of the world instead of rising up to experience Your heavenly heights. Amen.

April 23

"O wretched man that I am! Who shall deliver me from the body of this death? (Romans 7:24). Due to pride, unregenerated man is in constant competition with God, fleshly man is in pursuit of personal happiness and satisfaction regardless of the fallout, selfish man is looking to feel good about self, usually at the expense of others; and the worldly man is ever climbing some ladder of accomplishment to reach pinnacles, often leaving behind casualties.

When it comes to salvation, due to the flesh man finds his flesh at war with the spirit at various times, contends with worldly attitudes and must constantly crucify the old man. He continually needs to discipline himself to learn to give way to the Holy Spirit, step over foul attitudes, discern his spirit, and examine his ways and fruits.

The reality of man is that he is either in the midst of great conflict, contending with conflict, or finding refuge in the Lord to wait out conflict. It is for these reasons that Paul cried out in his wretched state, who can deliver him from the body of this terrible cycle of death. It becomes clearer each time one honestly examines their character that there is nothing within man that can withstand the purging of the fire of His Spirit, stand in the righteous judgments of His eternal Word, and expect to remain standing in light of His holiness.

Jesus stated we would have much tribulation and Peter talked about the trying of our faith. As long as there is some type of conflict, the benefits can prove to be far, few, and rare, but since all things are possible with God, such conflict for the believer will prove to be beneficial in the end. It ensures that God is having His way in them.

In such challenging situations, the saint is learning what it means to be an open vessel where the Lord can benefit others by having His life poured into and through them. The believer is coming into line with the will of God because the life of Christ is being established in them. He also will be confident in lining up to the plan of God because the image of Christ is being formed in their inner being, while bringing glory to God because the old has ceased and the new is being reflected.

In the end what others will experience is not man's best attempts to be good, but God's goodness to do all things well, whether it is within the believer, in the circumstances, in the conflict, or amid great darkness.

Prayer: Lord, we would like to think there is some good in every person. However, the good implies we have it within ourselves to please You. If we could please You outside of faith towards You, You would have never had to come and die on a cross for us. Forgive us. Just because we are not all that bad, does not mean we are good. The bad just reminds us we are sinners who need to be saved from ourselves. Amen.

April 24

"In all thy ways acknowledge him, and he shall direct thy paths" (Proverbs 3:6). The question I must ask myself is do I want to really know what is really happening around me, and if I do, is it to confirm my reality, or is it to be prepared to stand in the reality of what is really going on? So many times, we are bent on confirming what we know rather than ensuring we know Jesus. We major in the minors and minor in the majors causing us to miss making it to home base as to what is truth.

When it comes to the flesh the need to know is based on insecurities about being wrong and the possible repercussions of being rejected and mocked. When it comes to a wrong spirit because pride is behind it, then the need to know is about coming out on top and not being found to be foolish, ridiculous, inept, or obtuse. We need to clearly discern why we need to know and make sure we are not trying to stand according to our own understanding.

My NEED to know what God's choice or plan is in a matter is not to be right, but to be prepared to respond properly. I WANT to know because if or when major prophetic events happen, I will be standing on the Rock of truth, ready to be a voice of heavenly authority, Biblical reason in darkness, encouragement in despair, and a ministry of hope to those who find themselves in utter chaos and despair.

As a saint of the Most High, I struggle to remember it is about gaining God's perspective and not going with what I think I know or understand. I know in part and from that limited perspective I know I am not capable of making sound judgments without first seeking God's take on a matter. That is why I seek God about all matters, while trusting that as long as my heart desires to know truth, and is pure in receiving it, He will show me what I need to know to make wise judgment calls.

I have learned that when you operate according to God's perspective, you are probably going to stand out because you will not go with the flow of the world. You will not become part of the many voices of the world that are taking sides because your line is attached to the Rock of Ages that never moves from truth and righteousness, but you will also not be standing alone on your own zealous mound of opinions while lacking God's perspective and love. You are going to be walking a fine line as people either cheer you on or throw rocks at you.

I must admit, I fear becoming one of the many voices of the world that drown out the vulnerable voices. I become repulsed at the thought I might yell for the truth to be crucified, while mocking righteousness to silence all opposition. I shunned to think I do such things to maintain a fragile reality that can't afford to be shaken.

Prayer: Lord, we are pathetic. We think we know when we don't. We think we see when we have become blinded. We think we perceive when we are missing it. I love how Paul stressed that it is not WHAT we know that counts, as much as it is WHO we know. We must seek to know You, to see You, to hear You, and to gain Your heavenly perspective. Amen.

April 25

"And what concord hath Christ with Belial? Or what part hath he that believeth with an infidel? (2 Corinthians 6:15). I think one of the big

surprises for many people is just how pagan the world is in its practices and presentations. We are appalled at the half-time shows during some of the football games, recently sickened by displays of blatant wickedness at the Olympics, and have finally begun to stand up and sing the National Anthem at baseball games when they try to do away with it.

In many of our societies, this paganism has been covered with veneers of cultural refinement, religious garb, and a type of elite snobbery that we are not as bad as those we can compare ourselves to. Consider those barbaric, half-naked pagans with their various symbols often tattooed on their bodies, jumping up and down before their idolatrous altars, and swinging to the hypnotic musical beat or operating in some drug-induced, altered state in order to have some type of experience with the unseen world. The truth is we are worse because we are HYPOCRITES about it.

We compare ourselves with them while feeling smug we are not as obvious in our idolatrous worship as they, even though we are just as pagan. We judge them while condoning like practices in our midst. We can't imagine acting like them; yet in our refinement we prove to be just as foolish, cruel, and clueless about how our actions and ways are affecting others. Oswald Chambers referred to such paganism as "Civilized Paganism."

We can clearly see these "pagan" practices take place in our churches. For the most part they are ignored while a new generation of leaders who have been conditioned and indoctrinated by worldly emphasis are taking the reins. Obviously, the moral standard is not all that important. Consider how the old doctrinally sound and inspired hymns are being done away with, while the doctrinal issue may be used for accreditation but is rarely practiced. Clearly, the hard, narrow way of Christianity has been adjusted to appease the crowd and not please God.

What we have is now an Americanized version of Christianity that barely has any real Spirit or truth in it. In this "new" religion, we have been conditioned by a terrible mixture of Christian theology with worldly (pagan) practices. The problem is that it is all demonic, but many are failing to discern it.

Sadly, we are seeing much of the visible church fitting the criteria of the apostate church in the end days that will be taken away by a delusion sent by God to test the hearts of those who call themselves, Christians.

Prayer: Lord, we miss much because we are not seeking You. We get caught up with fleeting sentiment instead of growing more in love with You. We like our minds filled with knowledge about worldly matters but how many are seeking to know You? We want our religious notions upheld regardless of truth without being concerned about whether our foundation will endure the great shaking that will take place. Forgive us for having misdirected priorities. Amen.

April 26

"And what agreement hath the temple of God with idols? For ye are the temple of the living God' as God hath said, I will dwell in them and walk in them; and I will be their God, and they shall be my people" (2 Corinthians 6:16). In my last post I talked about "paganism."

It does not matter what refinement we cover paganism with and what religious activities we do to cover just how fleshly it is, we are not worshipping the holy God of the universe in Spirit and truth, while standing in holy fear and awe; rather, we are worshipping the god of this world, Satan. Paganism leads us back before the flood and eventually to a popular symbol that rose up after the flood—the tower of Babel where man was building a monument to himself to bypass God and any future judgments.

The core of this religion is humanism where man somehow obtains godhood on his own or a right status before some fickle idol. It is where the strongest survive, while the preferred idol is Baal, the altars have been erected to Molech, and where numerous children are being freely offered to appease the god of this world, Satan. We can't forget how the various lifeless, false deities of past nations have been renamed and reinvented by the times we live in and are now being constantly paraded in front of us, ever demanding that we bow before them. No matter how you look at it, the source is idol worship and the core is paganism, all of which creates oppressive darkness in the soul.

Am I shocked that paganism is raising its ugly head amid the spiritual vacuum of this day of great darkness? No, because it has always been there. It used to be hidden in darkness, but since the likes of "political correctness" and "woke," are being blatantly promoted, it is now on full display along with other abominable practices. Clearly, it no longer has a need to hide because man has been dulled down to its dangers and now has become receptive and tolerant of it.

Keep in mind, such paganism takes center stage when the church becomes more worldly and ceases to hold up the true standard of holiness. Lawlessness begins to rule societies, lewdness is a right-of-passage for the elite, rebellion becomes the norm, the mantra of hatred toward righteousness spews out like hot lava, and truth is an expensive rare gem that will cost much in the end, including one's life.

The reality is mankind will always regress into blatant paganism if he does not fill the spiritual vacuum with God and His holy ways. This paganism is clearly seen in churches, but we fail to discern it because we have been conditioned to tack God onto our fleshly, religious activities that allow the flesh to dance before pagan altars while paying homage to the idols of the age.

Prayer: Lord, we forget paganism is a natural worship of creation in one form or another that allows for lusts to operate unabated by any moral standard, imagination to reach heights of euphoria that will end in grave disillusionment, and the worship of lifeless idols that have no life in them. It is founded on superstition due to ignorance of You. It is doomed, and like the ages before it, civilizations that have given way to it and promoted it have been buried in the ashes of judgment and the dust of forgetfulness. Keep us from the natural and cause us to reach for what is true and righteous, ever proving to be excellent to You our great Savior, God, Lord, and Judge. Amen.

April 27

The poor little thing in my bathroom was determined to find an escape from the lifeless environment it found itself trapped in. Its frantic desperation noticeably increased with each passing second and I knew I had to try and help the lost ladybug return to the world outside where the golden sun kisses the morning dew, causing it to glisten like a million miniature diamonds arrayed on the grass and colorful flowers.

After a few tries with some soft tissue, I was able to take her out to the deck where I carefully placed her on a pansy. That is when I saw an incredible change in her actions. Realizing that she had somehow been rescued from a hopeless situation and transported to a place of life and beauty, she seemed a bit surprised, and then began to "savor" where she was with different motions culminating in "looking up" and waving her wee front legs as if in worship and praise.

It's okay if you call me a "nutcase" or an ignoramus when it comes to ladybugs and such, but the truth is, the Spirit of God deeply moved upon my heart and reminded me of what all creation was meant to do; that is, to worship and praise Him, and give Him all the glory, for one day, the redeemed and sanctified, just like that little creature, will be lifted out of this "body of death" and placed in the presence of His glory forever and ever.

1. And he shewed me a pure river of water of life, clear as crystal, proceeding out of the throne of God and of the Lamb.
2. In the midst of the street of it, and on either side of the river, was there the tree of life, which bare twelve manner of fruits, and yielded her fruit every month: and the leaves of the tree were for the healing of the nations.
3. And there shall be no more curse: but the throne of God and of the Lamb shall be in it; and his servants shall serve him:
4. And they shall see his face; and his name shall be in their foreheads.
5. And there shall be no night there; and they need no candle, neither light of the sun; for the Lord God giveth them light: and

they shall reign for ever and ever. (*Revelation 22:1-5*) – J. Haley

Prayer: Lord, You have made Your creatures to express emotions. We know that all of creation will ultimately praise You. Lord, thank You for letting me see Your intricate care and details when it comes to Your creation and its awareness of its Creator. Amen.

April 28

"And thou shalt consume all the people which the LORD thy God shall deliver thee; thine eye shall have no pity upon them: neither shalt thou serve their gods; for that will be a snare unto thee" (Deuteronomy 7:16). Diversity is the key word for today, but when it comes to Christianity, it is a dangerous snare.

We have been told we need diversity, so embrace it, for it is only right to have it to ensure a worldwide peace. Therefore, we must accept it and go along with it like a devoted disciple. This is the only way we will be one big happy family to ensure peace abounds. After all, we certainly must be intelligent enough that we can be open-minded about co-existing with one another regardless of difference in spirit or whether it is truth.

First of all, such a notion of world peace is a fantasy at best and the great lie at worst and will be so until Jesus sits on the earthly throne of Israel as King. Secondly, how many families of this world are in conflict and not all that happy, which begs the question of how can the world become "one big happy family" when it has even greater diversity? And the third part of this equation that will fall apart is that the problem is not in diversity but in the disposition of mankind. It is called sin.

Most people are willing to co-exist. They are like sheep. Leave them feeling secure in the pasture with enough grass and water and they will be fine. However, sheep also can be easily enough led astray if the pastureland becomes lean or corrupt and the water stagnant and muddy and the environment uncomfortable. At that point they can be led to the slaughter by promises of greener grass and clean, fresh water.

There are, and always have been, certain individuals and groups that will rise up to control, exploit, and use people who just want to co-exist. In their demonic delusion, they believe themselves to be the elite, the ones who know what is best (especially for themselves), and they are convinced that they are deserving of the best because they are superior in some way. They see people as a commodity to be used as they see fit, serfs to be indebted and exploited, and servants to serve their whims and agendas. Each person becomes some number or statistic as they remain faceless to them; therefore, it doesn't matter what happens to them because they are dispensable.

Our Creator does not see us as dispensable. He created us with a plan and purpose in mind. Due to sin, we have been separated from our real calling, but God redeemed us when His Son paid the necessary ransom for our sins.

As believers we no longer must co-exist as lost, wandering sheep in a doomed world. We cried out in great need of salvation, and our Shepherd heard us, sought for us, found us and brought us back to be put into His fold.

Prayer: Lord, we no longer have to fit in a world that is upside down. Your Spirit has prepared us to be fitted into Your Body so that we can bring You glory. Amen.

April 29

"And then shall many be offended, and shall betray one another, and shall hate one another" (Matthew 24:10). Are we all alike that we can forget what often separates us? Can we come into agreement without compromising what we know to live as one big happy family amid diversity? We would like to think that the differences are surface, when what separates us comes down to something that is much greater than color, race, or culture. What separates man is creed.

Man's creed determines his attitudes, his premise, his philosophies, and his belief systems. Creed is what man will die for. It also determines what he stands on and for, as well as what he will live by. Ultimately, creed in the mind of man gives him the edge to do what he must to get other people to agree with him. Until man agrees with him, there will be no agreement.

Diversity may be the mantra, appearing as tolerant, open minded, void of prejudice, and a promise of establishing a global euphoria, but the reality is that the only thing that can stand such a mixture, without being destructive to the souls of people or the soul of a nation, is goulash. The reality of diversity is that it is heading for the worst nightmare possible and will end in the same smothering reality that past nations have which imploded from within.

No matter how the Bible warns us of the dangers of parlaying with that which is not of the same spirit or lines up to Scriptural truths, there will always be diversity in the religious convictions of mankind. These convictions are not based on the Bible, but on cultural influence as to what god is acceptable and needs to be worshipped, what altar needs to be allowed to stand, and what religion needs to be allowed to dictate to the conscience of man.

Religions can promote diversity but when it comes to the real Church and Body of Christ, it can't give way to it because it would come under another spirit that will open the person up to a wrong Jesus and gospel.

Prayer: Lord, we have our creeds that make us right, superior, and worthy of writing off anyone who does not agree as dispensable, foolish, stupid, and unworthy of any real consideration. Forgive us for our dishonorable thinking and give us a heart for the lost, a vision for our true calling, and the inspiration to choose that which far exceeds the godless philosophies and ways of the world. Amen.

April 30

"Now therefore fear the LORD, and serve him in sincerity and in truth: and put away gods which your fathers served on the other side of the

flood and in Egypt; and serve ye the LORD" (Joshua 24:14). In the previous post, I talked about the worldly emphasis of diversity. Such a notion is a fantasy where everyone will somehow put aside all difference to get along and live in a quasi-state of peace. What is the real calling of God's people? Is it to water down all presentations to be acceptable to the world? Is it to confuse real love with tolerance so that the issue of man's sins is never dealt with but people feel good about "Christianity" and will come to religious places to be part of the crowd.

God has called His people, the nation of Israel, to be separate for a reason and He has called His Church to come out and be separate from the idolatrous world. For Israel, such mixtures were forbidden because the pagan nations around them would corrupt them spiritually. Like Solomon, they would be led astray to worship foreign gods and as in the case of the children of Israel in the wilderness, erect a golden calf in the name of the Lord.

The truth is regardless of the age, each generation has their own golden calf they can erect. For the Romans, all gods were acceptable, but there was one god above all others that all would have to bow to when one was to show their loyalty and that was to Ceasar. Many Christians of that time were martyred because they refused to bow to Ceasar. As we know, a house divided in loyalties, convictions, and agendas against itself will not stand.

Along with the idols people will naturally establish pagan altars where anything of innocence will be offered. Incident after incident shows that the spirit of the world succeeded in seducing God's people into a mixture that made them profane before Him, fickle and weak in the sight of other nations, and subject to judgment.

The truth is mankind will end up worshipping and serving one of two gods: the god of this world, Satan, or the God of the Universe, Jehovah. As Joshua pointed out in *Joshua 24*, the gods before the flood in his time still existed for there is nothing new under the sun, but we need to decide who we will worship and serve in order to quit standing between two opinions as an attempt to keep God "off our backs," while trying to keep peace with the devil. Such an attempt ends in paganism.

Prayer: Lord, we want to keep You around as fire insurance while making peace with the world so we can comfortably live in it. However, if we are not going come under the influence of this world, we must come out and be separate. Amen.

May

May 1

"And it came to pass, when the king of Israel had read the letter, that he rent his clothes and said, Am I God, to kill and to make alive, that this man doth send unto me to recover a man of his leprosy? Wherefore consider, I pray you, and see who he seeketh a quarrel against me (2 Kings 5:7). Every time I read this story it reminds me of a person that almost blew it. The person I am speaking of is Naaman.

The question is why did this person, Naaman almost blow it? Upon a young Jewish handmaiden's suggestion Naaman, a leper, went to seek out a real prophet in Samaria. This great and honorable captain of the Syrian host traveled by faith to seek out this man of God. However, he went to the king seeking healing rather than locating the prophet. Is that not how it is for most of us? We seek out those who are in an influential position for something only God can address.

Consider the pressure the king felt, he rent his clothes declaring, "Am I God, to kill and to make alive?" The king felt Naaman was setting him up to fail so that he could render some mischief against him.

We have the same tendency when it comes to leaders in our church. We expect them to be perfect, to do the impossible, or make matters right. These individuals may have a calling on their life to guide the sheep, but that calling does not include being God. They are not miracle workers, all-knowing, or the answer to any problem.

Every time one of God's sheep puts too much confidence in the pastor, they set them up to fail. Some pastors are like the king who realistically knows they are human and incapable of doing the impossible. Some become buried under the various attempts to carry the many problems of their sheep. As a result, some become burned out, while others become weary and despondent.

Now the real man of God, Elisha heard of the situation, and he asked the king why he tore his clothes when Samaria had a real prophet among them. The problem is, we don't always recognize the true men and women of God who labor among us.

We are always looking in high places where positions, accolades, popularity, and degrees play a big part in our attitude towards a matter instead of seeking the One who is above all in heavenly places to reveal the servant or the way we must walk to see a matter resolved. We are also looking around and about and not looking for those who quietly prove they are servants and instruments of God that will do His bidding.

Prayer: Lord, we often miss the miracle because we are too busy looking for someone to step on the scene and make it right in Your name. Forgive us for our preference to trust in what we can see, while failing to trust in You. Amen.

May 2

"But Naaman was wroth, and went away, and said, Behold, I thought, He will surely come out to me, and stand, and call on the name of the LORD his God, and strike his hand over this place, and recover the leper (2 Kings 5:11)." Naaman finally went to Elisha, but instead of Elisha meeting him personally, he sent a message to him with explicit instructions as to what he needed to do to be healed. How did Naaman respond? He was downright insulted. He expected the prophet to come out and give him some performance, but when it comes to God, it is never about performance but obedience.

Because Naaman was honorable, he could be reasoned with by one of his wise servants, and that is the only thing that often keeps a person from blowing it. Our natural tendency is to stick to our idea of how something should be delivered or carried out. However, God's ways are not ours and it takes wise individuals to tell us why not to obey.

The reasoning behind such matters is simple. What will we lose by believing the instructions and what if we gain what we are seeking? That should be the essence of our questions. We think we may be risking much, when, in reality, we have nothing to lose and everything to gain when it comes to believing God.

Naaman went down to the Jordan River as instructed to dip seven times, but not in faith. And guess what happened? The seventh time he dipped, he came out with the flesh of a little child and was clean. Sometimes we are faithless, but God will always be faithful to His Word. It is upon responding to His Word that we find that God is true to His Word in every way.

It is obvious that we blow it because we will not believe God. We often have our own ideas as to how God will bring about a matter to prove a point, but God has nothing to prove. We miss it because we will not follow His explicit instructions laid down in His Word, and when we fail to do what He says, we remain in the same state. In the end it will eventually destroy us as we become more skeptical towards the simplicity of God's instructions.

Prayer: Lord, we start out as heathens, but find ourselves desperately seeking some deliverance. We are shocked, a bit put off at believing that which is unseen. We wrestle with simple instructions, and are about to throw our hands up in the air as we get ready to walk away. However, reasoning somehow challenges us to try it. In the end we find salvation, and because You are faithful to Your Word, we are made new and whole. Praise Your name for being faithful to the end. Amen.

May 3

"And many lepers were in Israel in the time of Elisha the prophet; and none of them was cleansed, saving Naaman the Syrian" (Luke 4:27). In the last post I spoke of the incident of Naaman, the leper being healed. He almost blew it. He was so close, yet so far away because he had his own ideas of how his healing was to come about. He was insulted because the prophet did not meet with him personally and had simply given him some clear instructions that offended his notions about matters.

Jesus used Naaman as an example to the people at Nazareth. Even though Naaman almost missed being the recipient of a miraculous healing, he still became an example of a man who chose to believe the words of a prophet regardless of his heathen background. In obedience he stepped into the water, dipped himself in it seven times and came out clean.

Jesus pointed out there were many Israelites in the land that were lepers, but none were healed but a Gentile. Naaman was there because of the words of a Jewish servant girl. He was willing to travel far, and eventually even humble himself to receive the blessing.

We all usually begin like Naaman with our own ideas. We seek to hear the voice of the prophet, but if we don't like the instruction, we become offended and are ready to walk away without even trying it. That is where most people blow it, they fail to walk out the instructions to see if God's Word is true.

It is at the point we must realize that reason and faith finally motivated Naaman to obey the instructions. He reveals to us it is never enough to hear and even pursue a matter unless we are willing to obey the instructions.

It is so easy to miss God's move, promise, and blessing because we have our own ideas. The key is, is our heart open enough to be reasoned with? Are we honorable enough to see the reason behind something no matter how foolish and silly it may seem to us? Are we willing to step outside of what we know in good faith and simply do what we are told because not to would be more foolish than risking the insult or embarrassment of doing it?

Prayer: Lord, we get mixed up on what we think is honorable when we fail to do the most honorable thing of all, and that is to believe and obey You. Forgive us for holding onto honor that will fade with our self-importance. Amen.

May 4

"But he went in, and stood before his master. And Elisha said unto him, Whence comest thou, Gehazi? And he said, Thy servant went no whither" (2 Kings 5:25). There is another valuable example in this incident surrounding Naaman.

The final illustration has to do with Elisha's servant Gehazi. He could not understand why Elisha turned down Naaman's gifts. Certainly, Elisha should benefit from God's healing. Think about what I am saying.

Why did Elisha remain unseen? Because Naaman's healing was about him realizing who the true God was and not proving Elisha was a prophet. Elisha was a mere mouthpiece, but God was the source of healing. Elisha was not interested in receiving any accolades because all glory should go to God. He was not interested in receiving any benefits from an idolatrous heathen because God's healing is not for sale. It can't be bought, earned or deserved.

Salvation and healing come from God because of who He is and His right to be sanctified in the eyes of unbelievers because of His wondrous works. Naaman almost blew it, but Gehazi did blow it. Did Gehazi understand God's way in the matter? He was not one to see beyond his small world of service, but he did know it was wrong to ask and accept anything from Naaman due to Elisha's example of refusing it. He even hid it and lied about it.

God showed the actions of the servant to Elisha and the result is that unlike Naaman, who did not even see the prophet, when Gehazi stood before him it was to receive the declaration of judgment, not only on himself but his descendants. The leprosy that left Naaman in obedience came on Gehazi because of his disobedience.

Gehazi's deeds tainted the fact that God would be sanctified in the eyes of a heathen who the LORD knew would become a believer of Him because of the healing. How many times do we use the great work of God to benefit ourselves, bringing some type of glory and recognition to ourselves, instead of recognizing that it is God's doing? He ALONE will be sanctified in the eyes of others, set apart from all other gods in their hearts, while resulting in them benefitting from His incredible power to heal in order to bring another heir of salvation into His kingdom.

Prayer: Lord, it is so easy to make something about us. We look for what will benefit us. We desire to be recognized and exalted for any small part we may have in Your great work, ready to accept the glory You alone deserve. Lord, forgive us for being in competition with You, seeking to be exalted above You in order to receive undeserved honor that belongs only to You. Amen.

May 5

"For the vineyard of the LORD of hosts is the house of Israel, and the men of Judah his pleasant plant: and he looked for judgment, but behold oppression: for righteousness, but behold a cry" (Isaiah 5:7)" Israel is referred to as various living trees and vegetation. Here it is referred to as a vineyard that the Lord planted in a certain place, Jerusalem, while the men of Judah were considered a pleasant plant. Israel is also represented by the olive and fig trees.

When it comes to the members of the living church, they are referred to as branches that have been engrafted into the olive tree, Israel, in *Romans 11,* as well as the branch of the Vine. We know according to *John 15* that the Vine who also came out of the Olive Tree is Jesus.

The key to these illustrations is two-fold: 1) Israel and the church are both living entities and 2) they are meant to produce fruit. However, without being connected and abiding in the vine or being grafted in, a branch is useless because it is lifeless. When it comes to the vine or the tree, if it is not firmly planted in the right ground and properly cultivated, it becomes worthless, unable to produce any real quality of fruit. This is something that God was pointing out to Israel, and Jesus has made it clear to the Church.

There is an incident in *Matthew 21:19* where Jesus cursed a fig tree for lacking fruits. The main issue is that fig trees produced figs in early spring before producing the actual crop later on. Jesus was seeking the first fruits of it.

Remember the first fruits were to be dedicated to the Lord. It matters little how healthy the tree looks if it fails to reach its potential to produce quality fruit. Firstfruits were automatically dedicated to the Lord, for they had not been touched by the cultivation of man's efforts but were in their purest form. Even though Jesus cursed the tree, it gave Him the opportunity to teach on the miraculous ability of faith to tap into the impossible.

The fact the church was grafted into the olive tree, Israel, shows us that as members of the Body of Christ we are now part the blessings and promises given to Abraham's descendants. The promises of God came through the covenants that were established with both Abraham and David.

We are indeed blessed people, but it is not because we are branches grafted into the tree of life and promises; rather, it is because God by His mercy made the slit in the tree and by His grace, He engrafted us into it to partake of the divine, the miraculous and the eternal.

Prayer: Lord, we want to believe that as believers we display fruit that is worthy of Your consideration. We often think our religious works will bring sweetness to You, but the real test is how those around us are reacting to our lives. Are they tasting the sweetness of heaven or the bitterness of this world? My hope is that the fruit of my life will be pleasant to You and nourishing to those around me. Amen.

May 6

Then said he unto the dresser of his vineyard, Behold, theses three years I come seeking fruit on this fig tree, and find none: cut it down;

why cumbereth it the ground?" (Luke 13:7). In this parable in Luke, Jesus stresses that the owner of the vineyard expects to find fruit on every tree and if he doesn't, it means the tree needs to be cut down because it is taking up valuable space that could be used to plant a tree that brings forth fruit.

This example has caused me to examine my life as a believer. Am I taking up space in the Lord's vineyard or is my life being fruitful when it comes to His kingdom work? I may have great foliage that gives the appearance that I am a fruit-producing tree but if the fruit is not there to confirm it, then my life is all show that hides my hypocrisy.

As the vinedresser, God has every right to expect fruit from our lives. When it came to Jesus cursing the tree in *Matthew 21:19*, it is the only recorded time Jesus cursed something during His earthly ministry.

God plants, prunes and cultivates, but what kind of fruit is produced comes down to the relationship (response) the tree has to the vinedresser, and the branch has with the vine. The fruit will always tell on the tree or the branch; therefore, it can't be hidden. It does not matter how religious (healthy) we look to others, if we lack the right fruit, it will reveal that something is clearly missing in our Christian lives.

There are many that want to believe that the branches have grown into the Olive Tree and yet there is nothing in the branches that possess any seed of life to take root for it to become a tree. Branches get their identity from the tree and the vine, and those who arrogantly think different could find themselves separated from the source of life, fruitless and ready to be taken by the winds of judgment.

We must always consider our relationship with the Lord based on our attitudes and fruits and never on our ideas of who we think we are before Him. Our ideas of self can be greatly exaggerated, overrated, and like those of the Laodicean church, far from how He sees us. He not only said it once or twice, but in many ways and from different angles. We will always be known by the essence and quality of the fruit that comes out of our lives.

Prayer: Lord, we like to think it is about appearance and activities, but it will always come back to the fruit. Forgive us for keeping our Christian life about surface matters while avoiding going deep into the soil of our heart and checking out if we have been firmly grafted into You, our Vine of life. Amen.

May 7

"For if the firstfruit be holy, the lump is also holy: and if the root be holy, so are the branches" (Romans 11:16). In one of my latest posts I referred to Israel being represented by trees and the members of the Living Church represented by branches. Without Israel, there would be no salvation, for Jesus came out of Judah. Without Israel there would be no tree in which we could be engrafted to receive the life and promises that came by way of Jesus Christ.

To God, Israel represented His first fruits as a separate people, a holy nation, a royal priesthood among the pagan nations. When it comes to the church, Jesus is the first fruits of a new creation in which He will manifest His life through His branches.

Each illustration reminds us that, first of all, we have a purpose on this earth. It is not just about being some living entity, identified to some religion so that we can sit back on our laurels and wait for some great intervention or blessing from God. We are to be a conduit, a connection between heaven and earth that will become an avenue in which the Son of God's life can flow to others. If we lack the heavenly connection, we will be of no earthly use or good to our Lord or to others.

The life of Christ in us is pure and devoid of man's cultivation. God cultivates us with the pureness of His Spirit and truth, but it will come down to our relationship with Him that will determine the quality of fruit. What kind of fruits, if any, do we offer to Him in worship and others in service?

When someone comes up to us to see if we have anything of substance to offer but only finds fig leaves of religious appearance and platitudes, they are left with disappointment. If someone comes up to us to taste the fruit, but all they taste is something without flavor, substance, or value, they will walk away disappointed.

Heavenly fruit will never leave one feeling disappointed, dissatisfied, or frustrated making the claims of Christianity appear as nothing more than a big scam. God's supplies are never empty, His means never disappointing, or His ways a big joke or a terrible letdown. However, to produce the best fruit, we can't be partially connected to the vine or tree in half-hearted devotion or service; rather, we must be engrafted in and abiding in the source of life itself, Jesus Christ, to ensure our fruit benefits others and brings Him glory.

Prayer: Lord, we often simply want to get by, get through, and get any unpleasantries in life over with quickly. We want to give just enough to leave an impression without having our fruit really examined by others and tested by You. However, Lord in the end, our fruit will stand, fall, or be completely missing. Lord, I want to be a branch that will always offer the best of Your life to others because that is why I am here. Amen.

May 8

"And spared not the old world, but saved Noah the eighth person, a preacher of righteousness, bringing in the flood upon the world of the ungodly" (2 Peter 2:5). Although many people avoid the Old Testament with its laws, teachings, and examples, I constantly study, read, and cross reference it with the New Testament. I find myself sometimes shaking in my shoes, knowing God has not changed, and yet the God who is being presented nowadays seems to be getting further away from the God of the Bible.

God's holiness for the most part has been buried under false presentations of His love and grace to cover up the real issue that plagues mankind, destroys relationships, and breaks fellowship, and that is sin. The truth is, God has not changed His attitude towards sin. No matter what dispensation one lived in or now lives in, under the Law or grace, God has always maintained that in the end HE will judge sin that has not been properly addressed. The reason for the understanding is because man has always been saved by grace through faith and not by personal works.

In the Old Testament, there was sacrifice where the blood of animals made atonement to cover sin and in the New Testament, Jesus became the sacrifice to redeem us from the power, claims, and judgments on sin. However, to ensure that we have been cleansed from all unrighteousness entails true repentance and confession of sin that will bring us under the blood of the New Covenant to ensure pardon and reconciliation with God.

It seems that in today's Americanized Christianity, the attitude is that God will overlook sin because of love, but we must remember the angels lived in a perfect environment, but when Satan rebelled with a third of the angels, they fell from their estate of glory into darkness and damnation.

Noah found grace with God because he walked with Him before the flood, but he was aware that in the flood all creation was being destroyed because the imaginations of the people were continually wicked, and their way violent while he was being spared of all judgment in the ark because of his faith. Abraham was a man of faith, but he witnessed God judging Sodom and Gomorrah and prophetically saw his descendants taste 400 years of oppressive bondage. I could go on, but you get the point.

God has not changed His attitude towards sin. He has always shown long-suffering towards the sinner, contended with the rebellious to repent, with the wicked to consider their destructive ways, and with the evil to flee the wrath to come. It is His will that all be saved so that they can avoid the great judgment that will come upon all children of disobedience.

Prayer: Lord, we are faced with the challenge of keeping everything in perspective about our life here, our walk of faith, and our future with You in glory. However, we can become lazy and unprepared to face the challenges that come with faith. Lord, since there is much trouble in this world, refine my faith in the ovens of adversity to ensure that I am always standing on, and hiding in You as the Rock. Amen.

May 9

"And Enoch also, the seventh from Adam, prophesied of these, saying, Behold, the Lord cometh with ten thousands of his saints, To execute judgment upon all" (Jude 14-15a). This brings us to now. How many warnings are there in the New Testament that when the Lord comes back it will be as Judge to judge the whole world that lies in sin, lies, and rebellion?

We see that Enoch who walked with God prophetically saw the end of our age. Jesus is coming back with His saints to judge the sinners, the wicked and the evil. He also is going to judge the religious people who, like Cain, decide that their "unacceptable" sacrifice to the Lord should be accepted by Him. There are those who, like Balaam, sold their calling for filthy lucre, and people like Korah who, in spite of their high calling, was not content with their position and felt they deserved a place of greater prominence in spite of the fact God had not ordained it as so.

God's attitude towards sin and methods of judging remain undeterred. It is not His heart to see man perish in his sin, but man in his rebellion and sin chooses to believe his personal "Titanic ship" will never become shipwrecked and sink. I have no idea what these individuals think will keep their ship afloat when they run into the iceberg on their day of reckoning, but whatever it is will prove foolish in the end.

Keep in mind, Enoch was only the seventh generation from Adam when he saw this judgment. The question is, has sin in your life been properly addressed? Are you like Enoch who can be entrusted with the prophetic because of your walk with God, and like Noah you are finding grace because you have learned to walk with God in this wicked generation? Are you like Abram whose faith gave him the ability to intercede on behalf of two wicked cities and as a result Lot was saved?

You can't have this authority before God if you are walking in sin and maintain assurance in your position before God if you are walking in agreement with the sinner. You also can't have confidence about His deliverance if you are trusting the wicked world around you to save you when it can't because it is also doomed. And finally, can you expect a holy God to spare you from His judgment when you are toying with rebellion while parlaying with Satan and operating in unbelief and disobedience?

Prayer: Lord, we separate ourselves from understanding Your ways which are brought out in the Old Testament while trying to cling to some vague notions about Your love and grace in the New Testament. Lord, Your love addressed our sin by way of a cross, Your grace was shown to those who truly learned to walk with You by faith, and true faith and hope was given to those who simply chose to believe Your Word and Your promises. Forgive us for playing the fool who ends up being foolish in our ways, inept because of unbelief towards You, wicked in our actions and evil in our thoughts. Amen.

May 10

It's bright white metal with sharp black trim is the "latest" design in flower planters so now a three-tiered one, purchased for me to plant petunias in, is situated by our front door. It came as a surprise to me at what a conversation piece it became when the Bible study group first saw it, even though the baby petunias haven't had time to mature and display their glorious blossoms.

Listening to the growing number of compliments being made on the planter brought to mind how easy it is for we Christians to admire certain qualities in personalities for their appearance, personality, talents, usefulness or cleverness while missing the most important aspect of their lives—the Christ that lives within. In other words, what is there about you and me that draws people to us—is it US or is it the indwelling Christ?

Are we attracting people to ourselves, or is Christ in us, "the hope of glory" drawing people to us so we can share His life with them? I do hope that the petunias will grow and blossom profusely to the point that they, and not the planter itself, will be the point of attraction and delight, and so too, I pray that people will not see me, but Jesus in me. He said, *"And I, if I be lifted up from the earth, will draw all men unto me" John 12:32.* – J. Haley

Prayer: Lord, people are unique, and the reason why is because they are to be different members fitted in Your Body. However, we want people to be cut out of the same mode we are. I guess we what to admire our best instead of stand in awe of Your glory. Forgive us for our arrogance. Amen.

May 11

"Happy is that people, that is in such a case: yea, happy is that people, whose God is the LORD" (Psalm 144:15). There is nothing wrong with fun, but it is fleeting and there is nothing eternal about it. When it comes to happiness, we are told that the happy man is the one whose God is the Lord, which will prove satisfying to his spirit. If he seeks the Lord, he finds wisdom from above satisfying to the mind. He will live a life of substance for he will have mercy on the poor, satisfying the sense of goodness, and will fear the Lord which disciplines the soul, thereby satisfying it. Happiness comes down to having a right heart attitude towards God and the life He has entrusted to us.

What about contentment? We must learn to be content no matter the state we are in to realize that it is godliness with contentment that proves to be great gain for us. It is clear, to be content we must realize that all gifts come from God. For the gifts from above to become a blessing to us, regardless of our status in this world, we must learn to be thankful, as well as faithful and good stewards with them. We are told our main purpose here is to bring glory to God, but if we are dissatisfied in our life in Christ, aimless in our purpose before heaven, and unthankful towards the many gifts of God, we will fail to reach our potential, which is to bring glory to the Lord.

What is your heart's desire? We are told that we are to set our affections on things above and not on the things of the earth

(*Colossians 3:2*). If our affections are on the matters of heaven, our desires will line up to God's heart about matters. This allows Him to fulfill one of His many promises, *"Delight thyself also in the LORD; and he shall give thee the desires of thine heart. Commit thy way unto the LORD; trust also in him: and he shall bring it to pass" (Psalm 37:4-5).*

This brings us back to *Hebrews 11:1* as to possessing the substance of hope. It is based on the unseen, not on anything of or in this world. Hope that has substance also has expectancy that a matter will be so because heaven is behind it. It will possess an enduring confidence due to the evidence of what has already proven to be so when God is clearly the source and inspiration behind that which is pure, true, and right.

Prayer: Lord our hope is in You, because of Your great work of redemption, and we can stand confident in You. I am constantly reminded that the hope of the present and future glory is You in me. Thank You that You are the essence of all hope that stands sure in the past because of redemption, remains sure in the present due to the work of sanctification of Your Spirit, and will prove to be sure in the future when I am glorified with You. Amen.

May 12

"Thou wilt shew me the path of life: in thy presence is fulness of joy; at thy right hand there are pleasures for evermore" (Psalm 16:11). Paul warned us in the last days that men would be lovers of pleasure more than lovers of God. Where our affections are is where the focus of our heart will be, and it is what we will naturally pursue. If we love something we will desire it above all else.

In my latest posts, I showed how what we see can't bring real hope, satisfaction, happiness, meaning, or fulfillment to our lives. It is what we can't see that determines the quality of our life. It is important to note that we are being conditioned by the world around us as to our agendas, preferences, and pursuits. We have been accustomed to making our life on earth all about us, surviving this world, and getting the most out of it for ourselves. In our world it is all about what we think is right, and what will make our life happy and complete.

The problem with the world of self is that it makes for a small world that leaves us frightened at any type of change and disruption, insecure because our reality is fragile, and inept because we refuse to be challenged to reach our potential. We allow our fears to make us stubborn towards changes, our insecurities angry at any challenge, and our ineptness to excuse ourselves from stepping outside of our small perimeter to really discover the life God has for us.

God will never be found in the small world of selfishness. He will not be present in a world that is self-serving with the vanity of this world or self-absorbed with fear and uncertainty. He is found when we search for Him outside of our small worlds, seek His life amid a dying world, and find His abiding peace in what is typical for our temporary existence of trouble and tribulation.

The Lord is waiting for us to stop trying to maintain our life in this world and find Him to know life and to experience what is sure and eternal.

Prayer: Lord, we think we are looking for ways to recreate our life but the only thing that changes our life is when You make us into a new creation that will once again reflect Your glory. Amen.

May 13

"Now of the things which we have spoken this is the sum: We have such an high priest, who is set on the right hand of the throne of the Majesty in the heavens" (Hebrews 8:1). How small can our world become? It can become so small we can't move forward or breathe without experiencing panic attacks. It is for the reason of self-preservation of small worlds, paranoid realities and unobtainable resolutions that we have become comfortable with, that many fail to truly follow Jesus into the life He has called them to. It is for this

reason we must deny ourselves of the self-life with its rights, pick up a cross of personal discipline and learn to follow Jesus into the life He is calling us to.

We are told that Jesus is seated on the right hand of majesty. Consider what David said *Psalm 16:11*. That the Lord will show us the path to life. We know this path is called discipleship and can only be accessed and walked out by following Jesus. He stated that on the right hand of God are pleasures that will last forever. This revelation brings us back to the reality, that all we truly need, should be seeking, and must be willing to lose are any and all parts of this present life and world to know the true pleasure that can only be found in Jesus. It is from our life in Christ that we will discover the fulness of joy.

God is a God of order. Most people fail to see the order laid out in Scripture. Note the order in *Psalm 16:11* because to miss any step when it comes to the order of God, is to be out of order and out of step with God. We must first walk in the path of righteousness that He shows us Scripturally, before we can discover the joy that is attached to such a life. It is from this joy that we will discover pleasures for ever more.

Prayer: Lord, we want life to bow down to our self-life, but life is about revealing the smallness, emptiness and ineptness of such a life. Lord, give us a vision beyond the small world of self, the vain world around us, and the limited world of understanding so that we can catch glimpses of the pleasures that are attached to Your glory. Amen.

May 14

With so many changes taking place in our world today, (and most of them not for the better) it's a bit disconcerting when the familiarity of the mountain skyline you've become accustomed to suddenly changes. As I looked out the kitchen window at the now unfamiliar contour of the mountaintop, I realized that the reason for this new look was because the trees were being cut down.

The forested tops of the local mountains are reachable to loggers, unlike the formidable, high, jutting granite peaks of the Rocky Mountains which elicit awe and wonder. I told myself to get used to the "new look" for what else can a person do when changes beyond one's control seem to take place overnight?

It serves to remind me that we have to be careful not to put all of our confidence and assurance in people, places and things that are temporal, but instead trust in the Rock of Ages that never moves or changes as we build our lives upon Jesus Christ, the only firm foundation. While the experience of change begins at conception, and is part of our entire life's journey until death, the most important change that needs to take place in a person's life is that of being born again of the Spirit of God where all things become new, and making Jesus Christ Lord.

While the Christian walk is a walk of obedience and change from the old to the new, and as we are changed from *"glory to glory," (2 Corinthians 3:18)* we can rest assured that "*Jesus Christ [is] the same yesterday, and to day, and for ever*" (Hebrews 13:8). – J. Haley

Prayer: Lord, the world has nothing to offer us when it comes to something being immoveable and trustworthy. It leaves us grasping, drowning, and dying. Thank You for being the Rock that brings forth Living Water that will ensure my well-being during the storms of life until You bring me home. Amen.

May 15

"And said, Naked came I out of my mother's womb, and naked shall I return thither: the LORD gave, and the LORD hath taken away; blessed be the name of the LORD" (Job 1:21). Right now, what are you holding onto tightly? What are you afraid of losing the most? It is easy to cling to something without realizing it. It can be my idea of life, a relationship, my possessions, even my rights to have what I think I deserve when it comes to life. The reality is maybe what I am clinging to is not all that bad, wrong, or wicked, but it proves to be

oppressive because I can't move forward. It has become a hindrance because there is no personal growth, or a leanness to the spirit because it leaves me hollow.

I remember watching the story about how certain tribes find water in Africa. They cut a hole in a tree big enough for a monkey to get its hand through it and then they put the monkey's greatest enticement in that hole: Salt. The monkey finds the salt and reaches into the hole to get it but their hold on the salt keeps them from getting their hand out of the hole. They refuse to let go of the prize, and as a result they are caught. The other aspect of the story is that they are given the salt but are tied up until they become so thirsty they don't care who is following them to the water hole.

So many times, as independent thinkers and rebellious people who want to have life on our terms, life brings us to desperate states and places. It is only in a state of complete hopelessness and a place of utter despair that we, like the Prodigal Son, realize it is far better to be a servant at the table of abundance than a lost waif battling with the swine for pods. This is when we cast off the arrogance, lay aside our waning strength, and come home with our hat of repentance in hand. It is at that time we will be waiting to bow as a humble servant and ask for forgiveness to be restored once again at the communion table of our Father.

Prayer: Lord, the world may offer us a variety of tastes, but they are worthless and often poisonous to our souls. You offer us a seat at Your table of abundance and sadly we are too foolish or silly to know that the world is a pigpen that offers things only swine can appreciate and live on. Forgive us for our foolish thinking and ways. Amen.

May 16

"And Jesus said unto him, No man having put his hand to the plough, and looking back is fit for the kingdom of God" (Luke 9:62). Sometimes my greatest challenge has been to let go of that which is not beneficial to my well-being. Whether I am holding onto something

like a relationship that has become almost obsessive or a memory of something that has become a type of shrine, I must do everything within me to let it go, walk away, or step over or around it and never look back.

There are also those excuses I use to hold on to something, so I won't forget the type of distress it left me in and fall for it again. I must not forget those silly, sentimental articles that keep me looking back at what was but have long ceased to exist. There are always those claims to some right that insists I have the right to pursue and expect it, but all such faulty reasons and claims bring one back to the world and not God.

Let's face it, we want life on our terms, and the right to pursue what we want regardless of how wrong it will prove to be in the end. As long as we hold tightly to such things, we can't grab ahold of the blessings of the present. However, if we cling to such matters, we can't begin to cling to the Rock of Ages. If we worry about keeping or maintaining what we can't hold onto forever, we will fail to hold onto God's promises and follow Him into the life He has called us to. If it is not bad enough in looking back, we end up missing much of what is going on before us. Sadly, it is not unusual we also become fearful towards disruption, tormented about any type of loss, and miserable in the fragile reality that eventually we will be forced to let go.

Jesus made it clear, if we want to hold onto something, we must hold it lightly so we can easily let go of it if He should require it. If we are unwilling to let go, we will lose it, ending in bitterness, regret, and anger.

This reminds me of the fires on the altar. They were to be kept burning. I realize that for me, such holds on my life need to be put on the altar and what part the fire does not consume God will give back to me, purified and precious. Instead of the torment and misery that goes along with it, I now have a liberty to appreciate the blessings that come with things God freely gives.

We must not forget all gifts come from above, are beneficial to our spiritual well-being and will endure the testing, stand in the storms and withstand knowing everything we have is a matter of God's grace.

Prayer: Lord, I can't claim anything as being mine because You have given me everything. It belongs to You and I must be a good steward of it, but if You require it from me, I must be willing to let go of it so that my arms are free to reach up in sweet surrender and my hands are free to receive what You have for me. Amen.

May 17

"Folly is set in great dignity, and the rich sit in low place" (Ecclesiastes 10:6). Solomon, the wisest man had to become inundated by the vanity of this present world before he came to an understanding that it comes down to that which is eternal that determines how rich one becomes in this world. The constant lesson was that all is vanity that is attached to the flesh and this world.

The world offers much but it is contrary to God's ways. Its vanity warns that its promises are hollow, its ways destructive, its philosophies empty, its education foolish, its knowledge often based on opinions that are affected by various filters, and its emphases unfulfilling. Since all of man's pursuits in this present world prove to be temporary, it makes him often unresponsive towards any aspect of having hope beyond the age he lives in.

The reality of this world is it is upside down and therefore what is fair to the world is really unfair to mankind and what is sane to the world is insanity when compared to what is really going on. The world is inside out which means you can't trust the presentation of the world because its wicked ways have often been hidden in plain sight, but most do not know what they are looking at or for. It is imploding from within because it has no substance in which to uphold or maintain it.

Jesus came to turn the world right side up. He came to expose sin, touch the outcast, give hope to the hopeless, and a "leg up" and out of the vanity that consumes many. The early apostles preached a message that shocked the world, caused much of it to fall and crumble so that the Lord could put lives back together. Everywhere these devoted disciples tread, they left footprints and witnesses that would lead others to that which was eternal.

It is natural for man to travel the road of vanity, and if he becomes wise, he will see it leads nowhere and ends up leaving him nothing in the end. It is the bitterness from such vanity that causes man to look up, and when he does, he will see the light that penetrated the world over 2,000 years ago, penetrating his soul with warmth, hope, and faith.

Prayer: Lord we always look everywhere but up for our answers. However, the world always leaves us hopeless because it does not hold the answers. Praise Your holy name that You are the answer. Amen.

May 18

"I know that, whatsoever God doeth, it shall be for ever: nothing can be put to it, nor any thing taken from it: and God doeth it, that men should fear before him" (Ecclesiastes 3:14). The Bible warns us the way to destruction is broad, but it blinds us to that which proves to be folly. Folly will be brought to judgment and will end in damnation. The worldly way of folly looks good to the flesh, sounds logical to the carnal mind, and offers us various possibilities, along with false promises of happiness, success, and satisfaction to our empty soul.

Solomon realized the world puts great value on the folly of mankind. In this world, the powers to be can, for the most part, influence attitudes through culture, worldview through indoctrination, moral shortcomings through conditioning, and religious extremes through radicalization.

In folly man avoids standing for anything unless he knows he is on the winning side because it might prove to be silly or foolish in the end to those of the world. After all, for the most part he is a sheep that can easily be persuaded by ideas of the world's greatness or honor, but not prone to see beyond to the eternal. He can be stirred up by the many causes of the world but will not stir himself up towards the things of God. He can be happily led down a merry path by a pied piper but will not choose the narrow way of salvation.

Solomon explored all of the different promises of the world to find that if vanity is all there is in the here and now, life is a joke. He came to the end of all his worldly pursuits and had to admit that it was a waste of time. He came to the end of accomplishments and found out that the accolades attached to them were very fleeting. He came to the end of himself and found out that the one thing that will come through the storms with grace was dignity that could not be tempted with foolishness, bribed with promises of worldly greatness, and lured away by what ends up being the abundance of insanity. He realized that the world's insanity could easily wrap a person up into the destructive web of lies the world is constantly spinning to throw the unsuspecting off from its dark, destructive ways.

The wisest man came to the same conclusions all of the saints eventually come to, that the wisest person is one who fears God. The safest place for souls is humility and the richest person is one of sincere faith, while the most honorable person is a servant, and the greatest position in God's kingdom is at His feet ever learning what it means to love and serve Him. It is from these low places before God that one comes out clothed in dignity that ends up bringing glory to their Creator.

Prayer: Lord everything that is promised is contrary to the world's neon signs of false promises and happiness. There is no comparison, but so many times we must taste the bitterness of vanity in this world before we become desperate to taste Your goodness in order to embrace that which will enrich our lives for eternity. Amen.

May 19

Flapping his wings as if taking a bath, all the little bird managed to get wet were his wee feet as he stood on the flat rock in the middle of the birdbath. I chuckled to myself as I watched several other little birds hop into the shallow birdbath, quickly bob their heads into the water, then happily splash and flutter as the feathered onlooker tried to maintain his spot on the rock.

Finally, another bird swooped in and sent him flying up into a tree branch. A few minutes passed, and as I glanced out the window again, I saw either him, or another little bird just like him, standing on the rock when suddenly a rush of wings flying past sent him off his little platform—but then the most amazing thing to behold was how quickly, instead of flying upwards, his little legs seemed to run over the surface of the water until he reached the edge of the birdbath.

Watching God's creatures, whether wild or domestic, can be the ultimate in entertainment, plus they can teach us much about ourselves. As for the antics of the little "tweetie" birds, they quickly brought to mind those among the flock of God who claim to be standing on the Rock, Jesus Christ, but who merely go through the motions of being cleansed by His blood, and who want to appear "clean" to others, but have no heartfelt desire to surrender all—body, soul and spirit to the Lord.

These may "get their feet wet" in basic doctrine and comply with some outward ordinances, such as baptism and communion, but in reality, their hearts are divided, their minds are disconnected, and their emotions are turbulent and fickle. Therefore, like the wee bird, they cannot bring themselves to a point of total consecration and willingness to become a living sacrifice, totally immersed into the life of Christ and the baptism of the Holy Spirit. They refuse to "get wet all over" (washing of regeneration) and believe such Scriptures as *Titus 3:5* which says, *"Not by works of righteousness which we have done, but according to his mercy he saved us, by the washing of regeneration, and renewing of the Holy Ghost; Which he shed on us abundantly through Jesus Christ."*

Such people will always be on the outside in one way or the other, whether it's by quietly hiding among the congregation, or by giving lip service without adoration for God in their heart; by doing good works to appear righteous, (even as by feats comparable to "walking on water" in order to impress the undiscerning), gain a position among the leadership, or even come out on top with a lucrative "ministry." As for good works, *Titus 3:8* states, *"This is a faithful saying, and these things I will that thou affirm constantly, that they which have believed in God might be careful to maintain good works. These things are good and profitable unto men."*

The question is, what makes people think that they can fool God? If His "eye is on the sparrow," can He not see you and me, and can He not know the thoughts and intents of our hearts? Truly, it's not the people who give lip service, or do good works to be seen of men while trying to "fake it until they make it" that shall enter into the Kingdom of Heaven, but those whose names are written in the Book of Life because they have not held back, or reserved the right to live for themselves on the broad road that leads to destruction. *"Jesus . . . said unto them, This is the work of God, that ye believe on him whom he hath sent" (John 6:29).* – J. Haley

Prayer: Lord, when we live as if You are not seeing what we are doing or care what we are doing, we are living as if You really don't exist. We might be saying in our heart we will do enough that if You really exist, we can hide behind Your love and remind You of Your grace to show You we have some knowledge or religious background. But such attempts will be rejected because such actions were a matter of unbelief and rebellion. Amen.

May 20

"And the rain descended, and the floods came, and the winds blew, and beat upon that house; and it fell: and great was the fall of it" (Matthew 7:27). Solomon stated nothing is new under the sun. The things we see may appall us, but they should not be surprising. Many great societies have come and gone, and what they tripped over, bringing utter defeat, always can be traced back to a very simple reality: the morality of the soul of the country.

When you study nations' military advancements, you marvel at how great their armies, along with their feats were, such as Alexander the Great. You consider their victories and stand in awe or their accomplishments. As you study their history, you march with them through the countryside as they trample over enemies and push aside civilizations that once stood in greatness before their rise as a nation. However, you also know the end of such great societies. Like the ones before them, they have become buried in the annals of time underneath the dust of the world to remind each of us that outside of historical records there are not even gravestones to mark many of their existence.

It is important to note that what brought these societies down into the dust of the earth had nothing to do with armies, with their advancements, with their knowledge or even with the type of footprint they left behind; rather, it had to do with their morality. As you study these great civilizations, their slide became obvious when they began to give credit for their greatness to idols and started to believe they were infallible; therefore, were above reproach, accountability, and defeat. They gave way to and justified the most base and abominable practices.

Morally, these empires simply imploded from within because it is faith towards the true God and moral uprightness that holds homes, societies and nations together. At the end of wickedness is judgment that awaits, and at the end of evil is destruction that will swallow it.

It is surprising that great nations that followed these empires never learned their lesson. The reason why is because they did not believe or adhere to the God of the universe. They believed their power and armies were sufficient enough. Their confidence was in their idols that made them think they were infallible. They had no consensus that they were established on nothing more than shifting sand that would not only slide and shift from underneath them but become liquefied. The ground would open and eventually they would fall into the deep pit of judgment they had been digging for their own grave.

Without God as the center there is nothing to keep a nation from decaying from within and imploding when challenged because there is no character that will enable it to stand. The prayer of the righteous is that their nation realizes that God must never be cast aside, tacked on, or made mere mention of; rather, that people recognize that without Him, they are on a downward slide as a society that will leave them tasting the bitterness of judgment.

Prayer: Lord, nations think they are too great to fall, culture thinks it is too clever to be pagan, and people in abundance do not have any need for You. When society falls to this level out of pride, that is when one knows they are on a slide of destruction. Lord, thank You for ever being ready to show Your mercy to the foolish. Amen.

May 21

"That the land spue not you out also, when ye defile it, as it spued out the nations that were before you" (Leviticus 18:28). "We live in a world, not just a nation that seems to be sliding down into a cesspool of immorality and debauchery to such an extent that some are even becoming concerned about it that normally would not give it a thought. What is even more disconcerting is that there are some churches that have speeded through "stop lights" of Biblical instruction, crashed past barriers of warning, and are sliding towards ultimate destruction with their support for such debauchery in order to fit in with the godless ideology and philosophies of this world.

I must admit, I am having a hard time watching what is happening, especially in relationship to our children. It is hard to believe parents would expose their impressionable children to such debauchery as to teach them tolerance or some type of perverted concept of love, but as a society we have been conditioned to tolerate such loathsome practices to condition the upcoming generations to embrace it as being normal and acceptable.

Meanwhile, what is happening around us? God blessings can't be found, extreme weather abounds, and we are losing our children to an assortment of vain, numb-minding, destructive activities while the earth seems to be opening here and there, as much falls into some abyss.

Is the land spewing us out because of such debauchery? My Bible indicates it is. Is there no end to the insanity of such debauchery? Yes, there is, and it is called judgment. One day all of this will be put under foot when the King of kings and Lord of lords comes back to set things right. However, we need to make sure we are not on the slide because it is a one-way trip downward. Rather, we must make sure we are standing on the Rock, clinging to His truth, and remaining true to what is right and honorable.

Prayer: Lord, we do not realize how much this world conditions us to accept that which You have rejected and judged. Help us to remain sharp about what is right and true when it comes to the matters of Your righteousness and Biblical when it comes to true morality. Help us to always choose the side of what is Scripturally established as being so before Your throne. Amen.

May 22

"The highway of the upright is to depart from evil; he that keepeth his way preserveth his soul" (Proverbs16:17). Proverbs is a book of wisdom. Wisdom does a couple of things for those who seek it. First, it shows knowledge being put into practice to see if what we perceive to be true will stand when tested. Many people possess knowledge but how many truly walk it out to see if it works in practical ways. Many times, head knowledge proves to be nothing more than theories and not practical truths.

The next thing wisdom reveals is that it is a choice that eventually turns into a pursuit. For Christians that means I choose to know the One who is all wisdom to make sound judgment calls that will prove to be beneficial to all involved. When I see how wisdom works, it becomes a type of pursuit that will not settle for anything except for that which truly comes from above.

The third thing about heavenly wisdom is that it is confirmed by experiences. Since wisdom involves putting knowledge into practice, it ends in experiencing the fruits of such wisdom. In fact, the narrow path opens up into a highway where one's perspective is enlarged. This enlargement happens in light of God as one sees the possibilities are right on. They begin to see the answers or solutions to a matter so that wise judgments can be made in light of what is Scriptural, right and true.

Jesus said the way is narrow for those who are truly seeking God, truth, and righteousness that leads to the abundant life because it entails the person and work of Jesus. The wisest man before Jesus said that righteousness presents a highway for those who will walk in it.

We know the narrow way leads to life to keep us in the disciplines of the Christian life, but the highway enables the upright to depart from evil, as it provides a way out, around, and sometimes over hindering obstacles. Every experience that ends in wisdom is a learning opportunity that enlarges one's possibilities when it comes to challenges before them, allowing them to consider what is before them so they can choose not just the right way, but a better way as they make the right call.

We know that the Lord directs the steps of the righteous and it is for this reason, He is the one who preserves our soul, but we need to keep in mind that it is vital we keep in the right way so that our feet can always be aligned to the ways of wisdom and righteousness.

Prayer: Lord, thank You that in You is all wisdom and in Your ways are all righteousness. Remind me to ask for Your wisdom as I seek Your ways of righteousness and know that in the end I will be led to the highway that allows me not to just choose what is alright in order to simply get by, or even what is best to see good results, but what is better so that You will be glorified in the end. Amen.

May 23

"Then spake Elisha unto the woman, whose son he had restored to life, saying Arise and go thou and thine household, and sojourn wheresoever thou canst sojourn: for the LORD hath called for a famine; and it shall also come upon the land for seven years" (2 Kings 8:1). One of the events I appreciate surrounds the Shunammite woman whose son Elisha raised from the dead.

Elisha had a special relationship with this woman. It is due to this relationship that this woman was warned by the prophet to rise up and take her household elsewhere because there would be a famine in the land. How many of us in that woman's position would carry out such a feat? Clearly, she had to be a woman of great faith, trusting both the call upon Elisha's life and that the prophetic words he spoke truly came from God. Is there anyone in your life you could trust in such a fashion? For me there is only one sure man and prophet that I would believe and that is the Lord Jesus Christ. Since I trust who He is, I can trust His Word as well.

We do not see this woman debating whether she should believe, she simply obeyed and did as the prophet instructed. Oh, if we had such a trusting relationship with the Lord and would immediately obey in the same way, what blessings we might discover along the way. But how many of us immediately begin to debate the instructions found in God's Word with our own logic and reasoning to see if we can make heads or tails out of it? As a result, how many of us have missed the opportunities to obey and in doing so experience the blessings and protection upon our lives?

After seven years, out of faith the woman came back to the land. How many would expect to find their land unoccupied, taken care of, or available? So many people think the circumstances of life are a matter of chance and not of design. However, this woman's experience proves them wrong. God prepared the king to restore her land back to her after asking Elisha's servant Gehazi to share the stories of Elisha's miraculous feats, which included the raising of this woman's son. Just as the woman came in to ask for her land back from the king, Gehazi identified her as the mother of the boy that Elisha brought back to life. The king immediately commanded that her land be restored back to her.

This brings us back to an important principle. If you believe God, you will obey Him and if you obey Him, you will be brought to places of restoration in your life. What are you willing to leave behind in obedience? What are you willing to lose because you really trust Him, while walking in confidence towards what has been established as being so in your relationship with the Lord? Remember if you have the Lord, you already have gained it all and what He has preserve for you can never be lost in or to this world.

Prayer: Lord, we are often unwilling to lose what we have to discover what we can have in You. Forgive us for our foolish unbelief and help us realize that You are our real prize and You alone preserve what You have promised. Amen.

May 24

"He that dwelleth in the secret place of the most High shall abide under the shadow of the Almighty" (Psalm 91:1). As many know, my friend and co-laborer in the Gospel, Jeannette is a professional artist. Through the years she has sometimes shown me the importance of shadows in her paintings. To understand shadows, you must understand how light works and what direction it is coming from.

The truth is, until Jeannette pointed it out to me, I never thought much about shadows. Granted, if I was too hot, I looked for some shade, but I never thought about how that shade was provided by a shadow that was cast by some object, whether it be a tree, a big rock, or even a structure.

As I read this Scripture, I was once again reminded of the significance of shadows. The one truth that I was reminded of in this Scripture is not the shadow itself; rather, what is actually casting the shadow. A big rock does not cast a shadow like a tree does. The tree not only casts a shadow, but it also shades one from intense heat. In some cases, shadows allow one to blend in and almost become unseen, but what is the purpose for blending in? Does it have to do with hiding from the light, shrouding certain activities, bringing some type of dimension to one's perspective, or seeking a type of shelter?

For the believer, the reason we seek the shadow God cast with His light is to abide under it, but that can only happen after we discover the secret place of communion, fellowship, and worship with Him. We must first learn to dwell in that secret place before we can truly abide or continue to rest under His shadow.

Scripture reminds us that Jesus is the light of the world, and the object that has cast a great shadow over the land is His cross where

He redeemed us from the darkness of this present age so we can abide in the promises of His Word, while standing firmly upon the rock of His salvation. God's light is intense, but purifying to the soul, revealing to the spirit, and unbearable on the flesh. It will light the way in which the soul must walk and inspire the thirsty spirit to seek the water that refreshes but will judge and eventually consume what are the carnal ways of the flesh.

It is clear that to survive this world, we must be abiding under the right shadow, but first we must locate that shade which is the Lord, learn to walk in His Spirit to ensure we remain in it, and always stay within the shadow of His cross of redemption to know the true safety of abiding under it.

Prayer: Lord, thank You for Your light that cast the right shadows in my life where I can find rest and protection. Praise You for giving me that dwelling place where I can hide in the shadows of the glory yet to come. Amen.

May 25

At first the emerald green leaves began to surface in the planter box next to the colorful pink, crimson, and orange Impatiens and the bright yellow pansy. I've learned (and am still learning) that those small, fragile annuals that you carefully plant, care for and pray over in the spring can grow to some sizeable plants. In other words, you need to give them space to expand.

However, those perfect green volunteer leaves have now turned into dazzling white petunias with a plan of their own. Regardless of the competition for space in the over-crowded planter, it is a truly beautiful medley of life and color that I never planned, just like all the bright sunflowers that have popped up unexpectedly this year. Then there are the "Johnny Jump Up's" that did just that—they somehow "jumped up" into a tall planter full of marigolds, while way back in the vegetable garden petunias decided to show up. It's surprising and delightful, and in our minds, we are assured that the Lord put His own ideas and personal touches into it. After all, only God can create these marvels of nature, putting life into the seeds, some so small you can barely see them, that come forth and develop into complex plants.

When the pretty volunteers, however, begin to create an overcrowding situation, it makes you wish you could somehow enlarge the borders of the container they're in. Now, here's the analogy, or spiritual lesson, for us—what are we doing to "enlarge our borders?"

Of course, I'm talking about our spiritual borders, and the borders of our minds. It's so easy to get "root bound" or stuck in a rut, and never spiritually expand and grow beyond the mental channels and walls we've made for ourselves. Perhaps the cause is fear that keeps us bound up; or complacency and mental laziness. Maybe it's disinterest or lack of desire to learn and grow. The truth is, whatever the excuse is for not being willing to enlarge these borders in order to grow in Christ, it needs to be recognized for what it is, confessed to God, and overcome.

A. W. Tozer said, "The stiff and wooden quality about our religious lives is a result of our lack of holy desire. Complacency is a deadly foe of all spiritual growth. Acute desire must be present or there will be no manifestation of Christ to His people."

Paul wrote in *Ephesians 3:17-19, "That Christ may dwell in your hearts by faith; that you, being rooted and grounded in love, May be able to comprehend with all saints what is the breadth, and length, and depth, and height; And to know the love of Christ, which passes knowledge, that you might be filled with all the fulness of God."*

Therefore, let us "enlarge our borders" and with the Apostle Paul, *"press toward the mark for the prize of the high calling of God in Christ Jesus" (Philippians 3:14).* Time is short. – J. Haley

Prayer: Lord, very few of us realize how enslaved we are to small worlds, small thinking, and small advancements. You are always calling us from that which is limiting to that which will enlarge our perspective to see beyond this world. Thank You for always calling us higher. Amen.

May 26

"Flee also youthful lusts: but follow righteousness, faith charity, peace, with them that call on the Lord out of a pure heart" (2 Timothy 2:22). Proverbs 22:15 tells us that foolishness is bound in the heart of a child. That foolishness is selfishness that desires to be served, spared of any inconvenience, testing or tribulation, and ultimately worshipped. It lies at the core of our disposition due to the fact we are born into a fallen state thanks to the sin of our first parents brought on by deception and rebellion.

In our infant state we are vulnerable so all our needs must be met. In our childhood we are somewhat beginning to have a mind of our own but not wisdom to know how to handle what we feel or see. As teenagers, we perceive we have enough knowledge, plus an outcrop of hormones, along with arrogance, and strength to think we have the world by the tail if we just learn to play our cards right. We do not realize that these ingredients are nothing more than youthful lusts. In the upswing of our life, after teenage years, we think we have the world figured out, and by the time we have reached thirty, we may have been slightly humbled by life or disillusioned, embittered, or enraged by it.

We fail to realize the foolishness of selfishness plays a major role in each step of our life. Whether it is the foolishness that keeps us ignorant in our immaturity, self-sufficient in our strength, unteachable in our thinking, slothful in our ways, fearful of any change and challenge, skeptical towards true wisdom, angry or mocking at what appears to be a joke called "life," or hopeless in it all, it will all come back to the foolishness that continues to abound.

It is for this reason that it is vital from the beginning that a child is trained with good examples, challenged when it comes to wrong attitudes, taught to be respectful to others, and to be responsible for what has been entrusted to them. These disciplines are an important gauge that will guide their life and cause them to be wise enough to flee youthful lust and follow in the ways of true righteousness. Following the right path will help them avoid a past of foolish decisions, unwise choices, and irreversible consequences. Such measures will keep people from knowing the bitterness of regret that comes from wasting their strength, energy, and ability on vain, foolish things and activities that leave them empty and miserable.

Prayer: Lord, we are not born with wisdom. Wisdom is something gained through wisely learning from past experiences and walking in the ways of righteousness. Wisdom brings the necessary contrast between what works and what is a theory or formula on paper or in books that sounds good but has never been tested to see the end results. Lord, You are not a figment of the imagination, Your principles are not a theory, and Your ways are not an experiment yet to be proven. Lord, everything about You is Amen, so be it, for it is so. Praise Your Holy Name. Amen.

May 27

"Foolishness is bound in the heart of a child; but the rod of correction shall drive it far from him" (Proverbs 22:1). In my last post on foolishness, I referred to *Proverbs 22:1*. This Scripture makes it clear that there is only one way to address foolishness: DISCIPLINE. Without some form of discipline, man will remain foolish in every arena of his life.

Let's face it, in our fallen state our attitude is touchy, our emotions are undisciplined, our lusts can prove to be unmanageable, our thoughts erratic, our imaginations unrealistic and perverted, and our ways incorrigible. We try to comply to get along in this life, reform to somehow fit in, perform to throw people off from recognizing our insecurities, or conform so we can do what we want to in the end, but none of it transforms the mind, changes the inward disposition, or produces a right attitude. It takes discipline at all three levels: bodily, emotionally, and spiritually.

Children must have fair discipline to learn respectable boundaries to ensure proper conduct, while young people must learn to channel and discipline their lusts and strength to be taught responsibility through fair instructions, examples, and tasks to develop right attitudes. This entails learning how to work to gain self-respect for what they do.

Young men and women must be challenged as to their ways which requires them to understand there are recompenses or consequences for their decisions so that they can make sound judgment calls along the way. Older individuals must examine and guard their habits and thinking patterns to ensure integrity is being established in how they execute the different aspects of their lives before others.

When it comes to the Christian it requires the life of a disciple, who develops a healthy fear of the Lord to deal with foolishness at different levels. Our life in Christ involves changing our mind and direction through repentance, confessing our change of service from self and the world to Jesus by truly changing lordship and by faith, following Him in the narrow paths of righteousness through His Word. We must learn to line up to His perfect ways, be in step with His incredible timing, and to ensure that we are in the center of His will.

Keep in mind, the concept of "disciple" comes from the word "discipline." The life of a disciple is a disciplined, consecrated life that is marked by the excellent ways of the Holy Spirit that leads one into the four major areas of discipline, self-denial, obedience to His Word, sacrifice to gain what is worthy, and godliness in conduct.

Prayer: Lord, You have called us to a life of discipline that comes through discipleship, obedience to the ways of righteousness, sacrifice of self in light of all service to You, and to conduct ourselves according to godliness. Thank You for giving me the Holy Spirit who enables me to walk Your incredible life out in everyday living. Amen.

May 28

"The labour of the foolish wearieth every one of them, because he knoweth not how to go to the city" (Ecclesiastes 10:15). We are given insight in this Scripture in *Ecclesiastes* as to why foolishness

becomes such a burdensome matter to the soul because the labors of those who are being foolish will not only eventually weary them but everyone around them.

The problem with foolishness is that it hides its immaturity behind a veneer of "innocence," to justify irresponsibility. It often bullies its way through matters as it stands on a pinnacle of arrogance that will fall into a pit of depression. It will ultimately end in some corner cowering in self-pity as a victim, raging at circumstances or taking on the attitude of indifference to avoid getting caught up with the often-devastating results of it. The result always ends in emptiness of soul because there is nothing constructive that can be found in foolishness except a series of failures in life, and misery that finds itself standing alone in its small insipid world.

Since foolishness will not to be instructed at its height, or to take heed to warnings in its self-sufficiency, while refusing to leave its comfort zones, it ends up having no foresight to see beyond the dead ends. It is void of any sense that past this world is eternity, and in its state, it will often rush headlong towards its own ruin.

We all can be foolish at different times, but we must avoid ending up being a fool who fails to see our pathetic state. Without Jesus, we will find we are void of real wisdom to have any foresight as to where such foolish ways are leading us, and without His Spirit, we will not be teachable, discerning, and realistic about our plight to make any real wise decisions. We will we like a rogue wave on the ocean of life that is driven by the winds of time towards destruction, away from the life God has for us.

Prayer: Lord, I can't count the ways I have been foolish in my selfishness, but I am so thankful at the most important time in my life, You stood in the way to keep me from being driven out into the waters of judgment, by the winds of foolishness that ends in the waves of torment, despair, and hopelessness. Amen.

May 29

By humility and the fear of the LORD are riches, and honour, and life" (Proverbs 22:4). What kind of riches are your pursuing right now? It all comes down to what you desire to possess the most in your life. The desire to possess something must be great because to possess it will cost you something you might not want to give up, let go of, or lose along the way.

Most Christians will say, "I want all that God has for me." They say it with such sincerity that you know that is their desire, but do they have the maturity to recognize it will cost them things from their present life they may greatly value?

What premise must we get to or start from to truly possess heavenly riches? It all begins with **HUMILITY**. We must be brought to a state of humility before we can even begin to agree with God about what is important. This state is important because without humility our resolve to have life on our terms will never give way to the Lord's plan for us. With our stiff-necked attitude insisting on doing it our way, it will never bend in submission before Him, our knees will never bow before Him in awe, our arms lifted up in great need to receive from Him, and our tongues will never be able to sincerely praise and worship Him in **HONOR** of who He is and what He has done for us.

This state of humility operates within heavenly wisdom that comes from properly fearing the Lord. The **FEAR OF THE LORD** is the beginning of wisdom and maintains a healthy attitude towards God and life. Heavenly wisdom ensures discretion, sound judgments, and a heavenly perspective producing worship that comes by way of the Spirit in the true fashion of what is true, pure, and right.

And what has He done for us? He has given us **LIFE**. This life can experience the blessings from above, walk in confidence towards Him by faith, soar on the wings of His Spirit in the air currents of expectancy with great hope. This is accomplished because we know without a doubt all He has said and promised is "Amen, so be it on earth, for it is so in heaven."

However, we must make sure the life we are living is the life of Jesus that we have received by faith because of our great need to be delivered from the claims of the present world on our soul due to the wages of death. Death plagues mankind because sin abounds in those who have not been redeemed by the blood of the Lamb. It is because of the great work of redemption, we have been brought under the dispensation of grace by One who is the essence of the perpetual flowing work of grace in our life, the Lord Jesus Christ.

Prayer: Lord, as our Creator You alone give us life, as our Maker, You alone keep us in life, and as our Shepherd, You alone lead us into not only the abundant life, but everlasting life. Thank You for the life You have secured for me in this challenging age in which I live. Amen.

May 30

"There is a way which seemeth right unto a man, but the end thereof are the ways of death" (Proverbs 14:12). There are three ways in which a man may choose to walk in.

There is the wrong way, which is contrary to the ways of God, and then there is the ways of God which are perfect and will lead one in the path of righteousness. Finally, we come to the third way which is MY way, or in your case, YOUR way, and let me assure you that all our ways are different. I say this because the greatest arguments are not about what needs to be done, but the best, most reasonable, intellectual WAY to do it, and in the past in my mind, my way was always the best way.

The Bible is clear that our ways are clean in our own eyes and even though they seem right to us, they will often lead to ruin or destruction and death (*Proverbs 16:2, 25*). It was clear when it came to the children of Israel, they assumed that after their refusal to enter the Promised Land due to unbelief towards the Lord in *Numbers 14:37-45* it could be reversed.

It is understandable that in the logic of the children of Israel that it was a good time to change their position by deciding to be obedient by suddenly changing course and rising up to possess the land. In their minds, this repentance was necessary to avoid the consequences of a whole generation dying in the wilderness. This assumption led them to presume that God would naturally agree with their way of thinking, being, and doing, but many died trying and the rest had to flee in defeat.

Prayer: Lord, I know it is easy to take Your love for granted, but the truth is Your love was displayed on the cross, but Your judgment will be brought forth at the end of our lives. Obedience to Your Word symbolizes a small door of opportunity and we must rise up and immediately walk through it by faith. Sadly, once that door closes, it means the wilderness and judgment. Lord, You have always been longsuffering towards Your people but we need to remember faith comes before obedience to Your Word, and not after the consequences are pronounced. Lord, we so often end up with the cart before the horse. Amen.

May 31

"Wherefore I was grieved with that generation, and said, They do always err in their heart; and that have not known my ways." (Hebrews 3:10). Now you might ask, "What is so wrong with my way?"

Perhaps your way is not all that wrong, but unless it lines up to God's ways which are higher, it is missing the mark of being right. Remember, we have all sinned and fallen short of the glory of God, which means because of sin we have missed, or are missing, the mark of our high calling, potential, and purpose (*Isaiah 55:8-9; Romans 3:23*).

The only way to make sure we fulfill those three areas mentioned in the above paragraph, we must come back into line with our Creator based on His Word, according to His design for our life as the great

Potter. We must do this in light of His call on our life as our Lord, which points to Him as our Owner, Overseer, and Redeemer (*Romans 9:20-21; 1 Corinthians 6:20; 7:23*).

The problem with our way always falling short is because we fall short of simply doing it right beginning with what seems like small, insignificant things. Whether it is laziness, or ineptness due to not knowing how to do something (but unwilling to learn or admit it), or perhaps it is due to the habit of procrastination because we lack initiative or various other character shortfalls, we justify dropping the ball in some way from seeing a matter through in a manner that shows we have done it to the best of our abilities. We take short-cuts that may lack integrity, we end up presenting shoddy results and a nominal product at best. In the end, our character receives a rightful blackeye as we cross our fingers that our ways and reputation do not catch up with us.

As believers everything we do must be as unto the Lord (*Colossians 3:23*). Every attitude, practice, mode of operation, and our conduct must identify us to our heavenly vocation (*Ephesians 4:1-3*). We must never bring a reproach to our Lord Jesus because we don't have the necessary character and genuine faith to be true to our Lord, our word, our claims, and our godly responsibilities.

Prayer: Lord, You are so long-suffering with us. We fail to understand that when we repented, we turned from our way to face You. When we were born again, we were given a new spirit to walk in Your way as a new creation, and when we follow You into our new, consecrated life, it meant we were walking further and further away from our old way. Forgive us for wanting to run back to the old way in order to partake of the lusts and ways of this world. Amen.

June

June 1

"The way of man is froward and strange: but as for the pure, his work is right" (Proverbs 21:8). We are told in the last post that the children of Israel erred in their hearts towards the Lord because they did not know His ways.

God does not step outside of His holy character, His righteous ways, His eternal plan, and His perfect will to take care of matters. Because He never changes and there is no deviation in what He does and no ill-will in the reason for it, we can know and trust His ways. However, we must know His character, believe who He is and trust His ways are right and true to walk in them by faith. We must be assured that His glorious plan for us is redemption of our souls and His will is that we all be saved (*Jeremiah 29:11; Micah 3:6; Luke 9:56; 2 Corinthians 5:7; James 1:17*).

This brings us back to our way. Without knowing it our way is plagued with flaws that can be traced back to iniquity. Iniquity is that moral bent in our character that deviates from the ways of God. This bent will go the way of the flesh, the world, and/or the devil. Our way may seem right, but when we must manipulate others to get it, we become controlling without regarding the will and needs of others. This manipulation makes it a form of witchcraft that will prove to be divisive in the end.

When we insist on our way, we are in a wrong spirit, and when we demand it, we are presuming we have all the facts when in truth we know in part as *1 Corinthians 13:9* states. Clearly, we are limited in not only what we know, but what we can do about it.

When we can't imagine our way being wrong, we are operating according to our self-sufficiency. Such self-reliance is based on pride, which naturally assumes that God will surely approve of us because of our many "good" deeds we have done. Conclusions of this nature will reveal that we have failed to come into agreement with God, knowing that even our best outside of His inspiration, ordination, and anointing upon it is as filthy rags to Him and will be considered reprobate or useless (*Isaiah 64:6-8; Titus 1:15-16*).

If we want to make sure our way is true, our understanding correct, and our conclusions right, we must always come back into line with God's Word about a matter. If we do come into that place of agreement with Him, we will take on His attitude in greater measure. We will hate evil, love righteousness, insist on integrity in what we do, purity in what we think, and godly conduct in all our business affairs.

Prayer: Lord, we can think we are okay until You reveal our attitude about the issues of life. It is there we will come face to face with whether we are developing Your mind about matters that are close to Your heart. Lord, reveal any moral deviation in my way, thinking and conduct. Amen.

June 2

What was it? A UFO? A UAP? A supernatural mystery? After almost forty years of wondering and waiting for the answer to that question, the answer finally surfaced just a couple of days ago!

Even though I've read an eye-witness account of an identical experience, no explanation for it was offered. My encounter with the strange event took place one very dark night out on the Camas Prairie between Grangeville and Cottonwood, Idaho. It was summer, and two friends were leading a horse from one farm to another on a country road while I followed at a crawl in the car so I could bring one of the women back home.

This area is fairly remote, and is located close to the largest, continuous wilderness in the lower 48 states. (In other words, it's the perfect location for nefarious, governmental secret agendas.) Suddenly, a completely soundless, barely discernable cloudy light began to form about 40 feet above and in front of us. We all watched in amazement as a bright beam of light shot out of the formless, gauzy "whatever it was," and begin to shine around on the ground as if some "thing" we couldn't hear or see was searching for something. Then it withdrew its "spotlight" and all that we could see was the star-filled sky.

I remember watching the horse in the light of my headlights to see if she spooked, or nervously sensed anything, but she never so much as even flicked an ear. It's been my experience with animals, and dogs in particular, that they keenly sense the presence of evil, and by that, I mean wrong spirits or demons.

As it was, I was surprised when the woman whose farmhouse we were approaching calmly stated that "they" often "flew" over her house which was situated close to the deep Salmon River canyon. As for the "answer" it's called a hologram. (Check out "Project Bluebeam" and DARPA.)

Therefore, if you suddenly see terrifying or strange things in the sky, or what appears to be "Jesus," do not be afraid or deceived. I wrote this post for a couple of reasons, one being to share my joy in having finally received an answer to what I was a witness to, and to praise the Lord for His faithfulness to answer questions concerning His Word and ways if we ask Him.

The other purpose is to remind you of the days we live in and the great deceptions that have been, are, and will be taking place. Jesus told us, *"...if any man shall say unto you, Lo, here is Christ, or there; believe it not. For there shall arise false Christs, and false prophets, and shall show great signs and wonders; insomuch that, if it were possible, they shall deceive the very elect" (Matthew 24:23, 24)*. I hope you will read the entire chapter of *Matthew 24*, circling, or underlining, the word "Then".

God bless all who faithfully reflect the true Light of the world that "*shines in darkness*" (*John 1:1-5*). – J. Haley

Prayer: Lord, You always want Your people to be prepared, but if they fail to desire Your truth, seek Your face, and be willing to tarry until You show them, they will remain vulnerable and unprepared. Praise Your holy Name for Your faithfulness. Amen.

June 3

"And there went out fire from the LORD, and devoured them, and they died before the LORD" (Leviticus 10:2). This incident surrounds the High Priest, Aaron's two sons Nadab and Abihu. They offered strange fire before the Lord at the Altar of Incense that He had specifically commanded them not to do and they died for it. There are many such incidents in Scriptures where man showed a casualness towards the matters of God and were immediately judged.

When I consider the consequences for doing it my way, I remember the example of these two men. We talk about a wrong way of doing something, and these men definitely ignored what was set forth as ordained by God and showed utter contempt and disregard towards what He had set forth as to what was acceptable to Him.

Now, you may ask, what does this example have to do with you? God had very strict rules about everything that was dedicated to Him, including sacrifices. As Christians, we belong to Him and not ourselves, for we are redeemed by the blood of the Lamb. We are to offer our bodies as living sacrifices according to Paul in *Romans 12:1*.

We also have already been told as believers that we are to be His holy temples where His Spirit resides and we are to offer our bodies as an ongoing sacrifice to do as He will with them. However, if we are going to be an acceptable sacrifice that God can accept, our lives must be without spot or wrinkle. We are to avoid both physical and spiritual fornication, which is unholy agreements to ensure we can offer spiritual sacrifices which include praises to our God that would come out of purity that would truly honor Him (*1 Corinthians 3:16-17; 6:17-20; 1 Peter 2:5*).

As part of the Lord's priesthood, temple, sacrifice, and a worshipper, we need to come out and be separate from a world that makes what has been ordained sacred by God as common, foolish and unnecessary. It does not matter what the world thinks because in the end we will all stand before the Lord and give an account of our life to the just Judge of the Universe.

Prayer: Lord, You have given us many examples of the benefits of walking in Your way in light of the consequences of foolishly walking in our own way. However, many choose to walk in their own way due to unbelief, rebellion, and fierce independence. Forgive us for our arrogance. Amen.

June 4

"Then Peter said unto her, How is it that ye have agreed together to tempt the Spirit of the Lord? behold the feet of them which have buried they husband are at the door, and shall carry thee out" Acts 5:9)." As believers, we would like to think that God does not show forth such judgments as He did in the Old Testament. Consider Ananias and Sapphira in *Acts 5*. They lied about a matter that they had withheld a certain amount that they dedicated to the Lord, tempting the Holy Spirit, and immediately died for it.

Consider what Peter said to Simon the sorcerer who bewitched the people in *Acts 8* and wanted to buy the power that came from the Holy Spirit, *"But Peter said unto him, thy money perish with thee, because thou hast thought that the gift of God may be purchased with money" (Acts 8:20).*

All things that come from God including His great gift of eternal life can't be earned but has been given from above and is a matter of God's grace. Our responsibility towards any gift of God is to receive it by faith, and become a good steward with it that will not profane it by treating it as being common. We must not abuse it for our own selfish purposes, exploit it for our own personal gain, or neglect it because it does not serve our fleshly purposes.

Sadly, whether it is our bodies or our lives we have a tendency to treat the matters of our present life in a casual manner. Yes, some of the hardest work we do when it comes to our lives before the Lord is to justify doing it our way in order to dictate the terms of our life while we profane our temples, give way to unholy agreements, and compromise with the devil to taste of the temporary things of this world. In the end, we must consider what will be the greatest judgment.

Will it be His chastisement because we are His children so we can be partakers of His holiness, for without it we can't see the Lord as *Hebrews 12:10* reminds us? For me I hope so, but could there be immediate judgment in some way which, when and if it happens, is rarely mentioned, or even worse, will He simply turn us over to our desires as He did those in *Romans 1:24* to know the emptiness, as well as the despair of it as we face the reality that we will give an account for everything we do in our bodies.

The other aspect I struggle with is this: it is one thing to innocently fall into sin and another to walk into it after being warned, knowing full well it is wrong. How can we ask for forgiveness for something we did, when we knew it was wrong in the first place, but we wanted our way? Do we not realize when we insist on our way, we are showing utter contempt for God's way? How will He respond, what will He do, and what kind of reproach and shame will we bring on Him and our testimony in the end?

Prayer: Lord, we test Your love, try Your long-suffering, and become close to provoking You as we inch our way close to the line of rebellion in order to do it our way. We are hoping that the red light of Your commands and instructions will suddenly turn green to give us the go ahead, but the truth is the light doesn't change; rather, the gates guarding the crosswalks and dangerous railroad crossings in our life will go up to allow us to disregard all the restraints of wisdom and do as we please. We end up risking our life, our limb, and our soul. Forgive us for being rebellious against Your goodness and will. Amen.

June 5

"The thought of foolishness is sin; and the scorner is an abomination to me" (Proverbs 24:9). Today the idea of foolishness is watered-down. The presentations of it are avoided because of the attitude of "boys will be boys" and "girls will be silly." The consensus due to this attitude is that to highlight immaturity at this point is not necessary or that it is premature because it is a matter of someone simply sowing a few wild-oats here and there. I could go on but we always seem to have an excuse for people being foolish no matter how old they might be.

It is hard to avoid foolishness because we are in a state that operates according to foolishness and in a world that knows nothing but what is foolish. If that is not bad enough, we live in an environment where foolishness is anything but sin. It can be fun, a type of prank, silly fantasies, and godless causes with some fake cherry stuck on the top to give the impression that it is honorable. However, it does not matter how we see something; rather, it is how God sees it and anything that is inspired by foolish thoughts and ways is sin to God.

Keep in mind foolishness will use its strength to try to bluff its way through a matter instead of developing the integrity to be honest about it. It is too impatient to learn and too prideful to admit ineptness.

At the core of its selfishness is often a slothfulness that unless it feels a certain way, it will justify why it constantly "drops the ball," while failing to see anything through to the end. If it becomes confused, it will give way to fear and excuses, creating a cycle that ends in failure, often producing cynicism towards life that ends in one becoming a scorner.

I have encountered a lot of scorners in my journey. They may scorn your commitment to Christ, your desire to do right, your unwillingness to compromise, and your determination to avoid veering off course. The reason is because you are raising a standard that makes them uncomfortable, exposes their own level of fickle commitment, and greatly offends them because it shakes their pride, often causing anger or rage in them.

As believers we are told not to sit among the scorners. Without knowing it we can take on the same attitude towards matters they manifest. We are instructed to have the mind of Christ and not the critical spirit of a scorner.

Prayer: Lord, it is easy to become a scorner, but we are called above such a wretched state to see that which is eternal. The heights of Your glory reveals heavenly riches that will be discovered by the saint for ages to come. Amen.

June 6

"Correction is grievous unto him that forsaketh the way: and he that hateth reproof shall die" (Proverbs 15:10). What does it take to confront this ailment of foolishness in our life? We can see from this Scripture that foolishness in its rebellion and wickedness will not repent and that it hates reproof.

As believers we must test our own attitude to make sure we are not standing on the outside of the fringes of becoming a fool. To avoid being foolish, it foremost takes **truth**. One major discipline for any of us is to line up to what is truth, and right, regardless of how we feel about a matter. In fact, we must love or prefer the truth over all else, or we will end up sliding into judgmentalism, skepticism and scoffing towards what fails to line up to our way of thinking. There is nothing honorable when it comes to what God considers to be sin or iniquity. The problem with holding onto our right to always be right when we are wrong is the essence of foolishness.

The advice is simple and that is, **be sensible,** but that simple suggestion becomes debatable because people do not gauge foolish acts in the same way. Foolishness often chooses the hard way to try to prove it was right in its idiocy. It will hit its head against what is reasonable, rage against what is right, and kick up the dust to cause a ruse so others can't see how useless its ways are. Foolishness at its height will be anything but sensible.

Be teachable. Foolishness is a rebellious, unyielding infidel. It wants things on its terms and will not give way to something that does not support it regardless of how wrong it may be. It refuses to hear wisdom about a matter, and if it hears, it is for the sole purpose of coming out on top of something. Wisdom is discreet enough to recognize when wrong, humble enough to owe up in true repentance, astute enough to walk in what is right, and resolved enough that the last thing it wants to do is give way to foolishness.

It's a choice. We either choose wisdom from above or eventually we will slide into the foolish ways of the flesh, the folly of the world, or the traps set by Satan. The real fools are the one who are silently declaring there is no God in their heart.

We must therefore choose the ways of God to ensure we do not fall into the traps of foolishness. It is God's leading of the Spirit by faith, walking in the ways of righteousness by obeying the Word of God, and never settling for anything but truth that keeps us from being foolish and ending up being a fool in this world and before heaven.

Prayer: Lord, we start out on the road of utter foolishness, but when we encounter You, we come face to face with Wisdom Personified so it ceases to be a matter of what we think, but it becomes about the One we are following. You are our Wisdom; therefore, You are ever leading us in the wise ways of righteousness. Amen.

June 7

While the color red may signal for bulls to charge, perhaps the color red attracts hungry deer in the night. At least that's what happened to the pot with a red petunia in it. Thankfully, the deer did a perfect trim on it. Besides, it just so happens that this particular petunia, with its gangly and untidy growth pattern, seemed to insist on either being a wild thing, or was begging for a good "haircut."

Now, a short time later, that petunia has nicely made a comeback, and is neatly and proudly showing off beautiful red flowers. It's easy to guess what this little event reminded me of, and that is how sometimes, when you think you're "brightly blooming for God" and you're just "oh so lovely," smart, self-sufficient, and smugly "have it all together" is when the LORD allows you to experience a humble pruning.

This can take place deep within your innermost being faster than the deer nibbled off the top of the petunia plant. The Holy Spirit knows perfectly how to bring conviction to a proud heart, while the chastening of the Father is a reminder of His love for us. After all, without proper pruning plant life becomes an undisciplined jungle of wild, untamable, and unproductive vegetation; and the same is true for God's people if they resist the correction God brings into their lives through His Word and by His Spirit.

Remember, for the Christian, the color red represents the blood that our Lord and Savior, Jesus Christ, shed for us on the Cross for our sins. *"How much more shall the blood of Christ, who through the eternal Spirit offered himself without spot to God, purge your conscience from dead works to serve the living God? (Hebrews 9:14). "In whom we have redemption through his blood, even the forgiveness of sins" (Colossians 1:14).*

Is your conscious purged? – J. Haley

Prayer: Lord, purging can be painful but liberating for the soul. Pruning can leave us vulnerable but can ensure growth to our life in Christ. I would rather have the purging and the pruning to avoid the cutting and casting away that would leave me separated from You and lying in the lifeless dust of nothing while waiting for judgment. Amen.

June 8

"But he turned, and rebuked them, and said, Ye know not what manner of spirit ye are of" (Luke 9:55). This is the incident where

John and James wanted to call fire out of heaven against the Samaritans of a particular village. They had taken offense against them because they did not come out and acknowledge Jesus in the way that they perceived they should. Their offense seemed honorable enough, yet Jesus rebuked them, and they ended up with the name "sons of thunder" for their misdirected zeal.

There are many voices of offense today sounding all around us. People are offended towards this individual, that political party, or this group of people. Each offense is like stirring up an angry wave on the ocean. As it travels towards the shoreline it becomes increasingly larger because the type of momentum behind such offense is a growing vitriol that has one destination, and that is to crash on the shoreline.

What you hear are voices of anger and hate and what follows is a string of justifications for having such an attitude. You hear hissing of contempt, spewing out of accusations and name calling, and a string of merciless opinions, but the question is what would the Lord say about such an attitude? Granted, our words may sound right in our ears, it may seem like we are taking a noble stand, and what we are standing on is righteous indignation towards a matter that we assume God would certainly judge as being so in the end. But what if Jesus turned to you and stated, *"You know not what manner of spirit you are in right now?"*

Attitude does not point to being right or having righteous convictions; rather, it points to the spirit in which a person is operating. God weighs the spirit and not whether one is right or wrong. If one is in a wrong spirit, they are not open to being reasoned with and any opposition will cause offense. At such times truth is not important to these individuals; rather, it is the need to be right because to be wrong is unacceptable to their way of thinking.

Prayer: Lord, our arrogance is so great, it becomes clear why even the righteous are scarcely saved. We don't get it because we refuse to agree with You about all matters pertaining to life and godliness. Amen.

June 9

"Commit thy works unto the LORD, and thy thoughts shall be established" (Proverbs 16:3). In the last post we were considering the misdirected zeal of James and his brother John. They both were sure of their conclusions about the Samaritan's response towards Jesus. We all have our opinions and conclusions, but are they truth and do they maintain the spirit of what is important to God? Or, are they a summation of prejudices that are a product of the world we live in?

We all have our reasons for our attitude, but are they based on what we have learned to hold lightly because we see in part, or are they founded on shifting sand because they are merely what we think we see and presume we know? Sadly, we forget that the unseen realm of the spiritual world is what affects us the most, and the spirit of the world is working disobedience in the rebellious towards God that will lack the fruit of the Spirit (*Proverbs 16:2; Ephesians 2:2; Galatians 5:22-23*).

I personally don't trust anything I hear, and very little of what I see. I must soberly consider if what I see and hear are based on the propaganda of the world or on the Word of God. It is easy to discern by the fruit that comes out of my mouth and heart what spirit I am of. Jesus told us to beware of how we hear a matter because we have filters in which we hear something.

The fastest way to know what spirit I am in is to consider if there is vitriol in my attitude because that is opposite of love that can cover offenses. This examination is necessary if I am to see beyond the rhetoric of the present world and take on a meek attitude that can be open to consider and be reasoned with or challenged by the Word of God.

There are people I truly respect because of their love for God and His Word, but I don't agree with them a 100 percent, but it does not mean I am right and they are wrong. We all have our experiences and as a result we develop different approaches and convictions which do not negate other people's convictions. The only thing that would break that agreement is if they were leading one astray from the real matters of salvation. As long as we respectfully choose to respect the other without taking personal offense, we can agree to disagree without the breaking of any fellowship.

As Christians, we have a responsibility to discern the spirit we operate in and which one is influencing us the most. We must repent from taking on any attitude but the attitude of Jesus towards all matters. That is the only way we can be assured that He will not look at us and chide us with the words, *"You do not know what spirit you are of."*

Prayer: Lord, In the past, I have been in the wrong spirit many times. Thank You for looking at me and revealing it to me. There were times I thought my stands were right when in reality they were not founded on Your Rock of truth. I thought my ways noble, when they were not ordained by heaven. I thought my beliefs were right, but they lacked love, reason, and humility. I thought I was standing for Your truth when in reality I was simply voicing the world's attitudes. Forgive me for such nonsense. Amen.

June 10

"For the Son of man is not come to destroy men's lives, but to save them. And they went to another village" (Luke 9:56). What is God's plan in a matter? This is what is often missing when it comes to man. In recent posts we had the example of the zealous John and James taking offense for Jesus. It seemed noble enough, but what they were missing was God's perspective. Jesus did not come to destroy but to save. Fire would eventually come to the region, but it would be the Holy Spirit coming down on man and not judgment.

I hear a lot of people declaring that they want to know God's will or plan in a matter but how many ask Him what they need to understand? We naturally go with our opinions, what we think is going on, or with that which is most influencing our reason about matters. However, God's thoughts and ways are not our thoughts and ways, and yet how many of us assume God would agree with us and presume that we understand the dynamics behind everything that we are able to make sound judgments, while harshly judging others?

I will declare to you right now I don't know what is going on in much of the world and for that reason I ask God to show me what I need to understand to make sure I line up to His plan in a situation to avoid opposing what He is doing. We humans make it about who or what is right and wrong, and of course, in our thinking, we are right and that automatically makes the other person wrong. In fact, we can't understand why that person doesn't see it or get it and shake our heads at how can they be so "stupid" about it.

Let's face it: that is how we humans look at things. We look at it from one side through filters that we are not aware exist. However, as believers of the Lord Jesus, we must choose the higher ground by being realistic about our mortal limitations and remember even though such an attitude is normal for us in our humanity, it is also of the world. We must seek God's perspective, come back to His Word, and operate in the right spirit to ensure the right fruit in our lives.

Prayer: Lord, we are known by our fruits that come out the most in our attitude and actions towards those who may challenge and oppose us. We are to approach people in love, instruct in meekness, listen in patience, and be willing to be moved in our stands when You shine the light on our attitude. It is all about lining up to You. Amen.

June 11

"Not as though I had already attained, either were already perfect" (Philippians 3:12a). What was Paul trying to attain? We are told he was trying to attain unto the resurrection of the dead *(Philippians 3:11).* Resurrection is one of the six principle doctrines of Christ according to *Hebrews 6:1-2*.

As believers we are living in light of a better resurrection, one that will bring us face to face with our precious Lord Jesus who will rejoice at our presence before Him, and not in shame due to damnation (*Daniel 12:1-3; John 5:21-29; Hebrews 9:27; 11:35*). That is why in *Philippians 3:10* Paul wanted to know the power of our Lord's resurrection, but he also recognized there must be death, whether it is to the self-life or the physical life, which will entail loss and suffering along the way.

Paul knew that suffering was a necessary tool God used to refine His people. Our greatest example of this is Jesus. We see this when it came to Jesus' humanity, *"Though he were a Son, yet learned he obedience by the things which he suffered" (Hebrews 5:8).* We also have Paul clearly pointing out in *Romans 8:17*, if we suffer with Him, we will be glorified with Him and in *2 Timothy 2:12* that if we suffer with Him, we shall reign with Him.

We see that Paul admitted he had not attained such insight or that he had yet been brought to a perfect knowledge concerning resurrection, and for this reason he was pressing toward that high mark for the prize of the high calling of God in Christ Jesus. Is the prize Paul speaking of that better resurrection that each Christian should be pressing towards?

At the core of our faith is the expectancy of resurrection (*1 Corinthians 15:14-19*). We have a new life in us due to the Spirit of God, but we will be raised in a new, glorified body at the resurrection to partake of an eternal inheritance. We were raised up with a new life when we were born-again, and presently that new life is being formed in us by the Spirit so we can be conformed to the image of Christ (*Romans 8:29*). King David best said it in *Psalm 17:15, "As for me, I will behold thy face in righteousness: I shall be satisfied, when I awake, with thy likeness."*

Paul may have wanted to come to the perfect knowledge of resurrection, but I think he knew that until he experiences the resurrection of a new body, his understanding would remain incomplete. However, that never kept him from pressing forward as he reached towards that time in great hope, knowing that the resurrection promised will bring him into the fullness of life, as well as a place of worship that would be worthy of His Lord's acceptance.

Prayer: Lord, it is so easy to be reaching for what the world considers greatness, while missing what you have ordained as being great. Paul understood the prize: give me a greater revelation and desire to press forward by faith, reach upward with hope, and be prepared to embrace all that you have for me in my upcoming resurrection. Amen.

June 12

"...but I follow after, if that I may apprehend that for which also I am apprehended of Christ Jesus" (Philippians 3:12b). Have you ever considered what Paul wanted to apprehend? In the last post he wanted to attain unto the resurrection of the dead to possess greater awareness of God's power, but he also knew he had been apprehended by Christ but now he wants to apprehend.

To "attain points to reaching for something." Paul was clearly reaching forward and upward to attain the prize of resurrection unto eternal life. To "apprehend" something points to actually capturing it, overtaking it, comprehending, finding, and perceiving. It was clear that on the road to Damacus in *Acts 9*, Jesus met Paul and not only caught his attention but captured his heart and his soul. Paul may have been going the wrong way, but by the time his ordeal was over, he was on the right way, ready to take hold of his calling and his new life in Christ while ever pressing forward in the great race to gain the ultimate prize.

The reason many Christians are struggling is that they are trying to juggle the world and religion. They are tossing bits and pieces in the air and trying to catch them in order, but what they discover is that a person can't grab and hold onto two things at a time. They have to keep tossing all the different issues of life up in the air to keep everything going. Eventually, they wear down and will have to stop the act to finally settle down and make a decision as to what they are going to pursue and hold onto.

For a Christian it should not be a hard choice, but a war can take place between the flesh and the Spirit as to which one they will pursue. If one strives to apprehend the world, they will lose their soul, but if one decides nothing really makes sense in this world, then they can pursue that which is eternal.

What was Paul trying to apprehend—the knowledge, the ongoing revelation of Jesus Christ. In *Philippians 3:8*, he shared how he counted all things of this world and the life attached to it as loss for the excellency of the knowledge of Christ Jesus. In *Philippians 3:10,* he stated, *"That I may know him."*

If Paul was to attain the resurrection he was pressing towards, he had to know the One who stated, *"I am the resurrection and the life"* in *John 11:25-26*. Resurrection comes before life. There must be a quickening of life, but it happens when the Lord raises us up with His power to walk in a new life, and the life we are walking in is our Lord's life (*Galatians 2:20*).

Prayer: Lord, we often pursue what is wasteless to only taste that which is vanity. Lord, help me with priorities and keep me from chasing after that which holds no real substance for my eternal well-being. Amen.

June 13

"For the which cause I also suffer these things; nevertheless I am not ashamed: for I know whom I have believed, and am persuaded that he is able to keep that which I have committed unto him against that day" (2 Timothy 1:12). Have you ever counted how many times Paul stated the need to come to the knowledge of Jesus Christ? It is not the knowledge of doctrine, theology, Bible text, etc.; rather, it is the knowledge of the Person and Work of Jesus Christ.

We are told that Jesus is the same yesterday, today, and forever (*Hebrews 13:8*). John the Baptist, who was six months older than Jesus, made a declaration about Him as the Son of God who would take away the sin of the world in *John 1:29*. And in the following verse we are told that after him (John) would come a man which was preferred before him (Jesus): for He (Jesus) was BEFORE John. Jesus declared in *John 8:58* before Abraham was, He stated *"I am."*

Jesus in *Revelation 1:8* and *17* assured the Apostle John that He was the Alpha and Omega the beginning of all things as Creator and the ending of all things as Judge. He is the first in preeminence and will be the last in all matters (*John 1:1-4; Colossians 1:15-18*). We clearly see Jesus existed before His incarnation. He has always been, continues to be and will always be who He is, which is God who came in the flesh to be the sacrificial Lamb of God and now serves as our High Priest in the courts of heaven (*1 Timothy 2:5*).

What do you want to apprehend? Like Paul, it will always come back to what has apprehended you, captured the affections of your heart, taken hold of your mind, overtaken your thoughts, and becomes your main focus. Since Jesus is eternal as God, we can't comprehend the length, depth, and width of His power, dominion, and glory in our limited state, but because He took on humanity, we know He can indeed relate to us and we to Him. As believers we possess His Spirit within, and when we seek to know Him in greater measure, the Spirit will bestow greater revelations of Him in our spirit, causing us to come to a greater knowledge of our Lord as we are brought from glory to glory in the unveiling of His majesty to us and in us (*2 Corinthians 3:17-18*).

Has Jesus apprehended your heart? If He has than your main heart's desire should be to apprehend more and more of the knowledge of Him as Lord of your life, Creator God of the Universe, Savior of your soul, and the Son of God, who is the first-born of a new creation and the first fruits of the kingdom of heaven because He paid the price of redemption for us.

Prayer: Lord, we seek to know more about You, but the key is to know You more. Lord, keep me from simply searching to know about You and cause me to rise up out of my comfort zones of what I think I understand about You in order to seek to truly know You in greater measure. Amen.

June 14

"Two things have I required of thee: deny me them not before I die" (Proverbs 30:7). This is a prayer found in the last part of *Proverbs* that shows incredible wisdom. If you have not read about the two prayer requests, what would your requests be, and what would be the reasons behind them?

Would they be worldly or spiritual in nature? What would they say about the quality of your present life? After all, our prayers are often based on what we consider to be our present need in light of our future comforts, hopes and dreams. Perhaps you would find yourself quite confused because there are so many matters surrounding you and you can only have two requests. Let's just move some of those other possible matters from off the table. These requests do not concern others but you alone. What would they be?

Every time I read this section of Scripture I am brought back to a couple of places in my life: SIMPLICITY and the REALITY OF A MATTER. Perhaps such requests would bring people to other places of sound reasoning, but they always bring me back to these two places. So, what were the requests and the reasoning behind them? Consider the first request. *"Remove far from me vanity and lies: give me neither poverty nor riches."*

In the first request we see a contrast. The things that cause detours in our spiritual lives that often rob us of time and energy, and influences our pursuits are vanity and poverty, while the things that cause us much complication due to confusion, temptations, and desires are lies and riches. We fail to realize that there is much vanity in the riches of this world and that our attempt to change our poverty is based on an upside-down world that reinforces its many lies with false promises and ideas of temporary happiness, hollow success, and passing accomplishments.

Since we are in the world, it is easy to value that which has no value to it. Perhaps it might bring some temporary pleasure, but it is not lasting. There are those who look for a free ride through what they consider the theme park of the world. They want to pick and choose their ride, their activity, and their preferences. However, it will cost dearly in some way, and if its vanity does not lead back to the Lord, it will prove to be hollow, worthless, and bitter to the soul.

Prayer: Lord, we tend to think in our arrogance we know what is best, and in our ignorance of You we perceive we know what You will accept. Lord, we can't know anything about Your Kingdom, will, and ways until we know You. Knowing You produces humility, awe and repentance. I do not want to know about You or of You, I WANT TO KNOW YOU. Amen.

June 15

"Remove far from me vanity and lies: give me neither poverty nor riches: feed me with food convenient for me: Lest I be full, and deny thee, and say, Who is the LORD? or lest I be poor, and steal, and take the name of my God in vain" (Proverbs 30:8-9). In light of the first request, the individual makes the second request to the Lord, 'feed me with food convenient for me." In other words, when there is neither lack nor plenty to create any need or desire in the soul for the things of this world, then the person will look to the Lord to properly feed them what they have need of and what will sustain them. Spiritually speaking, for me the prayer would be, "Lord, feed me with what will keep me dependent on You while satisfying my soul and spirit so I have need of nothing but to focus on You and what is important to my relationship with You."

Here comes the reasoning behind the two requests, *"Lest I be full, and deny thee, and say, Who is the LORD? or lest I be poor, and steal, and take the name of my God in vain."* Worldly abundance causes one to perceive they have no need for Him, causing them to deny their need for God's continual intervention in their life. On the other hand, great lack causes one to feel the need to take matters into their own hands to bring a matter about however and with whatever means it takes, which ends in bringing a reproach on God's character.

I love this prayer in its simplicity of acknowledging and recognizing that too much of the world crowds out God, but great lack in it magnifies it, causing God to recede back into shadows of indifference in the mind. It all comes back to balance, for the great test of our faith is always found in extremes and as we can surmise, both sides of this coin have to do with faith. However, the establishment of faith is found in making sure we learn to value what is important, pursue what is eternal, and never settle for what is nominal in this world.

Prayer: Lord, You want us to know balance, but only You can balance all things out. Lord, feed me with Your food that is convenient for me to grow in my dependency upon You and in the knowledge of You. Amen.

June 16

Temptation quietly followed me into the bedroom. When I turned to face him, he remained silent, but his shining eyes said it all, drawing me in and holding me transfixed. As the intense longing in those penetrating eyes held me captive in their grasp, I felt overwhelmed by the power of his heart's desire.

Such boundless passion was hard to resist, but I had earlier made a firm decision not to be seduced into giving in when he was in such a state. Since he was positioned between myself and the doorway, I knew that my only hope of escape was to somehow sidestep him and walk away. Instead, I heard a strangled whisper escape my lips with a single word that I knew he would not accept: "Later."

Unphased, his sparkling eyes, still aflame with burning desire, unblinkingly stared into mine, and horror of horrors, I felt myself begin to melt like an ice cube in a hot skillet. I knew there would be no escape, no rest, no peace between us if I didn't surrender to his relentless demands. Sensing that he had successfully broken down my will to resist, he made no advances as I walked past him, but instead softly followed me into my den and patiently waited as I took the lid off of the precious plastic box that held the treasure of treasures—his dog treats!!!

"Ask, and it shall be given you; seek, and ye shall find; knock, and it shall be opened unto you: For every one that asketh receiveth; and he that seeketh findeth; and to him that knocketh it shall be opened" (Matthew 7:7, 8); "Pray without ceasing" (1 Thessalonians 5:17). – J. Haley

Prayer: Lord, we have many examples of what it means to approach You in prayer, be persistent in our requests, stand in silent awe of You while waiting, and know in confidence You will hear us. We also know that it is with great delight that You desire to answer our requests. Amen.

June 17

"Not that I speak in respect of want: for I have learned, in whatsoever state I am, therewith to be content" (Philippians 4:11). If you could put a main theme on my last few posts, it would be one word, "contentment." As I watch much of the world, it seems man is often driven, paralyzed, confused, fearful, and just plain lost in what seems to make less and less sense to him. Everything he hears is beginning to sound like a world going mad. How can you even begin to be content in such a world?

How important is contentment? Without it there is no rest because there is no satisfaction to be found and peace will seem far away because there is no order. The soul will find itself in upheaval because there is no respite from it all, and the spirit will be agitated because there is no hope.

One of the challenges of living amidst abundance is that man can begin to look for contentment in his outward environment. It is natural to perceive material goods as pointing to being satisfied, having stuff pointing to environmental control, and possessions can point to that which might constitute happiness and success. And yet all of these point to lifeless objects that can't change what really ails man or brings lasting satisfaction.

What ails man in his world is the vanity of all things when it comes to this present life. No one can find real contentment among all of it because contentment is a matter of heart attitude and not that of activities, things, stuff, or possessions. The Apostle Paul knew how to abound or how to be abased in this world no matter what was going on around him.

It was clear that Paul knew both states at different times in his life. He had abounded before his encounter with Jesus, but afterwards he was in prison, beaten, shipwrecked, and at times had to do his own tentmaking while still ministering to the flock. He knew how to be on the giving end of liberality, and the receiving end in a humble state in light of the great need for intervention and provision that would only come from his Lord and Savior.

Prayer: Lord, You are our Provider and how much we are willing to share with others of Your many gifts will often determine on how much we receive from You. If we want to heap things upon ourselves, we will know poverty in some way, but if we want to be avenues of blessings to others, You will entrust us with more, knowing we are a conduit of Your love, grace, and blessing to others. Amen.

June 18

"And having food and raiment let us be therewith content" (1 Timothy 6:8). The Apostle Paul knew the satisfying ways that came from being content no matter what state he found himself in. We know he suffered much for the sake of the kingdom of heaven. He knew that contentment was not based on having everything you desired; rather, it was appreciating what you did have at the moment, knowing it is sufficient for that time.

How could Paul be rich at one point and be brought to a state of poverty and be content? Again, the answer is he learned contentment but part of learning it is that he discovered it is attached to thankfulness. He recognized all things came from God who was faithful to provide all his needs.

He also recognized when he abounded, he could be assured of not being a burden on others and had more to give in order to bless others in greater need. On the other hand, when he was abased, God's grace proved sufficient enough to meet him in all of his needs regardless of what it was. When he had much or was in need, there was always something to rejoice about. In the case of the benevolent Philippians, he rejoiced over their giving while in prison. He also found great joy in the opportunities his present status always allotted him whether it was being a witness or witnessing their faith.

The question is simple for each of us, "Is the glass half empty or half full?" Those who have never learned contentment no matter the state, will always see it half empty and find nothing to be thankful for. They are busy looking at the lack and not at the fact they have need of nothing at that point, while those who see it half full are content with what they have because it is sufficient enough to keep them going.

I know I am living in a world that offers empty glasses with false promises of filling them, leaving many disillusioned, but as a believer, my glass is always half full and I have no doubt that it will remain so because God not only keeps it filled with the blessings of His life, but so many times He fills it to overflowing with His Spirit. I never fear lack because His grace is sufficient, and when I am in need of His Spirit, all I have to do is ask, trust, and wait, and at the right time He will give me what I have need of to satisfy my soul, sustain my spirit, and cause joy to abound in my heart.

Prayer: Lord, thank You for providing me with my glass of promises. No matter how many promises are obvious in that glass I am assured that Your promises will always be there, that Your life in me as Your vessel will never wane, and Your Spirit will prove to be not only sufficient to fill my life but will often prove to be overflowing beyond measure. Amen.

June 19

"For all that is in the world, the lust of the flesh, and the lust of the eyes, and the pride of life, is not of the Father, but is of the world" (1 John 2:15). The greatest conflicts that take place, where most wars are lost, are not on some great battlefield of the world or even the unseen realm, which is more real than what we see, but that which takes place within. There are three battlefields where great conflict rages within man. These are the mind, the soul, and the spirit.

The mind can be taken away from all sense of reality by the imagination (*2 Corinthians 10:3-5*). It often begins with the lust of the eyes catching the fancy of someone and then it graduates into the imagination of what it would mean to partake of it. From the imagination it can slide into obsession which is a step away from the insanity of being possessed by it. In such a seductive state, man will lose all reason and will do whatsoever to have it no matter the cost. That is why the mind must be transformed by the Spirit by bringing every thought into captivity of Christ, taking on His attitude about it in order to no longer be conformed to the world by its attractions and false promises (*Romans 12:1-2; Philippians 2:5*).

What about the soul? We are told in *1 Peter 2:11* that it is fleshly lusts that war against the soul. Those lusts, with their desires, will ever stir the soul up to pursue them under the illusion that the soul will be content with it, satisfied by it, and therefore needs it to experience it to know life and happiness. However, the world leaves man disillusioned, dissatisfied and empty, causing him to pursue it in greater means or seek other possible worldly avenues to find it, eventually leaving him in a greater state of disillusionment about life.

Such worldly pursuits can leave man addicted, cynical, and hopeless. It is for this reason the Apostle Paul instructs us to FLEE all youthful lusts and FOLLOW righteousness, faith, charity, peace, with them that call on the Lord out of a pure heart (*2 Timothy 2:22*). It is important to note that the company we keep will greatly influence our response towards what we choose to follow in our lives.

The truth is we are either fleeing something or following it. Many flee from God while following the world, but we must flee lusts if we are going to follow Jesus in the paths of righteousness.

Prayer: Lord, there are times I know I should flee but become complacent. There are other times I am clueless to the danger before me because I am not discerning. Lord, thank You for being faithful enough to keep me from slipping and patient enough to wait for me to once again focus on You so I can follow You in the right way. Amen.

June 20

"Thus saith God the LORD, he that created the heavens, and stretched them out; he that spread forth the earth, and that which cometh out of it; he that giveth breath unto the people upon it, and spirit to them that walk therein" (Isaiah 42:5). In the previous post I talked about the great conflicts that take place in the mind, soul, and spirit. When it comes to the mind it begins with unbridled imagination and for the soul it is unbridled lust.

What will be at odds with our spirit? When one is born again, they have the breath of God and the life of His Son in them. The spiritual can only affect the spiritual. We are told our flesh (the old man or the carnal man) lusts against the Holy Spirit in *Galatians 5:17* and vice versa. In other words, what the old man in us desires to partake of is contrary to what the Spirit desires for us and the two will never meet in agreement causing great conflict in our heart and with our conscience. In the end, it will twist our desires into a pretzel that entails a great struggle because we want what we want, but we know it is not right.

The spirit in us may be willing to do it God's way but the flesh is weak and will eventually succumb to the tormenting, unrelentless desires of the old disposition in us unless it is properly addressed. The Apostle Paul's solution is found in *Galatians 6:14, "But God forbid that I should glory, save in the cross of our Lord Jesus Christ, by whom the world is crucified unto me, and I unto the world."* He also stated in *1 Corinthians 15:31* that he died daily, pointing out he daily crucified the influences of the carnal man in him.

The Apostle John clearly pointed out in his first epistle, *"Whosoever is born of God doth not commit sin; for his seed remaineth in him: and he cannot sin, because he is born of God" (1 John 3:9).* It is not that we can't sin if we are born again, but we can't consciously sin without great conviction first gripping our soul. This conviction will not allow us to keep sinning without being utterly broken by it, or to remain in it for long. It will result in true repentance that will cause us to come back to our Lord seeking His mercy because His breath, life, and Spirit are truly in us.

Prayer: Lord, You tell us what we are at war with, what we need to understand about each battlefield and how to overcome our enemies, but how many of us take note and simply believe it in order to walk in it in obedience as a means to properly walk it out by faith? So many times, I can almost hear, "Ye of little faith" when it comes to overcoming the world in You by faith. Amen.

June 21

"A good man sheweth favour, and lendeth: he will guide his affairs with discretion" (Psalm 112:5). We live in a confusing world where either side of the coin spells gloom and doom. We don't know who or what to believe. We don't know how much of what we perceive is trustworthy. The more we hear the less we trust as to what we see and the more we see the more we question what we hear because none of it makes sense.

We live in a world of lies and propaganda because the age is under the father of lies, Satan. In the midst of our lives here, we struggle with the great desire to maintain some naiveness to believe there must be some good in man and some hope in this world that we can believe and actually cling to. Without believing "goodness" wins out in the end, there is no "hope" for anything to survive.

As believers, we must be realistic about not only the world we live in but mankind. Mankind will never save man. The darkness is too great to overcome in the natural strength, the evil too boundless for man to conquer, and the wickedness too deep to completely root out. That is why, as believers, our great hope is beyond this present age, clearly outside of man's limited reach, but not outside of God's domain.

To walk through this world we must have moral uprightness to properly handle our affairs with great discretion that only comes from godly wisdom. It is for this reason *1 Peter 2:11* reminds us we are to have the attitude of a stranger that is simply passing through our age and will see no need to get caught up with its wicked practices.

We must also have the disposition of a pilgrim. As a pilgrim we are seeking for a place where we have the freedom to truly worship God without the oppressive reins of government, the hindrances of man's traditions, and the endless detours and traps of the lies and philosophies of the age we live in.

As believers we should always be looking beyond this world to that which is eternal. We also realistically know we will not come into this place during our journey here on earth. It is for this reason Abraham's faith caused him to look beyond this world to the city made by the hands of God (*Hebrews 11:8-10*).

Prayer: Lord, we have no hope here. The world's ways and paths are dark, the night is long, and the terrain harsh, but You are the light that reaches the soul that will guide us to our forever home with You. Amen.

June 22

It had been a long and scenic road trip, but I'll never forget the time when, after a rise in the road, all the majesty of the Grand Teton Mountain in Jackson Hole, Wyoming, suddenly came into view. It was so incredibly awesome that unbidden tears came, and when we left that valley by the same road, I remember crying "goodbye" in the back seat of the car.

I was sixteen years old at the time. Mountains have always fascinated me; after all, I grew up in the Seattle area which is surrounded by mountains—the Olympic mountains to the west, Mount Rainier to the south, the Cascades to the east, Mount Baker to the north and on trips to Montana, the mighty Rocky Mountain range. Fast forward a few decades to 1996 where I found myself trying to find at least some "higher ground" in Houston, Texas.

The contrast between jutting mountains and flat land was stark. In fact, it was so painfully flat in every direction that we finally came to the conclusion that other than very tall buildings, a certain elevated freeway overpass offered the best "higher ground" experience we were going to get. I never felt "normal" living in "flat land" and was so thankful for every mile that passed when, six months later, we moved back to mountain country in Idaho.

I have to admit, what easterners point to as a "mountain" can cause us mountain folks to grin and refer to it as a "molehill," but that's beside the point. All of this got me to thinking about what "normal" means to different people.

No doubt where a person is born and raised, or wherever and however they choose to live for most of their life is what seems "normal" to them, whether it's a decent life, or one of debauchery. When it comes to choosing a church, it seems to me that most folks choose whatever they consider to be "normal" according to their ideas, beliefs or past experiences. Sadly, like birds nesting in their favorite environment, people often comfortably "remain in the congregation of the dead" for years (see *Proverbs 21:16*).

According to the Bible this is the result of wandering out of the way of understanding, or wisdom, but since they have no CONTRAST to challenge their perception of "normal," they are content to remain where they are. Contrasts are a powerful means of waking people up to think outside of their "little box of neutral, naïve, non-committed, normalcy" whether it's by bringing into focus, like towering mountain peaks, the heights of glory God is calling them to by His Spirit, or whether it's down in the valley to work in the vast harvest fields ripe for reaping.

Thank God His Word is full of contrasts from cover to cover so that those who truly desire to know what is "normal" to God for their own life shall find it. *"Ask, and it shall be given you; seek, and ye shall find; knock, and it shall be opened unto you; For every one that asketh receiveth; and he that seeketh findeth; and to him that knocketh it shall be opened" (Matthew 7:7, 8).* – J. Haley

Prayer: Lord, Your creation is breathtaking, but Your contrasts are distinct to bring value, and Your promises are glorious that color our future with indescribable distinction and beauty. Amen.

June 23

"I do not frustrate the grace of God: for if righteousness come by the law, then Christ is dead in vain" (Galatians 2:21). I have been reading a book about liberalism. It is amazing to me how labels are being used to identify everything from politics to religion, often masking what is missing from the equation, what is wrong about the presentation, and what is the truth to a matter. I realize the whole goal of any liberalism is to change one's worldview of God, life, and our purpose for being here.

The whole point of the book is how man has taken liberty with every aspect of Scripture and made cults out of religions, seduced men into mixing the secular with the heavenly, and fudged the lines of truth to dull man down to what is truth. Although the author himself is not aware that his premise, which is a certain man-inspired theology, has caused him to take liberty with God's Word by ignoring a large percentage of it in lieu of maintaining what he believes, his example, proves the subtly of all liberalism. It often gives the appearance of being true to Scriptural integrity, as well as reasonable in presentation while staying on the narrow way, when in reality, the person just has taken a detour from the Way of Jesus Christ.

So how do you avoid being swept up by the incredible wave of delusion that will catch man up in judgment in the last days? (*2 Thessalonians 2:10-12*) Being saved out of religious delusion has made me very aware of what the Bible tells me I must test. The first test is *1 John 4:1-3*. We are to test the spirit behind something. The Spirit of God has no agreement with the spirit of the world, Satan, and will not be found in an unholy mixture. Those who expose themselves to a wrong spirit will be dulled down and rendered ineffective from discerning spirits altogether.

It is important to constantly reiterate that the one main difference between what is right and wrong is the spirit behind something. The right Spirit will bring you back to the truth of all matters concerning salvation, while the wrong spirit will lead you down some other road.

This road could be good works, man-made doctrines, and religious affiliations to name a few, but the Bible is clear we are saved by grace through faith. To add to God's great work of grace and to downplay the way of faith that comes by believing God's Word is to frustrate His grace. In essence, it is to render Christ's death, burial and resurrection as not being true or as being unnecessary because man supposedly holds it within his means to obtain entrance into heaven without any intervention from God.

Prayer: Lord, we show disdain, contempt or unbelief towards Your great work of redemption when we decide not to believe what Your Word clearly declares, establishes, upholds, and repeats about it. Lord, You offer us life and we end up in the pigpens of the world chasing after the poisonous garbage of it. Forgive us for being fleshly, lustful, worldly, and foolish. Amen.

June 24

"As we said before, so say I now again, If any man preaches any other gospel unto you than that ye have received, let him be accursed" (Galatians 1:9). In the last post I talked about how easy it is to take liberty with the Lord's truth and great works. The first test has to do with possessing a right spirit in order to keep our faith, life, and works pure and acceptable to God.

The next test is who do they say Jesus is (*Matthew 16:13-19*). That is a question that is foremost in my mind. Are they taking away from Jesus as God in the flesh in any way. To take away from Jesus means you are undermining His great work of redemption. You most likely are failing to make it clear that all have sinned and must repent of it, and believe in your heart the Gospel is true to flee the wrath of God to come?

To be exposed to any other Jesus but the One in the Bible is to come under an anti-Christ spirit which will cause people to take on a casual or negative attitude towards the real Jesus. Keep in mind, if you do not get Jesus right you are building on a wrong foundation that will be shaken and will collapse in the end (*1 Corinthians 3:11*).

The next test is based on our commission as Christians. To call something Christian and maintain the legitimacy of it, it must clearly present the Gospel. Sadly, it seems few preach the true Gospel and yet how can people know what it means to be saved and from what? What is the purpose of any Christian presentation if it is not to see man saved?

A watered-down, entertaining, wrong gospel can't save. The Bible is clear: to present any other Gospel than what has been established in Scripture is to stand accursed before God. Remember, any presentation of God is also influencing and affecting those who are vulnerable or who do not know the truth. Presentations will affect how those in spiritual darkness end up seeing God, and whether they believe it is so will come down to our validity as a credible witness. Both the presentation and witness will mean nothing if we prove to be professional hypocrites by failing to walk out this extraordinary life.

Prayer: Lord, there are many "gospels" being presented by various religious sources, but there is only one true "Gospel" that saves, and it is the good news that changed my life and destination forever. Thank You! Amen.

June 25

"Be not deceived; God is not mocked: for whatsoever a man soweth, that shall he also reap" (Galatians 6:7). We have been considering what it means to test whether the message and the messenger is from the God of heaven.

The reason we must test all things when it comes to God and His Word is because every cult has been started because someone took liberty with God's Word. Every form of heresy hides behind some truth in the Bible but has redefined or broadened the path with "new insights," "greater revelations," or "deeper spiritual truths" that only those who are elite and special can even begin to comprehend.

The tests we have been given are simple and it does not take long for the imposters to fail one of them or all three of them. The first test is the spirit, the second test has to with possessing the true Jesus and the third test has to do with our commission to present the only true Gospel to the lost.

Many people fail the second test because there is a wrong spirit present because the Holy Spirit leads people to the true Jesus. If Jesus' death **for** our sin, His burial **with** our sins, and His resurrection in a new glorified body is not being presented to bring man to repentance and salvation, it will prove to be another gospel that can't save.

The next test has to do with principle. Principle reveals the law we are operating under and will ultimately determine the fruit that comes from our life. Jesus said we will know them by their fruits.

There are two laws according to *Romans 8:2*. There is the law of sin and death which is sown BY the flesh, and the second law has to do with the Spirit of the life of Christ Jesus in us which is sown IN the Spirit of God. Many of the presentations I see or hear today of Jesus appeals to the flesh and is void of the Spirit of God. Therefore, what principle are we sowing according to and what fruits will it produce in the end when it comes to our attitude towards God?

Finally, how much liberty does one take to fill in the empty spaces? Even the spaces in God's economy have a purpose and what will we end up filling them with: His inspired words, or our ideas? Empty spaces are to keep us from going any further because, past what is, there are often idle words that will be judged, ignorance towards righteousness that will not be tolerated, and presentations that could prove to be blasphemous.

Every time I consider the end results of taking any such liberty with God's Word so I can have my perverted way, I count the cost and have concluded that such liberty is not worth it. It is up to me as a believer to believe what is true, line up to it as being so, and walk it out every day of my life. This is where I have discovered that true liberty exists only in righteousness. It is the type of liberty that allows me to become what God has ordained me to be.

Prayer: Lord, we take liberty without knowing it. We have our ways of deciding what we will accept without realizing that unless we begin with spirit and who You are, we are apt to accept small bits of heretical poison here and a bit of perversion there, ending up dull of hearing as to what the Spirit is saying and becoming blind to what the enemy is doing. Have mercy on us and pull us out of the seductive lies and ways of this age. Amen.

June 26

"For ever, O LORD, thy word is settled in heaven" (Psalm 119:89). We are told God's Word is settled in heaven but on earth, it is anything but settled. Endless unprofitable debates rage when it comes to God's Word. The debate is not a matter of what it says, but how it is interpreted.

My friend's husband posed a very important question. "How much of the Bible must we do away with to get the rest of it to fit our understanding and different narratives of it?" That is a good question. Most people do away with the Old Testament, but never ask themselves where Jesus, the Apostle Paul, and the six principle doctrines of Christ outlined in *Hebrews 6:1-2* came from. They came from the Old Testament.

What about the examples of the Rock in the wilderness mentioned in *1 Corinthians 10:4*, Esau in *Hebrews 12*, Rahab and Job in *James*, Cain, Enoch, Noah, the children of Israel, Balaam, Lot, and Korah in such books as *2 Peter* and *Jude*? What about the great chapter about those of faith in *Hebrews 11*, and we must not forget about our God who never changes? They all came alive in the Old Testament casting incredible shadows and examples.

I knew a guy who was of the belief that anything before Acts was pretty much immaterial. (This belief is called "Mid Acts.") I had to ask myself, what does he do with the Gospels which are a record of our Jesus, who is all truth, and the many teachings, doctrines, and examples He left with us in those four books whose teachings are also found in Paul's letters? Everything has a source and foundation, or it would be nonexistent.

The question is what do you do with the complete counsel of God's Word? I admit I have my faithful Scriptures that I often turn to when it comes to discussing certain topics of the Word, but I know the subject matter is within context to the rest of the Bible. As one who shares the Bible in various settings and ways, I fear leading anyone astray. I know there is greater damnation on those who mishandle the truth.

I so appreciate how God established a sure foundation using real people while prophetically pointing forward to this time in which the New Testament becomes a fulfillment of the old. It is a time we can look back and prophetically see God in history, in events, and in establishing what will be so in the future.

There is not one aspect of the Bible that is not necessary, significant, and useful for instructions in righteousness. God does not waste time, play guessing games with us for some sick entertainment, or merely give us clues to figure it out. Everything we need to know is in His Word. There is no inconsistency from the beginning of Genesis to the end of Revelation. If an inconsistency is noted it is not because it exists in God's Word; rather, it exists in man's misinterpretation of it according to his perception and mishandling of it because he is in and of a wrong spirit.

Prayer: Lord, You Word will never be found in error. It is man's great error that he tries to adjust Your Word to his small, perverted reality. He often does it to justify his own uncertainty or unbelief towards You. Amen.

June 27

"But the word of the Lord endureth for ever. And this is the word which by the gospel is preached unto you" (1 Peter 1:25). I was part of a religious group that used the Bible as a front to present themselves as being Christians, but they had one of those clauses in their belief that basically stated the Bible was correct as long as it upheld their heretical teachings. You can't ignore those clauses because that is the loophole for not believing God's Word as the absolute standard when it comes to all truth that has already been settled in heaven. Such loopholes allow one to pick and choose what they are going to believe.

I have dealt with people who touted that they judge everything by the Word but when tested, you realize they are testing everything by their understanding of it. They are bound by certain theology, takes, and doctrinal beliefs that ultimately determines how they interpret God's Word. In the end, it limits them from seeing what the complete counsel of God says about a matter. It is amazing to see how such a limited plane keeps any of us from seeing the full counsel of Scripture that would shake what we presently understand and bring a more realistic perspective as to what we really know Scripturally.

The question is, can we know ALL truth when it comes to the Bible? To honestly answer that question, I can say I do NOT know all truth but I do know THE TRUTH, the Person of Jesus Christ. He is the essence of all wisdom (ability to comprehend), righteousness (standard), sanctification (heavenly work and identification) and redemption (salvation). I am often limited by what I do know when it comes to the eternal truths of God. I know that ALL Scripture has been inspired, and I believe it to be so, but I don't know every jot and tittle of it. However, what I do know I must rightfully divide to ensure the integrity of my understanding, faith, and ability to properly handle it.

I have concluded that it is not what I don't understand Scripturally that will count in the end, but what I know is Scripturally true that I will be held accountable for. If I can't be faithful to walk in what I know to be true now, how can I expect the Lord to entrust me with greater understanding and wisdom to come higher in Him?

Prayer: Lord, we always start out with a high opinion of what we think we know, but it is what we don't know that is going to ultimately humble us and bring us to a low state of realizing we can't begin to know the depth, height, and width of who You are and the eternal aspect of Your truths. Amen.

June 28

Excuses. Everybody has them, but some folks excel in the "art" of excuses. It's as if they have the ability to come up with an endless array of them at the drop of a hat, while others may fumble and mumble their way through a situation with less success.

As for me, I realized today that if, say fifty or so years ago I had had the foresight (that often comes from hindsight) I could've opened up a business and called it "Buy an Excuse for Every Occasion." Think of all the money I could've made by selling the perfectly written excuse, along with how to execute it, for almost any flub up, all categorized and easy to memorize.

Of course, we all know that excuses are usually hitched to a truckload of who-or-what to blame, so for an extra fee, I could've helped with that too. After all, there's the entire world, with everything in it, to somehow blame, and if that doesn't work, there's always the position of the moon, or the weather, or the endless mysteries of the universe. Generally speaking, however, just blaming the devil is probably easier.

When you stop and think about it, the Bible is full of man's excuses, right from the start. Adam's excuse was a "double whammy" so he wins first place for all time and eternity in the "Excuses Hall of Fame and Shame." His famous last recorded words which were spoken to God, are *"The woman whom thou gavest to be with me, she gave me of the tree, and I did eat" (Genesis 3:12).*

Thus, Adam blamed both his Creator and his wife for disobedience to God, and he apparently felt justified in his excuses because nowhere in the Bible do we read that he ever repented or received forgiveness so as to be restored into fellowship with God. He could've at least blamed the serpent, that old devil, the father of lies, but he didn't see it that way at all. *Job 31:33* gives us this insight into Adam. *"If I covered my transgressions as Adam, by hiding mine iniquity in my bosom".*

Therefore, no matter how eloquent, elegant or electrifying our "excuses" may be for disobeying the Lord, failing Him in some way, or giving in to temptation, God sees our heart, our innermost thoughts, and why we do what we do. If we try to justify ourselves with excuses, as did Adam, we only deceive ourselves. *1 John 1:8, 9* tells us *"If we say that we have no sin, we deceive ourselves, and the truth is not in us. If we confess our sins, he is faithful and just to forgive us our sins, and to cleanse us from all unrighteousness."*

So, instead of mentally fishing around for an excuse in order to justify self, why not just humble self and repent? – J. Haley

Prayer: Lord, we complicate our standing with You because we do not want to swallow our pride, eat crow when wrong, and owe up for our wicked ways by taking responsibility for them. Lord, thank You for being longsuffering with me until I repent after I have tripped over my pride and finally swallowed and choked on crow. Amen.

June 29

"These things have I spoken unto you, that my joy might remain in you, and that your joy might be full" (John 15:11). Jesus told us these things (Biblical Truths) have been spoken and then written to bring us joy. But how many, by faith, look to Scriptures to bring them joy?

The first thing I want you to note about abiding joy is that it is the Lord's joy. Imagine heavenly joy that can't be thwarted by this world. We may not know that we possess it because it is not an emotion like happiness; rather, it is a state. As believers we must remember that when it comes to something being a state, we must come to that place to experience it.

This joy will bring contentment that is a type of peace that exists within. There may be unnerving things going on around us, but we have an abiding confidence and peace that all is as it should be and that we will still find ourselves in the place of refuge of our Lord when the storm moves on.

Because of Scripture, I have the joy of my salvation for I know redemption is a finished work. It is in Scripture that I can stand in joy with great strength of confidence because God does not lie. It is joy that serves as my anchor that holds me close to the Rock in the storms. It is that joy that bubbles up in awe during worship, in hope during great darkness, and in assurance because of His promises.

Joy seeks Jesus, trusts Him as the Only One who can ensure its presence in our lives. It will cause us to ultimately stand confident that no matter what challenges such joy, it will remain because the one who possesses it knows the source behind it. Even King David understood that the source behind all joy sits on the right hand of God. In Him all pleasures will be unveiled, all promises will be realized, all hope with be brought to fruition, and all blessings will be experienced as one abides forever in the light of the glory of the only begotten Son of God.

Prayer: Lord, it is natural that man looks for that which pleases the flesh, exalts the intellect, and soothes the conflicting waves of the soul and conscience, but the truth is all pleasure of this world is temporary. To know and possess real lasting joy will always bring us back to pleasing You. This requires us to know You, believe Your Word, and by faith walk in Your righteous ways. Amen.

June 30

"For we can do nothing against the truth, but for the truth" (2 Corinthians 13:8). In my recent posts, I talked about man's endless debates over the Word of God due to personal interpretations based on what they Scripturally believe and have been taught. However, when it comes to the truth it is easy for any of us to fail to realize the spirit behind something conditions us to accept or buy what is often sold to us as "being the goods." Man's teachings and influences create the filters through which we see and interpret Scripture while religion subtly indoctrinates us through traditions, doctrines, and emphasis.

With this knowledge how can we really believe we have some corner on the truth of God's Word? Religious knowledge alone will often blind us to our ignorance of God and what constitutes real righteousness. It can become a garb that gives the impression of godliness but lacks the power to impact anyone.

In fact, religion with its theology and doctrines can keep everything surface but to know God requires us by faith to dive into deep waters that often become dark and frightening. We see aspects of God's character that unnerves us, shadows that make us uncertain about our standing in Him, and unsure about our footing when it comes to our walk of faith. The key to having sure footing in our faith walk always comes back to really knowing the God of the Word.

It is easy to hide behind religious platitudes, as we console ourselves that we are people of His Word, but the reality is our loyalty is often to what we believe or understand about His Word not to the truth of it. Such loyalty implies I am most likely going to defend what I believe to be true and not necessarily what the TRUTH is. However, we must always remember truth will stand on its own, hold its own, and will remain standing when all else is shaken and falls in utter destruction. Scripture on the other hand must be properly compared to other Scriptures to establish and discern what is truth.

Prayer: Lord, we are quick to hold on to a floating log of some truth as we bounce like a cork in the middle of endless waves of religious vanity and nonsense. Meanwhile, we can miss the opportunity of diving into the waters of uncertainty to become anchored to the immovable truth of Your Word. It is in Your depths we discover bits of Your beauty, Your majesty, and Your glory. Amen.

July

July 1

"When Jesus knew in himself that his disciples murmured at it, he said unto them, Doth this offend you?" (John 6:61). In the previous post we talked about how you can do nothing against the truth, only for it. Truth is eternal and since it has been established by the throne of heaven, one can never ascend to reach its heights or descend into its depths to witness its sustaining power to always stand no matter where or how many challenges come from the depths of hell. It will penetrate all darkness and stand when all has been shaken.

Truth will cause a reaction as it did with Jesus' disciples. There are three reactions to truth: 1) mocking because it does not fit the person's concept of God; 2) becoming fearful, confused, or insulted because something is challenging one's standardized conclusions about God and His Word, or 3) They know it is truth because God said it; therefore, out of faith they will submit before it and decide to walk according to it to make it their truth.

Those who mock the truth because it is contrary to their way of thinking are totally blind to it. You can take a person from Scripture to Scripture to show them what the Bible truly says about the matter, but they are unable to see it because they have chosen to believe a lie to serve as their standard of truth.

The ones who fit in the second category have, for the most part, created a doctrinal rut in which they are comfortable to stay. It is well worn and has been used to somewhat control any real challenges as to what they understand. They may not be wrong, but they are unwilling to step outside of what they perceive is sufficient enough for them to judge all spiritual matters. The problem with ruts is that they create their own darkness. These people may start out in the light, but because they limit the light, they move into shades of gray and end up groping in darkness because only the light of truth can lead each of us through the various dangerous, ever changing heretical terrain of the age.

Sadly, due to arrogance of not being right, the fear of being wrong, and fragile realities that couldn't hold up in the storms of testing, most people fall into the first two categories. Regardless, of how tightly we hold onto our particular understanding of God and understanding of truth, one can't do anything against the truth no matter how they adjust it, ignore it, deny it, or reject it. In the end God's truth will be what is left standing.

Prayer: Lord, in the past I have believed various lies in my life to live in this world, maintain my fragile realities, and ignore my insistency to be right in a matter, but You have maintained the standard of truth before me in Your Word. You are faithful to challenge me to choose who I am going to believe in order to come to terms with what I need to know about You, Your way and plan. Thank You for preserving my soul, bringing clarity to my mind, and renewing the inner man in me so I can embrace You and Your truth as my all-consuming reality check to all matters pertaining to You and the age I live in. Amen.

July 2

"He said unto him, What is written in the law? How readest thou" (Luke 10:26)? How much do you bother to stand back and really ask some pertinent questions of yourself when it comes to what you Scripturally believe? Do you discern the fruit of something to see if it is godly. Do you bother to see where something is leading you as far as your understanding of it?

Jesus asked many questions. It is not that He didn't know, it is because man needed to pause to really hear the question, stand back to mentally engage with what was really happening around him.

Man needed to become silent to ponder what was asked before answering the Lord's questions.

The problem is man is being conditioned to not ask questions, making him a mere sheep that can be easily enough led to the slaughter without any real opposition. He is being trained to know how to line up to the indoctrination of those who can't afford to be asked any question, especially the right ones. It would reveal that these individuals are evil in their agendas, opportunist in their wicked ways, and hypocrites in their practices.

Take our educational system. It represents the world's way of enslaving people through promoting an anti-God worldview. It does not teach people how to think, reason, and calculate; rather, it trains them how to think according to Socialist/Communist values and philosophies. It subdues any questions with bullying techniques to bring fear of isolation, rejection, and retribution that include mocking those who dare to ask questions, especially the right questions about the ineptness of such philosophies.

Jesus wanted the people who heard the question to be able to think outside the boxes that had clearly been established by the age they were living in. The hearers had been conditioned to hear only certain terms, phrases, and voices. These boxes seem logical enough and had enough religious implications that it sounded sensible to the masses, but for many they were being led into a ditch of destruction.

Paul warned us about the vain philosophies backed by traditions that are inspired by the rudiments of the world in *Colossians 2:8*. This simply means that these philosophies and traditions found their foundation in the world. Sadly, this is where many of the world and even those involved in religion find their source of understanding.

For the believer our attitude must be that of Christ and our understanding must come from the Word of God. Everything that we have available to us by way of our Lord's redemption was established before the foundation this world. It stands sure, will never waver, can't be moved, and will remain as the beacon of righteousness for all to see.

Prayer: Lord, we come to you with the logic of the world's philosophies. Instead of raising Your Word up as our standard to judge the ineptness of our worldly philosophies, we try to adjust its wisdom into the logic of such philosophies. This has caused me much confusion in the past until I realized that the world's philosophies pervert Your truths. Thank You for Your ongoing deliverance from such wretched influences. Amen.

July 3

"Beware lest any man spoil you through philosophy and vain deceit, after the tradition of men, after the rudiments of the world, and not after Christ" (Colossians 2:8). I made mention in the last posts about vain philosophies which are nothing more than traditions that are inspired by the world. To see this influence all you must do is consider religion.

In cults, leaders have been exalted to Godlike status and how dare we question them in their divine status! We have those "self-anointed" individuals who can't be touched in any way which includes doubting what they say without being threatened that if you dare touch "the anointed," you will die no matter how unscriptural they are.

For women who dare to question or challenge things that they discern to be off, they are accused of having the independent, controlling "Jezabel spirit." The most popular ones include being accused of being judgmental when discerning a wrong spirit and unloving when calling sin, sin amid the insane, decadent, pagan philosophies and practices of this age.

Another ruse that is put upon those speaking the truth is the accusation of being part of a cult because they won't go along with what is considered "acceptable doctrinal teachings" or the latest Christian bandwagon that is gaining popularity.

The organized church's way is nothing more than the world's way. It is about getting everyone to fall into line, march to their drumbeat, fit into the square boxes of conformity, and above all else, do not ask questions that would expose the shallow, fragile, pathetic foundation upon which something has been established.

It is clear there are two signs that are constantly put forth: 1) Don't ask questions and 2) it is not up for discussion. For the most part, when people ask questions, it is not to be independent and contrary but to bring reason to the forefront so they can rightly discern a matter. If they are sincere, they want to come to the right conclusion about an issue in order to make up their own mind as to what they can accept as being so. Such people are often found to be reasonable and will not insist you agree with them, but they do want a platform where discussion is possible, questions are necessary, reasoning welcomed, a time of exploration encouraged, and a desire to know that what is so is not considered a major crime or offense.

It is also obvious since Jesus asked pertinent questions, God has no problem answering them either, for He instructed us to ask. However, He will never answer those questions that intrude into His sovereignty. He will never bow down to unbelief or fear because people refuse to rest in His plan and will. He also will not repent or change His mind about what has already been clearly established in His Word as being the simple truth to a matter.

Prayer: Lord the great frustration of today is that no one wants to be challenged to explore the possibility of stepping out of their small worlds to come higher into Your glorious eternal truths. I accept the reality that my exploration to know You will be a journey I take with You, while accepting that others like me will end up taking their own journey. We all need to accept that we are walking down our own paths according to our own understanding, while learning how to hear what the Spirit is saying individually to us. Amen.

July 4

"For, brethren, ye have been called unto liberty; only use not liberty for an occasion to the flesh, but by love serve one another" (Galatians 5:13). Today is a day to pause. Clearly, for most purposes it is a regular day, but in this nation, it is a time to pause, count the blessings from above and then celebrate that despite men's

egregious attacks against this country from within and without, it remains standing as a country that still waves the flag of freedom. Granted, the flag is bit tattered by different forces that rage against any notion about man being free to govern himself according to his religious conscience.

I once read that there is only five percent of the population of the world that encounters any real religious freedom, and it is found in the United States. However, few in America understand freedom and how it is to operate. For years we have been told we are free while being enslaved by a few through taxation, while our personal rights have been frayed by wicked leaders, immoral agendas, and the profane.

We have been watching the moral slide of this country for years as it pushes out God in every arena, ever spewing out abusive "rights" are to the innocent. There is the ongoing nonsense about separation of church and state when it comes to Christians but ignored when it comes to Muslims. The separation of church and state is not between two distinct institutions, but a means to ensure the state will not dictate to the church its moral conscience and obligations to maintain the integrity of its beliefs. On the other hand, it does not allow individuals to push their religion as the rule of law on others.

Sadly, freedom to some means a free-for-all to push their ideas on others regardless of their conscience and religious beliefs. It is often what is considered the best of causes to those of the world that becomes the worse of nightmares to the true living Church of Jesus Christ. Many believers want to stay out of political arenas, but when the arenas become heretical, immoral, and insane, choices must be made. Saints are often being forced into a corner to decide whether to take a stand against evil forces while they can or face the evil forces at work in Satan's systems without preparation, authority and power.

Satan is a murderer, an accuser of the saints. He is brutal in his attacks against their witness. Where brutality rules, the slaves of the age taste oppression that is so heavy that it keeps many eyes from looking up. Despite the hope that believes deliverance will come to set man free from every wrong and bad master's rule, such slavery causes people to feel like there is no hope of ever knowing true liberty again.

As believers of the Most High we know that real liberty is spiritual. It comes from being reconciled back to God through the redemptive work of Jesus, and the reconciliation is what brings peace to an enslaved soul. The question is, do you know true liberty or are you struggling under the grave oppression of this world?

Prayer: Lord, many people desire freedom, but they do not understand what oppresses them and the harsh taskmasters of this world they serve. They see freedom to do as they please, but real freedom has to do with having the liberty to do what is right according to You and Your Word without persecution. Amen.

July 5

"Where there is neither Greek nor Jew, circumcision nor uncircumcision, Barbarian, Scythian, bond nor free: but Christ is all, and in all" (Colossians 3:11). In a recent post I talked about the conditioning of people based on the world's systems that may have the greatest influence on them. What we expose ourselves the most to is what we are prone to come into agreement with in a spiritual way. We will then come under the predominate spirit, influence, and attitude of what we agree with.

I talked about the conditioning of education and church systems. We are indoctrinated and not challenged and encouraged to make our own deductions after research. We do not dare to consider other views that might shake us out of our comfort zones, and we aren't open and willing to have our minds changed or enlarged if a matter can be shown to be truth. It is important to keep in mind once your mind is made up, you have no intention of it being changed whether it is a mere opinion, presumption, preferred reality, or a wrong conclusion.

Paul makes it clear in this Scripture, as well as others, we who believe the Lord are all in Christ. There is no separation between heritage, gender, background, or status as clearly pointed out in *Galatians 3:28*,. We are His vessels, instruments, and means to bring forth the work of His kingdom in this world.

One of the things that we have been indoctrinated not to question are those with certain names, titles, positions, labels, and degrees. We can come to the point of idolizing such things, which is nothing more than idolatry.

People with well-known names can create stars in our eyes that keep us from seeing that they too are human such as we are. They are likewise in desperate need of a savior, but the problem with them being the "star" in our limelight is that we can miss the Morning Star, Jesus Christ. He is the true star that can arise in our hearts and change our lives forever (*2 Peter 2:19; Revelation 2:28; 22:16*).

Prayer: Lord, we do idolize those who represent the type of prestige, position, and honor that belongs only to You. Lord, idols are lifeless and have no means of changing anything. Bring them down in all of our lives so we can fulfill the highest calling of all—to worship, serve and honor You. Amen.

July 6

"And that every tongue should confess that Jesus Christ is Lord, to the glory of God the Father" (Philippians 2:11). We must keep in mind according to *Philippians 2:9-11* that Jesus has been given a name above all names and at His name every knee will bow and every tongue confess that HE IS LORD to the glory of God the Father. We must also note that in the end, believers will be given a new name that is only known by them and the One who gives it (*Revelation 2:17*).

Man can be given titles by this world, but Jesus was given five titles by heaven according to *Isaiah 9:6*. These titles describe His glory that is too wonderful to imagine, revealing that He is the only wise counsellor to those who seek truth and healing. He is the Mighty

God who is creator of all, the everlasting Father who has established both a heavenly family and an eternal inheritance. Finally, He is the Prince of Peace that describes the kingdom He oversees which is void of the conflicts we encounter in this present world.

We will consider the other worldly standards we are prone to become enamored with due to the world's ability to magnify them and put improper value on them in the next post, but meanwhile we must realize that to be enamored or caught up with anything other than the God of the universe is akin to idolatry that we are told to flee. Granted, we are to have respect for people who are overseeing our well-being, but that is to ensure order and a proper attitude when it comes to those in authority. Such things must never supersede God's name, making it vain, common, or profane. To avoid blasphemy, any reference about the Lord must not downplay who the Bible has clearly revealed He is and must be to us.

However, it is up to us to keep things in the proper perspective according to Scripture. We are the ones who determine what pedestal we choose to put people on, as well as keep titles in their proper place when it comes to who we follow, exalt, and worship.

When all is said and done, we can't help but agree with the Apostle Paul's evaluation of the Lord Jesus Christ: He is indeed our ALL IN ALL.

Prayer: Lord, we are foolish when it comes to the emphasis we put on those who are worldly, while failing to give You due glory. We can easily be found to be fools in the end because we miss what is really important to You. Forgive us for allowing the insignificant things of the world to become what we think we need instead of seeing that You are all we need. Amen.

July 7

"He that descended is the same that ascended up far above all heavens, that he might fill all things" (Ephesians 4:10). In the previous post I spoke of how we become enamored with people who hold

certain names and labels. The question is why do we allow the glitter of our age, that will prove to be fading and disappointing, to eclipse the eternal Light of the world?

Jesus has the name above all names and yet how many of us give Him much thought? He carries the labels that in the end will not only stand but count for eternity, but how many of us stand in awe of Him?

When it comes to high positions, Jesus holds the highest in each realm. In the heavenlies He is worshipped as God, as well as the Lamb that will open the seals of judgment in *Revelation 6*. He is also LORD over all the heavenly Host. When it comes to His kingdom, He is King over all kings, nations, and people. When it comes to spiritual matters, He is the only Mediator between man and God, and the only High Priest after the order of Melchisedec who will serve as both King and Priest in the courts of heaven (*1 Timothy 2:5; Hebrews 7:1-17, 27*).

As promised, Jesus will soon rightfully sit on the throne of David when He comes back to reign. As Lord, owner, overseer of His household, He is LORD over all. As the soon and coming King, He will come back as Judge of all. Right now, He is sitting on the right hand of Majesty until His time comes to put all His enemies under foot and claim His rightful position as RULER over all (*Hebrews 8:1-6*).

The world may have its labels to categorize people in a caste system in order to judge their importance or significance when it comes to worldly matters. Those who give labels will often prove libel because they are hypocrites due to lacking the goods, being inept, unqualified, imposters, and so forth. But, as long as each person wears the acceptable labels, all gifts, talents, and abilities of the inferior will be ignored and regulated by the few, but our Lord has given His people a seal, the Holy Spirit.

The Spirit enables them in all of their abilities and talents to carry out His bidding. This seal unmistakenly, in the truest fashion, identifies the true saints to His kingdom and His household, but one must be born again of the Spirit and adopted to belong to His household (*John 3:3,5; 8:14-17*).

Prayer: Lord, man is always looking for heroes to inspire them and to pay homage to. However, I have learned, You alone fulfill all of those areas of my life, bringing inspiration, confidence, assurance, and hope that is unspeakable because I will be spending eternity with You. Amen.

July 8

"And seekest thou great things for thyself? Seek them not: for, behold I will bring evil upon all flesh, saith the LORD: but thy life will I give unto thee for a prey in all places whither thou goest" (Jeremiah 45:5). What about worldly degrees? There are those who can't see anything but the letters behind a person's name. I had a friend who humorously put the world's various degrees in a proper perspective. One day there was much discussion about those who held certain college degrees from the institutions of the world. My friend spoke up and reminded them he holds 98.6 degrees.

We have a friend who follows teachings of a dead heretic. She has been challenged to consider the error of his teaching according to the Word of God. Regardless of how the Word exposes the error of this individual, her justification for following him in the first place was that he had many degrees, and how can such an individual be wrong? To her it was clear that his degrees outweighed even the simplicity of the Scripture that also points to the Author who operates according to the Spirit and wisdom from above.

At first, worldly degrees may make everything seem a bit hot and heavy in excitement, but eventually they cool with time and only those who are impressed with degrees continue to hold them up as a standard to one's credibility. However, the one who holds all wisdom never had a degree from the world and was a carpenter.

This carpenter called men of low degree: fishermen, the outcast of society, a despised tax collector, and even a thief to follow Him while entrusting them with the greatest message that would turn the world upside down. He continues to choose those poor in spirit but rich in faith. He makes those who have great degrees ultimately look foolish and vain in their knowledge when compared to His incredible wisdom that is simple in presentation, but profound in its effect upon hearts and lives.

We are told that Jesus fills all things, that which is below, above and in-between. Why would any believer look to fill their lives with the non-essentials of the world when we each possess the fullness of heaven in our relationship with God through Jesus Christ?

Prayer: Lord, it is amazing what we value when it comes to this world. In light of You, they are trinkets, flimsy, silly, and temporary. The Apostle Paul even refers to that which pointed to You in the Old Testament as beggarly elements and shadows, but we can possess the real treasure of heaven which is You. Praise Your Holy Name. Amen.

July 9

It wasn't because she went to church every Sunday of her life if she could, or that she played the old hymns on the church organ that made such a powerful impact on my life: it was because she knew, loved and worshipped God and lived her faith with every breath she took.

That was my Great-Grandmother. My fondest memories of her were the things she sewed and knitted for the "mithanaries" in "Yerp" which was my way of pronouncing "missionaries" and "Europe" in my preschool years. She sent care packages to Africa, and only the Lord knows where else.

Great-Grandma taught me that there is no other book in the world as great as the Bible, and that no matter how hard I might try to hide from God, He could always see me. She was the one who enrolled me in Moody Bible School correspondence courses when I was in Jr. High School and bought me wonderful Christian novels for youth by Theodore Epp of Moody Bible School that all contained the Gospel.

Even though I took many detours through the murky swamps and tangled jungles of the world, that foundation she helped lay in my life held strong, and the greatest example she left to me, which opened the door to true, front-line ministry, was the simple, yet profound truth that you don't have to "be in a church or in the church system" to serve God. You don't have to have a list of impressive degrees, or a "big name," or be a "big shot" preacher, teacher, prophet, or so-called "expert" in secular psychology to serve God. In other words, you don't have to knock yourself out trying to somehow "fit" into the man-made, man-centered, man-controlled, religious establishment so you can somehow be, with the approval of man, "qualified" to serve the God you love. You do need to be born-again, baptized, filled with the Holy Spirit, trust and obey, walk in the Spirit by faith, have a testimony, and know the Word of God.

Thus, your mission field is wherever you are and whoever you see, or meet, on any given day. The Apostle Paul cautions us with these words, *"For ye see your calling, brethren, how that not many wise men after the flesh, not many mighty, not many noble, are called: But God hath chosen the foolish things of the world to confound the wise; and God hath chosen the weak things of the world to confound the things which are mighty; And base things of the world, and things which are despised, hath God chosen, yea, and things which are not, to bring to nought things that are; That no flesh should glory in his presence. But of him are ye in Christ Jesus, who of God is made unto us wisdom, and righteousness, and sanctification, and redemption: That, according as it is written, He that glorieth, let him glory in the Lord" (1 Corinthians 1:26-31).*

Therefore, rise up and follow Jesus, serving Him with all your heart, for the harvest is great, and time is short. – J. Haley

Prayer: Lord, I know You put the people in my life that would lead me to You. Your ways prove to be perfect in every way. Thank You for the witnesses of faithful saints that have been strategically placed in my life to bring me into a place of real service to You. Amen.

July 10

"For unto us was the gospel preached, as well as unto them: but the word preached did not profit them, not being mixed with faith in them that heard it" (Hebrews 4:2). The Bible warns us that in the last days deception will reign as king. This deceptive darkness will be all about us in ways we could never imagine. It has the potential to subtly overtake us without us even being aware of it. It will determine what we look to, depend on, and stand on and for when it comes to our beliefs. It will dull down our discernment to identify its form of deception by bringing us under a mixture of half-everything from taking the sharpness out of truth with heretical teachings and so-called "new" revelations. It will mix worldly practices with Scriptural doctrine and emphasize man's traditions and interpretations over His Word. Such a mixture reveals that unfeigned faith that comes from hearing the Word of God in the right spirit is missing, for faith comes by hearing and hearing by the Word of God (*Romans 10:17*).

In my recent posts, I wrote about our different attitudes towards truth and whether we are going to accept it according to our personal concepts of it, or what the Word states and confirms is truth. In my post, dated July 1st, I talked about three reactions to truth, and that many people fit in the first two categories.

In the first group are those who often mock the simplicity of truth and perceive the stories and events of the Bible as being fables or good stories. The second group have clearly adopted some of the Bible as being truth but due to their need to control what they do know, they will reject, ignore, or steer clear of anything that might shake their understanding.

The final group has decided to love the truth no matter the cost (*2 Thessalonians 2:10-12*). This is the only way one can combat the ongoing affronts directed at it. These individuals know they can be deceived, led astray, and are limited as to what they see, hear, and know. They know they can be insulted by the truth and that it cuts through the darkness of any preferred reality causing hurt at times. However, each time it wounds them, they know that it is setting them free from that which would eventually blind them to truth, wounding them in greater ways, enslaving their mind, or destroying their soul.

Those who desire to know the truth and nothing but the truth are willing to admit limitations of what they know. They willingly swallow pride when it comes to being wrong about something. They know that to be wrong means the wounding of their arrogance, which includes the possibilities of their fragile egos knowing the sting of embarrassment, as well as the unveiling of their selfishness that insists it must be right to maintain its seat of self-importance.

Truth is a luxury when it comes to the world. It is hidden among lies, ignored when it comes to fantasy, mocked when it comes to the world, and cast aside when it comes to reality. However, truth is the only sharp sword that can set us free from the harsh taskmasters of the world, the chains of the past, and the challenges of the present.

Prayer: Lord, we think we possess the necessary knowledge to direct our life amid its various challenges. We think we have the means to control our world, change the outcomes, and

July 11

"If the son therefore shall make you free, ye shall be free indeed" (John 8:36). We have been considering the different reactions that people have when it comes to truth. The Bible is clear that few will seek out, pursue, and desire the truth over false realities, philosophies, or presumptions. Since people struggle to control their reality, they prefer their own darkness and understanding to the light of the truth that will reveal ineptness, failures, and foolishness.

The light of truth penetrates, exposes, and reveals the source and motive behind all matters. Darkness must part when it is penetrated.. The fogginess of compromise must dissipate when it begins to expose the dangerous environment of rebellion, and ultimately it will reveal the quality of the work that has been going on.

When it comes to those who love the truth, they realize no matter what the light of truth exposes it is necessary to walk in the path of righteousness. They prefer the challenge of the hard way, the cutting of hard sayings, and wounding of the sword of truth that will expose all than the delusion of the world. They shun any preferred realities that are nothing more than fantasies, while refusing to buy the latest fables erected by man to subtly replace the truth as a sick means to console any religious conscience.

Truth will stand when all else falls before it. Idols will be brought down, lies will be silenced, and all false presentations will be dispersed in the end. We must choose to love the truth because that is where liberty, healing, and hope reside. To love the truth is not just about loving God's Word but loving Him. The Word of God is a revelation of Jesus Christ to bring us into a loving relationship with Him. It is made alive to our spirit by the breath and inspiration of His Spirit that not only reveals the Lord to us but allows us glimpses into His glory to bring awe to our souls and worship in our spirits (*John 6:63*).

It is for this reason that our pursuit when it comes to His Word should not be centered on intellectually knowing His Word to maintain our take on religious matters. Our goal should be to come to a greater knowledge of Him so we can discern His voice, understand His ways, recognize and appreciate His intervention, and enter into sweet communion with Him.

Do you love the idea of His Word or do You love His Word because you love the Lord?

Prayer: Lord, we can convince ourselves we love You, but do we love our personal concepts of You, while failing to fall in love with You? The only way we can discern that is by testing our attitude towards Your Word when it has tested, challenged, or revealed our understanding of You. Lord, I want to know YOU! Amen.

July 12

"I the LORD search the heart, I try the reins, even to give every man according to his ways, and according to the fruit of his doings" (Jermiah 17:10). Have you ever noticed the decisions we made in the

past affect our relationships in the present and could very well be setting us up for failure in the future? Instead of learning constructive lessons of the past, we make unrealistic determinations that may isolate us from life, create nightmarish environments in present relationships, and instead of controlling our life, it spins out of control into a downward cycle.

The tragedy is we don't always recognize those determinations that demand we take control of a life that is subject to a world out of control. We are not GOD and the best we can do is find ourselves in a miserable state, inept of having healthy relationships and in an existence that does not protect us from life; rather, it oppresses us from enjoying life and discovering aspects of it that would bring us liberty and joy.

When I first got saved, I felt like the weight of the world had lifted from me. I came to understand the weight was my sins. However, I did not realize what was in my heart. All my life I have been influenced by the world's ideas and ways. I knew I had sin in my life, but I did not realize it was a heart issue until my ways of thinking and doing brought me to a crisis of faith.

Defeat abounded, failure mocked me, and my Christian testimony was greatly tarnished by the perversion of the world that hung like a noose around my neck. It was then that the Lord revealed my attitude and the depth of my fallen state. At that point it was no longer about being saved from the wages of sin, but my great need of being saved from the entanglements and influence of the "old man" on me. I had to deny myself of any rights to life on my terms and become serious about daily crucifying the old man. I had to consecrate myself as a living sacrifice in order to follow Jesus into the life He had for me.

The Lord continues to try the reins of my heart. Every once in awhile He reveals aspects of my character I do not much like, but I know He is loving, faithful, caring, and just when it comes to dealing with me.

Prayer: Lord, You have always been faithful to bring me to places of repentance and growth. My desire is to be submissive so You can bring me to those places of maturity. Keep me on that straight and narrow path to life and righteousness. Amen.

July 13

"Search me, O God, and know my heart: try me, and know my thoughts: And see if there be any wicked way in me, and lead me in the way everlasting" (Psalm 139:23-24). What might we encounter when we give God permission to show us any wicked way in us?

We might find some of our past decisions could be based on unresolved issues. Whether we ignored, stuffed, or perceived we know about them is "good enough" or have tucked them nicely away in some corner of the basement of our soul or some closet of our mind. The problem is an unexpected memory, or a situation begins stirring them up and we find them once again tormenting and depressing us. Sometimes we even develop destructive behavioral patterns because of them.

Our great Physician knows all about such places, but we must come to Him and give Him permission to take His scalpel of truth to them. However, before He can we must also give Him permission to put His healing, purging light on every area of our lives in which these skeletons can be exposed. We must also realize that in light of His great healing balm of promises that can easily be applied with child-like faith, they also can be cast to the wayside by fear or unbelief.

The problem is we do not like our dirty laundry being exposed. What will others say, so we mask them with religious garbs. We put on the appearance of having it all under control as we become indispensable to others with our deeds. We also run about with great zeal to help others, become good workers in the church, or show our undivided devotion by being there every time the doors open.

Christianity is never about masking a problem with religion. It is not about good deeds because we can't make ourselves right before the Lord, therefore, the question is are we overcompensating for something we ourselves refuse to face? What are we hiding? What are we masking?

We must be like Jeremiah who confesses that the heart is deceitful and who can know it but the Lord who tries it to reveal it (*Jeremiah 17:9-10*). We also must always be like King David, willing to ask the Lord to take His light and reveal if there is any wicked way in us that would prevent us from seeing any corner, small closet, or space where darkness hides what truly ails us when it comes to our spiritual walk before the Lord.

Prayer: Lord, we like to think we are reasonable people but so often we are afraid of what we will see. Even though it is unnerving, we also know You will always bring us to places of seeing a matter for what it is to You. Lord, open my eyes so I may clearly see what is true in Your sight. Amen.

July 14

"…let us lay aside every weight, and the sin which doth so easily beset us, and let us run with patience the race that is set before us" (Hebrews 12:1b). What sins are being masked, hidden, or tormenting that could be stopping you from running the race set before you?

Through the years, I have watched many people whose lives before God seemed dead in the water or their faith shipwrecked on sandbars of disillusionment, along the shorelines of false hopes, or on the hidden reefs of unbelief. These people seemed traumatized, confused, and aimless.

There are three things that ails the soul: rebellion, sin (not just our sins), and Satan. In one of my latest Bible Studies, I compared these three things to what ails the body in this way: toxins (rebellion), parasites (sin), and environmental factors (Satan). We often mask what ails the body with drugs, but what about the soul? We mask what ails the soul with the doctrines of demons, traditions of man, and the rudiments of the world's inept philosophies.

In desperation we can find ourselves running here and there to find the answer to nagging questions about life that are ready to cause our faith to be taken down by some whirlpool. Meanwhile we are looking to worldly methods to bring resolution to that which makes our existence seem pointless. We can also, in grave confusion and disillusion, try grabbing ahold of some wishful thinking and fleeting promise and possibility that man can make the impossible happen when all his flattery, rhetoric, and promises cover up the fact he is powerless. The most man can do is offer us false promises and hope that somewhere along the line God will have mercy on us in spite of fleshly claims, worldly methods, and empty assurances.

We tend to mask the fact that there may be much activity in our religion, but no power. We may be dancing around the altars, but there is no fire to show any acceptance of any of it by God. We may be talking about revival in Churches but there is no move of God who is the only One that can bring revival.

This brings us back to why must we mask anything, unless it is to hide the fact that God is missing from most of it or perhaps all of what we are doing in His name. The emptiness of our activities implies whatever we are doing in His name means we are also using His name in vain.

We must individually answer these thought-provoking questions before we can expect them to become a match that lights the fire on the neglected altars of the hearts of others. I believe this is the great challenge of this time.

Prayer: Lord, I believe You are constantly putting forth the challenge to Your people, but can we hear it through all of our religious activities? Will we honestly examine the real fruits of it with the intent to repent of all such fleshly, useless activities and turn to You in true consecration of wholly offering up our bodies, surrendering ours souls for Your service, and giving way to the sanctifying work of Your Spirit? Amen.

July 15

One thing you can do in old age that you can't do in your young age is to remember a whole lot of "stuff" that occurred in your young age.

For example, it seems like just yesterday I was maybe twenty years old, and was dating a young, handsome, well-to-do single man that my stepdad had met in his auto repair shop.

He was hoping that it would be a "match" because the young man was from a very well-to-do family. In fact, his future potential was millions, if not more, because his extended family owned a well-known American snack company. The problem (if you can call it a "problem") was that my beliefs and ideas were well-established. Therefore, when we got around to discussing our individual ideas about future marriage and such, he let me know right up front that he expected his wife to be a career woman so that he could continue to live in the manner to which he was accustomed.

Thankfully, I wasn't "in love with him" at this point and thereafter let him drift off to find just the "right woman" to guarantee his plush lifestyle wouldn't be threatened or compromised. My stepdad was a bit disappointed, but I was "old fashioned" and believed that, if at all possible, wives were to be keepers of the home in line with what the Bible teaches.

Of course, the world is such a contrary mess in these end days because of sin and the wiles of the devil that we all know what has happened to God's order in this regard. The sad thing concerning the young man was that his total focus and goal was set on riches, and what money could do for him. The idea of having enough to provide for a modest "middle class American life" was beneath his perceived position and stature in life. It was also obvious that his desire for excessive abundance was a priority over relationships with others or with God Himself.

In our world today, with all of its perplexities, turmoil, strife and chaos, along with the battle that rages between good and evil, you often hear the statement, "Follow the money." If you do pick up that trail, do your research, examine all the facts, examine the "fruit," and discern the spirit behind it, you will inevitably discover that, indeed, *"...the love of money is the root of all evil, which while some coveted after, they have erred from the faith and pierced themselves through with many sorrows" (2 Timothy 6:10).*

If a person's love for money is greater than their love for the LORD Jesus Christ, then their heart is no better than that of Judas Iscariot who sold our LORD for 30 pieces of silver. – J. Haley

Prayer: Lord, we do not always know where our affections lie until we are faced with having to consider what we value in this life. The world has nothing to offer, but You offer us abundant life, an eternal inheritance, and a forever future in Your glory. Sadly, in our spiritual poverty and foolishness we can even gamble that away on vanity. Forgive us. Amen.

July 16

"Behold God is my salvation; I will trust, and not be afraid: for the LORD JE-HO'VAH is my strength and my song; he also is become salvation. (Isaiah 12:2). How can I keep from being afraid in a frightening world? Know that God is the total sum of my salvation.

I want you to note that God IS my salvation. Salvation points to deliverance. We must be delivered from the hold of this present world on our life, the wages of sin upon our souls, and the claims of Satan upon our minds. That means God is my present source of deliverance from that which is destructive, oppressive, and unbearable. As a believer, I have been translated from the kingdom of darkness into the kingdom of light, but by faith I must walk in that light to discover its benefits.

The second term I want to note is that the Lord is BECOME salvation to me. We ask God to save us, but has He become salvation to us? In the first declaration of salvation, I must recognize He is the way of salvation but in the second one HE IS THE ESSENCE OF MY SALVATION. Is there a difference?

The answer is yes. I seek Him to save me but once I come to salvation, I realize He is my Savior and that my hope is in Him, my life is hidden in Him, and my future has been secured in Him. It is His work of redemption that delivers me, but it is who He is and must be that He becomes the essence of my salvation.

So many times, we ask the Lord to save us or deliver us FROM something, but how many of us trust Him to deliver US THROUGH a matter that is not pleasant, overwhelming, and destructive? We may trust Him to a point with our souls, but fail to trust Him with our very lives, our inner being, and the circumstances that could greatly affect our life.

The challenge for Christians is to not only understand salvation is a complete work, but we have a responsibility to work it in and out of our lives. Our deliverance from the claims of sin and its wages of death on our life is present because we have the Holy Spirit working the very life of Christ in us.

Christ's life is eternal, always ongoing. His life is a gift, a matter of grace that flows from above, enriching our lives with its various workings. It is a point of identification with an eternal inheritance attached to it that we will discover in the ages to come.

Prayer: Lord, we can begin to know the great work of redemption when we are saved, the ongoing work of grace when we walk by faith and be assured of the future inheritance attached to it because of our hope in light of all Your promises. Thank You for securing my redemption. Amen.

July 17

"Therefore with joy shall ye draw water out of the wells of salvation" (Isaiah 12:3). Jesus' payment for our redemption was complete. It is for this reason that the Lord is the author and essence of my salvation. It is His life in me that gives me assurance, His Spirit that is my point of identification and inspiration, and His Word my food. The truth is the Lord is my all in all. It is for this reason He is enough when it comes to the essence of my faith.

For God to be my salvation, He must be my foundation, the source of my reliance, the Rock that never moves from what is so, as well as from what He says in His Word. He is the One who can flood my soul with such joy that it overflows even amid challenging times.

He is also the One who I draw all of my inspiration, hope, and assurance from Him, for He has provided the wells of salvation.

The wells of salvation to me are Jesus, and the many aspects of His work of salvation. Salvation comes by way of redemption because of Jesus' grace, in light of His mercy, in accordance with His Father's plan. The water that can be drawn freely from Him is the rivers of Living Water, the Holy Spirit.

My great desire is that God is your salvation because you have freely come to the wells of salvation to partake of them, to assimilate the life of Jesus. You came seeking forgiveness and life everlasting, but my hope is that He has become salvation to you because you continue to draw and drink of Living Waters from the true well of salvation.

Prayer: Lord, we stop at Your cross when it comes to obtaining salvation, but how many of us continue on to discover the fullness of that salvation that is found in You? Lord, I don't want to settle for a mere drop or sip of Your water, I want to bathe in its cleansing ability, drink in its fullness to know satisfaction, and get in its current to know the power of it to bring me into the fullness of the eternal and abundant life You have for me. Amen.

July 18

"And he said unto me, My grace is sufficient for thee: for my strength is made perfect in weakness" (2 Corinthians 12:9a). I often go to this scripture to remind myself that at the point of my weakness I will discover God is my strength. In a previous post I wrote about God being our strength and our song.

Lately, I have been struggling with my strength. Due to some physical things going on, I have very little energy, and strength requires energy to carry out the most minimal tasks.

When we are young, we often take our strength for granted. We can't imagine being without it. When we feel on top of something, we even can see our strength as making us invincible. The problem with personal strength is that we naturally rely on it to exercise abilities without thinking about the energy it takes. At such times we fail to consider our great need for God no matter what we do. This is when our strength becomes a point of greatest weakness as it sets us up in one way or the other to find out that it is limited even when it is operating at its peak level.

The Apostle Paul learned that oftentimes God allows infirmities in His saints' life to teach each of us about the limitations of our strength. It is in weakness we realize that it is God's grace that meets us, and that it is sufficient for whatever occasion to see us through to the end. The reason it is sufficient enough is because it is like a river that flows into different tributaries and channels.

The channels of grace bring that which will enable us to stand on what is so. It allows us to walk according to what is promised, and trust that it will see us through to the end of a matter because there is no disruption from its ongoing flow upon and in our lives.

Paul weaknesses brought disruption to his walk for him to truly learn how to walk in the strength of God's grace. It was for this reason he could embrace the weaknesses while rejoicing in his infirmities. He knew as weakness enveloped him that he would experience the strength of God to see him fulfill his calling.

Prayer: Lord, we often fail to realize that You alone are the strength behind all matters. We can feel self-sufficient until we come face to face with our weaknesses. It is then we realize we need You. Amen.

July 19

"...Most gladly therefore will I rather glory in my infirmities, that the power of Christ may rest upon me" (1 Corinthians 12:9b). It is hard to face our weaknesses because they cause us to feel vulnerable and out of control.

I have to admit that without energy and strength, it sometimes takes everything in a person to put one foot in front of the other, but the point is that those steps can cause one to become thankful that they can take them regardless of how slow and burdensome they may seem because there are those who can't. Every step reminds such a person that it is a gift from God, and that by faith one will gain the necessary spiritual strength to stand, continue on the course, and endure to the end. It is all about perfecting in me a testimony that will stand distinct and bring Him honor.

The thing that causes me to almost skip, even in my weaknesses, is that God is my song (*Isaiah 12:2*). It takes strength to talk and sing. Perhaps, I don't have the strength to dance before His altar but thanks to the breath of His Spirit, I will have the means to sing praises within my soul, to speak of those things that are precious to Him in silent prayer, to adore Him in quiet adoration, and to stand in awe of His majesty as I allow the worship of the heart to speak for me.

The one thing I have learned about an anointed song is, it often comes out of great darkness. Darkness points to some limitation, but even in such times, God is composing a melody within my spirit, a harmony within my soul, and lyrics upon my heart that I can sing back to Him in communion for His pleasure and glory.

Prayer: Lord, sometimes we are so shortsighted and miserable about what we can't do, we forget about what You want to do—to become our strength, to endow us with grace and to write a song upon our heart that we will be able to sing back to You in loving praise and worship. Amen.

July 20

"Then sang Moses and the children of Israel this song unto the LORD, and spake, I will sing unto the LORD for he hath triumphed gloriously. The horse and his rider hath he thrown into the sea" (Exodus 15:1). In the last post, I talked about the Lord being our song. He is composing the song in our heart that will speak of His glorious ways, intervention and deliverance.

The concept of songs in Scripture has caught my attention more than once. I recently read how the singing and chirping of the birds early in the morning is what signals flowers to open up to the sun to embrace its rays. How many times has your soul heard the call of the dove and marveled at how it affects you?

Depending on what time of day you hear the dove will determine how it affects your soul. In the morning, it can come across as seeking, during the day it can sound almost content as it stirs in the midst of the bird seed left behind, and at dusk, it sounds lonely. It can create a bit of expectation, anticipation, and melancholy in you.

We have also read the healing affects bells have on a person and the fact that in the music industry they will not promote artists who will not perform according to a certain megahertz that creates an altered reality that harbors anger, rebellion, and almost an insanity in the hearer. This of course is in accordance to wicked agendas. We know there is music around the throne of heaven and that the Lord gives us a new song according to various Scriptures in *Psalms.* In *Revelation 5:9* and *14:3* there will be a new song being sung around the throne.

I say this because in whatever God does, it is to bring us to perfection. "Perfection" points to purity. I have told my friend who has a tremendous singing voice that unless God inspires her and anoints the song, and it comes only from a pure heart, she must not offer it. When something such as an anointed song becomes a duty, it is made common. When something of God is rendered a fleshly exercise, it becomes corrupted. If it becomes a worldly performance that stirs up the flesh and emotions, it becomes profane.

Songs must not be a mixture of what man can do to help God in this world, as in the case of bringing down Satan or establishing a kingdom for Jesus to reign in. Anointed songs will be all about GOD and what He has done on behalf of man because of redemption, and what He will do because He has declared it as being so.

A song must be a testimony that must be void of nonsense that reveals the foolish thinking of man in light of his hypocrisy. It must show God's greatness and man's smallness to ensure humility. It must be solely about the LORD GOD ALMIGHTY who lived, was crucified, but now lives in possession of the keys of hell and death and who will live for evermore (*Revelation 1:18*).

Prayer: Lord, we have managed to make You small in what You can do, humanize You while deifying man in some way to lay claims to that which is impossible, and to give the impression the future rests in the hands of man instead of in light of Your sovereign ways and power to bring it all about. The changes seem harmless enough, but they are blasphemous to You and profane the truth and hope of a matter. Forgive us Lord, for our unbelief, our fleshly ways, and our arrogant opinions of ourselves. Amen.

July 21

"And they sing the song of Moses the servant of God and the song of the Lamb, saying, Great and marvellous are thy works. Lord God Almighty; just and true are thy ways, thou King of saints" (Revelation 15:3). What will the new song be and what are the songs of Moses and the Lamb of God?

As mentioned in the last post, I related how certain vibrations and megahertz promote healing and well-being, as well as bring destruction. Are such notions true? I believe so because God created music to inspire our spirits to soar, uplift our hearts in praise, soothe the soul in consolation, and bring us to a place of awe and worship.

Why must there be a new song? Because He is forever doing new and wondrous things in our life. Some will prove to be deep, bringing a greater awareness of His abiding care on our lives. Other songs will express the heights of God one has been exposed to that are too wondrous to express in mere words such as Paul and the third heaven. There will be those revelations that will inspire songs that will lead others to true worship.

We all have our way of expressing ourselves, but it is obvious that one of the means through which God reveals His great work in us is through song. When I look at the old hymns, I can see where many were written in the dark night of the soul, revealing how God proved to be their Rock when there was nothing else to cling too. Some were written in great despair when there was no hope but God. Some were rejoicing in His deliverance, revelations, and unfailing love, unending grace, and His mercies and compassions that are new every day.

How do you know something is of God? It usually comes with a personal price that allows one to know God in greater ways and it becomes a testimony about Him and His works. It ends in worship and not fleshly hype. It silences the flesh, humbles the soul, and ends in awe in the spirit towards God.

It is about what God is doing, not what man can do to help God so he can make declarations about what he is doing in the name of God. It is void of man's involvement, making it God-centered, and not man-centered. I say this because many of our so-called "songs" of today are minus the true inspiration of the Spirit that ends in worship of our true God. There is His truth that liberates the soul, giving liberty to the lips to truly offer up the sacrifice of praise to Him, taking away any fear of ending up being a Cain, who in the end became insulted because God would have nothing to do with unholy or unacceptable sacrifices.

It is time that man truly examines his religious exercises and experiences to make sure they do not prove to be useless. We must never settle for religious crumbs when we can feast at the table of His Word. We must partake of His holiness, come to the fountain of His salvation, drink freely of the water of His Spirit, and be part of His household, family, and kingdom, knowing an eternal inheritance of promises and blessings await us.

Prayer: Lord, I marvel at how You work with mere flesh. You can prepare man's fickle heart, anoint his lips with purging fire, awaken his soul, and quicken his spirit to provide him with a sacrifice You can receive for Your pleasure, an acceptable, good, and perfect sacrifice that will bring glory and honor to You. Amen.

July 22

"Therefore to him that knoweth to do good, and doeth it not, to him it is sin" (James 4:17). What motivates you? It seems like a simple

question, and you might recall that I have dealt with this subject in the past. We know that spirit, which is associated with attitude and intent, plays a big part behind motivations, but so do moods, feelings, and character.

There are four motivating factors behind what we do. The first one has to do with "wanting" to do something. People who want to do something will not let themselves be deterred from it whether it is to gain something they desire or pursuing something that they perceive will benefit them. "Wants" are often based on selfishness.

The second factor has to do with being "forced" to do something whether out of responsibility, commitment, or necessity. It may be something we would not do because of an indifferent mood towards certain matters of life.

Such a mood is often a product of laziness and ingratitude, as well as self-serving feelings that are based on how something will make us feel or look. At such times our character will also be exposed. We discover that the ways of life are choices that will not allow for shortcuts. But for one reason or the other we must carry something out or suffer possible loss, repercussions, or negative consequences that would not fare well. When it comes to this unpleasant factor, people can greatly resent having to deal with any unpleasant fallout.

The third factor is "self-respect." This is a term that is not used much, but for me I respect my life, reputation, and witness enough that I will do my best no matter how I feel about a matter because it will say much about the character of my person. Often doing something out of showing proper respect to maintain character can bring recognition that highlights the quality of what a person can and will do.

Honorable attitudes and conduct bring a certain amount of confidence and goodwill in what one does. It earns respect from others towards what the person accomplishes because of its integrity. As a Christian, my character must be beyond reproach, or I will not earn the type of respect I need for a person to trust what I say. Ultimately, I will not be able to have some effect on them that might make an eternal difference.

The final factor is "doing what is right because it is the right thing to do." I know very few people who will do something just because it is the right thing to do. It is easy to find reasons for falling short of doing right.

People are prone to do anything except what is right even though in the end it would serve their purpose well if they did. It is easy to give in to the excuses that allow me to stop short, evade, ignore, and brush aside what is right. However, as a believer I want to do what is right because nothing else makes sense when it comes to my walk with and before the Lord.

I don't do what is right because I must, if I did it would be in a wrong attitude that would make it wrong. I don't do what is right because I feel like it because doing right is not about feelings and will often come at a point of inconvenience or even with a cost that would reveal the real nature of my heart attitude. I don't do right to receive recognition, because doing right is not about me, but about God being glorified in the end because it is right to Him and a matter of faith and obedience on my part to that which is godly no matter the cost or inconvenience.

The question is what motivates you the most, especially when it comes to those things in life that will not bow to your wants, serve your purpose, and bring desired recognition to you?

Prayer: Lord, I like to think I do everything because I am "so wonderful," but the truth is I do everything because You are the One who is so wonderful and You deserve the best I can do towards others, knowing that the least I can do is what is right when it comes to the life You have given me. Thank You Lord for giving me all I have need of to experience You. Amen.

July 23

Is it really all that bad finding yourself all alone out in "left field"? I suppose the answer to that depends on a number of things, but to me, when I was in the sixth grade, it was literally as low as you could go when teams were chosen for a softball game.

There we all stood, out on the play field in the dust and the dirt, waiting for the team captains to pick their players. At that young age kids don't know the fine art of controlling facial expressions (and audible noises that can sometimes express more than words) so that other kids don't get a complex for life. Therefore, by the time everyone was picked except for me, I already knew what the outcome would be.

As for the game itself, my favorite part was swinging the bat. My second favorite part was pitching. After all, I pitched so well that every batter I pitched to hit a home run, so I was relieved of pitching. I never could understand that! The end result was I was told to go out to left field. "Where's that?" I asked. "Waaay out there" a kid said as he pointed to a distant spot that seemed at least a mile away. "What for?" I asked. More than one "instructor" yelled, "IF the ball comes your way, CATCH IT!"

It felt secluded way out there in left field and I felt "detached" from everybody. Plus, it was boring so I sunk into my own thoughts about I can't remember what, when all of a sudden, I heard the kids yelling and screaming, "CATCH THE BALL!!!"

Horror of horrors, I looked up into the sky and saw that descending ball heading straight at me! I only had a nano-second to make my move, but in that nano-second I knew it was going to hurt, maybe even break a finger or two or maybe even my wrist! There would be a lot of pain, but I'd gain some accolades, maybe, from the other kids. It was quick, but I had counted the cost. That ball was coming fast and furious as if it was aimed right at a spot between my eyeballs. That is when I "dodged the bullet" and let it slam into the earth.

Of course, the shouts of dismay and disappointment from the team was worse than sucking on a lemon, but it was all soon forgotten as most things are in life—except for that strange feeling you get when you know that, according to the world's definition of how things should be, you are definitely out in "left field."

The difference is, however, when you make Jesus Lord of your life, you have to count the cost, and part of that cost is being with Him "outside of the camp." You will have no love for the world, and the world will have no love for you. The games that people play to earn themselves popularity, power, and vain pursuits will not interest you, for you have been born again of the Spirit of God.

Jesus said, *"For which of you, intending to build a tower, sits not down first, and counts the cost, whether he has sufficient to finish it?" (Luke 14:28).* Count the cost, beloved: count the cost! *"And they overcame him [Satan] by the blood of the Lamb, and by the word of their testimony; and they loved not their lives unto the death" (Revelation 12:11).*

Have you counted the cost today? – J. Haley

Prayer: Lord, this world is always putting You somewhere so that You will not change the game plans that are fleshly, worldly, and evil. However, You will always hit a homerun when it comes to establishing the way in which we are to walk. I am so thankful You hold the reins of all events in this world. Amen.

July 24

"Now is the judgment of this world, now shall the prince of this world be cast out" (John 12:31). Three times I heard the word judgment the other night in my dreams.

We now, for the most part, live in a type of reality that runs from any concept of adversity and judgment. Unless it is positive, many people's attitude is "I do not want to hear it." Unless it is complimentary, they will shun it. Unless it fits into their small, narrow reality, they will ignore it or mock it. Unless it leaves them feeling good about life and themselves, they will become indifferent or angry about it. The Bible describes such a response as not loving the truth and if we don't love the truth, we will buy a lie and will be removed far from what is the reality of God.

The Bible speaks of three aspects of the world that will prove to be anything but pleasant in most cases: Judgment, tribulation and wrath. Judgment creates a separation. There are four types of judgments mentioned in Scripture: chastisements (separation from rebellion to holiness), judgment seat of Christ (separation of saints into kingdom position based on faithfulness and works), and the judgment of nations based on attitude towards Israel.

The final judgment is the Great White Throne Judgment. This is the separation of the unbeliever from all hope of heaven to the consequences of their unbelief towards the Gospel and the Word. This judgment will reveal all rebellion towards God's authority, as well as pagan and idolatrous practices inspired by the demonic realm. Judgment will always bring us to crossroads where we must decide the way in which we are going to walk.

The next word is "tribulation." Jesus told us to expect it in *John 16:33*. Tribulation comes in four ways. 1) the trying and testing of our faith to ensure the purity of it, 2) adversity and affliction that can bring us to maturity by causing us to take ownership of our lives, attitudes, and conduct, 3) suffering that comes out of usually great anguish and loss that perfects us in our Christian life, and 4) temptation that reveals the strengths and weaknesses of our character. Tribulation must not be confused with wrath. Despite the negative effects of tribulation, it is one of God's tools to do a deeper work in us.

Our flesh will never embrace adversity, and our pride will never bow before tribulation, but faith will resolve to trust God amid all storms of life. It will believe that despite darkness God has not forsaken us and in spite of the loss it leaves behind, God is still guiding us to a greater glory where we will never again know loss, suffering, and despair.

Prayer: Lord, we try to avoid that which would establish true character and unfeigned faith in us. It is natural to do so since the flesh throws a pity party, pride cries foul, and the mind goes into a dark place of depression. Lord, I need to walk by faith, knowing You are guiding me and in due time, I will clearly see Your light. Amen.

July 25

"And to wait for his Son from heaven, whom he raised from the dead, even Jesus, which delivered us from the wrath to come" (1 Thessalonians 1:10). In the last post I spoke of the three aspects of what we call judgment of separation when it comes to God. The first two are judgment and tribulation. The final word associated with separation is "wrath."

Wrath means "anger." There are three sources that wrath comes from: Man, Satan, and God. We must discern between these three. Man's wrath expresses itself in hate, cruelty (torture), vengeance, and destruction because there is no love for God. Satan's wrath is expressed in torment of soul, oppression of mind, possession of body, soul and spirit, and spiritual ruin because there is only hatred towards all of God's creation.

God's wrath is held back out of love to give man time to turn in repentance, flee His wrath to come, and avoid falling into His hands. Since He is an ever-consuming fire, He will burn up all that is profane to Him.

Sadly, man and Satan's wrath are often blamed on God, allowing man to unfairly judge Him, while turning on Him in unbelief, and shaking his fist at Him in defiance. Meanwhile, Satan uses such responses of man to accuse him before God. The enemy tries to use people's unbelief to make his case against God's supposedly "flawed" plan that there will always be that individual who will in the end choose to love Him despite the trials of their faith in this world.

Ultimately, the devil will smirk at the foolishness of man. Man's foolishness gives Satan cause to mock him for being a fool who chose to not believe in God, believe His Word, and in humility receive the truth of it that would remove him from under God's wrath. This brings us to the fact that God's Spirit will not always strive with man; therefore, we do not know how much longer God will give man time to repent for his unbelief, rebellion, and anger.

It is God who puts boundaries on Satan's wrathful advances towards such unbelieving individuals so that they can endure the trials in hopes they will seek out their Creator before the Spirit withdraws His presence. Once He does withdraw, all that person has to look forward to is the wrath of God.

Clearly, we are in times of tribulation where the patience of the saints is being greatly tried. However, God has given us the means to endure the testing of our faith and come out of the fires as a tried gem that indeed reflects His very glory.

Prayer: Lord, You made Paradise for us, but the first man was kicked out of it due to sin and set in the midst of a world that represents the barrenness of his soul and reveals the great judgment that rests upon the world. We are "sitting ducks" in this world until we decide to flee Your wrath by running to Your cross to seek Your mercy and to be saved from the wrath to come. Amen.

July 26

"For with what judgment ye judge, ye shall be judged: and with what measure you mete, it shall be measured to you again" (Matthew 7:2).
In the last couple of posts I talked about judgment. There are three platforms in which man judges a matter. I say this because many people use *Matthew 7:1* to silence all negative judgments against them. It is true we are not to judge unless we are ready to be judged in the same manner. The three platforms in which man uses to judge are opinions based on personal pride (standards) and prejudices, the world's attitudes based on family, religious, cultural influences and philosophies, and God's Word.

It is natural to judge according to personal understanding, but that also puts us in the place of being a judge over matters which include the unseen that we know nothing about. If we are not going off the basis of opinions and conditioned prejudices, we will be going off of fickle feelings that have nothing to do with what is just. Due to pride, man is often blindsided by truth and is brought to hopelessness by reality or driven into obsession by the endless demands to possess something that has no substance to it.

The world's judgments will line up to the agendas and philosophies of the particular age. These agendas are man-centered, which prove wicked and are based on profane philosophies promoted by the lies of the age that are found to be foolish and have nothing to do with truth and what is right and just.

Man does not always accept or promote these agendas, rather these agendas have been used to condition man to parrot them. They are based on presumptions that blind people to their intent and destruction, propaganda that twists the truth at best, and seduction that encourages another reality. Those who come under these agendas come under the spirit of the world, Satan, and not only are required to sell their soul, but eventually they will either drive them into great pits of despair or insanity from the absurdity behind their rationality.

We are told that the way we judge others will be how we are judged. There is no mercy in personal judgments and no righteousness in the world's judgments. If we lack mercy, we will mete out cruelty. When it comes to the world that is, for the most part, indifferent and mocking to God, we will mete out injustices due to the lies of the age and the prejudices against righteousness and the promotion of wickedness.

We must discern our platform before assuming any judgment is correct or presuming that it will be found true in the end because we can't imagine in our arrogance that it is not so. In the end, we will reap what we sow and find our personal judgments to be bitter and condemning to our soul, and our worldly judgments to be mocking, foolish, and intolerant to our spirit.

Prayer: Lord, we are told to examine ourselves, but we would rather judge others so we can be magnified in our own eyes, while making those who do not go along with us or serve our purpose small in our way of thinking. Lord, in the end You will show us how small we are while exalting those who we considered insignificant because the issue with You is, and always will be, humility. Amen.

July 27

"Judge not according to the appearance, but judge righteous judgment" (John 7:24). In the last post, I talked about the three platforms of judgments. There are personal and worldly judgments. These two platforms will exalt us as judges in our minds, but they both fall short of ensuring that we are making wise, just, and fair judgments. Sadly, such judgments are not based on truth and righteousness but untrustworthy rulers

The final judgment is based on God's Word. What most people do not realize about God's judgment is that each judgment towards wrong attitudes, wicked actions, and evil ways will stand no matter the age because they are based on His holy Law, moral character, and truth. For example, the prince of this world has already been judged, while wrong actions already have been condemned as being so by the Law of God. The penalty when it comes to offenses or sins made against God has already been determined: that of death; and that which God loathes and considers abominable have already been clearly defined.

There is also no recourse for Satan, for he is doomed. Man stands condemned in his sin unless he truly repents and lets each offense be addressed by the cross of Christ, for it is appointed for him to die once and then stand in judgment *(Hebrews 9:27).* Meanwhile, the world with its godless systems is subject to God's wrath yet to come.

We are to judge righteous judgment. This simply means we agree with the judgment that has already been made on the matter and will be found to be righteous in the end. Like our laws that have been established to be enforced, these judgments have been recorded as such in God's Word and in due time will be passed down on all offenders.

When we as believers call something sin, it is because the Word has already declared it as so and is not a source of hatred. When we call something an abomination, it is because that is God's definition of it and is not our judgment call. When we warn of the consequences to come, it is because the Bible has already established the penalty against it. We have not added to any of it to make a point, magnified it to try to get man to react, subtracted from it to make it more acceptable, or downplayed it so it won't appear too harsh and unloving. It all comes back to how God's Word presents it in light of God's attitude, character and ways.

It is time God's people quit trying to downplay the consequences for defying the Living God. It is time to cease being embarrassed and apologize for what is going to stand when all else is brought down before the God who will be the Judge all will stand before.

Prayer: Lord, we think that we have the means to judge when in reality our judgments prove to be biased, limited, and unjust. We lack the wisdom of heaven, the insight of Your Word, the discretion of the Holy Spirit to make just judgments. Lord, I want to always be on the side of Your righteous judgment which requires me to ask for more of Your Spirit who will confirm such matters according to Your Word. Amen.

July 28

"For this cause we also, since the day we heard it, do not cease to pray for you, and to desire that ye might be filled with the knowledge of his will in all wisdom and spiritual understanding" (Colossians 1:9).
What does it mean to make sound judgment calls?

As born-again Christians we have the means to judge but we must discern what spirit we are in. When we consider the lawful aspect of matters according to the Lord, they are based on moral integrity that is upheld by love and truth that is backed by wisdom and righteousness that understand discretion.

A righteous judge will declare a tough sentence in sadness because it could have been avoided and a merciful judge will reluctantly pass a just sentence because his preference was to show mercy, but it was not sought. In some cases, the judge will take offense for a grave wrongdoing leveled at the innocent and show great indignation by declaring that the person will be paying the sentence according to the fullness the law allows for such acts.

Man may do what he will with God's judgments according to the age he lives in, but they will stand in the end because they are recorded in His Word. They will be found to be righteous because they are just and will be used in judgment by the Judge of all. The main thing we Christians must be concerned about is the origin of our judgments.

As pointed out in a previous post, if judgments are personal, we will prove to be cruel, unloving judges even if there is some truth to our judgments. If it is based on the world, we will prove to be mockers, skeptics and scorners of those who don't agree with us because their judgments seem obsolete, ridiculous, and stupid. As Christians the only judgments we can stand on is what has already been established by God's Word.

Such judgments are not for us to pass sentence on others, but to warn, contend, advise, and counsel others as to their choices to avoid such judgments. This means pointing them to a sacrifice and a cross where Jesus took the judgment for our wrong-doings, offenses, and foolishness upon Himself and paid the ultimate price to satisfy the requirements and demands of the Law.

It is because I have received that great pardon from the Lord for my many offenses, that I can stand justified and forgiven for my sins, while being set apart for ongoing service, as well as preparing for the glory that awaits me as a citizen of heaven.

Prayer: Lord, it is by Your great work of redemption that I stand on what is true, withstand what was destructive, and now can't help but to continue to stand on because of what has been promised me. Amen.

July 29

Beware of the "Bait and Switch" scam from "parking lot" meat sales of "20 ribeye steaks for $40". You will end up paying about $9 a lb.

for thinly cut, squishy, tasteless meat about the size of a hamburger. Thanks to a courageous woman who dared to brave the cold wind here in North Idaho, and in spite of threats of police intervention from the glowering salesmen, she stood in the parking lot determined to warn potential customers.

We briefly exchanged first names, and when asked if she knew the LORD, she quickly responded, "Oh yes!" I love meeting brave Christians who will take a stand for what is right regardless of opposing circumstances in order to help others from being taken advantage of.

When you stop and think about it, Satan is a master at playing "Bait and Switch" with the innocent and those who have never been properly discipled. The "bait" he used on Eve was to assure her that *"Ye shall not surely die: For God doth know that in the day ye eat thereof, then your eyes shall be opened, and ye shall be as gods, knowing good and evil"* (*Genesis 3:4b-5*).

The enemy of God is forever trying to substitute a lie for the truth, call good "evil", and evil "good", and offer mankind the whole world if he will only sell his own soul. And, just as the slushy "steak" in the little packages is being passed off as a nice, thick, ribeye steak, Satan's "too good to be true" offers only lead to death and destruction. So buyer beware, and Christian be wise through knowledge and exercise of the Word of God, Jesus Christ. - J. Haley

Prayer: Lord, why are we surprised that most of the word is guilty of "Bait and Switch." We are living under Satan's oppressive systems that are always baiting us with facades and false promises to make a switch that robs us and leaves us devastated by the results. Lord, Your death on the cross has to do with the great exchange for what is excellent, but most people in this world would rather put their confidence in the "Bait and Switch" game of Satan. How foolish we prove to be when it comes to our preferences. Amen.

July 30

"Hear the word of the LORD, ye that tremble at his word: Your brethren that hated you, that cast you out for my name's sake; said, Let the LORD be glorified: but he shall appear to your joy, and they shall be ashamed" (Isaiah 66:5). What is your attitude towards the Word? I question my attitude because that is going to tell me a lot about my present attitude towards the Lord. After all, it is His Word that establishes the proper attitude towards Him and the right conduct towards others.

In *Isaiah* we are told about the brethren who may hate us and have evil intentions towards us. I don't know about you, but we have met some of those "Christian brethren" that took some type of issue with us. The truth is, most of the time you don't even know why such individuals took offense unless you were standing for some truth or not going along with the religious flow of a matter and bringing some contrast to them.

The first indication you know something is wrong is that they are behind some type of betrayal. Whether it is revealed through a false accusation, gossip or slander, it often blindsides you, leaving you stunned, because you have no idea that there was any such offense. Keep in mind, such offense is a matter of confusing jealousies, different viewpoints, wounded pride, or a point of embarrassment but whatever it is, it is of the flesh and not in accordance to the love of God and godly conduct.

Such persecution will come and must be expected if you are trying to establish and leave some testimony of your faith behind. The instruction is simple, let God be glorified by displaying Christian virtue during such times. After all, your testimony is not about you being Christian in a matter, but about God's good will towards man on displayed in Jesus and Him crucified.

There is a promise attached to the display of restraint in love and good-will in a challenging situation—that He will appear to us in joy. The joy of the Lord is our strength and our salvation. This points to the strength to stand, and the salvation that will ensure us of deliverance from the sting of betrayal that comes with the world.

And what about those "brethren" that give way to their base disposition and ways? They will be brought to shame. The main reason people are brought to shame is that they do not believe God's Word.

The unbelieving do not tremble before the warnings of the Bible or become sober and obedient about its instructions. They ultimately fail to recognize and become humble about their own plight before Him. In essence, they have never trembled at the aspect of falling into the hands of an angry God, who means what He says and says what He means.

Prayer: Lord, You are clear, the wise will tremble before Your Word and the righteous will walk lightly towards You, knowing they must discern where they are walking. The godly will line up to Your Word, and the good man will take note of his ways to make sure he is not missing the mark. Lord, have Your way and bring us higher in You. Amen.

July 31

"Who hath delivered us from the power of darkness and hath translated us into the kingdom of his dear Son" (Colossians 1:13).
During our time of morning fellowship, Jeannette reminded me it is often in the ordinary that some of the greatest moments impact our lives. We often look to accomplishments, events, years, and days to bring us some type of enlightenment, inspiration, or revelation when so many times it comes within those moments that quickly come and go.

I learned the significance of moments from my father who had Alzheimer's. His great challenge taught me about the importance of moments. The time that my father was actually in the present with clarity to interact came down to moments that had to be seized before the curtain enclosed him into a world that separated him from the reality around him. Those moments were small gifts from God that left me with priceless gems.

Jeannette was sharing how she remembered one incident in her life. It was ordinary in one sense, extraordinary in another way, and ultimately inspiring because of the impact it made on her. She was young at the time when she heard a guest speaker in church share his testimony. His name was Mitsuo Fuchida. Most who are not acquainted with WWII and Pearl Harbor would not recognize this name. However, he is the one who led the first squadron of Japanese bombers against Pearl Harbor and was instrumental in sinking the ship Arizona. It was at 7:53 a.m., he instructed his pilot, Lieutenant Mitsuo Matsuzaki, to send the famous radio message "Tora! Tora! Tora!" to the flagship Akagi, indicating that complete surprise upon the base had been achieved.

Fuchida was a successful and respected hero of Japan due to his many feats as a pilot in WWII to a point they even had a statue of him in his hometown, but what made the lasting impact on him was how he was often miraculously spared from death and why. There was more than one occasion that his life was spared.

When American aircraft hit his flagship Akagi, the resulting fires forced the evacuation of the bridge. During his escape, an explosion threw him from pending death, breaking both his ankles but sparing his life. I remember reading about an incident where he was recuperating from surgery in sick bay when the ship he was on was bombed, but he was thrown from sick bay into the ocean while others perished. He narrowly escaped death in Hiroshima, having left the city the day before the atomic bombing on August 6, 1945. The following day, he was sent to assess the damage, and remarkably, he was the only member of the assessment team who did not die from radiation poisoning. Amazingly, this once devoted and zealous pilot to the cause of Japan became an American citizen in 1960.

Why was this man miraculously spared and why the change? He had a greater mission and that was the Gospel of Jesus Christ. He met Jesus Christ and became a true heir of salvation that was translated from the kingdom of darkness into the glorious kingdom of the Son of God. He became an evangelist that traveled through the

United States as an ambassador on two fronts. He was an ambassador of peace and healing between two nations ripped apart by war, while advocating the only way to true and lasting peace and healing as an ambassador of Christ.

At the time Jeannette heard Fuchida's testimony, she was 19 years old. Keep in mind she is now in her early 80's s and was left overwhelmed by the power and inspiration of it. She went up to him, shook his hand and stated, "You're wonderful." His simple reply was a moment that became frozen in time and in her memory. He looked at her while pointing upwards and stated, "No, JESUS is wonderful."

Prayer: Lord, we look for great things to inspire us when it is those moments that make sense out of the senseless, bring awe to us in the midst of the ordinary, and remind us that nothing happens without a reason in the lives of Your saints. Amen.

August

August 1

For he is our peace, who hath made both one, and hath broken down the middle wall of partition" (Ephesians 2:14). Although this verse has to do with the partition between Jews and Gentiles, there are so many types of walls and partitions erected between others that can only be brought down by the Lord.

The truth is God can never allow these partitions to stand because we can never know how our experience will affect others. Have you ever heard of Jacob DeShazer? He was on one of the planes that was part of the Doolittle Raiders that were sent on a suicide mission to bomb Japan during WWII.

DeShazer was very outspoken about his hatred towards those who attacked Pearl Harbor. In fact, he declared that if could get his hands on the bomber, Mitsuo Fuchida, who led the attack against Pearl Harbor, he would slit his throat. Although most of his crew survived the expected crash landing of their plane, the USS Hornet, they were faced with the horrors of being captured by the Japanese.

DeShazer and the crew endured much abuse and torture by the hands of their captors, and DeShazer was one of the few who survived the 40-month ordeal. The one overseeing the camp was the worst of the lot when it came to torturing the prisoners and later managed to avoid being tried for his war crimes against humanity. This man's abuse caused DeShazer's hatred towards the Japanese to become all consuming, but it all changed for him when in his ordeal he was handed a Bible by one of the guards. Since it was the only material that they had to read, the crew took turns reading it.

DeShazer took full advantage of reading it when it was his turn, and eventually he had a real encounter with Jesus Christ.

The ironic part of the story is that DeShazer felt the call of God on his life. He married, went to Bible College and became a missionary to the one place you think he would avoid that many missionaries did at that time, Japan. Under his ministry it is estimated that 30,000 Japanese came to Christ including the guard who gave DeShazer the Bible. Even though he would meet and share Christ with the overseer of the camp, the man saw no need to repent in order for Jesus to be in his life and save him.

In 1948, another encounter indirectly took place near the Hachiko statue outside Shibuya Station in Tokyo. Mitsuo Fuchida, the one DeShazer vowed to slit his throat, was handed DeShazer's pamphlet about being a prisoner of war in Japan.

This pamphlet profoundly impacted Fuchida's attitude towards Americans, particularly after he purchased a New Testament the following year. By 1950, he met DeShazer, and this meeting further inspired Fuchida to become a Christian missionary. In 1952, he toured the United States as a member of the Worldwide Christian Missionary Army of Sky Pilots, declaring himself an ambassador of peace.

What caused DeShazer, a man from Oregon to have such a change of heart? It began with him pondering Jesus' simple request from the cross, "Father, forgive them, for they know not what they do." He realized that true freedom comes through forgiveness and not hatred. He begged God to grant him the same resurrection power to take away his hatred. The next day he woke up a new man, and it was said, that the guards even took note of it.

Two lives operating from conflicting poles, two men with like passions but on opposite sides crossed the great divide of hatred by way of the redemption of Jesus Christ. Two men who were enemies became brothers in the Lord. Two men sent to the other's country to be ambassadors for the same Lord and Savior. I don't know about you, but to me that is the miraculous work of redemption, the incredible manifestation of God great love, the power of the Gospel unto salvation, and the glorious revelation of how men's lives are completely revolutionized by one Person's great sacrifice on behalf of all, the God/Man, the Lord Jesus Christ.

Prayer: Lord, we have our pet doctrines, our platitudes, and our religious traditions, but do we possess that which is miraculous, walk in that which is incredible, experience that which is powerful, and have been revolutionized by that which is heavenly and glorious? These are the real marks that we have passed from the darkness of the old into Your glorious light to walk in the newness of Your life. Amen.

August 2

"Wherefore I was grieved with that generation, and said, They do always err in their heart; and they have not known my ways" (Hebrews 3:10). Recently, the word, "way" came up in a time of fellowship. There is man's way that he adheres to because he sees himself as being right and feels the conviction to hold to it no matter what. There is the world's way which makes logical sense and is acceptable to the masses; therefore, it seems normal. Man's way is often sought or desired while the world's way is preferred, but there is a third way, and that is God's way.

The Bible is clear that the ways of man seem right in his own eyes, but God weighs the spirit or motive. The world's way seems like it is the way to go if you want to be part of the in-crowd, but one can find themselves in a current of destruction like those who yelled for Christ to be crucified without understanding that they were in essence sheep being led to the slaughter. In the end sheep are ultimately brought to some altar where they are offered up in the name of some religious movement or cause.

Man's way tends to go with the flesh and when it comes to the world's way they tend to go with philosophies or logic of that time. When it comes to the flesh, we will go with what feels right and when it comes to the world, we will go along with what seems rational.

Sadly, the flesh is fickle and the world self-serving, and you can't trust either to hit the right mark.

When it comes to God's way, there is only one right way. If a man fails to walk in God's way, he will err in his heart and choose a way that may appear religious and acceptable, but it will miss the mark of doing what is right in the end.

God disciplined the way the children of Israel walked in the wilderness as they followed the pillar during the day and rested before the fire of God's Spirit at night, but they never really repented of wanting their way or in the end preferring the ways of the world. They maintained the attitude of the idolatrous world that served as their option and held on to their fleshly tastes that still held their affections.

What way are you walking in? Perhaps the question we need to ask ourselves is do we even know what it means to walk in the ways of God? The Bible tells us how to walk in the ways of God, but do we take note of it? Do we do everything we can to line up to it? And, finally, do we really believe this is the way of God and that we need to simply walk in it to ensure we finish our course that leads us to our final destination and inheritance?

Prayer: Lord, You have given us the map of Your Word to show us Your way. You have given us the compass of Your Spirit to walk in it, and the mileposts of Your life, examples, and teachings to follow along the way. There are no excuses as to why we are not in the way except we are void of the necessary faith to walk in Your way. Forgive us for our unbelief. Amen.

August 3

"And thou shalt remember all the way which the LORD thy God led thee these forty years in the wilderness, to humble thee, and to prove thee, to know what was in their heart, whether thou wouldest keep his commandments or no" (Deuteronomy 8:2). What does it mean to

walk in the way of God? The way has to do more with the person and work of Jesus Christ who stated, "I am the way."

Jesus clearly went before us and cleared the way for us to walk by way of redemption. He hung on a cross to show us the way. He went into the ground to not hide the way but to show that it leads to new life by way of death to the old and burial of it. Like Lazarus we may come out of the grave with the graveclothes of the old clinging to us, but we will be raised in a new life.

Resurrection allows the new life to come forth. There can be no resurrection without there first being a death. We even see this concept in relationship to discipleship. We are called to deny ourselves of the right to live the old life in order to be effective in crucifying it so we can follow Him into a new, disciplined life that leads to our eternal inheritance.

We see that the Lord led the children of Israel in the wilderness to first humble and prove them to reveal what was in their heart. And what would prove that they truly decided to love and follow the Lord was whether they obeyed His commandments.

Has the testing and proving changed when it comes to Christianity? Not really. Our faith is tested by the challenges of this life, and our devotion is tried by the harshness of the spiritual wilderness of this world. In the end it will reveal our heart towards the Lord. Jesus stated that if we love Him, we will keep His commandments (*John 14:15*).

This brings us back to whether we are walking in the way of God. We can conform to religion as long as it serves our purpose and the minute it doesn't, we will erect our own religious altar. We can perform our religious duties, but if God does not meet our standard, we can erect our own golden calf. It all comes back to the fact that if God does not pamper our fragile egos, protect us from ourselves by giving us our way, or keep us from the hour of temptation that reveals our real source of reliance and hope, we have our old idols to fall back on.

The key is, and always will come back to whether we love God because of who He is, or are we in love with the idea of what He can do for us. I have watched many people walk away from the Lord because in their way of thinking, He somehow failed THEIR test. They were testing God while He was revealing that they did not really believe His intention towards them and love Him after all.

Prayer: Lord, we act offended when You fail our test. We feel justified because we gave You a chance to prove Yourself. We failed to see the arrogance in our thinking, the foolishness in our evaluations and the blasphemy in our judgments. Lord, I am so thankful You know my frame, and You are longsuffering towards me in my foolish state and in light of my inept ways. Amen.

August 4

"...and the soul of the people was much discouraged because of the way" (Numbers 21:4b). I love to study the children of Israel's journey through the wilderness. We tend to be hard on them in our judgment of their foolish ways, but the reality is we are no different in our journey through this world.

Jesus warned us the way of the cross and true discipleship was hard, and like the children of Israel we can find ourselves grumbling about it. We would think we would learn from past examples, but the truth is we are often divorced from discerning our own heart attitude and reactions.

The main reason for our attitude is because we are living in the realm of familiarity that we often end up scorning. For example, every day God provided manna for the children of Israel, but they long forgot to see the miraculous in it and loathed it (*Numbers 21:5*). We, as believers, have been provided with the Living Bread from heaven, Jesus, but how many of us are grumbling that in spite of possessing Him we can only see what fails to serve our notions about the Christian life that is hard on the flesh, indifferent to the pride, and costs us our right to call the shots?

In this incident the children of Israel were experiencing physical thirst but instead of humbling themselves and seeking God to provide the water, they ended up accusing Him and Moses of playing a terrible joke on them. How many of us who experience some type of lack end up falsely accusing God rather than seeking Him and trusting Him to provide the need when necessary?

It is important to point out that in a like incident in *Number 20* is where you find the people accusing Moses and Aaron of leading them astray because they needed water. In the first incident Moses and Aaron were receiving the brunt end of their discontentment. However, it was the leadership that God tested in the second incident and sadly both the brothers failed to sanctify the Lord in the eyes of the people. In the incident in *Numbers 21*, it was the people's test, and we see where they foolishly came directly against God.

Instead of sending in water or bread, the Lord sent in serpents. The people were wise enough to see their sin and repent, but are we wise enough to see our sin of unbelief and repent, or do we justify ourselves?

The people of Israel asked the Lord to remove the serpents, instead God provided the solution. It is natural that after seeing the error of our ways to ask God to remove the temptation of sin, the test to our faith, or the sting of consequences, but the truth is God has already provided the solution, Jesus Christ. God's solution will require us to humble ourselves, confess our sin and ask the Lord to open our eyes so we can clearly see the way out He has provided for us.

The next time you read about the children of Israel, be careful how you judge them, because you could very well find yourself tasting the bitterness of your own rebellious ways.

Prayer: Lord, we often think we are an exception to the rule, exempt from such foolish ways, or too intelligent to be party to the same ways of the children of Israel, but the reality is they are our example as to what traps we can fall into. Give us wisdom to learn, faith to see, and discernment to know what we are looking at when it comes to our personal walk before You. Amen.

August 5

It's amazing how certain things remain in your memory through the years while other things simply evaporate. I guess it's the lasting impact, or impression on you that "sticks"—kind of like hay that sticks in your clothes after you slide down a haystack (which never makes your mother happy by the way).

What has come to mind lately is the common, ordinary, and often overlooked people who love God, and whom He loves and uses in ways that others miss, such as Beanie. I don't think I ever knew Beanie's proper name because everyone knew her by her nickname. She was married, and had two sons, but I never saw her husband in church. Perhaps you can remember way back when church was more about loving and worshipping God than about bigger buildings, bigger budgets, and bigger crowds.

Back then they actually had choirs, and if they could swing it, even choir robes. They practiced God-glorifying, sound doctrine hymns with the pianist and organist during the week and then stood up on Sunday mornings to lead the congregation into the presence of God. In my mind's eye, I can still see Beanie standing in the back row of that small church choir, singing her heart out to the Lord she loved, and I can also recall the anguished looks on the faces of the people around her because, sad to say, Beanie couldn't sing a single note on key!

Now, over 60 years later, I ponder the real message Beanie wanted to sing to the world. It is a message of selfless adoration of her Lord no matter what others thought or did. Her home and hospitality were always open to young or old, for all were welcome there. She glowed with love, joy and enthusiastic faith, as she unashamedly shared Jesus with everyone.

I believe that Beanie knew in her heart of hearts that "perfection in our performance" is not what pleases God, but instead, *"He hath showed thee, O man, what is good; and what doth the LORD require of thee, but to do justly, and to love mercy, and to walk humbly with thy God" (Micah 5:8)*. – J. Haley

Prayer: Lord, You put before us examples of those who truly love and worship You, but we often fail to recognize them as such because we are more in tune with the pitch and tones of the world and not that of Your heavenly altar. Forgive us. Amen.

August 6

"We are of God: he that knoweth God heareth us; he that is not of God heareth not us. Hereby know we the spirit of truth, and the spirit of error" (1 John 4:6). How many people do you know who struggle with their salvation? It is easy to encourage people to think that as long as they say the "sinner's prayer" they are alright and on their way to heaven.

Is it that simple? The answer is yes and no. It is that simple if one embraces salvation with child-like faith and is truly born again from above because they have repented by turning away from the old to embrace the new. However, it is not that simple if the individual was caught up with some type of sentiment that swept them up with the rest of the crowd to go forward as they followed some person in prayer.

There is a difference between mental **ASSENT** to accept something as being so and the humble **DESCENT** of a sinner who truly realizes in their heart, while receiving it by faith, that they are doomed and hopeless without God's intervention that was brought forth through His Son's redemption of lost souls on the cross. The first one may be enticed by the sentiment of the love and blessings of God, but the second one is seeking the mercy of God in the hope of experiencing the grace of God through the great gift of eternal life.

The problem with assent is that it misses the heart by 18 inches as it ascends upward on the steps of knowledge, and yet it is with the heart we must believe the Gospel and receive it into our very inner being as being so to ensure salvation of our souls. It is from the premise of humility wrought by God's incredible mercy that one realizes that the Christian life is a life of "ascent," but not intellectually, but in developing the attitude of Christ towards all matters, according to faith and obedience to His Word.

The Christian life is a life where one looks up and presses forward through the terrain of the present world. It is a walk where the soul becomes teachable and receptive to the Spirit of truth, which allows for their spirit to take hold of what is eternal in order to soar in the heights of His promises and glory in praise and worship.

The real witness that gives us assurance of salvation is the presence of the Holy Spirit, the very breath of God pulsating in our life that identifies us to our new birth. He is the heavenly witness that serves as our endowment and the earthly witness along with the water of the Word and the blood of the covenant that we are marked with the essence of eternal life (*1 John 5:6-12*, refer to *John 3:3, 5; Ephesians 5:26-27; 1 Peter 2:22-25*). It is the Spirit of God in us that enables us to discern the spirit of truth from the spirit of error as we learn who God is and begin to know the voice of His Spirit while trusting that He will confirm all truths by His Written Word.

Prayer: Lord, we struggle with salvation for various reasons, but one major reason is we do not have the assurance of it because we have never really learned how to hear what Your Spirit is saying. Lord, bring us to that place where we will seek more of You, knowing that You will give us more of Your Spirit to know with assurance our salvation is true, experience Your abiding love, serve with our whole heart, and worship You in Spirit and truth. Amen.

August 7

"For whosoever shall call upon the name of the Lord shall be saved" (Romans 10:13). What does it mean to call UPON the name of the LORD? We see that Abraham called upon the name of the LORD in *Genesis 12:8*, Isaac called upon His name in *Genesis 26:25*, and in the Scripture of Romans those who call upon the name of the Lord shall be saved.

Words are important and sometimes the smallest of words can prove the most powerfully used in the right context. I try to take note of such words. For example, in John 8:31 we are told many "believed ON" Jesus but He later goes on to tell the same crowd, *"And because I tell you the truth, ye believe me not"* (*John 8:45*).

Is there a difference between believing ON Jesus and calling UPON Him? It is clear the people in *John 8* believed on what Jesus was saying until their reality was challenged, and at that point they didn't believe Him. In other words, did they really believe UPON Him.

"Upon" is an interesting word. It is not a matter of just believing on something that fits our notions, it is about placing one's complete reliance and trust on that individual. In other words, people must first believe the source is reliable before placing their confidence and assurance on what they say. To believe UPON has to do with one's character and not one's words.

The word "upon" is a preposition that is used in relationship to another word. It implies seizing upon what is being said in relationship to the one being called on. In this case to call upon the name of the LORD means that the individual was seizing upon the one they were calling because of who He is. They were recognizing His deity, ownership, and covenant. It is not an intellectual acknowledgment or a conceptual agreement that something is so; rather, it is a sober cry to one who is able to do what is being sought. In the case of *Romans 10:13* it had to do with salvation.

Salvation is free, but the key is, have I really called upon the character of the LORD, knowing He alone saves or have I simply said some sinners' prayer without really calling upon Him to save me because He is LORD, Jehovah God? One may not initially understand all the implications of salvation, but there is clearly an awareness and desperation that if a person does not call upon the name of the Lord, they stand hopeless in their present state of condemnation under the Law of God and will perish in their sin.

Prayer: Lord, when we are first saved it is because of our awareness of the great burden of sin weighing down our soul. I am so thankful that You have heard my cry when I have called upon You because of who You are, faithful, true, righteous, and able to save me from everything that would beset and hinder my soul. Amen.

August 8

"I will take the cup of salvation, and call upon the name of the LORD" (Psalm 116:13). In the last post, I spoke about what it means to call upon the name of the LORD. The person in this verse understood what it meant to implore the Lord about the matter of his salvation. When the word "name" is used in relationship to the Lord, it does not point to His title, position, or actual name but to His divine, holy character.

To me the person in this Psalm is saying, first I receive the cup of promise in regard to salvation belonging to the LORD; I will offer it up to Him knowing He can fill it, while calling upon Him in light of who He is, and then receive it back by faith in order to partake of it. I fear too many people have a mere mental understanding of Christ's work on the cross and have believed on the promise of life but have not taken the cup of salvation to seize the opportunity to call upon His name to fill the cup with His eternal life.

For a Christian to seize a matter of God means they receive it in their heart as being so (*Roman 10:9-10*). In a sense the cup in this case is the heart that believes it by faith and receives it as truth. We are clearly told we must believe in our heart that God raised Jesus from the dead and confess He is Lord to be saved.

Confession has to do with not just agreeing with who Jesus is as Lord but eventually understanding that it makes Him the owner of our life because of redemption. We are coming into a contractual relationship of obedient service to Him out of love and great appreciation for His redemption.

The problem with having just a mental assent that Jesus died for me, and perhaps believing Him about His burial, is I can miss it all by failing to offer it back to Him because I really do not see the precarious plight of my own soul. He is the resurrected, living Lord and Savior of all who are heirs of salvation, and failing to call UPON His name to save us will leave each of us with an empty cup.

I often wonder who is walking about with an empty cup, assuming they have received salvation without really seeing their spiritual plight, thereby failing to call upon the ONLY ONE who can save.

Prayer: Lord, few heirs understand the real work of salvation until they grow in the knowledge of You and come to a greater revelation of Your redemption. But our initial understanding that we are sinners in need of a loving, great Savior that we call upon to save us, is enough for us to experience true salvation. Praise Your Holy Name. Amen.

August 9

"And the Spirit and the bride say, Come. And let him that heareth say, Come. And let him that is athirst come. And whosoever will, let him take the water of life freely" (Revelation 22:17). I appreciate how words are used in my KJV of the Bible. I have other Bible versions I consider but sometimes some of the words I am used to in the KJV are replaced with another word that may have like meaning but does not always have the same impact on me when I read them. We are influenced greatly by how words impact us.

One of the words I like to pause at is "whosoever." Have you thought about the implication of this word? It is boundless in one way, but very restrictive in another way. The concept of "whosoever" points to something that has no borders to it, but at the same time it points to a response to a particular time, event, or situation that will encompass those who do respond.

The problem with this word is that it may very well defy some of our belief systems. There are those who believe our destination has already been set in stone. It is true, God foreknows who are His because He is all-knowing about matters from the beginning of time to the end of time. Nothing will surprise Him, throw Him off or catch

Him off-guard. However, just because He foreknows a fact, does not keep Jesus' great invitation to come and drink from the fountain of the Living Waters of His Spirit from going forth to "whosoever" hears it, believes it, and responds to it from doing so.

There is no name attached to this word; therefore, it is not limited to one individual, a few selected ones, those of a particular ilk, a certain denomination, or group of people. It is for those who have the heart to hear, the desire to respond, and the willingness to embrace it.

This brings us back to God's foreknowledge of all matters. It is not God's knowledge that sets the boundaries of who responds, but man's free will and the choices he makes. It is true, unless the Father draws and the Spirit convicts, man will not hear, believe or accept Jesus' invitation to come, but the Father knows who has the heart to respond and the Spirit knows when man is ready to be convicted in order to respond. In many cases man has been brought to a state of real repentance and brokenness over his plight and sees his great need to be saved from his sin, but he must choose to respond. This was true for me.

It is also true that in God's providence, or sovereignty, He brings about circumstances so man can see his plight, but man chooses whether he becomes bitter about his plight or honest about his great need to be saved. A good example of this is the two criminals Jesus was placed between on the cross. They both started off mocking Him, but Jesus embraced the cross on behalf of mankind and brought one to the realization that he needed to be saved FROM his sin, while the other one taunted Jesus to save him IN his sin.

Jesus did not come to save man in his sin so he could continue to live as he pleases and then perish in his transgressions; rather, He came to save us from the wages of sin which is spiritual death by giving us His life that will separate us for a greater purpose.

I don't know about you, but I am thankful the invitation went forth to "whosoever" because I proved to be one who responded to it. My name was not attached to the invitation, but in the end, the invitation was big enough to encompass me into the promise of eternal life.

Prayer: Lord, we are waiting to hear our name, but You know it comes down to the heart and whether one is willing to hear the great invitation to come and drink, to come and live. It is and always will come back to our willingness to get up and respond to Your great call because we have the heart and need to do so. Amen.

August 10

"It was meet that we should make merry, and be glad: for this thy brother was dead, and is alive again; and was lost, and is found" (Luke 15:32). I don't know about you but the parable about the lost sheep in *Luke 15:3-7* is close to my heart. In my journey I have found that people can become lost in four ways. They can become lost to their families and inheritance like the prodigal son.

The prodigal son went out to find his own life outside of his real inheritance and do his own thing, and in the end became lost to his father, while the wayward son always knew where his father, home and inheritance was located. That is what happens to many people when they insist on their own way, they become lost to God, their Father and their real inheritance. For the prodigal, they must turn in repentance, come home as a humble servant so the Father can exalt them as a son and restore them back to their real inheritance.

The second kind of lost is the lost sheep. The lost sheep is the one who wanders away from the protection and flock of God, making them vulnerable and prey to predators. They might not even be aware they are lost until night comes upon them and they begin to realize the flock is nowhere to be found.

The prodigal son became lost to the father, but a lost sheep becomes lost to the protection of the shepherd. This happens when the Christian takes their focus off of the Shepherd and wanders outside of the boundaries of God's Word. It is important to keep in mind that the flock is where the shepherd is because it will only follow the voice of His Word to maintain the right distance to ever see and hear Him. The beauty about the sheep is that all they have to do is recognize they are now lost and begin to cry out in need of mercy, for their Shepherd will be seeking them out.

Prayer: Lord I was lost and You found me. As the song declares, "Your amazing grace never ceases to amaze me." We are told we will be learning about it for ages to come. Even though Your grace saves our wretched souls to the uttermost, we still can't fathom how great, how wide, and how deep it reaches in order to bring sweetness to our soul. Amen.

August 11

"Either what woman having ten pieces of silver, if she lose one piece, doth not light a candle, and sweep the house, and seek diligently till she find it" (Luke 15:8). I mentioned in the last post how there are four ways in which people and things can become lost. The first one is that people can become lost to family and their inheritance. The second way is that they can stray away like a sheep from the rest of the herd and become lost.

The third type of lost can be compared to the lost coin in *Luke 15:8-10.* Many times, people become lost amid religious activities. They fall through the cracks of neglect due to such things as assumptions about their salvation, indifference because of a lack of godly love, and judgmentalism due to denominational elitism.

The prodigal son became lost due to rebellion and the lost sheep became lost because of veering off due to some type of worldly attraction, but the third type of lost is due to a type of familiarity where the church simply does business as usual while losing sight of its high calling and commission to preach the Gospel by lifting up the true Jesus.

They also fail to teach the unadulterated Word or to disciple the followers to truly follow Jesus into the life God has for them. Keep in mind, God knows where we are at all times and where to find us, but we need to recognize that our life in God is more than religion.

The fourth type of lost is because of spiritual darkness. Mankind gropes in it according to what he thinks he knows and sees, but he is unable to see the light of the true Gospel because his eyes have been blinded by the god of this age, Satan. He walks in unbelief, with a veil over his mind. He stands condemned, hopeless, and dull of hearing because his heart has been glossed over by the pagan philosophy, wicked ways, and evil practices of the world.

As a believer of Jesus Christ, I have been found and possess the assurance of heaven. I have the status of a saint, the high calling of a servant of God, the assurance of a child of God, the position of an ambassador, and citizen of a kingdom made of a royal priesthood. Why would I prefer the world's glitter, its fading, vain attractions, its ways of doing business and its darkness to such glorious places in Christ Jesus?

Prayer: Lord, I have been lost in different ways, but Your arm of salvation is not too short to reach me, nor are Your ears closed to my cries for mercy, Your arms are not shut to me when I come home in repentance with a contrite heart, and allow You to take away the veil so I can see Your light of salvation, love, and hope. Praise the Lord. Amen.

August 12

"As it is written There is none righteous, no not one. (Romans 3:10). In my last couple of posts I talked about the four ways in which man can be lost. The big problem with mankind is not that once he realizes he is lost he sees his great need to be found, spared, saved, and reconciled, but what is hard is to get man in his self-sufficiency and civility to realize he is desperately and completely lost in the first place.

There are four things that keep man from seeing his need to be saved. The first thing is man's decency. If man is decent enough, treats his neighbor right, keeps his word, and is not some murderer and fornicator, he sees himself as a "good guy." As a "good guy" he does not see that he is all that bad or that he would deserve hell; therefore, in his reasoning he can't imagine God sending him there.

The Bible is clear when it comes to "goodness," there are none good but God. "Good" in this text means beneficial. Whatever God does is beneficial, but due to the flaw of iniquity in man's character he is not capable of being beneficial to God or others in all he does especially when it comes to eternal matters.

The second thing that keeps man from seeing his great need to be saved, especially from himself, is arrogance. Man in his arrogance sees himself as an exception to a matter and not subject to what he considers is inferior to him. He judges according to his high estimation of himself and concludes all must concede to him because he just knows he can't be wrong. In the end he becomes judge and jury to others including God as to what is the acceptable standard as in the case of salvation.

The third thing that keeps man from seeing his need to be saved is knowledge. If man thinks he knows all about a matter, he considers it a reality. For example, he knows Jesus died on a cross and that mental acknowledgement is good enough to assume he is saved. However, knowledge alone will not stand. It must graduate from just intellectually knowing something to believing it is truth and putting it into action.

We must keep in mind, knowledge that is tested to see if it stands becomes wisdom, knowledge walked out becomes discretion, and knowledge that remains standing proves to be true. Otherwise, knowledge about something is like a flat tire, it will get you nowhere.

Prayer: Lord, as long as we think we know a matter, we are confident it is our reality when in fact it is lifeless knowledge that has never been tested to see if it proves it is truth and can stand. Lord, save me from the high pinnacles of my arrogance that keeps me from seeing the worldly and demonic traps before me. Amen.

August 13

"But now we are delivered from the law, that being dead wherein we were held: that we should serve in newness of sprit, and not in the oldness of the letter" (Romans 7:6). We have been considering the things that keep man from seeing his need to be saved.

First, there are his fig-leaves of decency that man hides behind that will prove to be filthy rags to God. The second thing is his arrogance that leaves him naked before God but deluded about his state, where he sees no need to humble himself. The final covering is what I refer to as "the paper-doll coverings" of untested knowledge that falls short of really knowing the truth about a matter. It may give some appearance but there is nothing behind it to substantiate it as being valid.

The final thing that can keep man from seeing his great need for salvation is religion. Religion often proves to be the heaviest of garments to wear. Man usually tacks on, adds just enough, or surrounds himself with what he considers a good dose of religion that allows him to perceive he is okay with God regardless of how he is living. There may be other religious traditions that allow him to stand justified in his mind or cause some sentiment to rise up in him as a type of consolation, but God sees all matters differently.

The truth is, man is not saved in his decency, can't be saved by what he knows, will not be saved in his arrogance, and remains unsaved in religion that never causes him to address the real issue of his plight, *"for all have sinned and come short of the glory of God" (Romans 3:23).* If sin is not properly addressed, it does not matter how man regards himself, sees himself, reforms himself, and surrounds himself with religious activities, he still stands condemned in his sin.

There is only one who can save and that is Christ Jesus. It is His wisdom that stands as truth, His righteousness that serves as the only acceptable standard, His sanctification that ensures we are made acceptable, and His redemption that secures our salvation. It is for this reason that the way of salvation is narrow, and few will find it.

Prayer: Lord, we like to think we have something to do with our salvation, but it is truly Your gift, for it is a matter of Your grace that requires a measure of faith imparted to us by You to take hold of the hope You offer. Thank You for providing the way of salvation. Amen.

August 14

"If I had not come and spoken unto them, they had not had sin; but now they have no cloak for their sin" (John 15:22). As we consider man's plight in this world, we must consider the reality of all matters. In summation, what is not of God will prove to be useless, worthless, and insignificant in the end. What is not acceptable to God is under judgment, what is not ordained by God will prove profane to Him, and what does not ultimately glorify Him will prove to be a mockery to Him.

We are quick to assume if religion is somewhat attached to something, it must be okay. We presume if something looks decent, it must be counted honorable to God. If we consider good works a true test of the fruit of something, we are really missing that the test is a matter of quality not appearance or performance.

The reality of the Christian life is that it is not the product of our best and of our doing; rather, it is the product of the character and work of the Holy Spirit in us. When it comes to spirit it is more about environment that is conducive for the Holy Spirit to move, operate, and produce the right results.

These results entail a humble attitude, anointed worship, effective service, unfeigned faith, and acceptable fruit. The truth is that the Christian life will come back to the fruit it produces and whether it is sweet to the spirit and calming to the soul. However, the acceptable ways of God will always become bitter to the flesh, because it will call for the crucifixion of the old to ensure the complete exchange for the new.

The real work of God is to make us into new creations. He is not here to cover up the old with the new because the old will nullify the new and the new will compromise the old. He is not here to put fig-leaves on shame so man can avoid facing the consequences of his actions. He is not about putting some religious cloak over the moral flaw, failures, and arrogance of man; rather, He came to take away the cloak so that man will face His need, not for a do-over, but a complete transformation of his mind that entails receiving a new heart and spirit.

Man is used to sin and the environment of despair, death, and destruction. He finds comfort in what he is used to, uncertainty towards what he can't control, and can quickly become resistant to that which would move him out of comfort zones. However, the life that God offers man is hope, life, and blessings, but we can't partake of the fruit that possesses the seeds of death and expect those seeds to not corrupt the new life we have been entrusted with. We must deny ourselves of having life on our terms, and our way, crucify the old in order to exchange it with the new, and follow Jesus to secure the promises attached to our eternal inheritance that is found in our new life in Christ.

Prayer: Lord, we fail to see the whole picture of what You are doing in us, and the result is not only a mixture of ineptness, but one that proves to be powerless, nominal, and bitter to the soul. Lord, forgive me for wanting the "best" from both worlds because the world has nothing worthwhile to offer, while compromising what is excellent when it comes to Your life and calling. This is how I rob myself of experiencing what makes Your life worthwhile for me to pursue and possess. Amen.

August 15

The day that I found out our "talking" dog can also count was the morning after he had crunched up and gulped down three little dog cookies. Instead of a polite doggie style "thank you" he immediately began his dialogue.

His usual "talking" turned into agitated grumbling and all that because he got three, instead of his usual four, little cookies. So, to his way of thinking, I had cheated him out of one cookie and he wasn't going to be quiet about it no matter how hard I tried to ignore him—and you guessed it! He got his fourth cookie after which he retreated to his lookout post on the back of the couch.

This incident reminds me of how people sometimes treat the Lord when, instead of being thankful for the good things He does give them, they grumble and complain about what they didn't get. Our heavenly Father knows what things we have need of, and out of His love and mercy, He also gives us some of our "wants." But the key is, are we truly grateful for all that He bestows upon us?

Jesus' words concerning our basic needs are like a bright beam of light shining through the dark jungle of "stuff" most of us have accumulated, collected, hoarded or, worse yet, lusted after to "make our life happy and complete." Jesus said, *"Take heed, and beware of covetousness: for a man's life consisteth not in the abundance of the things which he possesseth" (Luke 12:15).*

We live in uncertain and "perilous times"—times when everything we have can be taken from us in mere minutes. To whom can we go but to the Lord in such a time? We have a good example of what our attitude should be in the Apostle Paul who declared, *"Not that I speak in respect of want: for I have learned, in whatsoever state I am, therewith to be content. I know both how to be abased, and I know how to abound: every where and in all things I am instructed both to be full and to be hungry, both to abound and to suffer need. I can do all things through Christ which strengtheneth me" (Philippians 4:11-13).* – J. Haley

Prayer: Lord God, thank You for Your bountiful goodness to us, and for our daily needs. Help us to be truly thankful and grant us a greater measure of faith to remain steadfast in our daily walk with You. I say this all in the Name above all names, Jesus Christ. Amen.

August 16

"And he said, Thou canst not see my face: for there shall no man see me and live" (Exodus 33:20). In the previous posts I spoke of four things that keep people from seeing their great need to be saved. Each aspect is deceptive when it comes to how God sees a matter. In fact, in each case, God is missing from the equation. For example, when it comes to man's estimation of his religious status, it is clear such a perspective is not God's holiness that reveals how far something is from Him when it comes to man's concept of his own decency. In such cases, God's righteousness also does not serve as man's ultimate standard as to what is acceptable. The sad conclusion in man's mind is that Jesus' redemption is not the only door that will lead to salvation.

The problem with decency is that in man's mind, it places him alongside of God where he, at best, considers God at a simple glance but in light of God's holiness his decency or best proves to be filthy rags. When it comes to arrogance, it exalts man above God revealing his utter foolishness that strips God of His glory according to a perverted, carnal mind.

There is knowledge about God that puffs man up in his opinions about his own idea of righteousness, but such ideas will always prove he is ignorant of God's righteousness. There is also man's self-righteous religion before God that shows itself to be insufficient as well as ends up proving to be a lousy substitute for a relationship with God. We could go on and on about how man measures himself when it comes to religious matters.

Man can settle for the decaying pieces of his decency that will eventually choke him, and the crumbling crumbs of his righteousness that will leave him hollow. There are also the poisonous bits of his arrogance that will leave him nauseated, and the lifeless worldly religion that sucks the very life out of the air of true service and worship. However, in the end, he will stand alone before the great Judge without any hope of salvation and recourse to change his destiny.

Prayer: Lord, man often compares himself to everything but the standard of Your righteousness which was manifested in Your humanity. Such comparison can delude us to such a point that we fail to see You at all in Your righteousness. Amen.

August 17

"The thing that hath been, it is that which shall be; and that which is done is that which shall be done: and there is no new thing under the sun" (Ecclesiastes 1:9). How many times has the present caused you to look back at the past and say "What if certain things of the past were different?" How many have asked of the present, "Why did this happen or why is this happening?" How many look into the future and say, "Now if this happened a certain way, it certainly would have altered the future in a way that surely would now prove to be well with my soul."

The truth is, if regrets of the past haunt us enough, we try to figure out how to sidetrack them in the present to have a future that will not haunt, taunt, and cause us to live in some mire of despair. Much of our despair is caused by foolish past choices and present decisions that are hindered by the lack of foreknowledge of how something will turn out. Are there things I would love to change in the past? You bet I would, but the question is how much of my past has truly shaped my present attitudes? My present attitudes are not based on past or present circumstances; rather, they are based on the decisions I made that now greatly influence the way I consider present matters.

For instance, I can't change the past, and it stands as it stood then, and there is no reversing it. Now, I can "cry over spilled milk," or lament over letting the "camel in the tent" that left an absolute mess behind. Or, I can choose to learn the lessons of the past and decide to change course. In summation I can repent before the Lord of how I look at something. Since repentance changes my direction, I can begin to walk in His way of righteousness and change my destination.

What is happening now is what is and I can't change present circumstances, but I can decide how I am going to respond to them. It is true that past regrets can pull me back, but as a believer I have confessed the sins of my past to the Lord and know in light of His great sacrifice, I can now stand justified. Justification comes down to as if I never committed the act because it all is under the blood of Jesus, which cleanses me from all unrighteousness.

My goal when it comes to Jesus is not to look back at what was, but face what is in light of my faith in who God is and what He has done for me through His Son. True faith stands on the foundation of a finished work that can't be changed, a present work that will stand regardless of circumstances, and a sure hope that when it comes to the past that what was then will remain so today and forever. As for the present, it will fade into the future, and one day soon, I will glory in His light, love, and majesty forever.

Prayer: Lord, it is easy to be chained to our past in regret and wrestle with our present fears about facing our future because so much is often thrown up in the air by the "what ifs" and the "whys," of life. But Lord all I need to do is quit looking back at what will not change, accept what is so today due to my faith and know that You have my back and You have already prepared the way in which I am to walk. My response is to take steps of faith towards You, according to Your Word, and I will be assured of reaching the glorious destination You have promised me. Amen.

August 18

"And the publican, standing afar off, would not lift up so much as his eyes unto heaven, but smote upon his breast, saying, God be merciful to me a sinner" (Luke 18:13). When you consider man's greatest plight in this world, it is not that his existence is on a constant downhill slide; rather, the plight has to do with him accepting what is so. It comes down to man facing a matter before coming to terms with the solution.

Man spends much time trying to avoid facing certain facts that include his own spiritual ineptness. This ineptness exists due to his mortality. This mortality reminds him of the miserable plight of mankind due to sin. He must also contend with the failures of his imperfect ways because of iniquity, the losses that plague him in an uncertain world, and the harsh reality of death that nips at his heels.

As we consider the mess man is in one must conclude that what man needs is a good dose of reality that anything outside of God's will, Spirit, Word, and presence is vanity and will end up proving to be as worthless as fool's gold. It is in light of the reality of God's greatness that man finally sees his smallness.

It is God's holiness that brings man down from any lofty concept he may have about himself to the safest place which is at the very foot of the cross of Christ crying out for mercy. In mercy he can experience undeserved grace, and receive God's forgiveness, realizing he will perish in his misery without it.

When man is brought to such realistic depths, he has no concept of any greatness in himself or any importance that could be regarded when it comes to God's glory. This constantly proves that he is not self-sufficient in and of himself. He becomes greatly aware that before God he stands completely undone, hopeless, helpless, and totally missing from the equation when it comes to his own salvation.

It never has been, nor will it ever be, God plus man in some way in any eternal matters. The cross of Christ crosses man out while lifting up our precious Jesus who became our great substitute before all of heaven.

One day soon, the demons along with worldly governments and mankind will have to acknowledge that the Lord Jesus Christ alone is God's solution to a doomed, dying world. He is also God's only answer to man's spiritual ordeal, and He alone is the power of heaven. In the end, He will receive all the glory heaven affords for He alone sits on the right hand of majesty.

Prayer: Lord, we have allowed certain leaders to be exalted, churches receive undeserved glory, man's self-righteousness becomes the standard, and religion becomes a sick substitute, but when all is said and done, You alone will stand in all of heaven's majesty, ultimately receiving all the glory in the end. Amen.

August 19

"There is no remembrance of former things; neither shall there be any remembrance of things that are to come with those that shall come after" (Ecclesiastes 1:11). Man desires to leave his footprint in this world. He wants to leave something behind that will cause others to remember him. I have often reminded people that at best we might be remembered by a couple of generations after we leave this world, but past that the most we might leave is a name on some family tree.

If we are fortunate to leave some historical notation or record behind to mark different mileposts of our life, it may prove to be commendable in some way for those who care to follow them. However, the greatest witness we leave has to do with what is marked by eternity.

When it comes to Christ, we leave a legacy behind for our children and a witness behind for those who follow in the steps of faith, but even that becomes consumed by a greater witness of saints that have indeed set a precedence. This incredible witness is something the world can't begin to understand, the flesh will naturally mock, and pride will scorn. It is for this reason Hebrews tells us the world is not worthy to even witness such faith.

This brings us back to what I pointed out in past posts of the "what ifs" of the past that will stand as is, so why look back, for in the end they will not even be remembered. What about the "whys" of the present? They will never make sense because we are not in control of events; therefore, the present is what it is now and will not change no matter what kind of fit we might have over it. The truth is any great feats or accomplishments will be forgotten.

This brings us back to the fact we are to walk by faith. When you consider what true faith says in light of God's promises, it does not say, "What if," because of the past or ask "Why" in light of the present; rather, it states, "Even so." Even so the past was bad, and I have even left some notable mileposts behind, what will it matter when I am no longer here?

What really matters when all is said and done, is what will be left standing in light of eternity. Regardless of my present challenges, the only thing I can possibly leave behind is the great witness of God's deliverance from them all. It matters little as to the notable losses I may have experienced in this world, my spirit is settled, and all is well with my soul because my God reigns and nothing will change that glorious reality.

We must keep in mind that the cross of Jesus crosses out the stain of regret from the past. The present hope of Jesus allows us as believers to walk in assurance even in the midst of unpleasant situations. Our sustaining faith declares that all the promises of God are "amen," for they will prove to be so. Faith gives us the means to state, "Even though I have lost all in relationship to this present world, I am hid in Christ, and because of His redemption, I have gained what is eternal and glorious. It will take ages for me to discover the fullness of His glory that is attached to all of His glorious promises.

Prayer: Lord, we are not to look back at what will not be remembered; rather, we are to look forward to what will forever stand in the annals of Your glory. Lord, thank You for covering my past with Your work of redemption, ensuring the present with Your Spirit, and establishing my future as being so with Your promises. Praise Your Holy Name for covering all the bases with Your glorious ways and works. Amen.

August 20

"A new heart also will I give you, and a new spirit will I put within you: and I will take away the stony heart out of your flesh, and I will give you an heart of flesh" (Ezekiel 36:26). This promise was directed towards Israel but when a person is truly born again, they will receive a new heart and spirit as well. This is necessary, for both a new heart and spirit point to a new disposition that shows the seed of a new life being brought forth, the life of Jesus which is eternal and abundant.

Heart has to do with inclinations and spirit tendencies. The deceits of the old heart are inclined towards the ways of iniquity, and the tendency of the natural spirit is to forever justify the wrongs of a matter to cover up unacceptable attitudes and actions.

The problem is that we are often so comfortable with the old that we tend to run back to its vomit. We can thwart, abort, resist, and reject the new work of God because it is not on our terms, according to our way of thinking, and within our comfort zones. We wrestle against, whine, cry foul, and sit down in a puddle of self-pity when the laser light of the Spirit and surgical knife of God's Word goes deep into our character. I know because I am guilty of such foolishness.

The truth is we forget what we left behind when our flesh is screaming for something exciting, our pride is chiding us that we can have all we imagined, and our eyes see a broad road of experiencing different aspects of the world that promises us success, happiness and satisfaction. On the other hand, the other road before us becomes narrower and more obscure as we try to see the end of it. We may know the promises, but we must choose to believe by faith they await us and that the experiences of this present world will end in despair.

I remember sitting in such a puddle in the middle of the crossroad of decision that greatly parted into two distinct roads. I was then reminded of an old life that taunted me and practically drove me mad because of its vanity and hopelessness. Then I was reminded of the new life that was imputed to me that gave me such hope, liberty, and assurance. It was then I knew I could not have both and I needed to choose to consecrate all to God so He could bring forth the new. To avoid casting off the old and settling for a quasi-state of dead-religion, while accepting, at best, a nominal Christianity would leave me lean in the end.

The choices are clear. There is no middle ground between this world and the unseen world of heavenly promise and bliss. For those who walk the fence or try to walk between the non-committal middle of compromise between this world and the next to come will find that the great Shepherd has left them behind, and the result is they have become lost in the vast nothingness of this present age.

Prayer: Lord, we miss it because we are too busy trying to stay on the fence or walk on the middle ground of compromise and foolishness. Cause us to see the old is not worth holding on to and the new is worth leaving behind all of the old to gain it. Thank You for keeping me on the straight and narrow. Amen.

August 21

Sudden panic! It strikes you in the pit of your stomach like a bolt of lightning, then quickly rises to constrict your throat as it numbs the mind. This can easily happen in any number of situations, and one of the worst for us is if we can't find our beloved fur baby.

Yes, we have a secure fenced yard, but sometimes we can't find him because he's good at hiding under a bush just to see if we miss him, and yes, he can also hide in the house if he has a mind to. Being mostly black makes it even harder to see him. Knowing that one out of every three dogs in America gets lost is a truth factor that adds to the "panic button" which is what took place a couple of years ago.

He was new to our little three-some family when he vanished. That's when you try to remember if he was in or out, because it becomes so automatic that you don't stop to make note of it. After a great deal of calling and searching, Rayola decided to go downstairs to Carrie's space and check, just in case, even though the door was shut. Happily, there he was! He had punched the door open, ran past it before it swung back and shut him in.

How panic works got me to thinking about the sheer panic Jesus' parents felt when they had traveled to Jerusalem for the Feast of the Passover, and after they fulfilled the days, and gone a whole day's journey, it suddenly dawned on them that Jesus was missing. They had assumed He was in the company of their relatives and friends (*Luke 2:41-52*).

If you think about it, Jesus was 12-years-old, so no doubt Mary and Joseph had the care and distractions of Jesus' half-brothers, James, Joses, Simon and Judas (or Jude) and even possibly his sisters. We can only imagine the kind of panic that set in; after all, they had been given the responsibility of caring for the Son of God, and they had lost Him! The frantic parents most likely left the other children with relatives, and then hurried back to Jerusalem, which was a day's journey, and then it took another three days of searching, (most likely everywhere except for where He was) before they found Him in the temple. *"And when they saw him, they were amazed: and his mother said unto him, Son, why hast thou thus dealt with us? Behold thy father and I have sought thee sorrowing" (Luke 2:43.)*

Even though they knew Who He was, perhaps they began to take things for granted where He was concerned, for they were "amazed" that He was in the temple *"sitting in the midst of the doctors, both hearing them, and asking them questions. And all that heard him were astonished at his understanding and answers" (Luke 2:46, 47).*

The question is, have you ever taken the Son of God for granted, and inadvertently left Him without missing Him for some period of time? It's easy to assume He is "traveling" with us as we go about our normal, busy daily lives, but is He? It's also easy to become so caught up with great, earth-shaking events, along with the myriads of small daily duties, chores, and challenges that we simply "leave Jesus behind" and figure we'll return to where we left Him when we have time and pick our spiritual life back up from there.

But who is following who? Do we expect Him to follow us, tagging along until we have personal time for just Him alone, or are we diligent to follow Him no matter where He leads? It's something to think about. After all, there's no deeper sorrow or terrifying panic on earth greater than suddenly realizing that you have left Jesus behind. – J. Haley

Prayer: Lord, You need to be the focus, the source, and the purpose for our Christian life, and yet we are prone to stray from You. Forgive us for allowing the glitter of this world to take our eyes off You. Amen

August 22

"And it shall come to pass in the last days, saith God, I will pour out of my Spirit upon all flesh: and your sons and your daughters shall prophesy, and your young men shall see visions, and your old men shall dream dreams" (Acts 2:17). The other night I had a vivid, disturbing dream. I don't remember most of my dreams which often

seem like a confusing mosaic brought on by body discomforts whether I am too cold or suffering from some indigestion normality.

The dream started with restlessness. The restlessness started with me. At first, I saw myself walking down long corridors to find my way out of the restlessness. Most religion is like wading through mazes or down long corridors of endless debates over various doctrines that prove unprofitable. However, the Bible stresses that we must have a correct vision, for those without vision will perish.

For believers, we have a commission and have been entrusted with the vision of Christ lifted up on the cross. The message is Christ and Him Crucified, and it is because of the hope of glory we possess which is Christ in us that we stand and continue to stand in the midst of a hopeless, dying, condemned world.

Eventually the main person that emerged in the dream made me an observer in it and not the main character. Out of restlessness this person left the safety of friends to walk out into the darkness among strangers. The next thing I was aware of was the person was in grave trouble. She had become lost and there were dark, evil forces and wicked men that had taken note of her and were about to prey on her.

The person suddenly became aware of her precarious plight and began to yell out for help. I could in fact hear her scream. I suddenly became a participant in the dream as I yelled at the people around her to help her or she would perish. Yet to my surprise the people I started yelling at to help her, for the most part, seemed aloof, indifferent, and totally oblivious to her urgent plight.

When I woke up, I was shaken by it. What could this mean? Suddenly the Lord gave me a picture. The lost person represents most of humanity, much of it wandering about in a restless state, seeking, but not sure of what they are searching for. Such individuals become lost and become prey to the terrible demonic forces that are all around them. Occasionally some of these individuals will begin to yell for help and in great distress scream, but those who should hear the pleas for help fail to do so because they do not care to hear it. They are content in their state and do not want to be bothered.

Sadly, some of these people represent the attitude of the organized church. Jesus may be seeking that one lost sheep but how many Christians are listening for the cries of lost sheep? The problem is not that we do not have the ears to hear the cry; rather, the problem is we do not love God and those He died for enough to open our heart to such lost souls. We may lay back on our laurels in church pews while people perish IN their sins, put our assurance in dead-letter theology as we turn a deaf ear to the cries of those who ARE perishing, and be content that we are not one of those foolish, lost sheep AS they perish.

However, the sad truth is we really do not love God, His Word or souls enough to see the urgency of our commission ever before us. We lack the authority and power of our high calling to get the job done. Sadly, without vision for the lost, we often waste the limited time we have to be the one who plants the seeds, casts the nets on both sides of the boat of life, and be a co-laborer with God in the great harvest field of humanity.

Prayer: Lord, forgive me for letting the world's demands drown out the cries of the lost, while the activities of religion leave me in mazes of ineffectiveness as others walk off into the abyss. It has become obvious that personal efforts of goodness always become a poor substitute for what it means to love and serve those around me. Lord, give me a love for You, a heart for others, and the ears to truly hear the cries of Your sheep. Amen.

August 23

"For our light affliction which is but for a moment, worketh for us a far more exceeding and eternal weight of glory" (2 Corinthians 4:17).
There are certain things that, when you hear them, cause you to take note as to their wisdom. I was listening to a man that was sharing what his father said when he asked him about what he could see about a kid's future. This is the gist of what his wise father said, "My grandfather walked ten miles to get to work every day, my father

walked five miles, I'm driving a Cadillac, my son drives a Mercedes, and my grandson a Ferrari, but my great-grandson will be walking again." The man asked his father, "Well, why is that?"

His father's answer was, "Tough times create strong men. Strong men create easy times. Easy times create weak men. Weak men create tough times. Many will not understand, but you have to raise warriors."

In my years in full-time ministry, we have faced some tough times, challenging times, great storms, overwhelming waves, and grave darkness that would cause our minds to faint if we did not consider or remember who we are in Christ. I initially complained, lamented, and occasionally felt sorry for myself, but the Lord would break through and either tell me to stand on what I knew was true about Him or simply trust Him with the outcome. I did not realize it then, but the Lord was making me into a warrior that would stand regardless of what was happening around me.

The truth is Jesus wants us to quit riding high in some worldly Cadillac that may give the idea of class and value but which greatly depreciates with the world. He wants us to quit striving for the fleshly preferences of a Mercedes to look rich and refined, while leaving us poor and leading us towards spiritual bankruptcy.

The Lord wants us to learn how to walk by faith. It is faith that allows us to soar in the current of the Spirit to know the excellence of the many heavenly riches that come with a cost but end up gaining dividends for eternity.

Prayer: Lord, forgive us for trying to compare heavenly riches to worldly wealth. One truly grows while the other one leads us down a dangerous path of destruction and spiritual poverty. Amen.

August 24

"No man that warreth entangleth himself with the affairs of this life: that he may please him who hath chosen him to be a soldier" (1 Timothy 2:4). When I consider the times that I live in, I fear for the generations that are following me. I grew up in the generation where

times seemed easy. I came out a bit spoiled and presumptuous about what I thought life was all about. I felt deprived of what I considered unfair, wrestled about what I thought were my rights, and plopped down like a spoiled child when I didn't get my way. In the end it always came back to trusting HIM.

I have watched the justification of each generation in their logic to make things easier on their children. However, we must ask ourselves what we are doing to our children if we fail to teach them good work ethics, moral accountability, and the willingness to sacrifice for what is worthy of all consideration? It is clear we are talking about something called integrity.

Without integrity man will never stand for anything. And if we fail to stand for what is right, what kind of legacy are we leaving behind if we do not really train our children to be soldiers in the ways of the Lord?

The greatest problem I see in those of the generations that are following me is their inability to stand for what is right. They go with the flow of the world, embrace wicked philosophies, and rage against anything that is contrary to their fleshly comforts, their indoctrinations, and their ways. They are mentally weak, morally bankrupted in their self-absorbed worlds, and willing to sit back as others make the sacrifices while they see no need to stir themselves up to reach any higher than their small-minded, miserable worlds of me, myself, and I.

It seems like each generation has failed to raise their share of warriors. How about the kingdom of God? The truth is, how many churches are raising warriors; or how many have deluded the weak into thinking that their "paper machetes" of knowledge, their proclamations of pseudo faith and false victory, their associations with the religious, and their set worldly methods will ensure that they are able to stand? Time will tell, but the casualties might be great in the end.

Tough times do create tough soldiers who are seasoned, realistic, and prepared to endure to the end. I am not as seasoned as I'd like to be, but I know that such strength comes from facing life's present troubles in light of what is sure, eternal and glorious.

Prayer: Lord, You have allowed enough troubles to season me, enough pressure to enlarge me, enough fires to establish me, and enough battles to prepare me. Forgive me for kicking, complaining, and whining and not trusting that You do all things well. Amen.

August 25

"Blessed is the man that trusteth in the LORD, and whose hope the LORD is" (Jeremiah 17:7). Where do you put your hope? As Christians we may say we trust the Lord with, and in, all matters, but is that where we put our hope? So much of the world, including the Christian world is finding itself amid storms that are emerging into a perfect storm where every type of force will come at a person from all angles, often ending in destruction.

In my last couple of posts, I spoke about living the easy life. Jesus told us we would have much trouble in this world. We read in God's Word about the affliction of the soul, suffering in obedience, persecution for the sake of Christ, loss of the present life, and grave challenges, yet many who have bought the American version of Christianity act as if you are a "good" Christian you should be immune from such trouble and challenges. When such challenges hit, these people, for the most part, are not prepared to stand and endure while coming to a place of compete rest in the Lord.

It is clear such a presentation makes for weak Christianity. Instead of preparing to stand, there are those who are ready to sit back in ease. Their hope is in the promise and not in the One whose brings forth the promise.

God's promises have conditions that prepare the person to walk in them according to the right spirit and truth. I have often wondered why Christians are so quick to lean back on the promises while failing to stand on them according to their conditions. Promises tell us how to stand and in what way to walk to possess them. In God's promises there are no such provisions that allows us to merely sit on them due to assumptions or lean back on them because of willful presumptions.

There are reasons man wants to sit on or lean back on God's promise, but the main one is unbelief. We would rather operate in wishful thinking instead of walk by obedient faith towards God whose promises will stand in the end. We would rather hide behind our concept of God's promises in light of the future, than possess them and know their fulness that in the end will enrich our lives beyond any measure the world could imagine.

The question is, are you sitting on the promises in hope of being spared from trouble or leaning back on them waiting for some future glory to fall on you despite the rest of the world falling into the abyss? Or, are you standing on them knowing that all of hell can come against you, as the times you live in may leave you utterly impoverished. The loss you may also experience will be almost unbearable to the soul. However, in the end, you will be standing because you have put your complete trust and hope in the immovable Rock of Ages?

Prayer: Lord, we have our reasons for sitting instead of preparing to stand and leaning instead of rising up to meet the occasion to stand on what is true, because of unbelief. Faith comes by hearing and hearing by Your Word. We may hear Your Word occasionally, but sometimes we don't believe You enough to walk in it. Forgive us. Amen.

August 26

"That ye be not slothful, but followers of them who through faith and patience inherit the promises" (Hebrews 6:12). In the last post I talked about the reason people fail to inherit the promises of God. The first one I mentioned was unbelief.

Abraham inherited the promise by looking for a city made by God and walking towards it by faith. In other words, by faith Abraham had to look beyond this present world and even the promises to possess the ultimate promise.

We have the example of Job's patience in *James 5:11* that allowed him to endure the great testing of his faith. When you study Job, you had to know it was sheer determination of trusting what he knew about God for him to not be removed from his faith towards God to ultimately endure his ordeal.

However, in Hebrews we are given insight into another reason why people fail to possess promises. It is something called slothfulness. Slothfulness points to a spiritual problem that comes down to an attitude and disposition. The problem is known as laziness.

At the heart of man selfish, unregenerate, disposition is self-serving laziness. If it does not feel good, he can become apathic. If it does not seem right, he can become complacent. If it is not fair, he can become irresponsible, unreasonable, and indifferent.

Slothfulness is the real reason for spiritual inaction towards God. Faith requires one to go against the flow of what is fleshly as hope enables one to take the initiative to rise in expectation. It is God's grace that becomes the avenue that allows us to freely walk towards and in the unknown to experience the miraculous and incredible. However, slothfulness is a complete opposite of any active faith.

Slothfulness can easily clothe the flesh when man fails to choose to walk out his Christian life by faith. The flesh wants life to be easy. It wants the walk to be a breeze, the terrain to be a park, the paths to be straight and not uphill, and the way without detours that would tempt man to foolishly veer off. Life is clearly made up of a series of crossroads that require the traveler to make decisions that in the end will expose his true character.

Man, basically wants the best of life handed to him without toil, work, and sacrifice so he can pretty well do as he will and avoid any real responsibility and accountability for the end results. This is why it seems that those of certain generations are without any concerns when it comes to selling their soul. The result is that they will easily come into line with a "Nanny State" mentality which is Socialistic in attitude, Communistic in philosophy, Fascism and woke in practices, atheistic towards religion, and agnostic towards any sure concept when it comes to God.

It is easy for spiritual slothfulness to clothe a man, but as believers we must be clothed in humility which comes from above. Humility is a state that allows one to be active, willing, productive, and godly in the matters of God. The question is what are you being dressed in?

Prayer: Lord, we can be active, engaged, and busy and still be clothed in slothfulness when it comes to truly carrying out Your kingdom matters. Lord, I want to be clothed in humility, so I am prepared to hear You despite endless activity, engaged with You despite constant demands, and obedient to You despite the busyness of this world. Amen.

August 27

"Take us the foxes, the little foxes, that spoil the vines: for our vines have tender grapes" (Song of Solomon 2:15). When we talk about slothfulness, we can't ignore procrastination.

Procrastination sits on the throne of good intentions. It is convinced that it is honorable about putting off a matter because it has all the intentions of doing it sometime, some day. Granted, we have good reasons to put off things that seem insignificant at the time considering how we feel or what is going on. After all, such matters are like little foxes that are there and can prove to be irritating up front, but they can be ignored for another day.

However, foxes can get in the henhouse. They are clever little creatures that know how to size up a matter and find a way into the equation. So how can the little foxes rob us in the end?

Many times, we make commitments with zeal but no conviction. Lack of conviction shows us we were not as engaged as we thought we were. We in fact thought too highly of our abilities and our intention. We offer meaningful words, but in the end, they prove empty because it was from the height of how something would make us look in the end. Up front such intentions can make us feel good about ourselves because we sound noble or honorable, but fleshly zeal is fickle.

Zeal is like a flash in the pan when it comes to seeing a matter through. It may have some excitement about something, but it fails to back up the matter with action. It quickly wanes as its emotional heights recede into the background to conveniently justify or forget what was said or promised. Such procrastination reveals that we didn't have the intention to do something in the first place. In the end our words have no weight, and our intention no conviction revealing that we lack integrity as well as being untrustworthy in all that we say. Our promises fall to the side as we end up doing nothing.

There is nothing that will destroy a person's testimony as a Christian more than not keeping one's word or vow. We may forget what we said, vowed, and promised others, but God has heard our words and whether we realize it or not they are being weighed as to if they are true, wise, and faithful in all communications and commitments.

Prayer: Lord it is easy to be content with mere words, but if one has integrity, they never settle for empty promises; rather, they fulfill their obligations. Lord, guard my mouth from foolishness, my ways from missteps, and my attitude from indifference. Amen.

August 28

"He also that is slothful in his work is brother to him that is a great waster" (Proverbs 18:9). A good way to describe procrastination is one who remains unpersuaded about doing what they said or promised due to slothfulness towards the matters of God.

Paul speaks of being persuaded, which is a matter of the will. It is not a matter of zeal that is riding high on some emotional wave that will quickly lose its power and strength as soon as it hits the shoreline of reality. It is not an intellectual persuasion after coming to an honorable conclusion that a matter is true or necessary but falls short of walking it out; rather, it points to a type of conversion that a matter is so. If a matter is true, it must be walked out by faith to ensure that the integrity of character and purpose of what is said is maintained.

As we can see in *Proverbs*, slothfulness is a brother to great waste and great waste is the fruit of procrastination where the foxes leave the evidence of debris behind brought on by destruction. How much do we swing from the heights of intention and land on plateaus of procrastination and end up failing to be faithful to our words, responsible in our actions, an overcomer of the foxes that can beset us with excuses and victorious in finishing the race?

Procrastination becomes an open door to wasting the time of others who take us at our word, a waste of opportunities that will never come our way again, and a waste of breath because our words will become idle and a judge to us. The truth is, inaction is unproductive action and indecision will go with the flow, causing a lethargy towards standing for what is right that will end up with the person falling for anything that goes along with their narrative, sentiment or comfort zones.

In such an indifferent environment, there are no absolutes, no real standards of justice, and no sure foundation in which to test the integrity of something. Enough procrastination will produce an aimless generation that will become lost in the insanity of their times, fall through the cracks of indifference, and be driven by the winds of the age into unbearable consequences and irreversible judgments.

Prayer: Lord, Your Word shows us the problem, the solution, and the way. However, we like to ignore Your way, as well as the conditions attached to Your promises, and the warnings of Your Word to make it more acceptable to our fragile realities. Lord the more I see, even when it comes to the best of man, the more I understand why Your Word points out that the righteous are scarcely saved. Amen.

August 29

"And he that was dead came forth, bound hand and foot with graveclothes; and his face was bound about with a napkin. Jesus

saith unto them, Loose him, and let him go" (John 11:44)" In the last post I talked about procrastination. We see the one thing that sinners put off concerns their very soul, well-being and spirit and that is salvation that comes through repentance. However, there is also much that can slip through the fingers of Christians if they put off properly responding to the matters of God.

In the last post I mentioned that fleshly man can be clothed in slothfulness. It can wrap around him like an embalming garment. Even though man stands completely undone before God, he tries to cover it up with garments. There are three type of garments that are mentioned in Scripture.

The first garment is a cloak that covers man's true spiritual nakedness. This cloak covers the "old life." It can be made up of fig-leaves of excuses, robes of self-righteousness, filthy rags that consist of man's best, and heavy garments of fear and depression.

It is not unusual for man to procrastinate when it comes to casting aside the garments of the old to follow Jesus. The excuses are unending, the religious activities are many that may soothe their conscience, the robes heavy but convincing that they are doing what they need to do to stand before the Lord, and the filthy rags decaying, leaving a slight stench. Man may begin by calling out to Jesus for mercy, but in order to rise up and go to Him, he must first cast off the old to receive the new and embrace it in order to follow Him into a new life.

The second garment is the graveclothes. If a person is born again, they must rise up in their new life, but they still can be encased in the graveclothes others put on them.

In the case of Lazarus' resurrection, Jesus told those around him to loose him. So many times, we feel responsible to convince people struggling with the old to cast it off. We may even try, without any success, to take hold and help them. If one insists on holding onto the old, we must let them because it is their decision, and then we trust that at the right time the Lord will deal with them. If they have been wrapped up like a mummy from others who attended them in their past life, we must be available to loose them from such hindrance with the Word of God so they can go forth.

The final garment is humility. This garment is not to cover up the old with fake nobility, to justify one's ongoing victimhood because of the old, or to excuse self from being an overcomer when it comes to the residues of the old life. Humility comes when one is broken over the waste of the old life, repent of its wicked ways, and become repulsed and contrite over the pride that has reigned from the throne of selfishness. Humility is a state that makes us open to hear the voice of the Spirit, possess the liberty to rise up in obedience by faith and truly follow Jesus into the new life.

The key to the overcoming life is not to procrastinate when we are called to follow Jesus. We must be quick to respond and if it means casting off something that seems insignificant or laying something aside that does not seem all that heavy, we must not give audience to debate about doing it; rather, we need to quickly do it so we can be prepared to follow Jesus.

Prayer: Lord, we get excited about the life you offer us, but how many of us really rise up, cast off the old and follow You? We are also around those who need to be loosed, but how many of them are we judging, rather than loosing them with the Word of God? Lord, forgive us for our inept ways, our self-serving attitudes, and our failure to love You with all our heart, embrace Your Word with all of our soul, and cling to Your ways with everything in us. Amen.

August 30

"No man can serve two masters: for either he will hate the one, and love the other; or else he will hold to the one, and despise the other. Ye cannot serve God and mammon" (Matthew 6:24). The other day I was reminded of the word "temperance." It is not a word we necessarily like because it points to discipline. It is not a discipline that comes out of some personal regimentation that is being controlled by a person's strength; rather, it is an inner discipline that comes out of meekness and integrity.

Meekness and temperance are the last two ingredients of the fruit of the Spirit. Meekness points to "controlled strength." For us to be in control of personal strength, our strength must first of all come under the control of some master. For us as believers, our strength must be under the control of the Holy Spirit. We are told even in *Zechariah 4:6* that all God does is not according to His own strength or might, but according to the Holy Spirit. This means God's strength is not kept in check; rather, to maintain the integrity of what is done, it must be properly channeled by and through the Holy Spirit to accomplish the plan or will of God in the right way.

According to what I read, "temperance" has four Greek words that are used to describe the level of it in a matter. The first word, "sophron" points to the person who is mastering their passions. This can't be so unless the person's strength is under proper control. The second word is "egkrates," which refers to a person who is fighting and struggling to gain mastery over their passions. This points to a person whose flesh is still lusting against the Spirit because one is still wrestling with carnal desires that have not been crucified.

The next word that is used is "akates". This word describes one who is losing the mastery over their passions. This points to a person who has not given up their rights to have life on their terms. They refuse to consecrate the whole of their life to God, while holding on to some notion that the world still has something to offer them.

The fourth word is "akolastos." This word describes a person who has lost mastery over his passions. This individual has walked in the foggy arenas of compromise. They have held on to the false promises of the world while juggling religious notions to maintain some semblance or façade of their spiritual status.

The Bible is clear that you can't serve two masters and in doing so, you will hate the one and love the other. The truth is the spirit may be willing to do right but the flesh is weak when it comes to letting go of the world. In spirit, you may have the best intention but without meekness and the willingness and determination to master the flesh, you will succumb to it in due time.

Today there are many trying to control their passions and are losing the battle because they have skipped over the part of being under control of the right master. The one who is your master will determine whether you are being controlled by passions or mastering them.

Prayer: Lord, we are told to be overcomers, but this is impossible until we master our passions. Lord, I know victory over the enemies of my soul begins with me humbly submitting to the work of Your Spirit. Lord, bring me down from the high tower of arrogance so I can truly submit to the gentle, glorious work of Your Spirit. Amen.

August 31

Long gone, and lost forever, so just live on the memories. That's the sad conclusion I finally came to concerning REAL watermelons. Perhaps you remember those big, juicy, sweet, bright red watermelons with the shiny black seeds (which are very good for you, by the way, if you chew them up.) Plus, way back in the "old days" before time-consuming technology kidnapped and held hostage the brains and creativity of most human beings, there was such a thing as watermelon seed spitting contests.

Since it was so hot and the thought of ice-cold watermelon still haunted me, I gave in and bought one of those "man-made" seedless things. As I cut into it, I lectured myself to be fair-minded, and even thankful for it before I took the first bite. However, all my good intentions went down the drain when the watered-down flavor of the pinkish pulp left a bitter aftertaste in my mouth. Disgust, like high-octane jet fuel, set fire to my mental list of woes against modern man's so-called "improvements" on God's creation in general.

Fast forward a couple of weeks, and guess what we found in the local grocery store? A huge box (with a sign that I read five times to make sure it really said what it said) of seeded Hermiston (Oregon) watermelons! There were only a few of them left which caused me to realize that I wasn't the only person left on this planet with a taste for the real thing.

Of course, our friend and co-laborer in the Gospel, Carrie had to do the heavy lifting. That thing weighed so much that we couldn't get through the check-stand in a normal fashion because the scale didn't go that high. Finally, the red-faced assistant manager, who was checking us out and who really wanted to get rid of us, only charged us for ten pounds! Later, when we finally cut into our blessed big "blimp" and saw, smelled and tasted that first juicy bite, we praised the Lord, *"Who satisfies our mouth with good things; so that our youth is renewed like the eagle's" (Psalm 103:5.)*

God knows what we have need of to bring satisfaction to not only our taste buds and physical needs, but to the cravings of our soul and spirit as well. *"For he satisfies the longing soul, and fills the hungry soul with goodness" (Psalm 107:9).* Jesus said, "*Blessed are they which do hunger and thirst after righteousness; for they shall be filled" (Matthew 5:6).* In *Psalm 34:10* we read, *"The young lions do lack, and suffer hunger: but they that seek the LORD shall not want any good thing."*

Wonderful are the promises of the Lord, but we must take note of the conditions that accompany them such as longing and hungering in our soul for goodness, hungering and thirsting after righteousness, and seeking the Lord in His Word and in prayer. Only God can satisfy the deepest longings of the human heart. – J. Haley

Prayer: Lord, we love to quote Your promises while ignoring the conditions. We don't realize that what brings the sweetness out in Your promises are those conditions. Without the conditions, promises are like a seedless watermelon that will leave a bitter taste in Your mouth. Amen.

September

September 1

"By faith Abraham, when he was called to go out into a place which he should after receive for an inheritance, obeyed; and he went out, not knowing whither he went" (Hebrews 11:8). Time is of the essence. Each day is not an opportunity to live as we please in order to experience some semblance of life, but each day is a gift from God to discover the life He has for us.

It is not unusual to see people barely holding on to their concept of life. Many are waiting for the time where everything will somewhat balance out, and they can go back to how things used to be. The question is, "Do we really want to go back to what used to be?"

In my years of serving the Lord, nothing seems to change and yet everything eventually changes. When you walk by faith, you are not walking according to some familiar drumbeat; rather, you are walking as the Spirit leads you and you will never know where you are being led.

Abraham had no idea about where he was being led, for he had never been there. What he did know was that he would end up in the Promised Land. We seem to forget that the patriarch did not have a road map. He had to trust God that He would bring him into the place that was being promised him.

We don't always know how God will direct our steps. Perhaps He will use circumstances, events, or personal challenges. When you follow Abraham, you realize that God caused Abraham's father to leave his home in Ur and move his whole family to Mesopotamia, which is the strip of land between the two rivers, the Tigris and Euphrates. In this region Abraham was still separated from the Promised Land by the Euphrates River that he would later cross over after the death of his father. In fact, the word "Hebrew" which was given to Abram by the Canaanites in *Genesis 14:13* comes from the word "Eber," which means "beyond, on the other side" or "the region beyond," because Abram had crossed over the Euphrates.

Jesus, after He was baptized by John the Baptist, was led out to the wilderness by the Spirit of God to be tempted. This was before His real ministry began. So many times, disruptions in life put us outside the box of what we are used to in order to force us to take steps towards greater promises. For Abraham, God was using certain events and situations to bring him into the land that would become the Promised Land for his descendants.

Our faith walk will often take us out of the familiar to experience the extraordinary or miraculous. It will lead us beyond unfamiliar territory where we are, in essence, forced to trust the Lord with the outcome. For Abraham, He would never see the fulfillment of his descendants inheriting the Promised Land, but he would know what it means for God to be his shield and the rewarder of his faith. He would understand that, for those of faith, it is not about a physical inheritance; rather, it is about possessing the spiritual reality of God and resting in His promises made towards those who are rich in faith and truly heirs of all His unseen blessings.

Prayer: Lord, we fight against the familiar to avoid change we can't control, but at the same time desire some change of scenery to avoid becoming stagnant and insane in the familiar. Lord, we can prove to be a bit fickle and ridiculous, but You know our frame and how we fear what might prove us inept but also contending with the fear of failing to realize the fulness of our calling. Lord, I am thankful, that You direct the steps of Your people. Have Your Way! Amen.

September 2

"I am a stranger and a sojourner with you: give me a possession of a buryingplace with you, that I may bury my dead out of my sight" (Genesis 23:4). In *Genesis 13:17*, the Lord told Abraham to walk through the length and breadth of the new land he was a stranger in because it would become the Promised Land for his descendants. We often must walk out what we have been promised by faith before we begin to even understand what we have been promised.

Abraham walked out the promised land in obedience, but it is important to note that all that Abraham purchased in the Promised Land was a burial plot. This plot not only held the former tabernacle of Sarah's life but it would hold Abraham, Isaac, Rebekah, Jacob and Leah's remains.

This burial place pointed to the seeds that had to be first planted by faith before the promises could take root to be brought to fruition. Remember what Jesus stated in *John 12:24*, "that except a corn of wheat falls into the ground and dies, it will abide alone, but if it dies, it will bring forth much fruit." That corn of wheat was His life. He was pointing to His death, burial, and resurrection, but this same principle applies to our faith.

We are told if we have faith the size of a small mustard seed that it can move mountains. As strangers to this earth, it takes faith to walk through it as pilgrims in search of our real inheritance that is not of this world. We are ever walking towards some type of demise in order for greater fruit to be produced in and through our lives,

My experience in this rewarding faith walk that I have been on for over four decades is that most of the time I had my ideas where I **wanted** to go, but God had other ideas as to where I was **called** to go. They were not only diverse, but in many cases, I was shocked as to where He ultimately led me.

Many times the Lord led to burial places where so much of my past was left behind in some unmarked grave. I began to realize He was preparing me to take greater steps into the unfamiliar as a means to cross over from this world to truly possess the fulness of life He was calling me to. Eventually the unusual terrain I crossed over became normal for me while the concept of "familiarity" became a foreign word that had no place in my spiritual journey.

The question is, is God shaking your present "box" in order to cause you to step outside of familiarity and trust Him with where He needs to lead you next in your newest adventure? He may never lead you from your present location, but where He wants to lead you as far as your walk with Him may take you in an area you are unfamiliar with and the question is, "Will you trust Him, knowing that it is all about gaining more of Him as He leads You ever so close to possess all of His promises?

Prayer: Lord, I had my druthers when it came to following You, while You had Your plan for my life, but in the end, I could do nothing more than cross over to Your plan and way. I am so grateful that Your plan proved to be the best for me in every way. Praise Your Name! Amen.

September 3

"For he looked for a city which hath foundations, whose builder and maker is God" (Hebrews 11:10). I have observed how many get caught up with the Moses's and Davids of the Bible. However, it was Abraham that God made a covenant with concerning his descendants. It was not based on law or great military feats that God called Abraham forth, it was because Abraham had faith towards his Creator.

It is Abraham's faith that led him to the Promised Land, and it was Abraham's trust in what God promised him that caused him to endure the long trial of his faith until God brought to fruition His promise of a son. In fact, Abraham had to wait a quarter of a century, and when all seemed as if it would never happen, God did the impossible by miraculously bringing forth a son that was named Isaac.

The beauty about unfeigned faith is not its ability to hold on but to trust regardless of how impossible it may seem that what God promised is already so in the light of heaven, and will, in due time, be so on earth. It is easy to have sentimental faith when everything is going our way, but real faith is only exercised when we can't see the promise ever really happening. Whether it seems too late or impossible to us is when God steps on the scene to bring it forth according to His time. In the end, there will be no doubt in the mind of the recipients that it was/is a God-thing, a God-matter, a God-promise and only God deserves the glory for it.

This is why faith endures because it knows God means what He says and will bring it forth. God's words are law, His promises sure, and His covenant, "amen" so be it for it is so. Abraham could have stopped with the impossible, became a cork on the waves of doubt because of circumstances, and gone into great despair because time mocked him and even his wife laughed at the prospects, **BUT ABRAHAM BELIEVED.**

Abraham had to cross over much terrain before he could enter into what God promised. He first had to leave behind the familiar and travel an unfamiliar road. He had to cross over a mighty river to even enter into the Promised Land. He had to be content to be a sojourner in the land promised him and a stranger to the people who would later lose it to his descendants. He would have to be as a pilgrim who would never settle for mere crumbs of this world but would seek a city beyond the borders of what was known, reach beyond regions that were limited, and embrace what would remain out of reach until he could enter it by way of his burial plot.

What powerful words, "**Abraham believed**." Yes, Moses gave the Law and led the nation of Israel to the Promised Land, and yes David conquered the enemies of Israel, but Abraham simply believed. as a result God moved aside the impossible, stepped on the scene to do the incredible, and silenced the mockery by turning the scoffing into joy.

May we, as Christians, believe God, believe His Word, and stand on the assurance that what was proclaimed as being so in heaven, will at the right time become so on earth. Meanwhile we continue to reach beyond what we know in this life to gain an inheritance we can't imagine, to ultimately possess that which is eternal.

Prayer: Lord, we have our ideas of what is significant, but You have Your promises that challenge us to look beyond our present terrain to consider that which awaits us in glory. Lord, help us to remember that to gain it all requires us to be an Abraham who simply believes You and walk towards it in obedience. Amen.

September 4

But the fruit of the Spirit is love, joy, peace, longsuffering, gentleness, goodness, faith" (Galatians 5:22). The fruit of the Spirit begins with the love of God because if the heart motive is not right, then what follows will not be pure either. We must remind ourselves that it is only those pure in heart that will see God. It is for this reason the ten commandments can be summarized in two commandments, "Love the Lord God with everything in you and love others as you love yourself." In other words, prefer others in the same way you prefer yourself when it comes to putting yourself first to make sure all of their needs are taken care of.

Jesus added a third commandment for His disciples to walk in, to love each other as He has loved us in a sacrificial way. Finally, we have the words of the Apostle Paul that love is the fulfillment of the law. In other words, it will satisfy the principle of the commandments which is to naturally prefer God and others over yourself so that you can properly honor or minister to them. That is why the first requirement to be a disciple is to deny yourself of being first, foremost, and honored. Without godly love being the principle motive in all we do, there will be no change in heart attitude and in what we end up striving for, which is to make sure we are being honored or recognized in what we do.

The principle of something has to do with what you are naturally bent towards due to that which influences you the most in the way you walk out your life. There are two principles or "bents" that influence us: iniquity and godliness. Iniquity is subject to pride, is bent towards feeding the lusts of the flesh, and wanting to come out on top in some way to receive honor. Godliness is subject to the Holy

Spirit, is bent towards righteousness, and desires above all else to bring glory and honor to the Lord.

We are born with a wrong bent. King David put it best in *Psalm 51:5, "Behold, I was shapen in iniquity; and in sin did my mother conceive me."* The only way to change that bent is to cease going along with it, and in real repentance turn from it and face God with the determination to change the direction of the natural bent in our character by doing what is right according to God's Word. When we truly come into complete agreement with God about a matter by taking on His attitude that is when true conversion takes place.

It is hard to understand that we are bent a certain way when we do not start out with wrong intentions, but it becomes obvious there is such a bent when something contrary to it tempts us to go the way of the selfish "old man's" disposition. Even though we may know what is right, we still want to find a way around it. Hence enters justifying ourselves in some way, only to feel guilty and condemned after we give way to it. Our justifications make our actions seem so right to us at the time. Remember deceitfulness is part of sin.

The question is, what does your present "bent" tell you about your life and walk before the Lord?

Prayer: Lord, we can reform the outside, but we can't transform the inside. We can try to control aspects of the old life of the carnal man, but as long as we try to control the old, we are not free to embrace the new. Lord thank You for reminding me that inward transformation is Your work and not mine. Amen.

September 5

And every man that striveth for the mastery is temperate in all things. Now they do it to obtain a corruptible crown, but we an incorruptible (1 Corinthians 9:25). I have been talking about the fruit of the Spirit which includes love, meekness and temperance. As pointed out, there is a natural bent in our character. To change the natural bent of the old man in us will take both meekness and temperance. We must be under the right master before we take mastery over our passions.

The Apostle Paul brings out our responsibility to master that which would keep us from finishing the course. In fact, he was quite adamant about keeping his body under control to ensure that he could bring it into subjection. This was to keep him from being a hypocrite in his preaching and a castaway when it came to his ministry and life in the Lord. (See *1 Corinthians 9:27*.) "Castaway" points to something becoming reprobate or useless.

This bent is not changed overnight and will require integrity, and something called patience. We must be willing to ever present our bodies to the Lord, die daily to the old man, and submit to the ways of righteousness. We must daily note our different responses to life to ensure that our bent is always being changed towards godliness. Once again, the bent is only changed as we agree with God about what is acceptable, good and right. This agreement is what causes our attitude about God and life to begin to line up to godliness. In other words, this is where the transformation of the mind takes place. Once transformed, we will not agree with that which is not right and true to God and His Word. It is as our attitude comes into sync with God's attitude that our conduct comes into line with His Word in Spirit and truth.

As pointed out in one of my latest posts, meekness is established first when it comes to the fruit of the Spirit which enables temperance to be exercised. For many, we try to get the cart before the horse. In our strength, we try to reform the natural man, control the carnal ways, and take charge of the fleshly lusts so we can outwardly conform to some religious or stoic presentation of Christianity without truly being changed through repentance, transformed by the renewing of the mind in the ways of godliness, and converted to righteousness.

The problem today is that many simply settle for some intellectual agreement about salvation, but they never come to the point of realizing salvation results in a changed bent towards life that lines up to the very ways of heaven as one grows in love with the God of the Bible and wants to please Him in all they do.

Prayer: Lord we are willing to accept surface religion that allows us to skim across the surface of what man ends up accepting as genuine conversion, but Lord You are the One who will go deeper in order to change the real bent of man so He will naturally choose Your way, Your Word, and especially choose to love, serve, and worship You in purity of heart and mind. Amen.

September 6

"Meekness, temperance against such there is no law" (Galatians 5:23). I made mention of meekness and temperance. These two factors make up the last of the fruit of the Spirit. Temperance is an interesting subject because as Christians our lives, speech, attitudes, thoughts, ways, actions, and conduct must be tempered. We can't live as we would like, display an unbridled tongue, ignore unbecoming attitudes, and let our thoughts wander the universe in search of something that will catch our imagination's fancy lest our ways become aimless, our actions wicked, and our conduct egregious.

One of the things that has fascinated me through the years is that in *2 Peter 1*, temperance comes after virtue and knowledge and then is followed by patience. Virtue has to do with character, knowledge with understanding, and patience with trials and testing that come out of experience. Clearly knowledge about God does not stand alone, it must have the type of character behind it that properly tempers what we do with it. Temperance must be surrounded by that which brings understanding as to how one is supposed to respond to a matter which requires a certain amount of patience and discretion to see something through.

We know according to *Romans 8:2* there are two laws: the law of sin and death and the law of the Spirit of the life in Christ Jesus. We read that if we have the fruit of the Spirit, there is no law that can rightly judge it because the law of the Spirit is not subject to the law of sin and death. The reason for this is because if we are walking after, according to, and in the right Spirit which is about possessing the life of Christ, we have brought ourselves under a better law, a new covenant that will prove excellent and satisfying.

Excellence is about looking beyond what is considered acceptable in the world, decent when it comes to the fleshly man and realistic when it comes to calling. As believers to walk in the way of excellence, means we are always choosing the ways of the life of Christ in us that require us to walk towards what is excellent. This means we will choose the path of righteousness and not the broad path and ways of the old man.

Clearly, the self-life must be denied from having any influence over us, the body offered up and kept in check. The flesh must be crucified to ensure we have become crucified to the world's influence, and the ways tempered if we are going to follow Jesus into the life we have been promised.

Prayer: Lord, we can lean back on doctrinal laurels, fall asleep in pews of religious practices, hide behind religious affiliation, and hope for the best, but the truth is we can only know and possess the fullness of Your life by establishing our life in You that is walked out by faith towards You and obedience to Your Word. Amen.

September 7

If there's anything that dogs have taught me, it's the fact that they have "select hearing." Take our super smart Yorkipoo, RayRay, for example. Even though I have Spasmodic Dysphonia I can yell if I have to, so when he's in the back of his fenced yard, hiding behind a bush, I can yell "Come" until the "cow jumps over the moon" and he won't budge. But, if I manage to blurt out words such as "squirrel," "treat," "fish," "chickie," "cookie," "cheese," "chewy" or "Carrie" he'll make a beeline for the door.

Thinking back on all the dogs God has blessed my life with, only one actually came when I called him. All the rest had the same aversion to the word "come" along with the ability to play "deaf" while looking this way and that as if to give the impression they can't quite hear what they're hearing.

This brings to mind how people respond to the Lord's invitation to come to Him, and how He must feel when they choose not to listen, or turn away, or simply ignore His invitation because of love for the world, the flesh and what the devil offers them. Of course, just as RayRay comes if he thinks he's getting something, crowds often followed Jesus because of the benefits He offered such as food or healing, and people haven't changed much from that time to this.

The prevailing attitude is if it benefits me, myself and I, with no strings attached, then maybe I'll think about it. We all love Jesus' invitation in *Matthew 11:28, "Come unto me, all you that labor and are heavy laden, and I will give you rest"* yet many hesitate to come because of the two conditions in the following verses, *"Take my yoke upon you and learn of me; for I am meek and lowly in heart: and you shall find rest unto your souls. For my yoke is easy, and my burden is light."*

Those two conditions require coming "under His yoke" and learning of Him. That requires a complete change of heart, attitude, worldview, identification, goals, and anything rooted in self-interest and self-preservation, plus it requires committed faith and obedience. Are you willing to answer His call and pay the price?

Prayer: Thank You Father, for drawing us to You, and for Your Son Jesus Christ who invites us to come, and for the Holy Spirit who convicts us of sins so that we can confess them and receive forgiveness and cleansing from all unrighteousness. Hallelujah! Amen. – J. Haley

September 8

"The way of man is froward and strange: but as for the pure, his work is right (Proverbs 21:8). The other day I was sharing with the Bible Study group about what I have learned about my way of thinking, doing, and being. It is natural to want our way about a matter. After

all, our way seems right to our way of thinking. We have looked at it from every angle, examined it from all sides, tested it according to all the possible resistance it might encounter, and we still come out with the same conclusion. The conclusion is how can we be wrong, and there is no way that any sound person can't see it my way in the end.

There is only ONE WAY in which we can operate according to, live effectually in, and ensure our walk proves to be beneficial and that is Jesus Christ. Jesus clearly states He is the way, and it does not just entail just a passageway either. He is the way that entails walking towards all truth and walking out His life.

The other part about our way is that the conflict that occurs in relationships does not always come down to what needs to be done, but the way it should be accomplished. The way is attached to our will to see that it is done, as well as our pride which can't perceive that any other way is right but our way.

The Bible is clear about man's way of doing. The reality is when it comes to our way, it may seem right, but it can lead to death (*Proverbs 14:12*). The problem with our conclusion about our way is that it may seem clean in our eyes, but God is weighing our spirit or motives behind why we are insisting on it (*Proverbs 16:2*). Our way often becomes a platform in which rebellion operates that ultimately defies God's authority and proves to be a form of witchcraft as we try to manipulate or control others against their will to see it or do it our way (*1 Samuel 15:23*).

The fruit is the same as the reality of our way. It leads to some kind of destruction or ruin (*Proverbs 16:25*). It is for this reason that God sees our way as strange or perverse. As I thought about God seeing our way as strange, I was reminded that Aaron's two sons were struck dead after offering strange fire on the altar. I had to consider when doing it my way in the matters of God am I likewise offering strange fire to Him that He can't accept and will ultimately cause judgment to fall.

We are told God's ways are higher than our ways and if we fail to walk in the ways of God, we never will learn what they are, and will ultimately err in our heart about what is truly acceptable to Him (*Isaiah 55:8-9; Hebrews 3:10*).

It is natural to want our way, but it can prove to be a type of spiritual suicide to insist on it. We must discern whether we are lining up to God's way in attitude, conduct and fruit. To do this we must walk in the way of the person, work, instruction, and example of the only true right way, Jesus Christ.

Prayer: Lord, we strive hard to be right, but we can't be assured of it unless we are in the way of Your redemption, walking out Your life by faith, and seeking to come higher in Your way of doing. Thank You for Your faithfulness to ever direct our steps as You put each of us in Your way of righteousness. Amen.

September 9

"And I, brethren, could not speak unto you as unto spiritual, but as unto carnal, even as unto babes in Christ" (1 Corinthians 3:1). The other night I was meditating on the word "side" in relationship to people. How many words is the word "side" associated with? For example, standing or sitting on the sidelines, standing beside someone, coming alongside of a person, taking sides, and standing on what we perceive to be the "right" side. You probably by now get the idea of the concept of "side" when it comes to others.

Through the years the famous side I have often stood on came down to "taking sides." However, the fruit that comes out of taking sides often proves unpleasant. We must consider why we take sides because it ends with division which comes out of carnality and discord which God hates. The fruits of it are conflicts and separation in relationships that could have been avoided if others had not fueled the fire by taking sides.

Let's face it, taking a side requires making some judgment call about a matter that we often do not have the full picture of, and finding ourselves becoming judge and jury to a situation regardless of our ignorance about it, especially when it comes to others' experiences. When we strip away the reason and nobility for taking a side, we often find what we refer to as "pride and prejudice" which brings us to an attitude that has already been conditioned in us by preconceived notions or assumptions from past experiences about that person or situation.

Prayer: Lord, we need to be delivered from our pride to flee our prejudice. Until we overcome pride, prejudice will continue to blind us to our arrogance. Lord, give me a hatred for my pride and never allow me to settle for my prejudice becoming my judgment call. Amen.

September 10

"For ye are carnal: for whereas there is among you envying, strife, and divisions, are ye not carnal, and walk as men? (1 Corinthians 3:3). I was watching a historic documentary about a man who was accused of murdering two sheepherders due to a land war between cattlemen and sheep owners because of how others perceived him. He proclaimed his innocence and even had proof, but those involved in the case would have none of it including a jury of his 12 peers.

His peers reasoned even if he was not guilty and hung, that such judgment was long overdue. Eventually his lawyer who believed in justice managed to get him as many as five stays of execution before they finally tracked down the two men who had killed the two sheepherders.

These two men confessed that they did it because there had been an altercation between them. Even when the truth came out, the people involved with his case did not want to let the falsely accused man go. They still wanted to hang him.

At this point one might realize that in many cases, taking a side is not about what is right or wrong, but about who needs to be right in order to make a wrong attitude acceptable. It is nothing more than a matter of pride and not justice, an issue of preconceived notions and not truth, and a situation of opinions and not facts. It is not that such people do not have strong convictions about a matter, but that they are blinded by those convictions and in the end will do injustice to something or someone.

As Christians are we supposed to take sides? I have often asked myself some simple questions before getting involved when it comes to taking any side such as, "Why am I taking a side," "Is this an eternal matter", "Is this about truth or a personal agenda or cause," or "Is this a mountain that God is asking me to risk life, reputation, and my witness for?"

When such carnality came out among the Corinthians as they took sides over who baptized whom, Paul would have none of it either. He told them their response were not that of mature Christians but that of babes who were still drinking the milk of doctrine. In *Hebrews 5:12-14*, we are told such babes can't rightfully discern between good and evil.

Prayer: Lord taking sides often finds us on the wrong side. Lord, that is why saints walk carefully, to not veer off on some sideroad that will leave them stranded and feeling foolish. Oh, I can't begin to count the sideroads I have veered off onto, but You used each one to show me the vanity of me taking sides. Thank You for being longsuffering with me. Amen.

September 11

It's amazing how little things can "make or break" how you feel at any given time. For example, perhaps you read one of my posts several months ago about "dingy Christians" which was "inspired" by the modern, "water-saving," but horrible, washing machine we had? That was one situation that threatened to "break" my mood every wash day. But now I'm happy to report that my "new" (but older) second-hand, refurbished washer with an agitator in it, and dryer do a great job on the laundry.

Just hearing that tough washing machine getting right down to business is one of those "little things" that makes me happy. Is it a really nice-looking machine? Well, at a glance maybe, but not really. Some places on it have been painted over, and there's a little rust inside the lid. In my younger years just knowing the machine wasn't "perfect" would've soured my mood, but today I'm so thankful for how good it works, despite the fact it isn't new and perfect, is no big deal.

This brings to mind how Christians tend to automatically view one another. Humanly speaking, even in Christian circles, we are naturally attracted to what our eyes see, or what our ears hear, when meeting people for the first time while others, who have obviously had a lot of "wear and tear" in their lives, and bear the scars, wrinkles, or broken hearts to prove it, aren't necessarily people we routinely gravitate to. However, these are the people who often turn out to be genuine gems in the kingdom of God—people who have paid a price to gain great faith, wisdom, and the anointing of the Holy Spirit in their lives.

Perhaps we need to pause and ask the Lord to help us see with His eyes, hear with His ears, and to grant us His heart of compassion for those whom we meet who are "less than perfect" outwardly, but who shine with the light of His glory inwardly. *"But the LORD said unto Samuel, Look not on his countenance, or on the height of his stature; because I have refused him: for the Lord seeth not as man seeth; for man looketh on the outward appearance, but the LORD looketh on the heart" (1 Samuel 16:7).* – J. Haley

Prayer: Lord, we are fleshly and tend to judge from this surface and often perverted level. Lord, give us the wisdom to pause, pull back and truly reason with ourselves about what we can see and understand and then seek Your perspective about the matter. Amen.

September 12

"And at midnight there was a cry made, Behold, the bridegroom cometh: go ye out to meet him" (Matthew 25:6). In my last post, I mentioned the word "side." As stated, the side road I often went down was taking the side of some person or situation that caused me to rise up out of passion rather than simply stand up to really consider what is so in a matter. When you refrain from taking sides, it gives

you pause to consider if the matter was any of your business in the first place.

There are other sides to consider. There is standing or sitting on some sideline or coming along side of someone. The truth is we start out sitting on some sideline waiting for something to happen, or we are standing on some sideline because of what is happening.

When it comes to sitting on the sideline it is because we are not involved in the actual situation. We may be observing something or waiting to be called on to do something but we are not involved in what is really happening. To be sitting on the sidelines requires us to be aware of where we are and what is going on but not to become judge and jury of it. It is a time to prepare for the call but not a time to lean back and take a nap thinking when the call comes, we will be ready to properly respond.

Take the five wise virgins, they were prepared while waiting for the call, while the other five foolish virgins assumed when they were called, they would be ready. This assumption required these virgins to slide by without being ready to rise up with a lamp that could be lit to find their way and meet the bridegroom in the lateness and darkness of the time.

It can be a bit wearisome to be ready at all times. When pressed, we can put such pressure on ourselves to make sure we are not wandering in darkness, left in darkness, or lost in it that we actually can become complacent towards it. We hate to admit when we are spending much of our time groping because we are blinded to the real matters around us. In such cases, we are often enfolded in chaos, confusion, and disillusionment.

The problem is that when we are not preparing to take action by being willing to step into the current, we are left on the sideline to try to direct the various happenings before us. The Bible is clear we need to be in the game, running the race, and advancing forward regardless of the obstacles, detractions, and battles.

Prayer: Lord, we do want to be on the right side but if we are to follow You, we must step away from the sidelines and follow You into whatever arena of this world that You are leading us into. Amen.

September 13

"But Moses' hands were heavy; and they took a stone, and put it under him, and he sat thereon; and Aaron and Hur stayed up his hands, the one on the one side, and the other one on the other side; and his hands were steady until the going down of the sun" (Exodus 17:12). We have been considering what it means to stand on some sideline. Standing on the sideline as a mere observer points to passive inaction. You may be considering what is going on around you, but it is from a distance. Distance is not always measured by feet or miles, but by indifference. Let's face it, man can distance himself in many ways.

He can distance himself in his mind, in his affections, and in his interactions with people. He will distance himself in familiarity, when disappointed, and betrayed. In the emotional arena man feels vulnerable, undone, and uncertain of how to act. To avoid being thrown into chaos, man stands on the sidelines while keeping his distance to avoid becoming involved.

As for standing on the sidelines as one prepared to jump into the events, it points to one who is ready to be called. Everything about them is on alert to respond to the situation at hand. They must be ready to not only hear the call but make sound judgments about it because they are prepared to meet the present challenges at hand. The reason they are ready is because they have within their possession the necessary instructions to move forward. In a way they already have the sense of what needs to be done. It is for this reason that when it comes to spiritual warfare, as believers, we are being called to stand.

The other side that we must take is that of ministry. Ministry requires us to come alongside someone in practical service. For Moses, two men lifted up his arms during the battle to ensure victory for Joshua and his army of men. This is the essence of most ministry.

Saints can become weary in their journey, soldiers have been wounded in the battles, and the downtrodden left in their misery. As ministers of the Gospel, we are to come alongside such people to lift them up in prayer and encouragement, bandage up wounds with compassion and gentleness, and take their hand and lead them to a place where they can drink of the Living Water and partake of the Bread of life.

Prayer: Lord, You have set before us the way we are to walk. There are times we are to rest along the way in preparation, other times we are to stand while waiting for the opportunity to advance forward and there are times when we just need to quietly walk up alongside one who is struggling along the way. Lord, the one thing I have always been thankful for is You. In my greatest need and struggle, You have been the Rock I could sit or stand on and the One who came alongside me to be my companion, help, and friend. Amen.

September 14

"Now faith is the substance of things hoped for, the evidence of things not seen" (Hebrews 11:1). What do you hope to gain in this world? Whatever you hope to gain is what you will pursue to possess it. What do you hope to experience in this world? Whatever you hope to experience you will seek it out in this world. What is the true desire of your heart? Whatever the desire of your heart is what you will set your affections on to know it in a personal way.

Occasionally, the Lord will bring me back to these simple questions. We often assume that as believers such matters are automatically taken care of, but when you read the Bible, you find that it is not the case at all. There are personal disciplines that must be put into place by each of us as believers to gain the life Christ has for us.

For example, do you want to gain the world or Christ? Whatever you want to gain, you must personally pursue. You need to keep in mind that in gaining the world, you simply gain an empty lifestyle that has no life attached to it and in the end, you end up with vanity and losing your soul. However, if you are striving to gain Christ, you will gain life eternal.

What do you hope to experience in this world, pleasure or purpose? Pleasure can have a lot of things attached to it like fun, happiness, and contentment. However, such things can't bring real purpose to one's life. For life to have meaning, there must be a reason for us to be here. We may be passing through this world, but to make sense out of our very existence, we must understand the reason for our existence, or life becomes not only empty but a bad joke.

The only thing worth gaining in this world is the Lord. However, to gain Him we must seek Him and if we are going to seek Him, we must rise up out of our spiritual lethargy to do so. We can't allow any indifference, dullness, or apathy keep us from seeking out the Lord. Without the Lord in our lives, there is no meaning to our existence, no purpose to our works, and no hope for anything past this world.

Prayer: Lord, we do miss it when it comes to Your kingdom. We fail to realize our life in You is not a matter of religion, but one of discovering what our life, purpose, and destiny is all about in light of eternity. Amen.

September 15

"But I fear lest by any means, as the serpent beguiled Eve though his subtilty, so your minds should be corrupted from the simplicity that is in Christ" (2 Corinthians 11:3). I have been talking about the matter of what side we are on. Through the years the Lord has had to deal with me over this issue in many ways. Even now, I must be aware of if I am standing on the right side or taking some side. The reason has always come down to the tendency for those with any kind of convictions, causes, and agendas to take sides.

Years ago, I was involved with a group of people who were trying to get Creationism into the school. We went to the capital and spoke to those involved in the educational system, but what we left behind were casualties. The Lord would later bring this to mind during a time when He was dealing with my attitude. As He showed me the division that was created by taking on a cause without really being called to do so, I found myself pitted against Christians who took issue with our stand for one reason or another, as the rest of the saints remained quiet.

In examining what happened, the Lord asked me, "Did anyone get saved?" The answer was, "NO." It was then that I was reminded of my real commission to preach the Gospel and disciple people to truly be His followers.

Through the years I have found myself caught up with debates over what we call "doctrine." In such debates we often leave those who are still young in the faith confused or taking sides instead of encouraging them to study His Word for themselves while seeking His face as to what they needed to know for their own personal growth. He showed me how unprofitable it all was. After all, it is up to the Spirit to bring such conviction to a soul and the Word to bring correction to their conduct and not up to me. I have learned that my way simply conforms people to some mere image while God's way transforms their inner man to the image of His Son.

It was when He brought this matter to my attention that He had me focus on the real issue. For instance, how many debates are there over "once saved, always saved?" The question is not who is right or wrong, but rather the question that needs to be asked of individuals is, "Are you saved?" How about pre-trib, mid-trib, post-trib? Instead of who is right or wrong, the question we need to ask those in the debate is, "Are you ready for His coming?" In other words, stop the debate and bring people back to the simplicity of Christ as to who they say He is and what He has done for them.

When you study the Bible, you realize this is the one issue the Lord would bring His disciples back to—the simplicity that surrounded the issue of His own identity and great work of salvation. In one situation He asked them, "Who do you say I am?" The matter of salvation is not who is right about a theological matter, some doctrinal debate that often ensues, or a particular issue, the matter comes back to whether we are founded on the Great Rock of Ages so that when all that we think we know is shaken, we will still be left standing on what is not only so now, but will remain so in eternity.

Prayer: Lord it is easy to get side-tracked, confused and then sidelined by matters that in the end will prove as vain as the debates that take place over them. Help me keep in the narrow way of Your truth that will set people free and not enslave them into a small religious box that has not served me well and will not serve them well in the end. Amen.

September 16

"For if he that cometh preacheth another Jesus whom we have not preached, or if ye receive another spirit, which ye have not received, or another gospel, which ye have not accepted, ye might well bear with him" (2 Corinthians 11:4). One of the problems with being human is that we can become so focused on a subject or cause that we can become disoriented in our spiritual life and almost become lost to our real commission and ineffective in our calling. This type of scenario causes our soul to be left in some dark place that leaves us confused or struggling to see where God is in a matter and hear what His Spirit is really saying to us.

In my last post I talked about the simplicity of Christ. His great work of redemption is clearly defined by the true Gospel which is the power of God unto salvation. To keep our understanding pure and right in all of our pursuits to know the truth, we must make sure that the right spirit is present who is the only One that is able to lead each of us into all truth about Jesus. All biblical spiritual journeys or roads do not lead us to a physical place, but to the way, truth and life of Jesus. To venture any further than the cause of Christ and Him crucified is to step out of the Way and take a detour.

This brings me to another detour He has revealed to me along the way and that is the matter of conversion. Am I trying to convert people to my way of thinking, which, like the Pharisees, will leave them falling into some ditch, or am I putting forth the seeds of life in order to bring heirs of salvation into His net.

Through the years I have discovered the passion behind personal religious causes could be anything from unresolved issues, whether caused by hurt, great loss, or feelings of betrayal by those in the religious world, or to pride and prejudice that is blinding us to what is important to God. It is up to me to examine my own heart motives and ask the Lord to put a spotlight on anything that would prove unbecoming to His great cause that was clearly manifested in His redemption. The truth is regardless of what I know, my position, or my convictions, it is up to me to consider the fruits I am leaving behind. Converts to our way of thinking often become casualties, while personal pride and prejudice will create division and judgmentalism.

Another great test when it comes to whether I have veered off is other saints. I have read many books and every time the writer gets on some personal detour in their doctrinal beliefs, I find myself bumping along with them until they come back to the real matters of God, which brings me back into the smooth current of the Spirit. However, there are certain writers that, as soon as they hit the bumpy waters, I have to close the book and go on because past that point, I find myself coming into a type of darkness that never leaves me edified.

God uses the silence of saints to sometimes pull me back when I get on some unprofitable bandwagon. It is a signal to me that I am on a detour, and I need to sideline myself and consider if I have indeed gotten sidetracked from my real commission. This is when I always have to consider if I have come under another spirit that will leave not only casualties behind but leave me standing alone on what will prove to be the unedifying mound of lifeless and non-essential convictions.

Prayer: Lord, You have been so patient with me through the years because You understand where I am coming from. It is not my heart to do wrong, to create casualties, or to fail to fulfill my great calling, but in my humanness, I can get sidetracked and disoriented by personal convictions and causes. Show me what I need to know about my own convictions to avoid any and hopefully, all detours. Amen.

September 17

"Then Moses stood in the gate of the camp, and said, Who is on the LORD'S side? let him come unto me. And all the sons of Levi gathered themselves together unto him." (Exodus 32:26). We have been considering different sides a person can take when it comes to life. The final matter as to what side we must be on comes down to making sure we are on the right side of eternity. I constantly mention this because the right side of eternity has to do with standing with the Lord in what is important to Him and not standing for, or on, what we think is right according to our thinking and our ways.

It is natural to think we are standing on the right side because we can see nothing wrong with our conclusions or understanding of something, but the Bible warns us that we are very limited in every arena of life. When it comes to God there is no way we can know all about the matters that concern Him because He is eternal and sovereign. We are asked to believe, trust and rest in the assurance of what we know to be Scripturally important to Him. I realize there are people who spend all their life trying to be experts at something, even His Word, only to find out that there is always something more to discover or learn.

There are people who want to know ENOUGH that they can do some justice to the truth and others who want to know JUST enough to get by and go on. There are those who take pride in their IGNORANCE of a matter because they don't want to be bothered with the responsibility of knowing something that might require them to stand. After all, such individuals can claim ignorance as to why they didn't stand for something, as well as to why they deemed something as being insignificant and unimportant in light of the fact it might require them to actually get involved with a matter.

Again, when we come up against something that might be important, we must make sure our approach is pure and not a matter of personal agendas and causes because such hidden motivations can cause a hardness of judgmentalism to come forth. Judgmentalism reveals we are too close emotionally to breach the matter in gentleness and meekness with patience (*2 Timothy 2:23-24*). Such hardness will cause confusion as to one's authority and witness.

It is important to remember we may be right about a matter, but it will come down to the spirit in which we approach or present something. If that is not right, in the end the fruits will not be pleasant to anyone who partakes of it and the Lord will not receive the glory.

Prayer: Lord, we can be right on and yet miss the target because we are not in a right spirit. Lord, help us to keep the right perspective as a means to approach a matter in the right spirit so we can hit the target head on and be assured in the end that You will be glorified. Amen.

September 18

"And be renewed in the spirit of your mind" (Ephesians 4:23). When it comes to God, what do you desire to be evident in your life in Christ: compliance, reformation or transformation? I was reminded of these three responses when it comes to meeting the expectations of those around us.

As a child growing up, I was for the most part compliant. I would do what those in authority asked. I would study them to see what would meet with their approval to ensure favorable responses. However, compliance does not mean obedience. It is more of a mechanism to get along with others. You avoid causing waves because you don't want the hassle or the turmoil. In a way, it is like keeping the contrary or unpredictable monsters of anger, rejection, and the critical ways of others at bay to keep them off of your back.

The second one is reformation. In the first scenario that entails compliance, you are trying to comply to other's standards. In a way, it is a game which points to a false way because it is not in your heart to be obedient or submissive. Since it is not from the heart such outward compliance can cause inward resentment, anger, bitterness, and outward rebellion down the line because you often wonder if people really see you for who you are and if they did, would they have the same favorable reactions. This causes one to consider if the love of family and friends is conditional after all, and when the compliant person rebels outwardly, it is often to test that love. When it comes to reformation, you are the one who is trying to clean up your act.

Reformation is just another outward reaction. This can occur because you want to meet some requirement to be accepted, meet personal standards to avoid rejection, and/or rise up to meet the occasion to prove that you can do something or attain it. Reformation is simply an outward adjustment of compliance but since it is the person's idea, it has the opposite effect of compliance. When people are striving to reform their act, they can become critical tyrants and harsh judges with others. After all, they are straightening up their act why are you not doing likewise.

The problem with compliance and reformation is that man may adjust the outside to some religious, pious form, but nothing is changing the inner man. It is the life of the inner man that will be ultimately reflected to the outer world. The Word is clear that the spirit of man must be quickened with a new life, and the soul of man must be completely transformed.

This change produces a complete conversion and revolution in the person. This type of radical change needs to be an ongoing work by the Holy Spirit who constantly renews the inner man. If the renewal is not done regularly, man's spirit will wane and the fire in his soul will grow dim as it is overwhelmed by the influences of the world.

Prayer: Lord, we fail to realize our spirit must be renewed and our soul uplifted daily. Thank You for Your Word that nurtures me, Your Spirit that renews me, and Your promises that allow me to live in expectation of seeing You as You are in Your glory. Amen

September 19

"For whom he did foreknow, he also did predestinate to be conformed to the image of his Son, that he might be the firstborn among many

brethren" (Romans 8:29). We are predestinated to be conformed to the image of our Savior and Lord. We must reflect His glory and not our best. In our fallen state, we reflect darkness and in our worldly ways, we reflect vanity and despair. We often cause our ways to comply to that which is base but allows us to get by in the world, and when it comes to our flesh, we try to reform it to appear like we are reformed. However, both attempts fall short of complete change of the inner man.

This brings us to the third and final evidence that we look for when it comes to the Christian life. The real and lasting process that needs to take place is transformation within. For believers, they know that transformation takes place when the Holy Spirit is doing the work. Their responsibility is to repent by turning away from the old, coming into agreement with God about the ways of righteousness and giving way to the ongoing sanctifying work of the Holy Spirit. It is true we need to have a change of heart, mind, direction, and conduct which occurs with real repentance, but we need to be transformed to change our fallen disposition as a means to become a new creation, and that work belongs to the Lord.

Transformation creates a wonderful environment where people come out with a new sense of destiny. Sadly, most choose compliance and reformation because they perceive that it is their responsibility, or they must be in some way in control of the proceedings to make sure it happens. Whichever way they look at it, they are missing the point.

Man can't make himself acceptable to God. He must concede that like the metamorphosis a caterpillar must go through to become a beautiful butterfly, he must be completely changed within before reaching the potential of becoming the creation he is called to be. This points to being born again of the Spirit where a person is completely changed from within to meet their greatest purpose yet: to be conformed to the very image of Christ.

Prayer: Lord, we want to be the one that takes the credit for any change in our life, but all lasting change comes from You. You alone change the inner man to bring every believer forth as a new creation.

Thank You Lord for being the One who so lovingly has changed me through the years to bring forth Your glory in and through my life. Amen.

September 20

Were you ever strangely enticed by a picture on social media? That is to say, even though there are hundreds of thousands of wonderful, beautiful, haunting, compelling, and emotionally moving pictures that tell a "story" or stir up fond memories, sometimes an image shows up on your feed that draws you in and stirs up something deep inside of you that makes you wonder about yourself.

Hence, the picture of a particular castle on Facebook and its surroundings caused me to see myself in it. It is as though I have been there in my mind. Perhaps it is due to the many travels I enjoyed when reading books that spoke of the places my ancestors migrated from. If I could rise from my chair and follow that pathway leading into the beautiful little castle in the picture that someone in the past built and lived their life story in, I surely would've done it! They say that our DNA holds certain aspects or "memories" passed down from our ancestors.

I realize that the beauty in heaven will make everything in this world pale in comparison, but this earth gives us glimpses into God's incredible beauty. In our present state, we can imagine ourselves in faraway lands where our ancestors lived, and even sense some pull or identity to it, but we can't begin to know the great inspiration and awe that God's heavenly beauty will bring to our spirit and soul. Meanwhile, we enjoy the paths of the past and the possibilities of the present, in lieu of the hope of the future.

Only God knows the totality of our complex and wonderful being, and what an awesome thought that is indeed! *"O LORD, thou hast searched me, and known me. Thou knowest my downsitting and mine uprising, thou understandest my thought afar off. Thou compassest my path and my lying down, and art acquainted with all my ways" (Psalm 139:1-3).* - J. Haley

Prayer: Lord, we never know how much of the past effects our desires, preferences, and points of inspiration, but the one thing I know is You know all about me. I was knit in my mother's womb by Your hand according to Your call on my life. I am so glad You are my true potter and that You will continue to shape my life until You bring me to perfection in Your glory. Amen.

September 21

"Wherefore, he saith Awake thou that sleepest, arise from the dead, and Christ shall give thee light" (Ephesians 5:14). It appears as if the contending for souls has become a lost cause in the present climate of religious activity. It is all about getting along with each other, while avoiding insulting anyone with truth. The goal seems to be trying to make the sinner comfortable in pews with their sins and offering those of the world enough spiritual scraps that they perceive they have had enough religion to get them by. It becomes increasingly obvious that it is not about saving souls, but about gaining several bodies to promote the success of personal kingdoms according to the world's methods and standards.

My question is how many are truly saved? People who do not believe there is a God in their heart use such practices as a possible "fire insurance" against hell, but do not realize that it is useless. They need to hear the truth about God, sin, and the vanity of this present life in a doomed world, along with the reality of future judgment so they can be awakened to their lost state.

The truth is many people settle back on their idea that they know there is a God. Some have enough religion under their belt to perceive they are good enough or in a good position with God to make it into heaven. Others have the right answers but lack the fruit of the Spirit to even interact with that which is heavenly. There are those who stand firm on what they believe, but is their foundation truly the Rock of Ages, or instead is it the shifting sands of rigid theology that lacks the right Spirit, doctrine that lacks love, or mere religious platitudes that end up proving to be indifferent because there is no connection with what is really happening?

The attitude the world has towards God, religion and life reveals much about the condition of the church of our times in America. Some of it shows little concern towards the lost soul that is wandering in a barren wilderness, or through some endless maze of challenges, trouble, and difficulties.

Jesus died for the sinner. He left behind witnesses and His promises to part the darkness of hearts and souls with the truth. He then ascended to heaven so the Spirit could be sent to convict the sinner of their sin and sanctify the believer that is born again. He preserves His Word so the heir of salvation knows what it means to be saved from all that holds each of us in bondage in the present world. It also allows believers to cling to the significance of their position in the heavenlies as they walk through a doomed world. Most of all it gives them great hope as they walk towards an eternal world of heavenly bliss and glory.

Prayer: Lord it is your heart, will, and commitment to save mankind, but they have put their fingers in their ears, closed their eyes, and refuse to respond to Your invitation. I am so thankful that You gave me the heart to seek, the will to know, and the revelation of Your commitment to cause me to respond by faith to come and drink from the rivers of Your Living Water so I can live. Amen.

September 22

"In whom we have redemption through his blood, the forgiveness of sins, according to the riches of his grace" (Ephesians 1:7). In the last couple of posts, I talked about salvation and sinners. God made salvation simple in understanding for the sinner and practical in how it works, Clearly, what is being greatly promoted when it comes to God, religion, and eternity is Universalism where all will be saved without coming by way of the cross of Jesus.

Due to the heresy of our times, such individuals don't have to admit sin that constantly lies at their door or nips at the heels of their fleshly ways. They do not have to confess that they are wrong about life-and-death issues, especially God. The most heaven can be to many who have bought this lie is a quasi-paradise where everything that surrounds a soul is what is based on the heart's desire they have developed in relationship to their present life on earth, such as fishing in the ponds of heaven, playing golf on some grassy turf amidst the gardens of heaven and having one big party.

My concern is that those who live in some religious bubble that is agnostic in attitude, gnostic in philosophy, religious in some practices, and views some type of church affiliation and movement as a shoe-in with the unseen, will end up pointing their finger on judgment day at a church, that for the most part, has been lulled to sleep. This spiritually dull state comes from those of the church compromising with the world, as well as being casual towards their high calling. They are conditioned to accept preaching that merely tickles the ears, while those preaching have become more complicit with the truth. Such individuals who have mishandled their calling and truth will not stand distinct in the darkness so the light of Jesus can truly shine through it.

It is not the church's responsibility to find some diplomatic way to tell man he is lost in his sin and on his way to an existence that will prove more distressing than the one here on earth. The Holy Spirit is the One who convicts of sin while revealing to the lost soul the need for a savior. He is the One who points people to Jesus Christ as the only Savior.

This proves man does not save; rather, man is the tool used to awaken the soul with the powerful preaching of the true` Gospel to reveal lost man's spiritual plight. It is the Holy Spirit who confirms all truth and reveals the source and way of salvation.

Prayer: Lord, when the church neglects its commission, it will lose its vision and its way. You are clear why we are here, and it is not to make people feel good in their doomed state, comfortable in their pews of indifference, and deluded by a false hope of salvation. Lord, shake Your people awake, cause the fire to fall, and a dose of healthy fear to cause them to tremble before Your warnings, admonitions and judgments. Amen.

September 23

"*If a man say, I love God, and hateth his brother, he is a liar: for he that loveth not his brother whom he hath seen, how can he love God whom he hath not seen" (1 John 4:20).* It is easy to promote the positive aspects of God's love and grace, but the Bible has many warnings about those who do not enter the fullness of God's kingdom.

We know truth sets people free who cease to insist on their own reality. We know that His love is available to whosoever will believe His great work on the cross. He has made it clear that He offers forgiveness and grace to all who will accept Jesus' invitation to come.

The truth of the matter is that there are so many warnings to those who call themselves Christians. The issue is not whether God loves us, rather do we love Him. We highlight that which allows us to comfortably walk in a nominal Christian life by hiding behind God's eternal qualities such as love and grace, while being indifferent to the fact real love never takes the middle road of commitment. It is sacrificial and those who possess it will do all to guard the integrity of it, knowing that its presence will manifest itself in worship of the Lord, and ministry and service to others.

To love God is to love and prefer His truth and His creation. The church must stand on the truth of what God has established. It must continue to stand with truth when it has been presented so the light can shine, as well as for truth so that man will see his great need for a Savior.

It is not to be the church's way to cause man to be comfortable in sin, but rather to awaken people to the consequences of sin. It is not the church's message to tell how God's loves us, but to stress that the love of God is found only when one comes to the cross of Christ. Man must see how this love has been extended to whosoever will come to receive it by faith, experience it because of redemption and walk in it because the Spirit of God truly resides in all who believe and assimilate the great message of the cross of Jesus.

The big problem is man confuses his part of child-like faith when it comes to salvation. He fails to believe the Word of God as absolute truth and stand on it as so, while trusting that the actual work of salvation is strictly the complete work of God in a lost soul. The blood of Jesus justifies, the work of the Spirit sanctifies, and the love of the Father reminds us we are His adopted children, heirs of an eternal promise with a wondrous future that allots each of us a destiny to meet and live in the glory and majesty of the One who sits on the throne of heaven.

Prayer: Lord, as believers we have such a wonderful future and yet we still tend to wallow in the pig pens of the world. We strive to not sink into the cesspools of its perversion, and hope that there is something other than vanity the world has to offer. Lord, save me from the foolishness of it all and bring clarity to the great hope I have in the work of Your redemption so that I can reflect Your heart and share it with others. Amen.

September 24

"For godly sorrow worketh repentance to salvation not to be repented of: but the sorrow of the world worketh death" (2 Corinthians 7:10). What does it mean to really repent? Jesus was clear you need to repent or perish. The question is, repent of what? What will cause one to perish?

We must define what repentance is not. It is not feeling sorry about something because you got caught. It is not about reforming yourself because you feel guilty about something in order to do better. It is not an intellectual acknowledgement that you are wrong and next time you will not do it because of consequences. Each of these represent a worldly sorrow that will lead to dead ends, failures, and death.

True repentance is about change that comes out of godly sorrow. Godly sorrow entails brokenness and contrition of the heart over something called "sin." There is a sense of desperation behind it because of the vanity it reveals about the present life, and becoming repulsed at the bitter fruit that it produces. This change is not some minor adjustment here or a bit of fine turning there. It is a revolutionary change that is necessary to ensure completion and success.

Repentance entails attitude, the thought process, and the way something must be in order to change conduct. People are creatures of habit. They naturally respond to matters the way they always have. The problem is that people do not see how their way causes offense or despair among those who must contend with the fallout.

Offenses leave a bitter taste and sometimes a broken heart to those that encounter its indifferent sting. Jesus said of such offense they cause bruising to the tender soul and wound the sensitive spirit. In fact, wounding the spirit robs one of real hope.

True repentance turns one from their way of doing to face the light of God. It is the light of heaven that exposes the destructive, selfish ways of man. The more one walks in the light of God, the more the deviation of their character and ways will be exposed.

Prayer: Lord, You have shown us the easy way back to You, but we often find that we first must end in a devastating situation before we will turn and crawl back to You, broken and pathetic. Thank You for being long-suffering towards me when my stiff-necked opinions and ways take charge. Amen.

September 25

"Lest there be any fornicator, or profane person, as Esau who for one morsel of meat sold his birthright" (Hebrews 12:16). Man is always trying to change the environment around him, instead of allowing God to change the environment from within. Man thinks outward reformation and compliance is a sign of repentance when it is man

just adjusting outwardly to some outward pressure or consequences. Such outward adjustment can be backed by great tears and distress. However, nothing has really changed, and the problem that produced some very unbecoming fruit is still present.

Those who try to change the environment for others by adjusting to something that is not pleasant for them can only keep it up for a couple of weeks and then they go right back into the same cycle, doing the same things. They end up conducting themselves in the same manner. The reason for this is because they don't see what is so wrong about it; therefore, they have not been persuaded that it is the real source behind the conflict. They see no need to change their attitude towards it. Without the change of attitude, there is no change of conduct.

Since they don't see what is wrong, their way of thinking has not changed. Any change is merely throwing their crumbs at others to quiet them. They will agree with what they think the person wants to hear to placate them, as well as agree to adjust to keep them at bay, but adjustment will never amount to real, lasting change because their perception of it has not changed.

It is natural to go the way of worldly sorrow when it comes to sin like Esau, but it lacks faith to believe what the Word of God states about it. Without a genuine change in attitude about that which is profane to God, such attempts fall short of the person taking the necessary responsibility for it. Without agreeing with God about a matter there is no assurance that a real change in attitude has taken place that will manifest itself in conduct.

Meanwhile, it is clear, we must repent of our sin or perish in our sin. Once we pass through the threshold of this world into eternity, there is no turning back from what will ultimately prove to be our destiny.

Prayer: Lord, we want to skip over, hedge around, ignore, and close our eyes to what it really means to repent and be saved, but in the end, there will be no excuse because You have made it clear in Your Word. Lord, thank You for opening my eyes to Your truth and pulling me out of the way of destruction and setting my feet on the true path of life everlasting. Amen.

September 26

"For though I made you sorry with a letter, I do not repent, though I did repent: for I perceive that the same epistle hath made you sorry, though it were but for a season" (2 Corinthians 7:8). This brings us to true repentance. As I've stated, true repentance begins with brokenness OVER sin, and not because of sin that results in consequences. We must see what sin does not only to ourselves, especially in our relationship with God since it breaks it and puts us at odds with Him, but when it comes to others as to how sin bruises, wounds, and causes despair to their souls.

True repentance is an about-face. It is coming to a PLACE of repentance. It comes down to facing God about the matters that concerns Him the most. It is where we allow Him to reason with us about sin to gain His perspective about something and not maintaining our own.

In the verse above Paul acknowledged that he was not sorry for making the Corinthian Christians sorry about a matter even if it was only for a season, but in a sense, he was changing his mind as to the impact it made on them. In the following Scripture, *verse 7:9*, he recognized that they sorrowed to repentance.

Like Paul I have seen Christians feel sorry for what they have done, but it has not always lasted long. Many figure that since they felt bad, that should be good enough and for a short season may change their conduct but their attitude about the matter remains the same. They may have even thought about it, but a lot of times they went back to their old attitudes and slid back to their former ways. So, what does it mean to repent?

A dishonorable matter between parties can't change until there is a change in attitude that will produce the right fruits. Paul was able to change his attitude because the Corinthians changed theirs, which produced a proper response and conduct from them.

Prayer: Lord, we are told to repent of our ways or perish in them. We have a hard time recognizing the destructive ways of our selfishness which blinds us to the devastation that we leave behind in the lives of others. Lord, forgive us for being insensitive and blind to our dishonorable ways towards You and others that are brought on by wrong attitudes. Amen.

September 27

"Now I rejoice, not that ye were made sorry, but that ye sorrowed to repentance: for ye were made sorry after a godly manner, that ye might receive damage by us in nothing" (2 Corinthians 7:9). Today there are many searching for answers to an upside world that is disrupting lives at every turn. Many individuals are falling into pits of despair because there is nowhere to go to find relief, peace, and rest. There are those who scream as loud as they can at the realities they are being confronted with, and others who live in false realities so they don't have to admit life is not a fairytale or a Hollywood production.

For believers, we walk by faith towards God. He is the solution to the mess of this world. Faith is not about changing our reality; rather, it is what will get us through this trying, difficult world and the times we live in. The reason we walk by faith towards God is that at some point, we truly repented and ceased to walk in our old way as we turned and began to walk in our new life towards the glory of God.

Changing a matter is not a matter of intellectual understanding but identifying with our new source and way of life. In fact, we begin to walk in the ways of the Spirit which makes us sensitive towards God and others. It is at that point we can begin to see the offense and hurt our "former" ways caused others. In other words, the Spirit helps us to make a correct estimation of a matter in light of the kingdom of God.

Clearly, the offenses our ways have caused others would not cause us any real harm or disruption up front, but in due time we would reap the consequences. In our new way, it is the Holy Spirit who will convict us of selfish ways.

This is why we must consider our attitude about what we were/are sorry about. We must think about where our attitude towards such matters as sin is leading us. As we think on the way we are about to take, we must make sure that ultimately, we come into agreement with how God sees a matter to change our perception or estimation of something. We must end up with the same estimation as God if we are going to be persuaded that it is wrong or missing the mark of bringing glory to Him.

Changing our estimation of something is how we change the wrong bent in our lives towards a matter. Once the bent is changed to line up to and come into complete agreement with God's attitude, it is then we will adjust our conduct to what is right in the sight of God.

It is natural for the flesh to show worldly sorrow and pride to show self-pity, but for the godly it creates a godly response towards God that reveals that in repentance one has not only turned from the old way but now is walking in the new way of excellence that reaches the heights of true righteousness.

Prayer: Lord, we are always trying to adjust to this matter according to what is obviously a wrong attitude, adjust to avoid feeling bad, and adjust ourselves to whatever to avoid feeling guilty so we can get along, but such adjustments have nothing to do with repentance. Lord, I need to make sure my bent is changed so I can line up to the excellent ways of Your righteousness. Amen.

September 28

"Awake to righteousness and sin not: for some have not the knowledge of God: I speak this to your shame" (1 Corinthians 15:34). One of the great struggles even for me is when does purity become cloudy and muddy? When does doctrine become unprofitable and when does high calling become a base cause? And, finally when

does good take a detour from what is best, and when does best, when given the opportunity, fail to choose the way of excellence?

We know that the flesh lusts against the Spirit and that there is conflict. We are told the spirit is willing, but the flesh is weak; therefore, it is easy to fall into temptation.

In *Hebrews* we are being told that it is God's heart to show us a better way in this present dispensation of grace. This is in comparison to the previous way of His holy Law and ordinances. To walk in the Spirit is a more profitable way than to walk in the flesh, and yet many insist on walking in the flesh and not in the Spirit.

If we are asleep to the dullness or stagnation taking place in our spiritual life, we must be awakened to that which is not lukewarm but to the path of righteousness that leads to godly conduct. It was clear in Paul's exhortation in the above Scripture that the great challenge to us as believers, is not to succumb to some comatose state where we are asleep to the true state of humanity. The question is, how many of us really need to be awakened to righteousness because we have not been totally converted to righteousness when it comes to our attitude about sin?

What does it take to be converted? It should be a daily pursuit. We are to seek God and His righteousness daily in Scripture. This practice points to ensuring we are of a right spirit which entails the necessary purity to see God in a matter to know if we are doing His will according to His Word. As we apply the cross to the old, fleshly ways, we will find greater liberty in our spiritual walk. All the time we are coming out from what is carnal and worldly to separate ourselves to what is truly acceptable to the Lord.

I must occasionally check to see if I am awake to righteousness when it comes to the matters of the Lord. How about you? Are you awake?

Prayer: Lord, it is easy to look around and guess who is awake and who is asleep. Some have been known to listen to Your words with closed eyes to discern or meditate on them, some shut themselves in with You when it comes to worship, and there are those who are thinking about worldly things and not on things above. You know who is who but the real issue is, am I awake to what is important to You? Amen.

September 29

"Sow to yourselves in righteousness, reap in mercy, break up your fallow ground: for it is time to seek the LORD, till he come and rain righteousness upon you" (Hosea 10:12). To me this Scripture is like a loaded gun. It is informative, the aim is clear, and the instruction will hit the target. However, the question is, am I ready to allow the Spirit to take it and make the right impact in my life.

What is the first thing we are told in this Scripture? We are told to sow in righteousness. When this was written, Israel was in grave sin. They were sowing in iniquity. Iniquity is defined as moral deviation from that acceptable way of what is right to God. They were basically sowing seeds in ground that was not properly prepared, in rows that were not straight, and in the midst of weeds that would overshadow and eventually choke out anything of substance.

When it came time to reap, it would not be mercy but judgment that would come forth from their planting and the type of seed they were using. They would know the bitterness of their own doing, the vanity of their ways, and the uselessness of the fruit that would be produced.

The instruction was to break up the fallow ground. The heart represents that fallow ground. It had become hard and it would take a pickax or plow to break through the hardness to make it possible for the seed to even take hold. Those who break up such ground will admit that it is hard work.

In a sense, what comes next is a warning. The warning is that it is time to do so. You have to realize that Israel was about to taste judgment. It was coming upon them in the form of a wicked nation called Assyria which would not show mercy, and what they did not kill or destroy, they would enslave and disburse through their empire.

What was it time to do: Seek the Lord. Israel had a short time to seek the Lord. Were they to seek God for a day, a week or a month?

We are told they were to seek God until He would come and rain righteousness upon them. It was obvious that Israel had become a barren wilderness, revealing even more as to the reason the ground of their heart was hard. They had let much slide by when it came to seeking God and making the necessary investment in their lives before God to keep their heart tender towards Him.

It is easy to put off seeking the Lord. We convince ourselves we have more pressing matters to take care of when it comes to this world. We convince ourselves that when all has been taken care of, then we will seek the Lord. Our responsibilities in this life will never cease and it is for this very reason there are those who lose out because they miss the opportunity to seek Him out while they are able to. Due to the hardness of Israel's heart, God ended up with ground that needed a sturdy plow put to it. Sadly, that plow came through captivity and oppression.

Prayer: Lord, I have missed opportunities in the past because I spent too much time trying to justify why I can't seek You out. It is not that You have bad timing, it is because I have my focus and priorities in the wrong places. Forgive me. Amen.

September 30

Drastic changes, hard challenges, and unexpected detours in one's life can cause, among other things, confusion, depression, and exhaustion. After hitting this point lately, it was mildly amusing when a mental picture surfaced in my mind of my dad's old Evinrude outboard motor. "That's me and how I feel right now" I said to myself. I used to call that thing "ever-rude" and here's why.

Back in the 1950's Dad loved to go fishing in Puget Sound. So, my parents and I would head out early to Haines Boat House in Meadowdale to rent a small boat to which he attached that unpredictable outboard motor. After getting it cranked up, it noisily propelled the tiny wood boat across the Sound to where the salmon fishing was usually good.

Back and forth we'd slowly "rock, roll and troll" with that sputtering, stinky motor making me sicker by the minute. (I always sat in the bow so all the fumes from "Rude" wafted my way.) The thing is, on every fishing trip, sooner or later, "Ever Rude" would conk out and refuse to start no matter how long and hard Dad had to pull, yank and crank on it. On top of that, with every fishing trip, when the tide began to turn, the situation would become more tenuous as the waves got choppy and often mounted up and crested over, becoming what we called "white caps".

Sometimes "Rude" would simply stop working in the middle of the Sound, and mind you, that is also a major shipping lane for merchant ships. Anyway, we all, by the mercy of God, survived those days.

Perhaps the Lord brought "Rude" to my mind recently because one of the things that it reminds me of is how fickle Christians can be when it comes to staying on course and seeing things through to the end no matter how "choppy" things get. Through the years we've watched more people than we can remember eagerly "crank up" their "motor" in eager determination to do some "great thing" for God, only to sooner or later lose their vision, weakly sputter out, and either aimlessly float through the motions of being religious or sink to the bottom in despair.

There may be different reasons for this, but by and large the fault lies at the doorstep of the Laodicean church system because it has failed in its commission to make disciples of Christ, opting instead to present "ear tickling" New Age, ecumenical nonsense and a "once saved, always saved no-matter-what-you-do" false gospel that embraces, promotes and teaches "another Jesus, another Gospel, and another Spirit." *"And Jesus said…No man, having put his hand to the plough, and looking back, is fit for the kingdom of God" (Luke 9:62).*

May the LORD help us to endure to the end. – J. Haley

Prayer: Lord, man-made motors fail in the oceans of this world, but hearts must not fail when it comes to You. Zeal will wane when it comes to great things, but commitments of love must hold steady when it comes to enduring to the end. Lord, cause love to grow in my heart and steady my faith so I can endure to the end. Amen.

October

October 1

"Whoso offered praise glorifieth me: and to him that orderedth his conversation aright will I shew the salvation of the Lord" (Psalm 50:23). How many times have you heard that our ultimate goal as believers is to glorify God? Yet, what does it mean to bring such honor to God?

We often think we bring glory to God through religious ceremonies, actions, or some type of pious conduct. We complicate the simplest things in the matters of God because we think we must do our part to highlight God by highlighting aspects of our commitment. We try to show how God brings out the best in us and therefore, we need to consider Him, but what are we told in this Scripture?

It is praise that we offer that glorifies God. In other words, it is not about us putting our best foot forward to show the greatness of God; rather, it is glorifying God because He is great. He does not need any help from us to try to get others to realize what it means for Him to be God.

What is praise? We all have our ideas but probably a good example is when we praise the people around us for carrying out certain tasks, whether it is our children, co-workers, etc. Do we praise them for just anything or the fact that their deed is worthy of praise? We praise them because they do not settle for just getting by in a matter; rather, they excel in it in such a way that their accomplishment even stands out more than they do. In fact, they make it look easy.

It is the way in which the person does something that we admire because it inspires us. We commend them for their accomplishment because it reveals their depth of character. Due to the way in which they do it, we are acknowledging them because they are worthy of such recognition. This type of praise is a way of paying tribute to them.

To praise God is to pay tribute to Him. We are acknowledging who He is, as well as recognizing the goodness and excellence in which He does all things.

Prayer: Lord, we have so much to praise You for, but our greatest point of praise is towards who You are. Praise Your holy name and all that You do on my behalf. Amen.

October 2

"Ye also, as lively stones, are built up a spiritual house, an holy priesthood, to offer up spiritual sacrifices, acceptable to God by Jesus Christ" (1 Peter 2:5). I often confused praise with worship. Praise and worship often walk hand in hand. Praise creates an environment of worship. It lifts our mind above this world in awe to consider the character, ways and works of God.

When we praise God, we are honoring Him for who He is. When considering Him, we are in awe of His great works, overwhelmed by the reality of His holy attributes and His perfect ways. When we consider God in His majesty, our mind automatically lifts heavenward, as our spirit takes flight in such adoration and our soul becomes overwhelmed by such gratitude that God is who He is.

It becomes obvious that the Lord stands alone in all He does and we can't help but pay tribute by glorifying Him. We are told when we are lifted up in such heights in our spirit towards Him by praise, we have just offered a sacrifice that God approves of and now we are part of an environment He can inhabit.

Notice how when one who honors God and orders the conversation of his life in the right way that the result is the salvation of the Lord. This shows us our Christian life is not to be a display that others admire, but a witness that bears record of One who is beyond description. It is not meant to outshine the best, but to shine through the worst with God's glory. It is not meant to lead the cause but to walk a path that often proves to be lonely at times so that when we come forth our life of service is not about us but reflects that we have indeed been in deep places with our Lord. These deep places allow us to leave behind the sweet savor of our Lord Jesus Christ as a tribute that will cause others to look up and consider Him in His majesty and greatness.

Prayer: Lord, we strive so hard to bring You glory when all You want us to do is become one who is consumed by the reality of Your life so that in the end, You will be exalted and honored before others. Amen.

October 3

"Then he said, Go, borrow thee vessels abroad of all thy neighbors, even empty vessels borrow not a few" (2 Kings 4:3). I was thinking about my expectation when it comes to God. We can have a type of morbid hope because it lacks expectation. The necessary fuel behind expectation that causes hope to become an abiding anchor to the spirit when it comes to God is active faith.

I have operated in what I call a "morbid hope." Morbid hope is, "I believe, but when it comes to me it does not apply." In essence, the hope of something is far from me, while it has been made available to everyone else.

"Morbid hope" at any stage is often rendered into self-pity. After all, how much have I strived, worked for, and tried to discipline myself to grab ahold of such hope to claim it as my own, especially during trying situations?

The truth of the matter is, such striving was my lame way of showing my waning, weakness of absent faith while unbelief pushed me closer to a dark pit of unbelief and despair. However, faith is not a simple matter of doing; rather, it is about standing in the darkness and only advancing to maintain the territory when commanded to do so.

This widow sought out the one who she knew could change the situation, the prophet Elisha. She shared her predicament with him, and he told her what to do. She was to gather every vessel she could from her community. In this case her search and obedience were a matter of faith, but the number of vessels revealed the quality of her expectation in doing so.

If she settled for a few, it would reveal her hope was close to being on life-support. If she gathered just enough that would show her trust in God had been shaken and her expectation would reveal a possible trepidation that dared not expect more. However, the fact she gathered as many as she could revealed her faith was active and her hope sure. It became clear that in the end, her expectation rose up to meet the test and God met her, not only in her need, but in abundance.

I had to ask myself if I was in the same situation how many vessels would I gather? I guess it would depend on a few factors such as if I am lukewarm in my faith towards God, or a procrastinator when it comes to obedience to God's instructions because I have no vision past my self-serving world. The final key would be if I was desperate enough to even take hold of real hope to relentlessly pursue God until I found Him and received the necessary instructions.

In times such as this is when I am honest that my faith is not sufficient enough, and that I need to believe in an all-sufficient God Who will give me the measure of faith that enables me to walk through the darkness, while trusting my loving Creator to work out the details.

Prayer: Lord, we have incredible examples in Scripture as to what can happen when one has expectations towards You. I feel so much falls short because I seem to stop short of experiencing not only You meeting me in my need but opening the flood gates to know Your abundance in a matter. Help me to avoid falling short, or taking shortcuts, and keep my temperament from becoming short because of irritations that stop me from finishing the course. Amen.

October 4

"Then said Jesus unto him, "Except ye see signs and wonders, ye will not believe" (John 4:48). We all know the first miracle Jesus performed. It was at His mother's request. She had no doubt in her mind that He could turn water into the best wine. She was a woman of faith and perhaps it came because of her relationship with Jesus. She ordered the staff to obey whatever He told them to do. How many of us have such a relationship with Jesus that we have assurance He will do what we ask of Him, and that it will be followed by some type of obedience on our part?

How many know about the second miracle that also was recorded in the Gospel of John? The second one involved a nobleman who came to the Lord on behalf of his dying child. Did he have such expectation when he approached the Lord about something so precious and dear to him? He asked in hope that was clinging to the possibility that the one He sought would resolve the matter. Perhaps it was Jesus' simple response that gave him confidence to trust Him, "Go thy way; thy son liveth."

Jesus did not heal the nobleman's son to prove who He was; rather, He healed his son to confirm the measure of faith the father had displayed towards Him which was manifested by his response of simply obeying Him. The Lord was clearly affirming that this man had not placed his faith in vain on Him. Now, note the nobleman did not tell Jesus what to do or how to do it, he simply asked Him to do it.

In the last post I spoke of something I refer to as morbid hope. Morbid hope is based on a wrong understanding of faith. Such faith is often based on what God can do. When people possess a wrong understanding of faith, they expect God to perform a certain way because it seems right and fair to them, while unfeigned faith is letting go of the method or the conditions, and simply trusts God to be God. It is prepared to obey the instructions that follow. Keep in mind Jesus often followed a miracle with some kind of instruction. The miracle may affirm faith, but the instruction was a test of faith to see if it would cause the person to rise up and walk towards, or in, the promise of it. In the end faith would become a witness to others as to why God counts faithful responses for righteousness.

So many times, we want God to prove to us who He is before placing faith in Him, but faith does not require proof, faith believes it is true and reaches forward to walk in it regardless how dark the time, and how impossible the terrain appears. To reach towards God without knowing the end results is what faith looks like, as it walks towards God in the expectation of hope to possess the many promises which are inherited by faith.

What does your life of faith say about your understanding of how it will manifest in your life?

Prayer: Lord, many perceive faith to be what will be handed to them. What is handed to us is Your blessings because of grace, but faith is about possessing or inheriting the promises and that requires us to walk towards You, knowing that all promises are found in You but they are to be inherited and that requires us to take possession of them by faith to benefit from them. Amen.

October 5

"Ye see then how that by works a man is justified, and not by faith only" (James 2:24). In the last post, I made mention of how people have the wrong perception of faith. There are those who can accept the idea of salvation but fail to receive it by faith in the heart as being so. The concept of heart points to there being a conviction that it is so, and we know that the issues and attitudes about life come from the convictions of the heart (*Proverbs 4:23; Romans 10:9-10*).

To receive something into the heart embraces a matter as being so, but it does not become truth until it is walked out in accordance to Spirit and God's Word. Once it is walked out, that is when it becomes established as a truth that affirms and shores up our foundation of understanding as to the will of God. We must remember that faith that is active is prepared to rise up in confidence and walk out a matter in obedience to what is right, acceptable, and considered pure before the Lord.

When it comes to expectation that comes out of faith it is clearly not based on what the Lord can do, but on the reality that He will always do what is holy and perfect. He will faithfully execute a matter according to His will and Word. The expectancy of hope is based on His promises because God does not lie, change His mind, and will accomplish what He has said in due time.

Such hope will not move from His promises no matter what, ever giving way to expectation that will trust God in His timing and ways to bring it forth. During this time faith will continue to walk towards the Lord in obedience, knowing that each step is bringing a person closer to experiencing the fullness of His Work and His promises.

As I am reminded from previous posts how the poor widow of the Old Testament who was desperate and clinging to hope along with the man whose son was sick in the New Testament who dared to hope, I was reminded of how expectation operates. The woman came to her only source of hope, the prophet Elisha, while the nobleman sought out Christ. Due to the relationship the prophet had with God, and the Person and Work of Jesus in the New Testament, these two seeking individuals both took hold of the source that miraculously changed the situation.

As believers do we dare to hope in and approach the Lord about the matters of the heart? The other question is how far did both these individuals have to travel to find that one individual who would surely intervene for them to bring about the miraculous results? Did distance matter at that point? All we know is they found the one they were seeking. This shows how faith will rise up, seek out, and will not stop until it finds the one it is pursuing.

As I thought about both examples, I had to ask how far am I willing to travel to find the One I am seeking? I know it requires me to rise up out of comfort zones, and push past points of convenience, knowing that at the end of the testing of my faith is salvation.

Prayer: Lord, our expectation wanes because our hope has succumbed to a whimper and our faith to a limp because we have based our confidence in You on works, our assurance towards You on Your performances, and hope in You based on meeting our conditions. Forgive us for not letting You be God, knowing You are God, trusting You will uphold unfeigned faith, allowing us to stand confident that You are perfect in all You do. Amen.

October 6

We've all heard our name called, but the tone and sound of that call depend on who, or what, is calling us. No doubt most of us will never forget those times when we were kids out playing when suddenly you could hear your mother's voice calling your name. If she was calling you to come home for dinner, that was a good call, but if she happened to yell your full name with a volume that you swear could be heard for miles outside of the neighborhood, that's when you became numb with dread.

Life is full of a variety of calls--most importantly, the call of God upon your heart, which can happen, as it initially did with me, even at a very young age. As for the world, there is the call of the wild, the call of the sea, the call of the mountains, the call to explore, the call to duty, or the call to excel in some business venture, sports, art or what-have-you. Some calls are less lofty or challenging, such as the call of the local woods that seemed to call me many years ago.

It was a pleasant day, the rain had ceased, and the fresh air was exhilarating. I took my wonderful shepherd dog and off we went—just he and I, all alone on a dirt trail that led into a thick, undeveloped, forest. Curiosity as to where the path led caused my steps to pick up speed; that is, until I suddenly became aware of the fact that, besides deer tracks, I was inadvertently following fresh bear tracks! That is when the heady "call of the woods" evaporated and my four-legged companion and I turned and ran for home.

Then, a few years later, I received another call--the call of the Holy Spirit to ministry. While there have been no bears to confront, there have been other opposing forces, some great, some small, but regardless of who, or what wages war against the call of God in our life, one thing remains sure, and that is we have the victory through our Lord Jesus Christ. (See *1 Corinthians 15:57*.) Jesus said, *"I beheld Satan as lightning fall from heaven. Behold, I give unto you power to tread on serpents and scorpions, and over all the power of the enemy: and nothing shall by any means hurt you" (Luke 10:18-19).*

Is Jesus calling you today? – J. Haley

Prayer: Lord, we encounter many different calls in this world. Some we rejoice over, others bring a feeling of sorrow, and there are those we ignore altogether. However, there is one call that is a matter of life and death, and that call will determine the quality of our existence and future and that is Your call upon our life. To fail to adhere to it means we miss life, miss the right way, and the promises of a glorious future in Your presence. Amen.

October 7

"And every earthen vessel, where unto any of them falleth, whatsoever is in it shall be unclean; and ye shall break it" (Leviticus 11:33). What is in the vessel of your life? The Apostle Paul tells us in *2 Corinthians 4:7* that we are nothing more than clay vessels. In the service of God there are many vessels, some to do His most honorable work and some for the purpose of doing that which is dishonorable to bring about His plan. Either way God will have His way and in the end His will, will be done on earth as it is in heaven.

The other morning, I woke up with a challenge, "Are you willing to be broken or will you become more so resolved to continue to do it your way?" I did not feel that God was putting forth the challenge that I was resolved to have life on my terms; rather, He was reminding me that the life of Christ in me can't be freely emitted from my life unless I am once again broken.

The truth is we can't break ourselves. All breaking will come from outside of our best attempts to make ourselves presentable to Him. To survive this life, we often become resolved to hold it together so we can come across as a polished vessel, one that is more about appearance and outward show than about being used by God.

Many avoid the breaking, but the breaking must first come before we can once again become pliable in His hands as clay that is ready to be shaped by Him for His most honorable purpose according to the times we live in.

I have learned that being broken brings tremendous liberty because all my attempts to hold together all matters of my life in God is what adds the greatest pressure and distress to my life. I must not only be broken to release me from any attempts to keep it together, but to let the life of Christ flow freely from me and serve as that sweet fragrance that God is bringing forth in my life through the working of the Spirit for His glory.

It is easy to say, "Have Your way Lord", but we must keep in mind for Him to have His way, He may have to break us so He truly can shape us. As He did me this morning, I must ask are you willing to be broken or will you maintain a resolve to keep it together, and in the end, become a cracked vessel of inconsistencies that will reveal that you really do not have it altogether?

Prayer: Lord, I know what it feels like to be a cracked vessel and a broken vessel. To surrender myself to Your way will mean brokenness in some way, but as I am reminded, I am simply the clay vessel and You are the Potter. You know what You are doing and can bring forth an honorable vessel that can be used for Your glory. Have Your way Lord because I am confident of one thing: You do all things well. Amen.

October 8

"Now therefore thus saith the LORD of hosts; Consider your ways" (Haggai 1:5). One morning, I woke up from a dream in which I was

witnessing to someone. It started out with a crisis and somehow ended with some emergency surgery of the heart. The doctor performing the heart surgery was the best in his profession. His abilities had drawn world-wide recognition.

I can't say exactly who he did this surgery on, but it had to be someone close to me because I was grateful to him for his abilities. Somehow, I ended up in a one-on-one conversation with him at his residence which appeared to be an unkept small room. At the time he was relaxing on a couch looking somewhat despondent, while I was seated in a chair.

I started out expressing my gratitude, but I could see by his cluttered room, his countenance, and his attitude there was so much more going on with him. It was at that time I saw his spiritual barrenness, and that he was in a grave crisis. That is when I said to him, "You have accomplished much but something has been missing from your life. Yes, you have experienced all the world can offer but you are empty, the accolades have become hollow to you, the successes no longer satisfying, and the meaning of life is now turning into a personal crisis because nothing makes sense to you because it all seems useless and insignificant."

He looked up at me with tremendous despair and torment in his eyes and I could even sense a tear breaking forth. It was then I said to him, "Years ago you heard about that which is satisfying, but the world's attractions won out and you have pursued them ever sense, but in the depths of your soul you know that only God can satisfy you and that satisfaction has been provided by His Son, Jesus Christ.

"You are like the prodigal son, you now see the world as a pigpen and what you are feeding on is nothing more than the husks that litters it, but you need to believe that the invitation put forth to sit at the table of Jesus years ago still holds and that the loving Father awaits you to return to your real home. But you must turn from your reckless ways and return seeking forgiveness, admitting you don't deserve to sit at the table as a son for you have squandered your inheritance, but now you would be content as a servant to serve at His table." My dream ended with him tearfully dropping to his knees, crying out for God to have mercy on his wretched soul and asking for His forgiveness.

In Haggai, the message to God's people was to consider their ways. "Consider" points to coming back to center, which will require His people to examine if they are in the way of truth and life. The truth is many have strayed from what needs to be the center of their life. They have been detoured from walking in the way that leads to a true, satisfying life that is not littered by the emptiness of the leftover husks of this world but leads to the One who is the essence of everlasting life.

Are you one of those strays who are weary with the matters of this present world? The invitation still holds. The Father beckons you to turn in repentance and come home, and once again sit at His table of fellowship as His child.

Prayer: Lord, time is running out, and the invitation is becoming more of an echo that seems further away as the dark times we are living in are becoming greater. Lord, perhaps the opportunity to turn from this present darkness to face Your light is also ebbing away, but I know if we can still hear the invitation, there is time to still come home. Give me the ears to hear what Your Spirit is saying so I never miss the invitation, the instruction, and the opportunity to sit at Your table. Amen.

October 9

"Again, the devil taketh him up into an exceeding high mountain, and sheweth him all the kingdoms of the world, and the glory of them; And saith unto him, All these things will I give thee, if thou wilt fall down and worship me" (Matthew 4:8-9). It seems that no matter what time of year and season we find ourselves in the middle of the political conflict that regardless of whether it is an election year or not, it constantly rages because in essence it is the kingdom of darkness against the kingdom of light. What can we trust, what can we abide by, and what side must we take to be on the right side of eternity?

We have been conditioned to look at labels and titles, but the Bible instructs us to test the spirit. We have been indoctrinated to look at platforms, while the Bible tells us to discern the intent or agenda behind something. The truth is, we have been fitted with various filters in this world to influence our attitude that will determine what side of the coin we choose to side with, but it is time to realize it is the same coin, just a different side and approach.

What I have become aware of is that regardless of the label and title, our political system, especially on the national level, is run by those who have the same agenda regardless of the party. We must keep in mind all systems of this world are under Satan who can pose as the cunning serpent that plant seeds of unbelief and rebellion or he can come as an angel of light who covers up wicked agendas with noble deeds, honorable causes, and great feats to blindly lead people towards the same abyss. However, the fruits of both sides reveal that it is being done for the same reason or agenda. The difference is the speed of the train.

One is on the fast track, while the other one is on a side track, but both are leading to the same place. Both are running us over a financial cliff, while morally dragging us down into a cesspool that, in His holiness, God can do nothing more than withdraw His presence and blessing from this country, leaving it for the wolves, vultures, and tyrants.

Humanity spends much of their time arguing over matters that in the end will prove useless. The reason is that regardless of the side we are on in this world, both are heading towards the same end of destruction. I think it is time that Christians step outside of the debates and honestly seek out how God is looking at matters in order to make a sound judgment call about the times they are living in.

Prayer: Lord, it is so easy to get caught up with the nonsense of this world, but we have greater giants to overcome and greater battles before us. Keep me from wasting my time and energy as You prepare Your people for what is coming down the track. Amen.

October 10

"The Spirit of the Lord GOD is upon me: because the LORD hath anointed me to preach good tidings unto the meek: he hath sent me to bind up the broken-hearted, to proclaim liberty to the captives, and the opening of the prison to them that are bound" (Isaiah 61:1). In a post I talked about my dream concerning a man who had come to the end of himself to realize that regardless of his accomplishments in this world, he still possessed nothing of significance. He was empty, depressed, and living in a small, cluttered reality that held much of nothing to show for his life. Sadly, this is true for most of humanity, even those who call themselves Christians.

I know the emptiness of such a life because as a "decent individual" or one who was "not such a bad person," I realized I was not good enough even to meet my most pious standards. When I finally faced the reality of being a sinner, I realized my pursuits in trying to do what was right mocked me because when integrity was lifted up as a standard, my offenses against God became obvious. It was when I compared myself to the "worst" of the world, I perceived I was not so bad after all, but when Christ became my standard of righteousness, I became the worst of the lot. Each pursuit eventually brought me to the same conclusion that I was in dire need of a Savior.

Man has a way of putting himself in a better light when the spiritual darkness about him is both great and blinding to him. He compares himself to those whom he considers inferior to himself, allowing him to become smug in his own arrogance towards them. When he sees someone he admires, he tries to emulate them in order to cover up his lack of character and abilities.

We are told the Holy Spirit came to reprove the world of righteousness. In essence the Holy Spirit lifts up the standard of Jesus Himself as to what is acceptable to God and when man looks at the true standard of righteousness, all he can do is see how far away from the mark he is from that which is heavenly and glorious. And, when man sees that great gulf between his best and God's righteousness, there is only one reaction, "God have mercy on me."

Prayer: Lord, in You we are saints, holy people set apart by a holy calling. However, in our humanity we are often reminded of why You came: To show us mercy by saving us from ourselves. Thank You for changing my status. Amen.

October 11

"Wherefore let him that thinketh he standeth take heed lest he fall" (1 Corinthians 10:12). The Christian walk possesses the same traps as the world. As a new zealous Christian, I thought I had reached an important pinnacle of understanding, only to find out I had not even begun to climb the mountain. In my time of spiritual growth, I thought I gained the necessary insight to stand only to discover I would have to first fall to realize what it meant to stand on what was right. When I felt infallible because of what I knew, that is when I had to be broken so I could be pliable in God's hands. It was then I realized I lived in a cockeyed reality.

This is because we live in a world that is upside-down in how it views all things. It views it through spiritual darkness that is highlighted by shadows that are void of the Rock of Ages. It is the Rock that determines if spiritual light has any substance in it. The Rock casts the shadow of the cross of Christ in the midst of humanity. If the Rock is missing, the light will prove to be a false light that blinds one to the destruction that awaits them.

As I observe people, I see those who struggle in the mass confusion of trying to wade through an upside-down world in lieu of the righteous values of an unseen world. They wrestle with maintaining some type of association as a "Christian" in light of maintaining some identity to the life or world they are acquainted with. They hold tightly to some type of independence which serves as that one point of decency, sanity, hope, and purpose they have managed to cling to when it comes to their life. In their thinking it brought clarity to them, but in reality it eventually ends in confusion if their idea of rightness falls to the wayside. It is at that time they struggle to not come under a blanket of hopelessness that causes a vexation of spirit.

I have heard the silent cries of the souls of many through the years. Some are clinging to being a Christian in fear and uncertainty while trying to hold on to some semblance of meaning. Others are hiding behind labels of religion hoping that will be enough to stand before God. Many are on a dead run, busy doing the "good works" so they will make themselves worthy before God, but in such cases, there is that one thing that is often missing and it is the assurance of salvation. So much of what they possess clutters their understanding of that glorious joy that comes with salvation.

Meanwhile, our great Physician waits to heal the broken heart and bind up the bruising caused by vexation of the spirit. He longs to set the captives free from their small worlds of insanity and give them the liberty to look beyond the present in order to be lifted upon the currents of His Spirit. This is what allows believers to see beyond this world a city made by the hands of God that has been prepared for His children who also make up His bride, the church.

Prayer: Lord, there is much going on, but the hope we have is not in this world or whether our preferred side wins; rather, it comes down to if we will in the end be sitting at the table with You in celebration of Your redemption being secured, Your Work being completed, Your way being accomplished, and Your promises being fulfilled. Amen.

October 12

I killed it. I didn't mean to, but there was no one else to blame. After all, it was my idea this past summer to put the aloe plant on the deck where it was nice and hot in the sunshine. Who would've "thunk" that there was such a thing as a desert plant that got sick simply because it was put where it could enjoy some sunshine? Then again, perhaps my haphazard off-and-on again watering of it didn't help.

Whatever the cause was it began to just simply give up, and then one day all of its puffy green "arms" looked strange and simply detached from its little root stump when slightly touched. As I put the whole thing in the garbage, a little nagging thought surfaced in my mind, "So now what're you going to do if you get burned?" Not to worry, I assured myself. I rarely ever get a burn even though most of my life seems to orbit around in the kitchen.

A few days after the aloe funeral, it accidentally happened! My hand flip-flopped, fainted and forgot how to handle the electric hot water kettle while pouring boiling water into my teacup, which slightly tipped to one side causing my thumb and part of my hand to be the target. Cold running water helped and thankfully the burn wasn't too bad, just somewhat red, and sore.

This incident brought to mind how just a little negligence "here and there" in our spiritual lives can have far greater disastrous results. *Hebrews 2:3-4* tells us, "*How shall we escape, if we neglect so great salvation: which at the first began to be spoken by the Lord, and was confirmed unto us by them that heard him; God also bearing them witness, both with signs and wonders, and with divers miracles, and gifts of the Holy Ghost, according to his own will?"* Just as I assumed things about the aloe plant, which led to negligence and ultimately its end, so too when Christians assume that just because they repeated some prayer to "accept Christ" and perhaps were baptized and attend a church that they're saved.

But that is not what the Bible teaches. When reading, believing and studying the Word is neglected, as well as prayer and obedience to the commandments of Jesus, then what avenue of "escape" (God's judgment) is left? There is none. Truly, negligence leads to the "broad way that leads to destruction" (see *Matthew 7:13-14*). – J. Haley

Prayer: Oh Lord, forgive us when our assumptions and self-serving tendencies give way to negligence of Your great salvation. Amen.

October 13

"Strive to enter in at the strait gate; for many, I say unto you, will seek to enter in, and shall not be able" (Luke 13:24). I was thinking about salvation this morning. It seems like a simple word, but how many really understand what it means. It seems like today this simple word is probably the most misunderstood word in religion.

For example, "salvation" means deliverance. It points to the idea of being rescued from a dire situation that involves life or death. If you consider the implications of being saved, the very work of it would bring a certain sobriety to one's soul. After all, the person was on the brink of perishing in some way, and because of intervention was pulled from the clutches of it in the nick of time.

As I watch people, the concept of salvation seems far from them. There are those who do not care if they are saved because they have no sense that they are lost and need to be saved from falling into some great pit of judgment. There are others who hope they are saved because they try to live a decent enough life that surely the good will outweigh the bad in the end. These people are often living in denial that true salvation is not a matter of trying to be good, but the reality that there is nothing "good" in mankind that can save him.

Some are assuming they are saved because of religious affiliation, but it is not a matter of affiliation that saves but being identified to the great work of redemption that was brought forth through the cross of Jesus. Then there are those who live in some ether wave of delusion that, due to some religious experience or encounter with the supernatural, they perceive they are surely saved regardless of whether there was any real repentance, confession and brokenness on their part that caused them to cry out to God for His mercy because they are perishing in their present state. After all, we are all sinners separated from God, doomed in our state, and facing the dreadful prospect of facing a holy God in His wrath if we fail to receive His pardon that can be secured when we receive Jesus as our Savior and Lord.

Jesus is clear about "salvation" in *Luke.* Many will try to enter into the place of salvation but will miss it in some way. There is only ONE WAY that man can be rescued from his state of doom, damnation, and ruination. Therefore, we must strive to enter through that one narrow gate that God has provided.

It is not enough to come up to it because of an intellectual understanding, look into it because of some religious affiliation, and hope our best attempts will cause us to be close enough to it. Instead, we must enter into it before we can experience true deliverance of our soul from the claims of sin upon it. This will spare us from the judgment of spiritual death or separation from God, allowing us to experience its great work of complete deliverance as it enables us to reach our destination of living in the presence and glory of God forever.

Prayer: Lord, thank You for revealing to me that I was perishing in my lost state, missing the entrance of salvation in my delusional state, and passing by the entrance in my state of denial about what it means to be truly delivered from my wretched plight. Amen.

October 14

"Then Agrippa said unto Paul, Almost thou persuadest me to be a Christian" (Acts 26:28). To me the most misused, misunderstood, and abused word in religious and secular circles is the word "Christian." How many times was this word used in the King James Version of the Bible? I looked it up and it was only used three times, once in *1 Peter 4:16* in relationship to suffering as a Christian for the sake of one's faith and twice in the book of Acts where the disciples were first referred to as "Christians in Antioch. The final time it was used was when Agrippa accused Paul of trying to persuade him to be a Christian (*Acts 11:26; 26:28*).

The word "Christian" was to identify those who were walking in a New Way. The new way pointed to those who were not merely imitating the way of Christ but living a Christ-like life that clearly distinguished them in the world as not being part of it.

The Apostle Paul clearly stated in *Galatians 2:20* in light of one who has truly been born again of the Spirit, that such a person will be living the life of Christ by faith and not their own life. In *Romans 8:29*, we are told that we have been foreordained to be conformed to the image of Christ to reflect Him to the world.

Today the word "Christian" is not a term that describes those who walk in the righteous ways of Christ according to the Word of God, but those who for one reason or the other simply wear the label without having any real consensus as to what it means. Granted, they may hide behind a slanted concept of decency, have some religious notion behind them, and possess some intellectual agreement with it. Neither of these tests identify one as being a Christian.

Ultimately, the one thing that shows that they are simply using the term "Christian" to give them some legitimacy is that they never really line up to a Scriptural aspect of who Christ is. This includes the moral standard of His righteousness, and the sobering reality of the judgment to come on the unbelieving, disobedient, fearful, and idolater.

Christianity is not a term, a religious notion or a point of denominational identification, it is the life of Christ present in a person. This life is brought forth by the Spirit, walked out according to truth and will manifest itself in obedience that comes out of faith.

Prayer: Lord, Your Word identifies what a real Christian will be like in their attitude and walk, but how many of them that use that label consider or discern if they are truly walking according to Your life so they will ultimately reflect You. That is the true test to all who claim to be a Christian. Amen.

October 15

"And they that be wise shall shine as the brightens of the firmament; and that that turn many to righteousness as the stars for ever and

ever" (Daniel 12:3). Those who wear the title of "Christian" to give some legitimacy to their unscriptural claims, shore up their shaky authority, or maintain some sanity when it comes to their confusing logic, have often broadened the narrow path into the broad path to justify their worldly narrative.

Many are confused because what they thought was truth is not panning out to being real in a world that appears to be going mad. They are doing all they can to adjust the present tormenting reality into their understanding. It is their way to hold on to that small thread of sanity is slowly unraveling as they desperately cling to the last horizon of hope that is dissipating before their very eyes.

I have often told believers they can't walk in this world unless it is in light of eternity. I remind them as citizens of heaven, our hope is not in this world, but in the next.

The concept of being on the winning side is the world's way of looking at a matter, but God's perspective is, are we standing on the right side of the cross of Christ to ensure salvation? Due to the life of Christ in us, His righteousness will shine through us, attracting others to Him. It is walking in the light of Christ that we maintain our testimony and know that we are in agreement with Him and His Word. This assures us of standing sure in and on heavenly authority.

Keep in mind, the world appeared to win when Christ was crucified, and the anti-Christ system of the world will wear down the patience of the saints, while the person of the anti-Christ will prevail against the saints according to *Daniel 7:21* and *25*. However, we have this wonderful promise in *Daniel 11:32b, "but the people that do know their God shall be strong, and do exploits."*

Prayer: Lord, it is easy to wear labels, learn to talk the talk, but what will reveal whether we know You is whether we are walking the walk. You are clear, if we abide in You we will walk as You walked in Your humanity. Keep our feet on the narrow way of truth, our faith established on who You are, our focus steadfast on You, and our ways lining up to the moral rightness clearly founded and grounded in Your Word. Amen.

October 16

"And being made perfect, he became the author of eternal salvation unto all them that obey Him" (Hebrews 5:9). Have you ever thought about what disobedience looks like to God? I thought about this the other day. We must begin from the conclusion that the opposite of disobedience is obedience. This conclusion seems easy enough but think about it, there is no wiggle room. From the perspective of obedience and disobedience there are no shades of gray, just black and white, or walking in darkness or light.

The truth of the matter is, we humans like to operate in gray areas to justify any questionable or dishonorable attitudes about the way we think, live, and conduct the affairs of our lives. It is true we often stand as rigid judges of certain moral issues that we can pridefully uphold because we are not tempted in that way. We can appear tolerant or understanding about moral deviation that we often wade in and out of because it serves our fleshly notions, our worldly practices, and earthly ways. In fact, we can transpose our deviations on others by accusing them of what we are guilty of, throwing others off as to the hypocrisy that exists in our own life.

However, God's Word is clear as to decisive boundaries we must never overstep. In a sense we tend to dance around moral, ethical, and righteous ways that do not serve our purpose.

Jesus suffered in His humanity in order to come to perfection as the Lamb of God. As a result, He is the author of eternal salvation. However, we must note there is a condition when it comes to salvation: We must be in obedience to Him to be saved.

Prayer: Lord, obedience is not the means to earn salvation but to show that we have truly received Your life by faith and now in love we want to please You by being obedient to what You have set forth in Your Word. Praise You for Your merciful ways. Amen.

October 17

"And he that doubteth is damned if he eat, because he eateth not of faith: for whatsoever is not of faith is sin" (Romans 14:23). The Word is clear that when we are not willing to line up to what is Scripturally right, it reveals that we are void of unfeigned faith.

We are told that what is not of faith is sin and it is because of our faith that God is able to count our standing before Him for righteousness' sake, and our obedience as being righteous. It is for this reason, we can't please God without faith, for faith is manifested through obedience to His Word. As Paul stated, *"Faith comes by hearing and hearing by the Word of God" (Romans 10:17).*

The problem with being black and white about religious issues is that we Christians are often accused of being unloving and intolerant, which makes us draw back in fear. Fear not only reveals a lack of faith, but it is a form of worship.

It is fear that has caused many to be quiet about matters that prove to be life and death when it comes to the soul of man. Yet we are told to stand with truth and hold the line of righteousness because souls are on the line. After all, the wages of any sin, regardless of how we might measure it in this world, is death. It is not a matter of any of us judging it as sin because God has already judged it as being an offense to Him.

God will be the ultimate judge to all matters and in the end, we will stand before Him to give an account of the deeds we have done in our lives. For believers, fire will be put to their works to see what they are made of—that which will burn or that which will be refined, but for the sinner, their deeds will convict them of breaking the moral law of God. That is when every sinner will face the judgment of the Law as to the death sentence that hangs over them.

Prayer: Lord, we avoid looking into the just face of Your holy Law and realize that it reveals that we all have sinned, but You have provided a way to spare us of our inevitable sentence of death through the redemption wrought on our behalf on Your cross. We cry out to You for mercy knowing You desire to pardon us from a death sentence and show us grace by giving us Your eternal life. Meanwhile, like Paul we ask for greater boldness to stand in these dark times with the sword of Your truth. Amen.

October 18

"No man can come to me; except the Father which hath sent me draw him: and I will raise him up at the last day" (John 6:44). God's attitude towards sin makes Him appear unloving and yet how many times do we purport the love of God to attract people to Him?

We speak of His desire to bless and His long-suffering that gives us time and opportunity to turn to Him in repentance, so we don't perish in our sin. However, the one thing we often forget in our desperation to get people to see God's love is that the Father must be drawing us to the Son before we will even consider what Jesus Christ has done on our behalf.

I must admit I was not drawn to Jesus because the Father so loved me; rather, I was drawn to Jesus and His great work on the cross because I was hopelessly lost in my sin. I acknowledge it was the love of Christians that gripped my heart, but it was my need to be saved from my miserable plight that opened my heart to the Gospel message.

We try to arouse some type of sentiment or emotional response in people to cause them to rise up and seek the Lord, but it is the Father who truly must first draw that person towards His Son. It only seems right when you consider that the Father was the One who introduced Jesus as His Son at both Jesus' baptism and the Mount of Transfiguration. At the Mount of Transfiguration, the Father's instruction in *Matthew 17:5* was to *"hear him."*

The concept of hearing someone is not just for the purpose of hearing what they have to say, but it is also for the purpose of doing what the person's says. I recently talked about obedience and disobedience. We are either disobeying what we know is right because we do NOT believe, or we are obeying God to ensure the integrity of our life before Him because we DO believe. Again, to obey points to obeying God's Word.

Prayer: Lord, we like to talk the talk and act out our religious best in front of others. Sometimes we are so good at it that we even can deceive ourselves about our real spiritual status. Lord, put Your light on the truth of all matters so I can't live in denial and darkness about my spiritual plight. Amen.

October 19

"Then Peter and the other apostles answered and said, We ought to obey God rather than men" (Acts 5:29). There is no real hypocrisy in true religion. We, as Christians, clearly must not operate according to some twilight of compromise. Compromise occurs because we are stepping outside of what is true to somehow water down, adjust, or twist the meaning, instruction, prophecy, and intent of the Bible.

We tend to move in and out of the black and white areas of what is acceptable to God to avoid being honest about our own depravity. And in so doing we lose our edge of discerning what is really happening in the environment around us, rendering us somewhat ineffective in discerning the times and dangers of the age we live in.

It is clear from *Hebrews 5:9* that Jesus is the author of salvation to those who obey. As I stated and must reiterate obedience is not a requirement for salvation but a manifestation of our faith towards God that walks hand in hand with love that pleases. It possesses hope that lives in expectancy, and an attitude of worship and awe that dreads to bring any displeasure or reproach to God.

As Paul stated, we are saved by grace through the belief of faith when it comes to knowing what is true, the exercise of faith expressed in obedience, and the standing of faith towards God that can't be moved because it is founded on the one true foundation of Jesus Christ. (Refer to *2 Corinthians 13:5.*)

Prayer: Lord, thank You for Your Word. You have hidden nothing from us that we need to know, and You give us the measure of faith to trust You with what is unknown to us to keep us in the way of Your love, blessings, and promises. Amen.

October 20

"For we dare not make ourselves of the number, or compare ourselves with some that commend themselves: but they measuring themselves by themselves, and comparing themselves among themselves, are not wise" (2 Corinthians 10:12). It is natural to look for some exemplary example to model our lives after.

As a young person I looked for such people. Many times, the ones who caught my eye were those who had a certain personality. They were personable, likeable, and seemed to have that winning personality that I felt I lacked. I wanted to emulate them, but I realized in my later years, I was not like them.

In order to grow up I needed to establish my own identity, and in time I realized that such emulation of someone was a sign of immaturity on my part. Another word for emulation is "idolized" which is a word that is the same as "idolatry." Paul clearly points out in *2 Corinthians* that such comparison is unwise.

Sadly, the example our young people have ends up being nothing more than mere images erected by the vain culture we live in. These examples are based on talents that need no integrity to verify their legitimacy. Many times, these individuals lack real character, but their natural abilities are what stand out, often hiding moral flaws. If people are honest, these "so-called" heroes lack true heroic qualities that would be worthy to take note of and honor.

I always tell people I have one hero, and His name is Jesus. There is no one that can defeat Him, outdo Him, and outshine Him in His abilities, ways, and glory. He is not an imaginary cartoon hero. He is real, living, and still doing the incredible and miraculous.

Prayer: Lord in our immaturity we look to the world for heroes, to heroes for inspiration, and for inspiration that will cause us to reach beyond ourselves for some great feat. However, all these things leave us disappointed, disillusioned and in despair because what we admire is an image. We don't have to look any further than You, for You alone are genuine and real. Amen.

October 21

"For we which live are always delivered unto death for Jesus' sake, that the life also of Jesus might be made manifest in our mortal flesh" (2 Corinthians 4:11). As Christians we still tend to look for godly examples. We are looking for what is real, and occasionally we may see a person with genuine grace. It is natural desire to be like that person because we view them as a real Christian without understanding that such grace is established under great pressure.

We might see a person who displays great inner strength of character without realizing that such strength is often the result of great tribulations. We may want to be like that individual who stands in light of incredible power, but who fails to know that the great power of the Spirit comes through suffering and testing.

The question we must ask ourselves when it comes to admiring certain characteristics that we silently wish we possessed, "Do we really want to go through the process to gain them?" Being around someone may cause one to imitate them, but they will be void of possessing the particular point of character or virtue that would clearly make them that person.

The key about the process God must often take us through to bring out our character as a believer will have its own way of expressing different Christian virtues. We may possess grace, but it will manifest itself differently than someone else. We may have had character forged in us, but it will not show itself in the same way that someone else displays it. In fact, the way we express godly virtues will seem natural to our person because they are formed in us by the Spirit who will not go against the grain of how God made us.

The truth is the process may be hard, but the end result will reflect that one image that verifies if we possess the real light of heaven. Or, on the other hand, if we fail to pay the necessary price it will eventually become obvious that all we are doing is turning out our best presentation based on our own ideas of what a Christian looks like.

Prayer: Lord, I want to emulate the image of heaven and not the best my flesh can present or the world's notion of greatness. However, I know that without Your touch and Spirit I will never accomplish such a feat in my own strength. Have Your way oh Lord. Amen.

October 22

It had gotten to the point that it was just downright disgusting, dirty and depressing, but trying to tackle the job of cleaning it was a bit too physically challenging for us two older ladies so we had to wait until our younger and taller team member could find the time to help clean it. After all, the fall weather seems to be sinking faster than usual into the cold grip of winter, and we'd be stuck trying to clearly see out of the big living room window for months.

Just the thought of trying to enjoy the "great outdoors" from the warm safety of our house through that filthy window was discouraging. Besides, my grandma was right when she said, long ago, "If your floors and windows are clean, you whole house looks clean." I'm beginning to think more like her by the day.

Being able to see clearly is a priceless blessing, as anyone who struggles with vision problems, or is blind fully knows. Even more precious is the spiritual ability to see clearly, but how many of us truly value the spiritual vision of the Holy Spirit?

When Jesus said, (among other things) that He was anointed to recover the sight of the blind (*Luke 4:18*) He meant spiritual sight, even though He healed many physically. Why should we desire to have clear spiritual eyesight? The answer should be, so we can "see God!"

Jesus said, "*Blessed are the pure in heart: for they shall see God" (Matthew 5:8". "Follow peace with all men, and holiness, without which no man shall see the Lord" (Hebrews 12:14).* The Apostle Paul wrote, *"For now we see through a glass, darkly; but then face to face: now I know in part; but then shall I know even as also I am known" (1 Corinthians 13:12).*

Oh Christian! What are you seeking to see in these troubled and perilous times? Just remember that no matter what you hear, or what you see, or what you are told to believe in the coming days, the world, the flesh and the devil can offer nothing of eternal value.

Be mindful that many people, even professing Christians, are blindly pursuing their vain, unbiblical fantasies; but the children of the true Light of the world seek, by faith, to keep their spiritual vision as clean and clear as possible so as to remain established on the foundation of Jesus Christ through the Word and prayer. *"Beloved, now are we the sons of God, and it doth not yet appear what we shall be: but we know that, when he shall appear, we shall be like him; for we shall see him as he is" (1 John 3:2).* – J. Haley

Prayer: Lord, there are many who are physically blind that have a better heavenly perspective. Sadly, many are spiritually blind to the deadly path they are on. I want to thank You for giving me the spiritual eyes of faith to see You in Your Word, Your examples, Your ways, and in Your creation. Amen.

October 23

"For consider him that endured such contradiction of sinners against himself, least ye be wearied and faint in your minds" (Hebrews 12:3). Have you ever had one of those days you failed to be patient. You couldn't find meekness anywhere around, struggled with all temperance because your mood was being bounced around in bumpy waters and it was as though you were getting motion sickness that was causing you to nurse the mood with self-pity? Well, I had

one of those days recently and I could just write it off as such, but lately I have been having my share of them.

I would like to look around to blame something and there might even be a few legitimate reasons for my mood, but the Bible tells me I must resist giving into, giving way to, and giving up to the attitude and excuses that I am tempted to clothe myself in to justify my wrong responses. The only way I can do that is quit looking at my circumstances, stop giving audience to my logic, avoid the temptation of looking within, and rein in my imagination to take my thoughts captive. Once I take thoughts captive, I can then bring them into subjection to Christ. Finally, I need to get out of the unmoored boat to keep my emotions from being cast about.

As we know, to take charge of such moods is not a mere exercise of getting past self. It requires one to take the disgruntled old man and silence him with the cross. We must face our boastful pride with the light of truth by simply considering the great length Jesus went to secure our redemption. He experienced the contradictions of the world that seemed insane, unfair, and wrong against Himself so that He would not allow Himself to become weary in His mission or faint before He finished securing redemption for us.

Getting past my right to feel sorry for self, picked on, or isolated in the morbid reality that "no one knows the trouble I've seen," requires me to look to the Perfect One. Jesus took it upon Himself to identify not only with the great trouble that mankind experiences but to become identified with man's plight by becoming the sin offering.

Christ experienced much because as my Redeemer and Savior, He paid the price I could not pay. He became identified with me in order to stand in the gap on my behalf as High Priest and He drank the bitter cup of judgment as the Lamb of God so that I wouldn't have to. Through it all He experienced it all in His humanity that I would experience, except the corruption, perversion and ruin brought on the soul by sin. He did it all making Him my example in all matters concerning God and life.

It is important to remember that I can't outdo, out suffer, out give, or out run the Lord. He alone stands as my example and only by complete surrender to His will, the transforming of the mind, the sanctification of the Spirit, and the work of the cross am I able to line up to His true example of righteousness.

Prayer: Lord, my interpretations of life are based on that which has impacted me the most. Lord, I seek You out so that Your ways will impact me the most, Your Spirit will lead me, and Your Word will become my standard. Thank You for the promise that if I seek You with my whole heart, I will be found by You. Amen.

October 24

"But put ye on the Lord Jesus Christ, and make not provision for the flesh, to fulfil the lusts thereof" (Romans 13:14). Are you an imitator of Christ or one who is being conformed to the very image of Christ? Years ago, I was part of a Bible Study that used what many called a watered-down version of the Bible. Although it is nowhere to be found today, this Bible, at that time, was part of the latest fad that seemed to be taking Christendom by leaps and bounds, and when we came to the part about being a Christian, this Bible version related it to being a mere imitator of Christ.

At first, I was somewhat impressed with the presentation of the concept of the Christian life. All I had to do was imitate Christ. However, as I began to meditate on the concept of imitating Christ and being conformed to Christ, it was then I began to see that one concept did not address the real intent of Scripture.

"Intent" has to do with the spirit of something. We are told that as a sword the Word of God cuts deep down into the soul and exposes the intent of the heart. This is when I began to consider the type of impact words make on one's soul.

Did the impact simply reach the intellect with the idea of something, reach the heart with some sentimental notion, and/or the logic with some rational conclusion that made sense? Or did it reach the spirit with a revelation that would revolutionize how one would consider or approach a matter. Did it bring the subject matter to a higher or more excellent way of looking at it?

The truth is we are quick and able to imitate something, but such a portrayal makes us an imposter. Imposters are able to entertain in some way, but they are not able to give real credence to what is being advocated. We do not trust imposters because we can't believe what they say since their words have no authority behind them.

Are you willing to simply imitate Christ or do you want to take on His attitude and walk as He walked? Walking as Christ walked is the only way we will possess the necessary authority as an overcomer of the old life and way to give credibility to our calling, testimony, and new life in Christ.

Prayer: Lord, we often find ourselves in a battle with the old as we try to reform it and make it acceptable to You. However, the old can't be reformed and the only way we can overcome it is to crucify it daily. If we don't, it will eventually overcome us. Amen.

October 25

"And that ye put on the new man, which after God is created in righteousness and true holiness" (Ephesians 4:24). This Scripture is clear that the new man must be recreated in us if we are going to reflect the real image of His glory. To create something means a transformation from something of a different form into something that speaks of its highest potential, such as in the case of a butterfly.

As I considered the idea of imitating Christ and being conformed, I realized that actors and actresses imitate characters in plays or on the screen. At one time these professional performers were called "hypocrites" because they portrayed characters while failing to be such individuals. They were a portrayal of a mere image that lacked substance and not the real thing.

As Christians we are not to imitate Christ; rather, we are to be conformed to the very image of Christ so that we can be like Him. "Conform" has to do with being shaped a certain way to not present a mere image but to be made into the very likeness of that person in order to reflect a certain character and traits.

I decided at that point I was not to be an imitator but an actual reflection of the person of Jesus to a lost world. I would not be reflecting my best performance or portrayal of Jesus; rather, I would be reflecting the very attitude, example, and ways of Christ.

This example brings me back to the question. Am I merely imitating Christ at different times or am I being conformed to His very image by the sanctifying work of the Holy Spirit?

Prayer: Lord, we are often quick in settling for imitating You, but we are called to be conformed to Your image in order to present Your attitude, righteousness, and ways to a world that is always finding mere fading images. The world's best portrayals pan out to be a façade. I choose what is real and will prove to be true in the end. Amen.

October 26

"Now the God of patience and consolation grant you to be likeminded one towards another according to Christ Jesus" (Romans 15:5). In my last post I pose the challenge of whether we as Christians want to merely imitate Christ with our best presentations or whether we are willing to submit to the sanctifying work of the Spirit to conform us to His likeness. As believers, we must remember that the only reason we can be conformed to the likeness of Christ is because we have His very life in us. His life in us also points to the breath of God, His Holy Spirit being in us.

The more we live the life of Christ in us the more we will be conformed to His likeness. Although we may know this intellectually, we must question how many are being conformed by the life of Christ and how many are trying to present Christ by putting forth their religious best?

It is the Spirit of God in us that not only is working the life of Christ in us, but He is empowering us to walk out this life. Without the Spirit, we have no power to walk out the new life in us, and any attempts to live like Christ instead of being conformed by His life in us will end in utter failure.

This brings us to the subject of the Church. Is the church supposed to present a mere imitation of Christ or reflect the real Jesus to the world? Whether the church presents an imitation of Christ or reflects Him comes down to how many people who call themselves Christians are mere imitators of what they perceive the Christian life to be, or are they being ever challenged to be conformed to the very likeness of Christ? The real point of identification to Christ, even in the church is if the Holy Spirit is present.

Once again, we must remember that the Church is the body of Christ and Christ is the "head" of the body. The Body can't function without the "head," and the head is what ensures the body functions properly.

The One who brings each member of the Body into unity is the Holy Spirit, which is the breath of God. The Church is also a spiritual building that houses the presence of God. The believers who are living stones are the ones who offer the spiritual sacrifices, the service of real worship, and reflect the real glory of Jesus to the world. That is our real high calling as saints.

The world sees enough imitators, but what the lost need to see is the real Jesus being emitted from our lives as believers, and His glory from His true body, the church.

Prayer: Lord, our bodies are empty shells without Your life, and as Your body we are lifeless and ineffective without Your Spirit. Lord, it comes back to You being our all in all and each of us being Your open vessel and willing instrument. Have Your way. Amen.

October 27

"She's really on fire" a friend wrote in an email one summer. Naturally that piqued my ever-present curiosity, so to make a short story shorter, I arranged to make the acquaintance of this "fireball."

What I wanted to know was if she was "on fire" for Jesus, or just another fiery comet zooming through space. Upfront she was a friendly, very determined, young woman who was openly interested in a Bible study. So far, so good. However, after just one meeting it became visibly and verbally apparent that her burning flame was indeed "strange fire."

Not only was it fueled by an odd mixture of Old Testament traditions, misapplied Scriptures taken out of context along with typical cultish conclusions, but her "fire" verged on what some in the medical secular arena call "religious mania." Obviously, this poor woman was driven by the "fire" of a false light which is typical of an antichrist spirit.

The sad thing about people who are "on fire" with the wrong Jesus, wrong Spirit and wrong gospel is that any Living Water you try to pour on them in the hope of dousing the "strange fire" they are operating under, the more "heat" and "smoke" you have to deal with.

This brings to mind a verse in the powerful *Book of Jude* where he admonished in verse *23*, *"And others save with fear, pulling them out of the fire; hating even the garment spotted by the flesh."* To be honest with you, I often wonder when the organized "church" is going to wake up and smell the smoke.

The typical "fireless-ness" of the average fun-loving, self-serving, self-satisfied, half-hearted, half-asleep Christian in this nation is more dangerous to the continuance of our Republic and freedom to worship the one true God than any other group of people, however evil, because "judgment must begin at the house of God." (See *1 Peter 4:17.*)

There is a fire coming to reveal every man's work—fire that separates, purifies and consumes. (See *1 Corinthians 3:12-15.*) Since our service to God will be put to the test of fire, how can we be sure our works are acceptable in His sight when He rises to shake both heaven and earth, wherein only "those things which cannot be shaken may remain"?

Hebrews 12:28, 29 gives us this insight, *"Wherefore we receiving a kingdom which cannot be moved, let us have grace, whereby we may serve God acceptably with reverence and godly fear; For our*

God is a consuming fire." Here again, with the tragic incident of "strange fire" in mind (*Leviticus 10:1, 2*), we learn that there is an "acceptable" way to serve God. We cannot enter into His presence in the same manner we'd casually stroll into a sports arena, theater, or social gathering; instead, we are to serve Him *"acceptably with reverence and godly fear."*

Do you want the fire that God will accept? John the Baptist declared, *"I indeed baptize you with water unto repentance: but he that cometh after me is mightier than I, whose shoes I am not worthy to bear: he shall baptize you with the Holy Ghost, and with fire: Whose fan is in his hand, and he will thoroughly purge his floor, and gather his wheat into the garner; but he will burn up the chaff with unquenchable fire" (Matthew 3:11, 12).*

Therefore, let us *"gird up the loins of our minds,"* (see *1 Peter 1:13*), and resist the urge to succumb to mind-numbing traditions, habits, and routines of the flesh with mental proclivities that are not actively engaged in focusing on the reality of God and who He is: praying that our "fire" will be acceptable to Him as we deeply desire to unreservedly offer ourselves to Him with "reverence and godly fear." – J. Haley

Prayer: Lord, we want the fire without it be consuming to our old man and ways. We want the water, without having to lose control and flow in the current according to Your Spirit. We want it all, but we do not want to lose any part of our life and this world. The result is we end up being spiritually poor cringing beggars that live like vagabonds instead of children of God. It is what it is Lord. Amen.

October 28

"For the which cause I also suffer these things: nevertheless I am not ashamed: for I know whom I have believed, and am persuaded that he is able to keep that which I have committed unto him against that day" (2 Timothy 1:12). Are you in a state of resignation, or in an

attitude of acceptance, or perhaps you have taken on the mind of living in denial?

In today's world there seem to be many who are in a state of resignation. This particular state is a result of hopelessness. My brother told me that when he was in the army, stationed in Germany, the message according to the political times was one of retreat instead of holding one's ground. When we consider resignation, it is a type of retreat and not standing or holding one's ground.

Such resignation occurs when people are looking at the circumstances or events instead of the One who sits on the throne and sovereignly has the final say over all matters. They retreat to some corner and hope that the enemy will be stopped at some point and let them remain in their "so-called" safe zone. They never really come to a point of faith and simply submit to God and seek Him as to what they need to do to endure to the end in a victorious fashion.

When it comes to those who accept their lot, they are the ones who are waving a white flag of surrender to the enemy of God. They are stating that the odds against God are too great and therefore they will accept the oppressive condition of the enemy as he makes them slaves to a wretched system to taste the corrupt ways of the world, and drink of its judgments.

Prayer: Lord, You told us to choose life, but often we choose oppression in order to hold onto this life which will end in disgrace. Lord, I choose to pursue and know the life You have offered, which is eternal for now and forever, and abundant for the time I live in. Amen.

October 29

"And said to the mountains and rocks, Fall on us, and hide us from the face of him that sitteth on the throne, and form the wrath of the Lamb" (Revelation 6:16). Man tends to hide from both life and God. He hides from reality because he does not what to face it and he hides from God because he never wants to look into His holy face.

To hide from life is to never know it and to hide from God is to know only darkness. For man to hide from this life entails living in denial of the wicked ways and destruction of this world. They often hide in no-man's land where they just get by to avoid conflict, or they get behind causes as a noble gesture to hide their fear of life. Those who hide behind causes see themselves as being honorable, which gives them reason and purpose in this world, but because these causes are of the world, it pits them against God, revealing that they are enemies and not friends or servants of God.

It is important to point out we are called to be overcomers and not one who slides into some quagmire of this world and allow ourselves to be taken down into some pit of despair. We are living in precarious times, but our life is hid in Christ, our ultimate citizenship is not of this world, our hope is not in this present life, and our destination heavenly.

If we despair, it is because we have put our hope in something besides Christ. It we find ourselves wandering about in aimless confusion, it is because we have relied on our own understanding and have failed to seek God's perspective in His Word about how He views matters. If we find our foundation is shaking, we must examine how much of it is truly founded on the person and work of Jesus Christ.

The Bible is clear that only the overcomer, the ones who finish the course are going to receive the blessings and promises of heaven. Those who are resigned to the lies of this world will never know the blessings that await them. The ones who accept their lot in this world will never know what it means to be victorious, and those who live in denial will never be overcomers of their true enemies.

Prayer: Lord, we often forget You are the One who fights the battles for us and will win the war in the end. Thank You for the victory of the cross, the defeat of the enemies, and that Your enemies, my enemies in the end will be put under Your feet. Amen.

October 30

"Restore unto me thy joy of thy salvation; and uphold me with thy free spirit" (Psalm 51:12). Do you remember when you first got saved? I do because I felt so free in my spirit, zealous in my soul about life, and glorious joy because I knew something real had happened to me. However, that was what many refer to as the honeymoon of Christianity, which does not last forever.

Through the years I have experienced the great depths that come with swinging on limbs of immaturity and finding oneself hitting some insurmountable tree of reality and crashing to the ground of defeat. I also know what the growing pains feel like when God begins to put His finger on your limited personal strength and reveal the depth of your pride. Such pains not only make you uncomfortable and uncertain, but they can be painful to one's ego and vanity.

Keep in mind the person who wrote this. It was King David. He had a heart for the Lord, and we see where his beginning started in obscurity when as a young shepherd boy, he was being prepared to take on a giant. It was played out in humility as he admitted that the battle belonged to the Lord. He was prepared to be king when he was on the run from Saul for over a decade. However, at the height of his reign as king, he fell into the sin of adultery and tried to cover it up with murder.

King David walked in the path of self-denial and self-delusion about his sins and it was only after the prophet Nathan confronted him that he was truly brought to a place of repentance. However, the consequences that followed David's sins proved to be bitter to the soul.

There are a couple of things that will rob a person of the joy of their salvation, sin and complacency due to spiritual stagnation brought on by a lack of love towards God and His Word. There are two things that will cause one's spirit to come into bondage: sin and unbelief. Sin is a matter of an independent attitude that insists on having its own way, while the absence of love for God and His Word will lack any real motive or inspiration to come higher and to do something right. When it comes to unbelief, it is because one lacks genuine faith to walk obediently in the righteous ways of God and His Word.

Although sin is rampant in our world, the one thing many Christians lack is faith that overcomes the world. It is faith that stands on the right foundation regardless of the storms, it is the walk of faith towards God that leads us through the darkness of this world, and it is active, obedient faith that will endure to the end, allowing us to finish the course.

Are you like King David that started out with great faith but now you find yourself weary with the world around you? Remember, God is waiting to restore the joy of your salvation and set your burdened-down spirit free to once again soar above this world in great expectancy of the hope of the life that has been promised to us.

Prayer: Lord, thank You for Your faithfulness, because when my humanness is taking center stage, You are being put in the back seat. Lord, forgive me for being the culprit when it comes to retaining the joy of my salvation and to ensure the liberty of my spirit to soar above this world. Amen.

October 31

It was utterly shocking! The hard, black mass in the cast iron skillet in no way even remotely resembled the colonial dessert I thought it would be. After all, I had very carefully followed the recipe a woman had sent to the Everett Herald Newspaper for Apple Pandowdy.

I may have been young in the mid 1970's, but I knew how to cook, bake and follow directions. I well remember the hassle of trying to remove that inedible "homemade road tar" out of that pan! No amount of hot water would loosen its grip. After trying to pry, chip, stab, and scrape at it, I had an idea. Why not just put it outside in the chicken pen and let the hens do the work for me? After all, everybody knows that chickens will eat anything. Besides that, over in western Washington it rained most of the time, so surely that would solve the cleanup situation. Did it work? NO!!!

Even after three days or so, not one peck mark was visible. I'll never know what went wrong, but I do remember being irked with the woman who sent in the recipe, but then, how could I be sure it was her fault? Maybe the newspaper failed to print it properly. In my mind somebody, somewhere goofed, (not me, of course) and so it goes with us wonderful human beings when irritating, bad, terrible or disastrous things happen. The question usually is, "Whose fault was it?"

Now, we all know that the Day of Judgment is coming wherein we shall stand alone before the LORD and give an account for our lives. There will be no one to blame for our failures and disobedience, but ourselves. Because we still have the true Word of God (Holy Bible translated from the original Hebrew and Greek) we will have no excuse for believing any one of the plethora of lies blowing and flowing through Christendom.

We can't blame the false, demonic, New Age teachings that are immensely popular in so-called "Bible" studies these days with all of their dangerous, "new" this or that occult-Hinduism-inspired "methods," or the fact that church leaders leave out most of the Bible in their weekly sermonettes.

We can't blame the wolves, heretics, and false prophets on TV or those reaping great benefits from demon-inspired books. Such "teachers" and "leaders" will answer for themselves and receive their own damnation, (see *James 3:1*). It is our responsibility to "test the spirits" and to "search the Scriptures" to discern what is truth and what is error no matter how "ear-tickling" it may sound. Therefore, seek the Truth, hold fast the Truth, and love the Truth to the end, because time is short. – J. Haley

Prayer: Lord, we must love the truth if we are going to survive the great delusion of our time. Loving the truth is not just knowing it, knowing about it, or holding bits and pieces of it; rather it is loving it, loving You, and prizing You above all other persons, things, and matters of this world. Amen.

November

November 1

"The LORD is my light and my salvation; whom shall I fear? The LORD is the strength of my life; of whom shall I be afraid" (Psalm 27:1). We are living in uncertain times. For some they may have more optimism when it comes to the future, while others are afraid or sense an ominous feeling. No matter how we approach the future, we must acknowledge that we are seeing prophetic signs all about us concerning the end of the last days.

We do not know when Jesus will part the clouds, but we do know there will be great spiritual darkness engulfing the world. Whether this darkness takes ahold of minds, grips hearts, or causes many to hide in fear or rage in total anger and despair is hard to say. We know that as believers we have been told to make sure our lamps are filled with a sufficient amount of oil so that when our bridegroom comes, we will be ready to rise up in the darkness and meet Him.

The problem is that many are looking for a man or government to save them. They are holding their breath as they wait to see if the path our nation and the world is heading down will be somehow thwarted as evil agendas are stopped, allowing us to once again go back to some normalcy. However, my Bible tells me that there is no going back to what has, is, or will be judged. We must go forward by faith into the life God is calling us to.

God's Word tells us we will walk according to the light in us. We must always test and discern our life by the type of fruits that are being manifested in it. Without the light of Christ there is no fruit, and without the water of the Spirit there is no cultivating the inner man to ensure a healthy life and desirable fruit.

Prayer: Lord, we can get caught up with whether we are being religious and pious enough but fail to test our true fruit according to Your Life and Spirit. Fruit will tell on us as to our character and will always speak louder than our words. Lord, we need Your light and Spirit to ensure our fruit brings You glory in the end. Amen.

November 2

"In him was life; and the life was the light of men" (John 1:4). This Scripture clearly tells us the life of Christ in us serves as the light that will manifest itself in our life. We must walk this life out according to the Lord's life in us. However, the oil of the Holy Spirit is what must be present for the light to shine within us.

Our wicks of devotion must be trimmed with love for God and the love of God to ensure that we have what it takes for the fires from God's altar to set us aflame. We must have this flame in times of darkness when we are being called to rise up in faith and obedience, and move forward regardless of the times, the darkness, and the events taking place.

The Lord is not only my light, but He is my salvation. As Savior He died for me, as Redeemer He paid a price for me, and as the Promised Messiah He became my hope. His salvation was completed at the cross, was confirmed by His resurrection, and will be brought to full fruition when He comes back in glory.

If I am hid in Christ, I am assured of my future in glory with Him. If God is for Me in this life who can be against me in this world. Greater is He that is in me than he that is in this world; therefore, what should I fear with such great promises as my anchor which holds me tightly to the Immovable Rock in this life?

Prayer: Lord, thank You for being my immovable Rock. In faith I cling to You, in hope I reach up for that which is heavenly and excellent, and because of Your love, I can take hold of You. Amen.

November 3

For there shall be no reward to the evil man; the candle of the wicked shall be put out" (Proverbs 24:20). Darkness abounds in this world and man walks according to it. Yes man is groping in it, hiding in it and prefers it because his deeds are evil but in the end it will be snuffed out in judgment. It is for this reason that man's particular understanding of life is considered light to him, even though it is spiritual darkness that encases his soul in the grips of death.

As believers we walk according to a heavenly light that does not rely on logic, intellectual understanding or the false lights of the world. The light we walk by is truth, possesses hope, penetrates darkness of the soul, and will lead us to excellent places of wisdom and insight.

The main reason each of us as believers must keep our life in Christ in the right perspective is because that is the only thing that will keep each of us steady in the dark times. Granted, Jesus is our anchor, but we must have the faith to keep our focus on Him when nothing else makes sense in this life. Let's admit it, less and less about this world makes sense as we get closer to the end of this age.

The Bible tells us that many will faint in their minds as hearts grow cold, and everything begins to shake both in heaven and on earth. Only that which remain standing on the Rock will endure the shaking, survive the times, and ensure that one becomes an overcomer in this age. May our minds remain sound, our hearts sure, and our course steady as we keep our focus on our precious sweet Lord and Savior Jesus Christ and our feet in line with His Word.

Prayer: Lord, we have so much hope in light of Your glory, so much assurance in light of Your promises, and so much to rest in, in light of who You are. May we avoid the traps of fear, the entanglements of the world, and the false lights and promises of Satan as we strive to keep our eyes on You. Amen.

November 4

"Beloved, follow not that which is evil, but that which is good, He that doeth good is of God: but he that doeth evil hath not seen God" (3 John 11). The Christian walk is pretty simple, but we complicate it. We are told here that we are not to follow that which is evil. It seems simple enough, but we are told in *Hebrews 5:14*, that we must discern between good and evil because even evil has a beautiful or attractive, side to it. How do I know this? We have been warned in *Isaiah 5:20* that evil will be called good and good will be called evil.

We are seeing this today. There are those who call good evil because any opposition to it supposedly lacks love and tolerance. We also see people calling evil good because it appears to be tolerant towards certain sins. For the response to be considered "politically correct", as well as in step with the times, this profane presentation of love has been conveniently adjusted to fit into the religious and cultural narratives of today.

I realize that the offense taken against good has nothing to do with rejecting people based on their status, race, gender and etc.; rather, it has to do with not agreeing with certain moral practices that have already been judged as being an offense towards God. It is not God's will that people perish in their sins, but that they come to repentance. God holds back both judgment and wrath to give people time to repent, turn from their blatant offenses, and like all lost or prodigal children, come home.

However, the Bible makes it clear that if one does work and promote evil, they have not seen God. If one has not seen God, then they have no real knowledge about Him. Remember it is only the pure in heart that can see God and when you are involved in evil, there is nothing pure about it.

You can make all kinds of religious claims, but if you are taking the side of the profane, you must question your understanding of God, your standing before Him, and whether you are truly an heir of His salvation. The reason for evil being considered "plain evil" is because the agendas behind such evil are of Satan's design and will always end in complete spiritual ruin in the end.

So, what is your attitude towards good and evil? This is the real test to all matters. That which is good will be found to be in agreement with the agendas of heaven, while evil will oppose righteousness as it seduces people into another reality that will not only confuse what is right and true. It will ultimately pit these rebellious individuals against the great Creator and Judge of heaven and earth. Such people will find "no standing" in His court.

Prayer: Lord, we can delude ourselves by talking the talk, but what we stand for or fail to stand for in the end, will reveal our real standing with You. Oh, Lord, take all of the wretched blinders from off of our eyes so we can see You for Who You are. Amen.

November 5

"It is written, Man shall not live by bread alone, but by every word that proceedeth out of the mouth of God" (Matthew 4:4) Jesus was quoting *Deuteronomy 8:3.* The question is do we believe what Jesus stated, that EVERY WORD that proceeds from God's Word is true? When God's Word is involved, all we can say is "Amen, so be it on earth, for it is so in heaven." This would mean that God's Word will always remain so, which makes it law, establishes that it is absolute, and it will stand when all else falls (*1 Peter 1:25*).

Peter also backed up the absolute authority of God's Word in his second letter when he stated, "*Knowing this first, that no prophecy of the scripture is of any private interpretation. For the prophecy came not in old time by the will of man: but holy men of God spake as they were moved by the Holy Ghost" (2 Peter 1:20-21).* Once again, the Bible is not a collection of man's thoughts and interpretations; rather, it is a recording of God's prophetical Word that came upon holy men as they were moved by the Holy Spirit.

My co-laborer in the Gospel, Jeannette, made the statement that many people scripturally err because they edit the Bible in such a way that it will agree with their interpretation and reality about the issues of God and life. I know some people that have edited out almost three quarters of the Bible to fit their small-minded narratives.

It is amazing that man thinks he can interpret the Word of God without any enlightenment from the Spirit of God who leads us into all truth. The Word is spiritual, and Scriptures must be compared with spiritual truths and principles to ensure that they line up with the whole counsel of God's Word. Those who fail to rightly handle God's Word will piecemeal it until there is no spiritual nourishment or life in any of it.

Prayer: Lord, we piecemeal Your word so we can feel on top of it and think we have a corner on Your truth. But Your truth is eternal and the more we learn, the less we know, and what we do comprehend comes from Your Spirit who must enlighten our spirit about what is so. Amen.

November 6

"For I testify unto every man that heareth the words of the prophecy of this book, If any man shall add unto these things, God shall add unto him the plagues that are written in this book: And if any man shall take away from the words of the book of this prophecy, God shall take away his part out of the book of life, and out of the holy city, and from the things which are written in this book" (Revelation 22:18-19). Have you piecemealed the Bible? Have you decided what You will agree with or what you will ignore? Some discard the Old Testament even though it is the foundation that brings dimension to the New Testament, verifies prophecy, and establishes sound doctrine. There are those who edit out all the warnings so that they can placate worldly tastes, lukewarm preferences, and half-hearted devotions. Some only hold to the promises of God so they can operate in a feel-good religion that does not require them to face the harsh reality of sin, repentance, and judgment.

There are others who only read the red letters of Christ in the Gospels instead of comparing spiritual truths with spiritual truths that would ensure the intent or principle of the depths that truth can take one into when it comes to greater revelations of the Lord. Some edit out all of the Bible except part of the book of Acts and Paul's letters and yet Paul quoted a lot of the Old Testament and established teachings that only line up to Jesus' teachings in the Gospels. There are some that rely on the entertainment industry to fill in all blanks when it comes to who God is instead of obeying His Word by studying it to know who He is for themselves (2 *Timothy 2:15*).

Like Jesus, Paul is clear about the validity of the complete counsel of God's Word in *2 Timothy 3:16-17, "All scripture is given by inspiration of God, and is profitable for doctrine, for reproof, for correction, for instruction in righteousness: That the man of God may be perfect, thoroughly furnished unto all good works."* We must note the words "ALL SCRIPTURE."

The question is why is it that man takes such liberty to edit the Bible? The answer is simply, he does not believe it to be God's absolute, final Word on all matters. There are grave warnings to those who mishandle the Word of truth in unrighteousness such as that found in *Romans 1:18* or add or take away from its commands or prophecies as found in *Deuteronomy 4:2* and *Revelation 22:18-19*.

Prayer: Lord, it is man's careless ways to use, abuse, ignore, and adjust Your Word to fit their religious take on a matter or their carnal, worldly realities, but it is clear that when all is said and done, Your complete counsel will still be standing when all else shakes, crumbles and falls at Your feet. Amen.

November 7

"To every thing there is a season, and a time to every purpose under the heaven" (Ecclesiastes 3:1). We have been going through the book of Ecclesiastes. It is a very interesting book because it brings man face to face with the essence of his life. For the most part man is in pursuit of making sense out of life. He wants to find some meaning to it according to the life he is living in his particular age.

A person may start out trying to find satisfaction in the flesh, or purpose for their existence in the activities of the world, only to discover that such pursuits leave the flesh in a state of greater dissatisfaction IN their life, while the matters of the world leave one in disillusionment ABOUT their life. As the preacher in Ecclesiastes points out, all proves to be vanity when it comes to the pursuits of the flesh and the world.

As one pursues life in light of the flesh and the world, they discover the vanity of it all, and when they do, they either go into denial that it can't be so or in despair because it is so. Perhaps the greatest casualty in it is the fact that the person did not redeem the time they had to make sure their life counted in light of eternity. Time reminds us that the life we are living is not forever, but a gift of God. It puts limitations on our doings, our activities, and our accomplishments.

It is hard to face the harsh reality that our life will fade into a vast emptiness called time because it eventually leads us to the door of death and eternity. Time marches to a drumbeat, and it has been known to lead one practically ANYWHERE since it can't be controlled. It causes others to become lost in SOMEWHERE due to the fact it can't be stopped, and it leaves many in NOWHERE because it appears as if it has no real destination.

Prayer: Lord, it is obvious that the life we have in this world is temporary and leaves no real footprints behind. Lord, I need to value the footprints You made on Your way to the cross. It is your footprints that require me to follow You in this life as Your disciple, as well as lining up to the imprints You have made in Your Word to establish Your eternal life in me. Amen.

November 8

"I know that, whatsoever God doeth, it shall be fore ever: nothing can be put to it, nor any thing taken from it: and God doeth it, that men should fear before him" (Ecclesiastes 3:14). We often fail to realize in the initial years of our life that time points to a beginning and an end, to the changing seasons in life where age takes hold. When we

sense there is an end to life as we know it here, we tend to squander it. This often happens when we think we have ALL THE TIME in the world to live our lives.

We may gauge time according to projects, plans, or events to discipline our time, and yet we are rarely aware that for the most part we are just PASSING THE TIME. When we pursue the different avenues of the flesh and world for pleasure, we often look back and realize, for the most part, such pursuits were a WASTE OF TIME. Such a realization throws us into a crisis of questioning the reason for our very existence, and for some it causes them to hate their existence and their labor that they see as temporary and fruitless.

When we get older, we sometimes will consider that much of what we did reveals that we have WASTED MUCH TIME. We even might look back and identify some of those missed opportunities and regret WASTING OUR TIME on something that proved non-essential in the end.

It is vital for man to realize that God is the timekeeper in all matters. He has GIVEN US TIME to discover that there is no meaning to life outside of Him, no greater time to know Him than now, and no waste of time in discovering the life He has for us. Clearly, man gauges his time according to this life, but he will never know the real purpose and meaning of this life until he considers his life in light of his Creator and eternity.

Prayer: Lord, we only have SO MUCH TIME in this life to get it right. This means we must get You right and make sure You hold the right place in our hearts, minds, and activities. Amen

November 9

Papers everywhere! Books, files, office supplies, art prints, and a lot of stuff littered my office space. It seems chaos has to erupt before order and organization can become somewhat of a reality.

As I sifted and stacked papers and files, a short summary on suffering caught my eye. It was as if the Holy Spirit caused it to surface at this time due to the misery of my current eczema situation. The surprising thing is I had written it decades ago as a result of a far worse situation, and I had forgotten all about it.

Perhaps it can be a blessing to others, so here it is: "God's ways and His plan for your life are far, far greater than your ways and your plans for your life. Suffering has a way of forcing us to dig deep down into the inner resources (bedrock) of our very existence while, at the same time, reaching upwards beyond our grasp to gain an entrance into the very presence of our Creator.

Suffering strips us of everything in our life that is made up of vanity, fake nobility, insufferable pride and intolerable self-righteousness and independence (sin). Suffering is the one doorway into the harshness, tragedy and glories of reality. Suffering has the ability to stretch person's soul as nothing else can.

No, not even hours spent in emotional fantasies or far-reaching grandeur; nor days and years spent searching and exploring the wonders of creation; nor even a lifetime spent in avid devotion to gathering mind-boggling facts can plummet your soul into the abyss of consciousness as suffering can. The essence of suffering is to reveal you to yourself and to reveal your God to you in His Omnipotence and Sovereignty." - J. Haley

Prayer: Lord, we resist the testing of fiery ovens, the trying of our souls, and the anguish of the spirit brought on by suffering. Lord, I know suffering is Your special tool and I choose to trust the type of work You are doing with it in my life. I know in the end it will bring glory to You. Amen.

November 10

"He that made every thing beautiful in his time: also he hath set the world in their heart, so that no man can find out the work that God maketh from the beginning to the end" (Ecclesiastes 3:11). God has made everything beautiful and yet we live amid great darkness where

wickedness defiles what is beautiful and evil calls it suspicious and ugly.

The question is why does man miss God's beauty or defile and redefine it? The answer is that God has set the world in their heart. What does that mean? It means that God put it within the heart of man to pursue the world.

Mankind often deifies aspects of what he sees and knows. You will find him dancing around "so-called" worldly acceptable (pagan) altars to worship some concept of a god. If man does not exalt aspects of creation to worship, he will exalt himself in the delusional state that every man possesses the divine within and through certain enlightenment he can realize his true status. However, like man's existence in this present age, the world is temporary and therefore is limited as to what it can offer man. However, mankind still relentlessly pursues it, making the true Creator a footnote at best after mentally erecting some image of Him that ends in idolatry.

Mankind may silently look to the world to satisfy their desires, while considering its ways to give them direction and purpose, its education knowledge, its philosophies of wisdom, and finally looking to its systems to save them. In their search, they hit different peaks to only end up in valleys and canyons that lead to dead ends, endless rabbit trails that lead to nowhere, and disillusionment that leaves them in emotional pits of despair.

Sadly, despite the same wasteful results, man still prefers the flesh and the world over God. After all, he is free to do it his way while swinging from foolish limbs of wishful thinking causing him to fall into valleys of hopelessness because his ideas of life keep evading him.

Prayer: Lord, we are a stubborn, obstinate group that would rather hold on to foolish dreams than seek You to know the life You have for us. Lord, it is a miracle You can save any of us, but it is through impossible acts You make Yourself known. Amen.

November 11

"Unto thee will I cry, O LORD my rock; be not silent to me: lest, if thou be silent to me, I become like them that go down into the pit" (Psalm 28:1). Man rarely looks up until he finds himself in the darkest pit, nowhere to go, no place of escape, and no hope, and yet there is hope but it is beyond this world. The Lord put within man's heart the world but why? We are told that within the conscience of man is a knowledge that God exists and His creation verifies it.

If they have not been conditioned and indoctrinated by godless philosophies and religions, man even has an inherent knowledge as to what is right and wrong. What we have when it comes between the conscience of man and his heart is a contrast. Man can listen to his conscience as to what he knows is true and choose the right way and discover and seek after God to personally know Him, or he can go with his heart that is far from God and miss Him altogether.

We are given another contrast in this Scripture and that is man can't and will not know God if he is functioning from a worldly influence and perspective. Man can't recognize the works of God. They can't understand them because to their mind it is foolishness to believe, but they do not realize that His works are beyond man's comprehension.

Since God's works are beyond knowing, His ways will prove foreign, and His intervention will be missed. This shows us that man has the spiritual capacity to know God in a personal way, but he must step outside of the world's understanding and ways to seek and know God for himself.

The world's ineptness shows us it is not of God and can't save us. Man's limitation reveals he can't and will never be found or proven to be God and is unable to save himself. And time lets us know that everything associated with this world lacks the touch of eternity which identifies and distinguishes the one true God of the universe from the rest of His creation.

Prayer: Lord, man is always trying to bring You down in some way to pigeonhole and humanize You, while deifying his understanding of You so that he can control his idea of truth and realty. However, when we come to the end of everything, there is nothing else we are able to consider that would make sense except that there is a God and He is Creator of all things and one day we will all stand before Him. Lord, this present world is about us being allotted a certain amount of time to discover what is true, right, and eternal. Thank You for revealing Yourself to me. Amen.

November 12

"Surely he shall not be moved for ever; the righteous shall be in everlasting remembrance. He shall not be afraid of evil tidings: his heart is fixed, trusting in the LORD" (Psalm 112:6-7). In these Scriptures we are told that a good man will not be moved from what is right, and that it is the righteous who will be remembered forever in the annals of God. After all a "good" man knows where he stands because of godly wisdom and sound judgments, and the righteous know what they are standing on the Rock of Ages.

Keep in mind righteousness is a standing, an attitude and a way. The standing has to do with uprightness before God. God is the Rock and righteousness stands on what it knows is true and right. It will not be moved from that sure place.

The attitude has to do with the deep conviction of heart when it comes to doing what is acceptable to God. When one has such an attitude, doing right is the least they can do because they see it as their reasonable service. And when it comes to righteousness being a way, it points to doing something in an honorable way that ensures it is being done in the right spirit, while maintaining the integrity of faith to walk it out. To walk something out in this manner points to godliness.

If we as believers have such a standing, why would we be afraid of the evil tidings of this world? We shouldn't if our life is godly, our ways upright, and our Rock, Jesus. This world is not ours to quibble over, get caught up with, or to try to save. Granted, like the good man we must keep our wits about us in this world so we can show proper responses and remain a witness of heaven, knowing it is the righteous that leave a record behind.

As saints, we must fix our heart on what is right as we trust the Lord to bring forth His promises, stand on truth and for it, while avoiding getting caught up with evil tidings. We must keep in mind what others do with wise responses and righteous ways will be a decision on their part and not our business.

Prayer: Lord, we have all we need to finish the course before us, that is as long as we keep our wits about us and do not believe the tidings of this world. However, we must choose to believe the promises of the next and trust You to bring them all about, to avoid falling for the lies, trembling at bad tidings, and cowering in some hopeless corner of despair. Amen.

November 13

"And now for a little space grace hath been shewed from the LORD our God, to leave us a remnant to escape, and to give us a nail in his holy place, that our God may lighten our eyes and give us a little reviving in our bondage" (Ezra 9:8). We often perceive that grace was not a predominate factor in the Old Testament but those who understood Jehovah God knew that all of His works on their behalf and blessings bestowed on them was a matter of grace.

Ezra was part of the priesthood but was in bondage in Babylon. However, the king of Persia gave the necessary permission for the Jewish captives to resettle in Jerusalem and build the temple. The first group of almost 50,000 were led by Zerubbabel and other leaders in 539 B.C, but it was Ezra's desire to travel to Jerusalem after the temple was rebuilt to minister as a priest. He led over 1,700 people back to the Promised Land in 458 B.C.

Ezra knew that he needed space in which God's grace could be shown on behalf of a remnant to escape the bondage that they had lived under. Sadly, for many other Jewish people they preferred the bondage, rather than the liberty to once again worship the LORD God, while they truly establish their true spiritual legacy among the people of the Promised Land.

The priest noted in the Scripture that it would only entail a remnant, but God still needed to lighten their eyes and revive them in their bondage. The truth is not many are willing to leave comfort zones. They fear the unknown more than the bondage. They don't know what it is going to cost them in the end; therefore, they will continue to rest in the simmering juices of bondage. Granted, they may complain and murmur occasionally, but at least they know what their day holds for them. Ezra knew that even the willing remnant needed to be revived to move out of bondage to seek out their heritage.

The Jews were to be both the witness and light in the land. However, their light had been dimmed by challenges and there was no authority in their witness. In order to erect both, they would have to come back to the center of all life: God and His Word.

Prayer: Lord, we forget our calling and commission and as a result we fail to become the witnesses and reach places of excellence in our calling. Our theme should be, "lest we forget why we are here" instead of focusing on how great we can be in Your kingdom as a way to impress ourselves and others. Amen.

November 14

"They answered him, We be Abraham's seed, and were never in bondage to any man: how sayest thou, Ye shall be made free" (John 8:33). God never sets His people free to simmer in bondage but to establish a witness in their midst. He never put them in large places of freedom, to once again bring them under some other slavery, whether it be some idea or standard of piousness or religion. Jesus came to ransom us from the claims of sin on us and the judgment of

death on our souls. This was to set us free to become all that He ordained us to be to bring glory to Him.

The problem is we are in Satan's world, under his systems, and bound by unseen chains of demands and the tempting snares of the world. We spend much of our time struggling under oppression, thinking that such oppression is not really slavery but what is normal.

I often wondered how many Christians live in bondage. It is clear in observing this world that bondage is something we humans can become used to. We have an uncanny way of just getting by in slavery, and even though we sense we are enslaved in different ways we are willing to put up with it because we know what to expect from it.

To step out of comfort zones to face the unknown when it comes to seeking a new way and life is a bit overwhelming. It is unnerving and will often undo us as we realize that we must trust in something bigger than we are to survive some of the challenges.

What we fail to remind ourselves is that as true disciples of Christ, He will call us out of the normalcy of comfort zones to follow Him into an extraordinary life. This life will allot us to not only see how His grace works but will enable us to be witnesses of the impossible as God leads us past the enemies, around obstacles, and through the challenges of this world into His glorious promises.

Prayer: Lord, there is much we must overcome in this world, but if we follow You, You will victoriously lead us through the various terrains so as overcomers we will come into the fullness of Your promises. Amen.

November 15

Let's face it, we're all human whether we're born again or not, and there are times when you just simply "hit bottom" and everything within you wants to quit. Sometimes hitting bottom may only last for a short time, and a few tissues later you're okay.

But at other times it seems like there's no relief in sight for days, but regardless of the time element, there are some things we need to remember about hitting bottom, and one of them is this: Everybody's "bottom" is different. Rayola (my co-laborer in the gospel) taught me that many years ago when the battle was fierce, the forces against us relentless, and the challenges overwhelming. In other words, "hitting bottom" for one person may not be the same situation as it is for another because we all have a breaking point.

Thankfully, the truth is, God knows us all intimately and He knows our capabilities, he knows where our breaking points are, and He knows just how much pressure, sifting, boiling or refining we can take when our faith is being tested. "Hitting bottom" however, must be discerned for what it is, whether the cause is physical, mental or spiritual and dealt with accordingly through the Word and prayer.

The wonderful thing is the Holy Spirit is with us when we're in a pit, and therefore He either brings peace and rest, comfort and renewed vision, the Living Word, or convicts us if we need to repent.

Finally, let's be sure that, as Christians, the next time we get derailed and hit bottom that we 1) resist the temptation to have a pity party; 2) resist the temptation to pretend everything is "just fine" because if it isn't, it isn't and we need to be humbly truthful, and 3) *"draw near to God and He will draw near to you," (James 4:8)*. Ask Him for wisdom (*James 1:5*), and be thankful. "*Then shall ye call upon me, and ye shall go and pray unto me, and I will hearken unto you. And ye shall seek me, and find me, when ye shall search for me with all your heart. And I will be found of you saith the LORD." (Jeremiah 29:12-14a.)* – J. Haley

Prayer: Lord, we need to learn to discern the matters of Your kingdom. Discerning entails standing firm on the Rock of Your truth to determine the spirit behind something. Lord, give me wisdom to discern, to properly hear, and make sure it hits the right mark in my life for my edification and Your glory. Amen.

November 16

"Blessed are they that keep judgment, and he that doeth righteousness at all times" (Psalm 106:3). God's judgments about all matters are just. This goes for the judgments He has established when it comes to sins. People have a hard time facing the fact that we are born into an ungodly state and our tendency is to insist on our own way which will offend God. This offense is known as sin.

This Scripture tells us those who keep His judgment will be blessed. To keep His judgment requires us to take on His attitude about a matter to ensure purity in what we stand for. To keep judgment in the right perspective begins with us holding the line of righteousness for ourselves. It is true we can warn others of the consequences out of love, contend with them over the insanity that rebellion causes out of genuine concern, and pull others out of the fires when they cry out for mercy, but we can't expect people to hold to God's judgments unless they choose to believe what God says about it as being true and right.

The truth is most people, including those who operate in a religious world, ignore God's judgment and adjust what is considered right and true to their own idea of self-righteousness. From this point they operate in a type of self-delusion that blinds them to the fact they are now on the broad path leading to utter spiritual ruin in some fashion.

The Bible is the only source that reveals God's judgment. We must approach it by faith knowing that everything it says is "Amen, so be it (on earth), for it is so (in heaven)." "Amen" is the same as believing it has been established in heaven and will be in due time executed on earth. When it comes to the Bible there is nothing more that can be said, added to, or minimized, and to put a "but" while adding a doubt, and minimizing its absolute authority with personal judgment and debate is to go into unbelief that will end in spiritual bankruptcy.

We are to follow after righteousness to ensure that we do what is right all the time. As you can see, it is not just a matter of knowing what is right but doing it because it is truth that has been established by God's judgment in all matters concerning heaven and earth.

Prayer: Lord, we so want the matters of Your kingdom on our terms, according to our thinking and ways, but in the end Your judgment will be left standing for Your truth is forever. Amen.

November 17

"And Jesus answering said unto them, Do ye not therefore err, because ye know not the scriptures, neither the power of God?" (Mark 12:24). We live in the days when it seems many are falling into some type of Scriptural error. In this case Jesus was talking to the religious Sadducees because they did not believe in resurrection in spite of the fact that the saints of old such as King David, Job, and the prophet Daniel specifically made reference to it *in Psalm 17:15, Job 19:25-26*, and *Daniel 12:1-3*.

Such error should not surprise us because deception has plagued mankind since Satan deceived Eve in the Garden, and in his fallen state man can easily fall into it without realizing that his premise is wrong. We also must not forget Jesus' various warnings about deception in the last days.

We are clearly living in the last days and the deception that will be predominate will not only come out of ignorance of God and His Word, but there will be many substitutes claiming they are "the Christ," when in fact they are imposters who possess an anti-Christ spirit.

Error of any nature is subtle and hard to recognize unless one is able to properly discern it because they know God and His Word. They clearly stand strong and immovable on what His Word says about all matters concerning life and godliness. Above all, they love God's Word because it is a revelation of who He is, and He is the only Rock that never moves from truth, sways from what is real, or tries to adjust what is so to fit into what is nothing more than a lie.

Prayer: Lord, we miss it because we do not approach Your Word as the only absolute truth and standard to all matters. Forgive us for our arrogance to demand You must agree with us before we will by "profane" faith embrace Your Word as TRUTH. Amen.

November 18

"But all these things will they do unto you for my name's sake because they know not him that sent me" (John 15:21) How do people err when the truth is in black and white, especially to those who choose to believe? Why would they mock heavenly wisdom that is full of common sense to those who look at a matter without any self-serving filters as being foolish? In *Hebrews 3:10*, we are told that the children of Israel err in their hearts because they did not know the ways of God. However, in *Mark 12:24*, we are told the people err in a couple of ways. The first one has to do with not knowing Scripture.

If one does not know the Word, they will error in their heart because Scripture shows us how God operates. In other words, it shows us the ways of God. He will never stray from His ways because they are righteous since they are in line with His holy attributes, His perfect will, and His eternal plan of redemption.

When we understand the ways of God, we can properly follow how He addresses and deals with matters in Scripture, confirming that He never misses a step or a beat when it comes to fulfilling His plan. When people do not know the ways of God because they are ignorant towards Him, they fill in the blank spaces with their own sentimental ideas of Him, causing them to reaffirm or erect a wrong concept of Him in their heart. Sadly, their heart will win out when it comes to who God is regardless of what the Word states. After all, the issues of life are determined by the heart attitude.

Finally, those who do not know God, will never believe the extent of His power, trust Him to show Himself mighty when necessary, and stand assured that all that God does will reflect His goodness that will prove to be beneficial. We know that God's power is manifested in and through our lives as believers by the Holy Spirit. Nothing is too great for God to deal with nor is anything too small for God to overlook. The key is not what God can do, but that He does all things well in light of who He is. He wields His power to fulfill His will and bring forth His plan to perfection for His glory.

Prayer: Lord, we know You do all things well, but we have a hard time believing that You will bring forth Your perfection in our lives according to Your will and timing. We often believe You can do it, but to show forth Your goodness on our behalf sometimes has us admitting that we believe You can, but help us in our unbelief, trusting that You want to do it on our behalf. Amen.

November 19

"Take heed therefore unto yourselves, and to all the flock, over the which the Holy Ghost hath made your overseers, to feed the church of God, which he hath purchased with his own blood" (Acts 20:27). This instruction from Paul was to the elders overseeing the church of Ephesus. This Scripture caught my attention because the real exhortation to the elders of every local body is clear: feed the flock.

Today it seems that some leaders in the churches are more interested in building up the church with numbers instead of feeding the flock spiritual food. We know that the one who truly builds the church is the Lord, while elders are responsible for ensuring the sheep's growth and welfare. In fact, a true elder is to show hospitality and is apt to minister the Word of God whenever given the chance to do so.

After observing some of the leadership in local churches, I have questioned whether the leadership is more interested in building worldly kingdoms for their personal exaltation and benefit when the Bible is clear as to the responsibilities of the leadership.

Peter was given the same challenge in *John 21:13-17,* when he was told by Jesus three times to feed His lambs, feed His sheep, and feed His flock. Likewise, the Apostle Peter exhorted the elders to feed the flock of God in *1 Peter 5:1-4*.

These shepherds were and are not to take oversight of the sheep by some brute force, to lord over them or serve among them for filthy lucre but as examples. He went on to remind all shepherds that the Chief Shepherd will appear and when He does his desire is to see them receive a crown of glory that will never fade.

Prayer: Lord, You are clear about the qualifications of leaders in Your kingdom. Sadly, we humans like to move the bar as we see fit and as a result, Your sheep suffer, the Church seems to become weaker, and true Christianity is mocked, put down, and cast to the side because it lacks standing, authority, and power. Amen.

November 20

"And he gave some, apostles; and some, prophets; and some, evangelists; and some pastors and teachers; For the perfecting of the saints, for the work of the ministry, for the edifying of the body of Christ" (Ephesians 4:11-12). God set forth a pattern when it comes to leadership in His kingdom. As to the Apostle Paul's instructions about pastors there seems to be some confusion about the necessity for this position in the Church. In fact, some local bodies have moved away from using the term "pastor" and just have elders even though *Ephesians 4:11-12* clearly stipulates that one of the positions in the body is that of a pastor.

A pastor holds the same position as the elder, but his main responsibility is to be a shepherd that is a faithful overseer of the flock. Like any good shepherd, pastors are to ensure that the sheep are properly fed, led, and protected. They are to simply be an extension of Jesus when it comes to the flock.

Without the central figure of a pastor who are the sheep to look to as their shepherd? Who will the responsible elders hold accountable for the condition of the sheep? The pastor has the responsibility to properly minister to God's people according to God's Word so the sheep will know they are safe in the environment, feel the caring touch of a shepherd, and hear the voice of the true Shepherd. Hearing the voice of the true Shepherd will ensure that the sheep do not scatter to other pastures, leaving them vulnerable to the predators of the age.

The Bible is clear about the distinctions of the positions in the Body of Christ, but sadly not every leader or shepherd adheres to the instructions. When this error happens, the Body will prove to be out of order, the physical church will lack true power, and the sheep will greatly suffer because there is no place where they can truly rest.

Prayer: Lord, when we fail to adhere to Your order, we find ourselves in precarious places. The lambs become vulnerable, the sheep flee or wander off, and the flock is scattered because they can't hear Your voice in the teaching and preaching of the leadership. Lord, when will Your people believe Your Word is true, Your ways perfect, and that in good faith they will obey what has been set forth in Your Word? Amen.

November 21

"And said, I beseech thee, O LORD God of heaven, the great and terrible God, that keepeth covenant and mercy for them that love him and observe his commandments" (Nehemiah 1:5). This is a prayer of Nehemiah. We are told this is how he approached God after learning of the despairing condition of Jerusalem. He sat down, wept and backed up his great distress with fasting and prayer for several days.

We can see where he beseeched, implored the God of heaven. He called upon Him as (Jehovah-Yahweh) LORD God (Elohim) who was and is Creator. Nehemiah acknowledges God is great which points to being higher and more excellent, as well as terrible which has to do with having reverence, a healthy fear towards Him.

Our approach to God is an indication as to whether we truly know Him. The reason I say this is we do not casually approach someone we do not really know, and we are not flippant with someone who deserves our respect. When people approach the Lord in a casual way, they reveal that they do not really know Him, but they are assuming or presuming they do because of some religious notion, association or experience. However, if they truly know God, they would know that they must approach Him in reverence of who He is, in awe of His greatness, and in dread of bringing any kind of reproach to or against Him.

The second thing we must note about Nehemiah's prayer is that he approached God on the basis of Him keeping His covenant with His people, and His desire and willingness to show mercy. We as believers are Scripturally told we can only approach the Father through Jesus. The reason for this is because Jesus is the essence of the new covenant of redemption that allows us to seek the mercy of God, knowing that in the end we will find grace.

We are also told in Nehemiah's prayer that the reason we approach God with a sober attitude, is because of His covenant. This covenant allows us to know mercy, and mercy properly utilized, produces a love for God. Godly love allows us to approach Him in confidence, knowing that we will be able to stand before Him without fear of judgment.

We are also told if we love Him, we will obey Him. Many people perceive obedience as a terrible burden, but when love is present obedience becomes a way of showing love. Love takes great pleasure in doing that which will delight the heart of the one who is loved. Such love is kind, selfless, and sacrificial.

Prayer: Lord, we are blessed because You have provided the way through Your cross in which we can appeal to heaven and know we have standing, authority, and confidence that we will be heard. Amen.

November 22

"Every good gift and every perfect gift is from above, and cometh down from the Father of lights, with whom is no variableness, neither shadow of turning" (James 1:17). This week marks the countdown to Thanksgiving. It is supposed to be a time of remembering what we have to develop an attitude of gratitude.

Since we live in a country of abundance, we often can take for granted the blessings we have been entrusted with. Granted, for some they have labored and sacrificed much to possess such blessings, but the truth is, if God did not touch, multiply, and open the door to usher such gifts in, people would not be enjoying them as blessings.

We must believe what *James 1:17* tells us that every good or beneficial gift that graces our lives and every perfect, pure gift that enriches our life comes from the Father above. A gift can't benefit us if we don't use it properly and a perfect gift can't enrich us unless we humbly accept it as being from the Father's hand, otherwise we will think everything we have we deserve. In such flippancy, we tend to think we do not have to be good stewards of such gifts, and we can do as we will with them. We do not need to be responsible servants with them to ensure they will benefit or bless others, revealing that we have no real gratitude towards them being provided for us.

Part of being thankful is realizing that all gifts are a matter of God's grace. We do not deserve them because we worked hard for them. We do not earn them because we made the necessary sacrifices for them. It is God's grace that He blessed us with an open door to pursue them and multiply them despite the god of this world constantly robbing us of enjoying them, oppressing us in our pursuit of them, or causing bitterness to take root in our soul because they can become illusive to us.

This brings us to the fact that our greatest gift is the life God gives us. We can't enjoy the gifts that benefit and enrich our lives, unless we recognize that our very breath and life is a gift from God. Each day is a gift, and it is a gift in the sense that we can discover, enjoy and rest in the life that has been provided by the sacrifice of God's Son. Our life is enriched because of the many gifts from above that grace our life such as forgiveness, mercy, compassion, pity, and love. In the end, these unseen gifts prove satisfying to the soul, beneficial to the spirit, and rewarding in our walk.

The question is, are you being prepared to be thankful or are you going to prove to be unthankful about what you have because you have become a miserable miser who misses, exploits and abuses the blessings from above?

Prayer: Lord, we like to think we earn all things when in reality, You must touch everything for them to become a blessing. The truth is if the things of our life are not touched by what is heavenly, they will prove to be temporary as the joy of fickle gratitude, based on worldly things, quickly lose their luster. Lord, Your light never changes, Your commitment towards us never varies, and Your love for us never changes regardless of the neon lights and shadows cast by the world. Amen.

November 23

"Oh that men would praise the LORD for his goodness, and for his wonderful works to the children of men! And let them sacrifice the sacrifices of thanksgiving, and declare his works with rejoicing" (Psalm 107:21-22). Our countdown to Thanksgiving continues for the next couple of days.

How does one develop an attitude of gratitude? Certain *Psalms* give us a wonderful insight into being thankful as in the case *of Psalm 107*. What must we begin with to develop the right attitude? We begin with praise. Praise is the wings that take flight because it is based on who God is.

All thankfulness finds it springboard in praises that lifts the mind above the present world to consider the greatness and majesty of God. The praises are based on the goodness of God and His wonderful works that are too great to describe. It is as our mind is lifted by the wings of praise that we find thanksgiving lifting our heart towards how God's goodness and works have indeed touched our lives.

The truth is, we must be lifted above this present life to even begin to see how God has blessed us. We are often too close to both His goodness and works to recognize how He has indeed touched our lives. We are so caught up with the current of life associated to this world that we fail to see how God uses His power to direct the current with His many graces.

Once we gain the perspective of God's continual intervention into our lives, we can begin to appreciate His many gifts. However, the greatest gift comes with knowing that God has provided us the life through redemption to experience the heights of such praise.

When the heart is lifted in thanksgiving in light of God's greatness, we will offer a sacrifice of thanksgiving. Old Testament offerings require a sacrifice of thanksgiving to show the necessary recognition that man finally gets it—that God has provided everything a man needs to experience life, know and rejoice in his Creator, and walk in the life of true worship and service before Him.

The question is, have we even gotten off of the ground of religion to truly experience the heights of praise so we can begin to offer the sacrifices of thanksgiving to our eternal, glorious Creator as we rejoice in His many gifts?

Prayer: Lord, we fail to get out of our pews, lift our arms so the wind of Your Spirit can lift us into the heights of praise to see from a heavenly perspective just how much You have blessed our lives. Oh, if only we would praise You, we would know how to worship You as we offer the sacrifices of thanksgiving for all Your incredible gifts. Amen.

November 24

"Because thou servedst not the LORD thy God with joyfulness, and with gladness of heart, for the abundance of all things: therefore shalt thou serve thine enemies which the Lord send against thee, in hunger, and in thirst, and in nakedness, and in want of all things and he shall put a yoke of iron upon thy neck, until he have destroyed thee" (Deuteronomy 28:47). We have been doing a countdown to Thanksgiving.

When it comes to this time of the year we can get caught up with the trimmings, the activities, and the ways of the world. There is nothing wrong with appreciating some of the happenings around this time except how many times do we leave the meaning of some of the celebrations in the rear view mirror as we partake of what will prove to be vanity in the end.

One of the few traditions of this time that remind us of why we take time out to consider something of significance is Thanksgiving. There is indeed a history to it, a purpose for it, and a solemn reminder that its significance should not be taken lightly.

I started off reminding everyone that everything we have need of and is necessary comes from the Father above. These two scriptures in *Deuteronomy* also point this very fact out. It is because God has provided everything that we in turn should be joyful and glad for any opportunity to serve Him. True service also points to worship. Joy and gladness truly point to an attitude of gratitude that has been established in praise and comes from a thankful heart.

I appreciate these two Scriptures because they take a very solemn turn to bring an ominous awareness. If we fail to serve the Lord in gladness, we will end up serving our enemies in bitterness until death takes us away. We must consider how much time we spend in vanity and how much time do we spend in offering thanksgiving to our Lord in our service and worship.

Perhaps if we took more time to remind ourselves as to why we are really here, we may find ourselves in the heights of the heavenly and not racing through the base ways of vanity. The tragedy is that in the end we do end up serving our enemies in some way without really recognizing it. I don't know about you, but for me in my younger years many of the events surrounding this season ended in family feuds rather than families being blessed to be together so they truly could recognize the many blessings bestowed on them by their Creator.

Prayer: Lord, praise, worship and thanksgiving are all personal matters, but as Your people, praise should be continually on our lips and worship a normal response in all things pertaining to Your kingdom because thanksgiving is in our hearts. Amen.

November 25

"In everything give thanks for this is the will of God in Christ Jesus concerning you" (1 Thessalonians 5:18). Today will mark another

Thanksgiving. Thanksgiving will reveal what possesses us. So many people value things and not what is valuable in light of eternity. Because of what we value, we often miss what will prove significant in the end. Due to the fact we don't recognize what is significant, we miss what would enrich our lives.

Often our hindsight of matters leaves us in a state of regret, and the present haunts us with "if only" while we have a hard time looking forward because we are being pulled back to the foolish ways marked by immaturity and ingratitude. The problem with being raised in a society of abundance is that we are made weak by much, often spoiled by vanity that comes from having too many things while possessing nothing of substance such as integrity. This, in the end, produces ingratitude towards all things.

One of the purest offerings is that of thanksgiving. For it to exist it must come from a pure heart. The idea that thanksgiving is the will of God is not about the fact He deserves and expects such an offering; rather, it is more about our well-being. It is true He deserves such a pure offering that is borne up by praises, but true gratitude brings contentment to the soul, delight to the spirit, and peace of mind to the weary.

Consider what Paul is saying, "it is the will of God in Christ Jesus CONCERNING you." In Christ we have all we need, but if we do not have a pure heart in which to believe, receive, and know it is so, we will miss the blessings and become lean in spirit and miserable in our being. We will lament rather than rejoice and we will cry "woe is me" rather than rise up in praise towards the Lord. In a low state, we will fail to come to the conclusion that Paul so often came to, but clearly expressed in *2 Corinthians 9:15, "Thanks be unto God for his unspeakable gift."*

Prayer: Lord, we do miss it because our eyes are not where they should be, our heart is not set on what is eternal, and our mind is not settled on what is sure. Bring us back to the center of all things, and that is You are our unspeakable gift. Amen.

November 26

This is the time of year when most, but by no means all, of the people in America are focused on turkey dinner and turkey leftovers. As for us, we love those leftovers for turkey soup, turkey sandwiches, turkey stir-fry, turkey salad, and turkey casseroles. Having said all that, however, this post is really about "eating crow."

Believe me, even if you don't like turkey, eating crow is far worse! Remember that old saying "I had to eat crow" which meant, "I was wrong, and had to face it, admit it, and apologize"? Well, way back when I was about half my present age, I had to "eat crow." Not just a wee bit of crow, or two-feather's worth, but a whole three-course meal's worth of crow. (My fiction book, *Rose of Light, Thorn of Darkness* is based on this whole saga.)

Let's just suffice it to say, that I seriously considered writing a "Christian Crow Cookbook" but I couldn't even begin to create enough, if any, interesting recipes for crow meat or beaks, feet and feathers, and as it turned out in my own personal case, I didn't have to just sort of taste "eating crow," I had to swallow the entire bird. WHOLE.

The glorious thing is just this: God didn't fall off His throne over my plight, but rather He used it for my good and His glory. The Lord will take that which Satan plans for evil and turn it into good if we let Him.

In *Genesis 50:20*, Joseph said unto his brethren who had sold him into slavery, *"But as for you, ye thought evil against me; but God meant it unto good, to bring to pass, as it is this day, to save much people alive."*

God is Almighty, and nothing is impossible for Him. Therefore, if you love God with all your heart, but are facing a situation where crow is on your menu, trust and obey the Lord, knowing that, *"...all things work together for good to them that love God, to them who are the called according to his purpose" (Romans 8:28.)* – J. Haley

Prayer: Lord, crow is hard to eat but facing You without such experiences of humiliation would lead to such great despair of the heart and soul. I would rather choke on crow and learn how to properly swallow it with repentance and confession than face You, knowing I brought such reproach to You because I would not humble myself when I was wrong. Amen.

November 27

"I therefore, the prisoner of the Lord, beseech you that ye walk worthy of the vocation wherewith ye are called" (Ephesians 4:1). In a recent post I talked about how real leaders of the church are to feed the sheep to ensure the health of the flock. We know that for the Church it is the spiritual food of God's Word.

It seems the instruction to feed the sheep is clear enough, but challenges arise because the Word of God is not always the main diet for leaders and sheep. It seems that many, including leaders prefer to read and teach from many other books rather than the Bible.

There are various tastes, even among the sheep, that are attracted to "foods" other than the Bible. There are those who like the fleshly fluff of sentimental religious worship, the milk of dead-letter doctrine, or the milk toast of worldly compromise. Although there may be bits of nourishment in each of these diets, they can't bring spiritual growth. The meat of the Word is what brings sustaining growth, and the meat has to do with doing the will of God.

When you consider that what we spiritually eat will determine our growth, we start by realizing that Christianity is not just a title or a Sunday activity. It is living the life of Christ. To live His life is a daily requirement and requires spiritual nourishment. It is for this reason the Apostle Paul refers to the Christian life as being a vocation, a profession that is an intricate part of all we do.

The key in growing into this life is that we must seek to know God's will as a means to walk in it in order to abide in it. It is only as we assimilate His Word through obedience, walk it out according to the leading of the Holy Spirit, and learn to abide in sweet fellowship with the Lord, that we will know the benefit of the meat of His Word.

Prayer: Lord it is about being in Your will, walking according to it, and abiding in it that we can begin to understand how it is a vocation that will eventually become natural for us to walk in. Amen.

November 28

"Jesus saith unto them, My meat is to do the will of him that sent me, and to finish his work" (John 4:34). How many Christians are being prepared to chew the meat of the Word? It can initially prove to be hard to chew the meat of truth because people have not developed the teeth to chew on it due to being constantly fed the doctrine of milk.

There are some who would never dare swallow the meat for it would choke them because they have never learned how to chew it to find out the acceptable, good, and perfect will of God. My concern is that leaders have lost or never had a vision for the lost sheep of Jesus to understand what it means to lead them to the green pastures and pure waters.

This brings me to the other problem I see among those who hold a position of overseer in the church. The position has become a worldly profession and is no longer a matter of a high calling from above.

These individuals are often not anointed and empowered by the Holy Spirit to properly wield the sword of the Word to ensure it hits the right targets. Many leaders seem to use the methods, attractions, and gadgets of the world to attract people into their midst instead of exalting the true Shepherd, Jesus Christ. We are told that if Jesus is lifted up, He is the one who will draw the lost, wounded, and wandering sheep to Himself.

True church growth will come down to how effective the leadership adheres to the true Shepherd, but the church must not settle for half-hearted, hireling shepherds. On the other hand, local bodies can't expect a committed shepherd if they are not committed to following the true Shepherd. The heights the local body reaches will be determined by how low in humility the leadership becomes before the Only, true Shepherd, as well as their level of sensitivity to the Spirit and their obedience to His Word.

Prayer: Lord, You are the Maker of this world, the Shepherd of Your sheep, the Lord over the spiritual household, the head over the church, and the Master who shapes Your people for Your glory. Lord, I choose to be an instrument for Your use, clay in Your hands to shape, and a servant that serves You with my whole heart, strength, mind, and soul. Amen.

November 29

"Let thine ear now be attentive, and thine eyes open, that thou mayest hear the prayer of thy servant, which I pray before thee now, day and night, for the children of Israel thy servants, and confess the sins of the children of Israel, which we have sinned against thee: both I and my father's house have sinned" (Nehemiah 1:6). I have heard that there are many prayers going forth for revival. I would love to see it, but upon studying Scripture, repentance born out of true brokenness must be the first order of business for there to be any revival, salvation, and restoration.

Nehemiah was born in captivity because of the sins of Judah. He was a trustworthy man for he was the Gentile king's cupbearer. However, when he heard about the condition of the great affliction of the Jews in Jerusalem, his heart became so burdened with the knowledge that although some of the people had gone back to the land decades before, Jerusalem was still in a precarious position.

The walls of protection that had been broken down and the gates that had been burned by the armies of Babylon had never been erected. The king noticed something was wrong with his cupbearer and that is when Nehemiah bravely confessed his concern. The ruler showed great favor when he gave Nehemiah permission to leave his prestige post and travel to Jerusalem.

Nehemiah's prayer is worth studying. However, what we must note is that he stood in the gap as a mediator, but for anyone to do that they must first become identified to the plight of the ones they are interceding for. This required Nehemiah to become identified with the sins of the children of Israel. He goes on to say that the people had dealt corruptly against the Lord and had not kept His commandments, statutes, or judgments, and as a result they had been scattered. However, he knew if they would only once again turn to the Lord in sincere repentance and brokenness, He would restore them.

Prayer: Lord, in prayer we start out with wants and after silence, we ask for our needs. However, the real calling of prayer is intercession on behalf of others. This intercession is about seeing Your will done in a matter. Amen.

November 30

"So the wall as finished in the twenty and fifth day of the month Elul, in fifty and two days" (Nehemiah 6:15). How important is intercession? It is all about identifying with God's heart about a matter to ensure His will is carried out in the lives of His people. In such prayer we become co-laborers with our Lord. It is important to point out that Nehemiah's enduring intercession day and night had a lot to do with God blessing him to carry out the burden that was on his heart.

Nehemiah was truly one who understood the great betrayal of those before him and his own limitations in seeing a matter through. He knew he had to have that right standing before the Lord to ensure his authority in carrying out his commission.

What was Nehemiah's commission? It was to build the wall and erect the gates. Due to great opposition he had to have a sword in one hand and his building tool in the other, but since the Lord was truly behind the restoration, the wall was finished in 52 days.

We would all like to see repentance in this nation, but it must start among God's people recognizing how much they have failed to adhere to His Word and now have broken down walls in their life and burned gates that provide no protection. It is clear they truly need to repent in brokenness. Once that happens the Nehemiahs need to step up with the Word in one hand and their callings and gifts in another to be part of the restoration that truly needs to take place in the lives of God's people.

Prayer: Lord, so many of Your people are in affliction but are overlooked because there always seems to be much more important pressing matters to take care of when it comes to the affairs of the Church. Lord, forgive us for ignoring the broken-down walls and burnt gates of those struggling in their Christian walk. Amen.

December

December 1

"And Joshua did unto them as the LORD bade him: he houghed their horses, and burnt their chariots with fire" (Joshua 11:9). I have heard testimonies of those who had to walk by faith. The key to walking by faith is that such a walk means walking through fires that refine faith to the point of consuming it. It also means facing the lions in the den of opposition knowing you can be devoured. It entails enduring the storms of uncertainty that could leave you utterly devastated, and standing in the battle, recognizing that the victory is not in you surviving it, but in leaving a witness behind that there is true faith, even in the midst of an unbelieving world.

Faith is tested, refined, and enlarged when there is nothing left that you can believe or trust in when it comes to the world and the flesh. It is at the point of where everything you had dependency on in this world has been houghed and burnt that you find out just how much you do depend on God in all matters.

I have said this many times, faith is a choice, and it is when all worldly and fleshly options are no longer on the table that a person will either give way to crawling into some corner in utter fear, despair, hopelessness, and anger or choosing to trust God because of that small seed of faith He has planted in their hearts.

Prayer: Lord, You have given us faith so we can stand when all is falling around us, but it must be enlarged and that only happens when it is being tested. Lord, I trust You to put the right type of fires to my faith to bring it to maturity. Amen.

December 2

"To Titus, mine own son after the common faith: Grace, mercy, and peace, from God the Father and the Lord Jesus Christ our Saviour" (Titus 1:3). All believers possess a common faith because it is directed toward the one true God, but faith needs to be tested to reveal where our real reliance is: the world or God.

We see in yesterday's devotion where Joshua understood the great need of God's people to depend solely on the Lord to ensure victory in securing the Promised Land for themselves. However, it is man's natural tendency to depend on personal strength, wit, worldly ways and measures instead of depending on God, while resting in His promises that all He declared, HE WILL DO!

I know for me that in the past I have ignorantly depended on "horses" that pointed to personal strength and understanding, and "chariots" of the world to bring about a matter, but it was not until all such things were removed that I could land and rest on what God had shown or promised me in the past. It is when I chose to trust God that I had the great faith-building pleasure of watching Him bring the miraculous forth.

The refinement of faith is a matter of individuals casting doubt and debate aside, laying their best plans on some altar, getting out of the way and letting God be God while trusting Him to work out what seems like impossible details for His glory.

Prayer: Lord, I have foolishly depended on fleshly means and worldly ways to advance myself through the formidable territory of this age, but each dependency left me feeling foolish and in a state of despair. It is only when I walked in light of You and Your Word, that the faith You gave me would grow amid testing, endure the storms of this life, and remain standing in the midst of what the world would consider a point of mockery and defeat. Thank You for giving me the necessary measure of faith that assures me that in the end I will finish the course. Amen.

December 3

"All good things must come to an end," was one of the old sayings my dad often said when I was growing up. Even though it's true, in a worldly sense, it never was what I wanted to hear or think about, but then the day came when the "good thing" I loved so much had to be given up for my health's sake. After all, I fell in love (when I was in elementary school) with the "good thing" that was to become a major basis for much of my life when given a paint by number oil painting set.

I still remember the smell of the linseed oil, paints and turpentine as I carefully brushed the smooth, shiny colors onto the thin canvas. Over four decades later, after years of art exhibits and teaching painting my "art career" climaxed when honored with the task of painting the murals for the Chapel of the Resurrection in Bothell, WA. Eventually the buildup of toxins from chemicals and heavy metals, dietary ignorance, along with months of working on the paintings, and long hours working evenings and weekends in ministry, took its toll. (And that is another story.)

The point is, I had to face the heartbreaking fact that this "good thing" that I loved so much had come to an end, but know that, when God calls you, the "good" you know is inferior to the "better" of God. This brings to mind the ultimate question Jesus asked the Apostle Peter.

You no doubt remember the story of the third time Jesus showed Himself to the disciples after He had risen from the dead. At that time Peter had stated "I go a fishing." Why? I believe it was because fishing for Peter was just like oil painting for me. It was that "good thing" in his life that he was used to, that he was familiar and comfortable with, that he was good at, that gave him a means of support, and although it could be difficult and challenging, it defined, in a way, who he was.

At this point, Peter did not know what else to do, and he had no clear vision of what the Lord wanted him to do either. But, when Jesus appeared to him and the disciples who were with him, He brought him to the place of decision by filling the net with "great fishes, an hundred and fifty and three: and for all there were so many, yet was not the net broken." (An example of ministry when under God's control.)

Then, after eating the meal of fish and bread with the risen Lord, *"...Jesus said to Simon Peter, Simon, son of Jonas; lovest thou me more than these?" (John 21:15).* Before moving on past this crucial junction, we need to stop and consider how important Jesus' question was.

Jesus knew that if Peter did not make a conscious decision to let go of what was such an integral, important, and "normal," if you will, part of his life and something he knew, depended on and loved (because the sea has a way of captivating people) that his heart would be divided between the ways and persuasions of the world, and the Person and work of the Lord Jesus Christ. Then He went on to ask Peter three times if he loved Him.

The question is, when we encounter Jesus, when we believe who He is, and when we decide to follow Him, do we truly love Him "more than these" people, places and things that play such an important role in our life, or will we go back to "fishing" our way. *"To him be glory and dominion for ever and ever. Amen" (1 Peter 5:11).* – J. Haley

Prayer: Lord, we often choose what we are used to, but You are forever calling us upward to that which is better, excellent, and glorious. Amen.

December 4

"Neither did he leave of the people to Jehoahaz but fifty horsemen, and ten chariots, and ten thousand footmen: for the king of Syria had destroyed them, and had made them like the dust by threshing" (2 Kings 13:7). In a previous post I talked about how it is natural for people to depend on the different aspects of fleshly strength and the power the world promotes. When it comes to individuals depending on fleshly and worldly means to save, protect, and deliver them from their enemies they will ultimately taste bitterness in the end.

There is only One who can truly save, protect and deliver us and that is the Lord. We usually do not discover this until after all our strength has been ebbed out, our options left in the dust of despair, and we have been brought to a place of utter ruin. Up to that time we rarely consider looking up and throwing ourselves on the mercy of God.

Let us consider the plight of Jehoahaz. The resources he once had were greatly rendered down to a mere impression that a sufficient military force existed to ward off Israel's enemies. Clearly, Israel did not have the power to present any real opposition, especially to the king of Syria.

It is important to note it was a Gentile king who humbled the Israelite king. Sadly, this Jewish king never looked up to seek the one true God of Israel. He settled for a mere impression and never knew victory.

How true is this scenario when it comes to Christians? I know for me, after I was born again, I still possessed a high opinion of all my abilities and relied on worldly options. It was only after the ways of the world brought me to great weariness and upended all my options that the ineptness of my strength and worldly ways was revealed.

We often think we depend on God, when in reality it is nothing but an assumption. Until we are tested by that which is out of our control, we will never know whether we are standing on the shifting sands of nonsense or the eternal Rock of ages.

Prayer: Lord, we are deluded about our spiritual standing. We fail to realize the sands of self-sufficiency must be pulled out from underneath us for us to realize that our standing is not really on You after all. Send in the waves of testing until I am grounded on You. Amen.

December 5

"And if any man think that he knoweth any thing, he knoweth nothing yet as he ought to know "(1 Corinthians 8:2). When I became a Christian, I was so enthusiastic about Jesus, I could never imagine

not having faith towards Him. I was immaturely swinging from various branches of zeal that was setting me up for a big fall.

I must admit eventually I hit a real crisis when it came to my faith. I was confused and felt a great blanket of depression come over me. I knew I held the answer to my plight, but I had never been brought to the place where God was the only solution left to address my pathetic state. I was at a crossroads. Either I needed to exercise faith by believing upon God and His Word or I needed to go into unbelief while maintaining some impression of my Christianity.

A mere impression may keep others from knowing one's vulnerability. It will also cover up the fact the person will have no real victory to declare in the end, revealing the ineptness of that individual's inability to overcome the slavery brought on by the failure of never looking up in recognition of God and actually exercising unfeigned faith towards Him.

Prayer: Lord, we always like to think we have faith but unless we are brought to the place where You are our only solution, we will never see how we are still dependent on the ways of the flesh and the world. Lord, I want to choose the way of faith no matter how hard it is on my pride to face how inept I am in all matters. Amen.

December 6

"Thus saith the LORD: Cursed be the man that trusteth in man, and maketh flesh his arm, and whose heart departeth from the LORD" (Jeremiah 17:5). In the last couple of posts, I have been talking about faith. This verse in Jeremiah shows us that the trust factor is a matter of the heart.

We are told in *Romans 10:9-10* that we are to believe the Gospel in our heart to be saved and even though trust is a matter of faith, it also involves that part where if one does not really trust the character of the individual, they will harbor suspicion and doubt, and eventually stray away from them. They will be unable to walk out their faith in confidence.

We see that if one departs from trusting the Lord in their walk of faith, it is because they have made a choice to put their reliance on something else. Remember when it comes to the heart, a person can't serve two masters at the same time. This is true for dependency.

The focus of our heart comes down to what or who we put our hope in. The intensity of that hope will determine our level of devotion. When we put our hope in man and his ways after "supposedly" trusting God, we will depart from the Lord being our source to pursue the life we think is available in the flesh.

It is clear that man's source of reliance will determine the quality of his life here. If he depends on man, he not only will be disappointed and disillusioned, but he will put himself under a curse where everything will eventually fall apart and prove to be vanity, bringing misery to his soul and vexation to his spirit.

Prayer: Lord, there is no hope in this world, and no answer will be found in man's best or greatest attempts to make life count for something. You alone are THE answer and our only hope to experience any kind of life here. Amen.

December 7

"Blessed is the man that trusteth in the LORD, and whose hope the LORD is" (Jeremiah 17:7). "Blessed" points to an attitude of contentment. Another word for it is "happy."

We must note that cursed is the man that trusts in man. The concept of curse comes down to the type of environment that will be produced in rebellion, as well as unbelief that will prove to be anything but beneficial. There will be oppression, failure, despair, and misery. In the end hope is nowhere to be found, and all will prove to be vanity.

It is for this reason Jeremiah made it clear that real satisfaction in this life is experienced when one puts their full trust in the Lord. It is natural for us to put our hope in what we see; whether it is the arm of flesh, which includes ourselves, our leaders, or even governments, but to do so is to come under a curse of misery and despair. One source of reliance will prove to be foolish, while the other one will reveal wisdom.

We must repent of misguided dependency and once again know that our only hope is found in the Lord. We need to stop our foolish reasoning and independence and make the choice to trust the Lord with our whole hearts, and by faith and obedience come into line with what His Word says about such matters.

Prayer: Lord, as believers, we imagine and hope we are totally dependent on You, but trials often prove that such thinking is a fantasy. Lord, I choose to trust You because You never lie and You keep Your Word. Amen.

December 8

"And Jesus said, Somebody hath touched me: for I perceive that virtue is gone out of me" (Luke 8:46). Through the years I have greatly valued those times the Lord touched me. I have felt such things as His gentleness to comfort, His power to heal and revive, and His firmness that comes with some chastisement. Those times are what have made the greatest impression on my life.

When I come to the incident of the woman who had the issue of blood, I am reminded of how vital it is for me to not just touch the Lord, but to take hold of Him. This brings me to a very important point when it comes to the example of this woman. The intensity behind me taking hold of the Lord comes down to how desperate I am to possess His solution.

Consider the plight of this woman. She had this medical problem for 12 years. Because of it, she could not enter places of worship for she was considered unclean (*Leviticus 15:19-27*). It is clear her life was far from "normal" for her. In many ways she was isolated by something that was beyond her control. It also was clear she sought help from man, but man's means and methods could not address her plight. In fact, such means leave a person in a greater state of hopelessness that becomes a boiling pot where utter desperation will occasionally spill out in despair.

Prayer: Lord, we need to touch You and be touched by You. However, we are too busy being an observer in the crowd. We may see how You feed the hungry and heal the sick, while missing that we have need to encounter Your touch in a personal way to experience what we have need of to follow You. Amen.

December 9

"But unto you that fear my name shall the Sun of righteousness arise with healing in his wings (fringes)*; and ye shall go forth and grow up as calves of the stall."* (Parenthesis added.) The woman with the issue of blood sought out her only hope and that was Jesus. What she grasped were the borders, fringes, or "wings" of His prayer shawl.

These fringes represented the Word of God. It is clear she didn't simply touch the fringe of His shawl, but she took hold of it to such a point that Jesus felt the very virtue of healing leave Him.

Genuine faith works from the premise of desperation that comes out of the awareness there is no other hope to be found but in the Lord. It will take hold of what God has said and promised and not let it go until the Lord takes note of it from His very throne. Many suspect that this woman was grabbing a hold of the promise of God when she grabbed ahold of His fringes.

How desperate are you for God to step on the scene and touch you. The woman with the issue of blood gives us valuable insight. This woman walked away from the Lord healed because of her faith that had been embroiled in a crisis. Keep in mind she was the one who stood up, pursued Jesus through crowded obstacles and grabbed a hold of Him for herself.

It is our tendency to whine, display self-pity, and become angry and embittered over the obstacles before us, the storms that never let up, the losses that abound, and challenges of our life, instead of rising up to seek out the Lord and truly take hold of Him for ourselves.

Prayer: Lord, we often miss it because we are looking down in despair, looking around in desperation, and focused on the bitter taste life leaves us. Thank You for walking in our midst at the right time so we can take hold of Your promises by taking hold of You. Amen.

December 10

"Glory ye in his holy name" (Psalm 105:3a). What are you seeking? If you are truly searching for something by pursuing it with everything in you to obtain it, you are doing it because it is in your heart to do so.

This brings us down to your real commitment. What are you committed to, to ensure that you obtain or possess what is within your heart? The truth is that our searches will come down to what our heart desires. We may not even know what that desire is, but our soul is restless to secure it, our spirit remains lean while we struggle to find it, and our emotions make us feel like we are on some roller coaster because they never can land on what is sure. It is in this type of spiritual environment that discontentment reigns, self-pity seethes beneath the surface, anger simmers, and misery is the byproduct.

This brings us to the goal of all searches. It is about securing some type of glory that will bring distinction to the meaning of our existence, our way of life, our way of doing, and our heart aspirations. The Bible is clear that the only One who deserves such distinction, attention, and adoration is God, our Creator.

God's glory penetrates all darkness. It subdues all other types of glory, and in the end, it will be the only glory that will stand in judgment, withstand in storms, and continue to stand when all hell comes against it.

Our great potential is to reflect the glory of the only begotten Son of God. Until we reach the fullness of our high calling we will twinkle like the stars. One minute His glory will be seen by others in our lives, while there will be times the light of His glory will be at such a distance that they can't see the light. However, just because they can't always see it doesn't mean it has ceased from shining in hearts and through lives.

Prayer: Lord, Your light is eternal and can't be snuffed out. It may seem too far away, but it can quickly draw close once we decide to focus on it. Thank you for Your faithfulness. Amen.

December 11

"...let the heart of them rejoice that seek the LORD" (Psalm 105:3b). There are various distinctions in the world that catches our eye or our imagination. Since everything in this world is temporary, the glory attached to any part of it begins to fade. The light becomes dim and the reflection somewhat blocked. When it is blocked that is when the flesh is in the way, and when it becomes dim it is because the world is taking us out of the way.

Regardless of the world's attractions, we must keep the Lord ever before our eyes. It is a discipline and that discipline is highlighted by the word, "let." Let your heart or let your mind be in a certain way or place. I must release my heart to rejoice in seeking the Lord, knowing what brings great delight to the heart is awaiting me. I must let my mind be focused on what is significant to keep in the right way.

Keep in mind, searching is about discovering, finding, and obtaining something. When it comes to Christianity and walking it out by faith, discovery points to finding the unexpected and miraculous. When it comes to finding the unexpected, you will secure what has been promised you and when it comes to obtaining what has been promised, it points to satisfaction.

As believers, the desire of our heart should be to ever seek the Lord. I know that when the Lord is the one sitting on the throne of my heart, that I will seek Him out above all other attractions that the world can tempt me with. I will seek to find Him in every storm, know Him when all is shaking, and possess Him so that in the end I will joyfully abide in the One who truly holds and possesses my heart.

Prayer: Lord, we have many attractions in this world that lead to nowhere and will leave us empty. However, when I seek You out with my whole heart, I am assured that You will be found by me and I will encounter Your glory that will make sense out of my searches in this confusing life, in this dark age, in this doomed world. The promises are before me, knowing You are our true portion when it comes to our heavenly inheritance. Amen.

December 12

At this time of year, we tend to remember and think about our family times. I have memories of camping and fishing. Camping back in the 1940's and 50's, when I was a kid, was a lot different than it is today.

Back then, on our trips from Seattle to the Bitterroot Valley in Montana my parents and I may have been "cramped" together in a little bitty tent, but we sure weren't "cramped" in a designated, government-controlled "campground." No way would my dad ever pay hard-earned money to pitch a tent with scores of other campers when there were miles of forest alongside the two-lane highway for hundreds of miles where one could pull off the road somewhere and find just the "right spot" to camp.

Therefore, I have no clue as to where we were when, in the middle of a pitch-dark night, something woke my parents up making scratching noises on the tent. Panic hung in the air as my parents whispered back and forth while "shushing" me to be quiet.

"Bear" is one word I remember hearing as my dad grabbed his ever-ready big pistol, and a flashlight. The scratching noise quit as soon as he exited the tent, and all my mom and I were aware of was the light from his flashlight bouncing around in the darkness.

Finally, Dad returned unscathed and announced that all it was, was a chipmunk that had been running up the tree we camped under, then jumped off onto the top of the tent so it could slide down and repeat the process. I remember thinking to myself how I wished I had been able to watch that cute little forest creature amusing himself in such a manner.

Now, in today's world, it's worth noting that there are times when we hear things that sound ominous and threatening. Maybe such sounds are not as harrowing as hearing a bear roar in your ear, bombs exploding, sirens wailing, or people screaming, but let's face it, certain words can be worrisome, disturbing, and downright fearful at times even though they really don't amount to anymore than a "chipmunk" size lie, rumor or bit of propaganda that scratches its way into your environment via some "news" source.

When this occurs, your "weapon" and the "light source" for your soul, is God's Word. *"And they overcame him by the blood of the Lamb, and by the word of their testimony; and they loved not their lives unto the death" (Revelation 12:11). "Behold, I give unto you power to tread on serpents and scorpions, and over all the power of the enemy: and nothing shall by any means hurt you" (Luke 10:19). "Thou wilt keep him in perfect peace, whose mind is stayed on thee: because he trusteth in thee" (Isaiah 26:3).* – J. Haley

Prayer: Lord, our imagination always plays tricks on us. It can make chipmunks into bears and humanize You and make You small in some way so people do not have to rightly regard You, properly worship You, and with all their heart serve You. Forgive us for letting our feeble, perverted imaginations define You. Amen.

December 13

"He must increase, but I must decrease" (John 3:30). I believe in something called "regressing in order to progress." In short man must lose his influence in the lives of Jesus' sheep so those who are seeking can progress forward in the life they are called to. Every denomination has its limitations depending on leadership and politics, and it is not uncommon for believers to hit the unseen ceiling that consisted of man's emphasis and influences. In one church I was given a good foundation, in another I learned about operating in gifts, and in another I was being prepared as a soldier to stand.

However, when I consider today, the one big question I hear the most is "What church can I go to?" I must admit, I don't know what to tell them. The Bible is clear that the sheep will scatter, and the reason why is because they can't hear the voice of the Shepherd, Jesus.

We hear the voice of our Shepherd through the pure, anointed preaching and teaching of the Word and through adherence to the pure doctrine that ensures us the will of God is and will be carried out. The Holy Spirit must be present to ensure purity in service and worship and to stir up those asleep, convict those in sin, and expose those with other agendas.

The truth of it is there has always been "Lone Rangers" such as the prophets. They walk according to a different drumbeat (the voice of God) in light of a higher calling that brought them out from the normal religion of their day to seek what was excellent to fulfill that calling.

If you are on a journey to discover your complete life in Christ, you have probably found yourself to be a "Lone Ranger" on more than one occasion. Don't let the critical voices of religion deter you. You keep listening for the voice of your Shepherd. He will not lead you astray.

Prayer: Lord, we must not let the voices of our age keep us from listening for Your voice. If we are Your sheep, Your voice is the only voice that matters. Speak on Lord and may my heart be stirred up by Your voice, my ears be attentive to Your voice, and may I never lose focus of You so that I can't hear Your voice. Amen.

December 14

"My meditation of him shall be sweet: I will be glad in the LORD" (Psalm 104:34). One of the main themes of the New Age is "meditation." However, the difference between meditation in this verse and the one the New Age presents entail a different spirit and focus.

Psalm 104:34 tells us what we must meditate on. It is not a theme, a religious notion, spiritual experiences, or religious affiliations or beliefs. We are to meditate on the person and work of our Creator

God. It is from the foundation of who God is that meditation becomes a point of heavenly inspiration, expectation and revelation.

If we start with who the Lord is, we are inspired to reach higher and higher for He is eternal. If our thoughts land on His marvelous ways, our expectation will put out its wings to soar in them. And, when we finally obtain a greater revelation of Him, we become like an eagle that will only settle for the heights of God and not the base valleys of human limitations, practices, and worldly understanding.

When it comes to New Age Meditation, you are encouraged to empty your mind and wait to see what inspirations come to you. Note, if you do not start out with the right foundation to test and discern a matter, anything will go. It is important to point out that there is no foundation to such godless meditation. At this point one opens themselves up for a wrong spirit, such as an anti-Christ spirit, to easily enough come in and erect a different God and Christ that will seem more real to the individual than the one presented in the Bible.

Prayer: Lord, we are surrounded by the foolishness of liars, heretics, wolves, and despots. We need Your abiding protection, but we must love Your truth and discern the spirits in our midst and the times we live in. Amen.

December 15

"These are murmurers, complainers, walking after their own lusts; and their mouth speaketh great swelling words, having men's persons in admiration because of advantage" (*Jude 16*). Jude warned the saints in his epistle that certain men had crept in among them without them being aware of their wrong spirit and evil designs.

We tend to believe in labels, titles and degrees without testing the spirit. If we fail to test the spirit and fruits of a person, we have no real barrier in place to protect the vulnerable from the wolves.

Sadly, there are New Age practices in operation in the church. These practices have come in under the guise of "exercise" and developing greater spirituality. There are those who are trying to warn Christians, but they are often accused of being judgmental, intolerant, and unloving. To those who are involved with these practices, they perceive themselves as being capable of not buying the error that is behind such movements, but the problem does not rest with intellectually separating earthly matters from the spiritual but recognizing the spirit behind it.

We must keep in mind that when it comes to the battle that takes place between the flesh and a wrong spirit, the flesh will eventually succumb to it. The only protection we have when it comes to a wrong spirit is to test it, separate ourselves from it, flee to God and stand on His Word and abide in His authority, knowing that in the end every one of His enemies will be put under His feet.

Prayer: Lord, our intelligence blinds us to our ignorance about spiritual matters, our pride blinds us to our vulnerability, and our self-sufficiency blinds us to the foolishness still present in our character that treats those things contrary to our wrong way of thinking with a casual attitude. Lord, forgive us for our stiff-neckedness. Amen.

December 16

"Finally, brethren, whatsoever things are true, whatsoever things are honest, whatsoever things are just, whatsoever things are pure, whatsoever things are lovely, whatsoever things are good report: if there be any virtue, and if there be any praise, think on these things" (Philippians 4:8). In my first years of being a Christian, I was encouraged to memorize this Scripture. At the time I did not know how important a role it would play in my life until later. When it comes to Scriptural meditation it will come down to trained thoughts and not unbridled imagination.

To open our minds up to something and wait in silence without having the right foundation and focus is to empty them so that whatever comes in will write on our imagination strong impressions through experiences that will become more real than God's Word. Once the imagination is taken captive by something that is seductive, these beguiled individuals will be like those at the Tower of Babel, *"...and now nothing will be restrained from them, which they have imagined to do" (Genesis 11:6b).* In their mind, they can't imagine how they could be wrong or that they can't make it come true because it is supposedly from God.

The problem with unbridled imagination is that it will exalt itself against the knowledge of the true God. It will pervert truth, twist what is honest, justify what is wicked, profane what is pure, and cause that which is beautiful to become confusing and dark. Sadly, such an imagination will invade every aspect of how people see a matter. In the end of the last days, man's darkness will be as in the days of the Noah, *"that every imagination of the thoughts of the heart was only evil continually" (Genesis 6:5).*

Our thoughts must be inspired by a godly foundation that will direct and discipline our focus to ensure the right conclusion about matters. When it comes to our thoughts as Christians, they are a result of thinking on that which is true and what has been established by God's Word. These thoughts must adhere to honest meditation about what is real and what is unacceptable to God. They must be just in their handling of matters, pure in their motives, as well as lovely, becoming, or beautiful in light of God's estimation of the matters at hand. In the end, it will end with a "good report" when it comes to one's life and testimony.

The beauty about *Philippians 4:8* is that when you add all the virtuous qualities together, they all point to Jesus Christ. Clearly, we must think and meditate on Him for He is the absolute truth to all things pertaining to life and godliness.

Prayer: Lord, we don't need to let our imagination run wild to find some semblance of purpose or hope to this life. All we need to do to avoid the confusion, rabbit holes, and the abyss is to think and meditate on You and on what Your Word says about You. Amen.

December 17

"Remember his marvellous works that he hath done; his wonders, and the judgments of his mouth" (Psalm 105:5). In previous posts I talked about meditation. We must realize that meditation is a

discipline that determines what we think on to gain perspective, inspiration and revelation.

Such meditation will have a source in which to draw from and it is the source that will determine the quality of meditation. It is for this reason that to open the mind to "whatever," instead of first disciplining its focus, is dangerous. We must be sure the spirit in which we operate in is the Holy Spirit who will guide us into all truth about Jesus and teach us about those things to come, but we must make sure the source and focus of our meditation is the Lord.

In this Psalm we are told what to remember. It is in meditation we will choose what we remember in order to direct our thoughts. We are told in *2 Corinthians 10:3-5* to avoid letting our imagination define who God is; rather, we are to bring every thought into captivity in obedience to Christ. Once again, we see the necessary discipline to ensure meditation that is heavenly inspired.

This brings us to what we need to remember in our meditations and that is God's marvelous works, His wonders and righteous judgments. When we meditate on God's works, we are reminded of His power and when we meditate on His wonders we are reminded of the miraculous and when we think on His judgments, we will remember His judgments are righteous. His righteous judgments also point to His transparent holiness that will expose all uncleanness to purge and sanctify it for His use and glory or consume it in judgment.

Prayer: Lord it is up to us to remember who You are so we can meditate on that which will inspire us heavenward as we consider all of Your marvelous Works and glorious ways. Thank You for providing us with the means in which we can meditate upon You. Amen.

December 18

"Beloved, now are we the sons of God, and it doth not ye appear what we shall be: but we know that when he shall appear, we shall be like him; for we shall see him as he is. And every man that hath this hope in him purified himself, even as he is pure" (1 John 3:2-3).

Have you ever thought about what you shall be when this part of your earthly journey is over with? After all, as believers we are supposed to be preparing to reach that ultimate goal of what we have been designed and called to be.

Through the years I have related calling to doing, and my potential to reaching some great height in ministry, but I have learned that my calling reaches far beyond doing. When it comes to my potential, it involves that which reaches beyond the best to what is better which will lead to that which is excellent. However, to get beyond doing, I must test the spirit or intent behind what I am doing. If I settle for anything other than what would be coming from a pure heart to God, I will miss the target.

When I consider any type of service to God, I must make sure it is a matter of ordained works that He has set forth in His Word before the foundation of the world, or they will be considered profane works to Him. The truth of the matter is if I am not willing to consecrate all for the glory of God, I will end up throwing mere crumbs at a holy God who calls for and deserves that which is the best. The best only comes out of unfeigned faith that manifests itself in obedience to His Word.

John tells us that even though we may not know how we shall be when our journey is over, we must remember that we start from the position of being His children. As children we have been imputed with a "spiritual DNA" that comes with possessing the life of Jesus in us. We know we do not belong to this world and that our inheritance is heavenly and eternal (*1 Corinthians 15:46-49*). We must realize that with His life we are a spiritual man that has a calling to walk in the Spirit as He leads and guides us, and not a fleshly man, driven by carnal, lustful ways.

The whole purpose of the great work of God in us is to conform us to the image of His Son. We get glimpses of the glory of His Son by the Spirit through His Word, but it is limited. We are looking through the limitation of the flesh, but one day the flesh will fall to the side, and we shall see Him as He is and when we do, we will see His image upon our life being reflected back to Him.

The question is are you being conformed to the heavenly man or are you remaining an earth-bound person that may be religious, but will not have any heavenly distinction in your life?

Prayer: Lord we are used to walking according to the flesh, but our spiritual birth identifies us to the heavenly. Lord, I desire to reach my calling and potential by being conformed to Your image so when I stand before You, I will be a mere reflection of You. Amen.

December 19

"Thou wilt shew me the path of life: in thy presence is fulness of joy; at the right hand there are pleasures for ever more" (Psalm 16:11). What does it mean to please or delight God? The first thing we must note is that to please another, we must put aside what will please us and focus on the one we desire to please.

One of the main reasons for pleasing anyone is to honor them because of love. We know that faith is what pleases God. Those who believe God, walk after His Spirit and in obedience to His Word will bring great pleasure to Him.

David understood that the Lord had to show him the path to walk. We know that the Word of God is the lamp unto our feet that will guide us each step along the way, but we must believe it is true. It is a map that clearly defines the path of righteousness, but we must Scripturally identify it in this world by focusing on the One we are to follow. And where will this path lead us: Into the presence of the Lord.

Oh, how we need His presence to enfold us in rest, establish us in communion and prepare us for the terrain ahead. The terrain can be wrought with steep places. There are enemies along the way that want to rob, kill, and destroy, as well as unseen forces that want to hinder us. We must be aware of and watch out for the various temptations and traps of the age that want to thwart any advancement.

However, note what is in the presence of God: the fulness of joy. How many realize in the fruit of the Spirit, love and joy come before peace? How many are seeking peace because they have not received God's love and as a result, know no joy?

Prayer: Lord, we want joy without knowing peace. We want peace without knowing the reconciliation that comes out of love. Lord, we have it backwards, but Your sacrifice on the cross shows us the proper order. It begins with love on the cross, learning peace that comes through reconciliation and hope so in the end when the morning comes there will be rejoicing. Amen.

December 20

Christians love to sing "I've got a mansion, just over the hilltop" while picturing in their mind an exquisite architectural wonder, all pristine and bright surrounded by perfect landscaping, crystal clear streams, fragrant flowers, green pastures and woodlands that never fade away. Or something similar to satisfy their own personal tastes and desires.

While all that may be a lovely, but temporary, mental escape from our present reality, the question is, is the "mansion over the hilltop" we've all heard about for most of our lives really a huge estate in heaven that we can only dare to imagine? Thanks be to God, if we believe it's just that, based on *John 14:1-3*, then we're wrong! The truth is it is far, far greater.

Historically, in the days of King James, a "mansion" meant a room in a big, fancy house, not the house itself. Since we haven't seen heaven, we like to equate the most beautiful and the best we can see on earth to be somehow what is waiting for us to move into when we "fly away." The meaning Jesus was conveying to His disciples is that there is plenty of room with God. He was not referring specifically to heaven, because our God is omnipresent. He is everywhere.

The Bible tells us that not even *"heaven and earth"* can contain Him (*1 Kings 8:27; 2 Chronicles 6:18-21*). In the Old Testament God's "house" or "dwelling place" refers to places where God's presence is manifest such as the temple, or even the whole creation, or universe.

"Lord, you have been our dwelling place in all generations" (Psalm 90:1), and *"He that dwelleth in the secret place of the most High shall abide under the shadow of the Almighty" (Psalm 91:1).* (*See also Psalm 71:3; Deuteronomy 33:27; Psalm 31:20.*)

What Jesus was conveying to them, and to us, is that it is about the Person, not the place. Therefore, the only person in whom we can find perfect peace is Jesus Christ—the Prince of Peace and Lord of the Sabbath, our place of perfect rest. – J. Haley

Prayer: Lord, we equate what is unimaginable with things that we understand but will prove to be inferior and insulting in the end. Lord, we may try to imagine the unseen world of Your presence, angels and perfection, but we can't begin to comprehend its beauty, its wonder, and its glory. Amen.

December 21

"There is no fear in love; but perfect love casteth out fear: because fear hath torment. He that feareth Is not made perfect in love" (1 John 4:18). Many people make determinations based on fear of something and end up living in insipid worlds of fear. They fear losing their small sense of control over their world without realizing that fear controls them. They fear circumstances instead of God. They fear death and thereby fail to embrace life. They fear losing aspects of the world but not their soul. In the end they live in a world of paranoia, where they can't see anything but FEAR.

Fear is worship of the god of this world, Satan. The altar of it is lies and the power of it is found in the imagination. Fear is magnified by all the reasons for its existence. You have the endless parade of the "whys" or possibilities of what could go wrong, and the "what ifs" surrounding the unknown.

Those who worship it fail to see the big "I" that sits in the middle of the word "sIn" and the vowel that rides high while forming the word "prIde." Both fleshly tyrants must have their way, according to their terms to make sure everything turns out in alliance with their fears and concerns, or there will be "heck" too pay.

Such fear is what makes their realities so fragile that there is no reason to it or reasoning with it. Everything must bow down to one's particular fear as they cower before its sick demands as its darkness permeates the environment it creates. Because fear is all consuming, demanding, and controlling, it is clueless to the many fruits it produces in others: resentment, anger, bitterness, frustration, and hopelessness.

However, for the most part, the person does not care about what it does to others because they must keep their fear from tormenting and driving them. Others must bow to it and do all they can to please it to keep it from proving to be the wimp it would prove to be in the light of God.

Fear is opposite of faith and is a product of unbelief. Fear's main goal is to magnify itself in such a way that faith towards God can't take hold. It wants people to bow before it to keep them from taking steps of faith to discover it is nothing in light of God. It wants to keep others subject to it so they can't know the freedom that comes in the Spirit.

Fear's biggest fear is that the one will discover that faith knows how to walk through it because of God's great love shown in redemption. It knows how to soar high above it because faith is not subject to it, and it will overcome it because the person no longer believes its lies. Instead of bowing before fear's insipid tactics, it will replace all of them with the promises of God's Word.

Prayer: Lord, I know the oppressive power of the lies of fear, but I also know the power of Your life, Spirit and Word that enables me to see through it, above it, and around it in order to walk through it. Amen.

December 22

"For even hereunto were ye called: because Christ also suffered for us, leaving us an example, that ye should follow his steps" (1 Peter 2:21). Jesus' life on earth is our example of what we must be willing to do to do the Father's will.

It takes faith, obedience, and complete submission to God's plan, will, and way to complete the course in front of us. You may have the best intentions, but without the conviction of the Holy Spirit, and the willingness and resolve to lose it all to gain Christ, you will end up choosing the base way. Granted, you might have zeal at first to do it God's way, but if you do not have a willing, humble spirit and the firem conviction and resolve to lose all to gain all of God's best, your flesh and carnal way will win out.

Your pride will get caught up in the mix and somehow justify that whatever becomes your desire or pursuit. You will think you deserve it since you have the right to secure it for your happiness. You will be convinced that you can't do without it, or that God will understand in the end. However, He will not understand because He came from the glories of heaven to give His best on your behalf, to give it all for your redemption, and as a result, He is worthy of like commitment from each of us (*Philippians 2:1-11; 3:7-10*).

We are not here to get our way. God is not some Santa Claus or Sugar Daddy at our beck and call to see that we have our way so all will be "well in our soul." Others are not here to carry out our way so we can remain comfortable and aloof to those around us. Life is not present to make sure we end up getting our way so we can sit back in ease.

We are mere clay, the dust and dirt of earth, that God as the Potter must conform to the life of Christ. We are a mere pawn to the world that can be used and sacrificed accordingly, and a dispensable slave to Satan. Our choice never comes down to having our particular way, but what master will have His way in our life. The master will come down to who we serve and what we decide to please—the lust of our flesh or our righteous Lord (*Romans 6:8-20; Hebrews 11:6*).

Prayer: Lord, we want our way because we don't trust Your way to comply to our way, and rightfully so, for we have such a high opinion of what we think we know, we become foolish in our limited ways. Lord, forgive us for wanting and trying to be God in our small insipid worlds. Amen.

December 23

The spirit of man is the candle of the LORD, searching all the inward parts of the belly" (Proverbs 20:27). Right now, there are various celebrations going on that include lights. How important is light?

We know without LIGHT there would be no LIFE. The life we have in us is determined by the type of light we are walking in. Jesus warned us that our light could be darkness, that of ignorance, delusion, and death.

Notice how *Proverbs* states that the spirit of man is the candle. Spirit has to do with breath and fire. Without air there is no fire. The Holy Spirit provides both the air that ensures interaction with the Lord and the fire that points to some type of warmth, as well as that which lights the way.

For the believer that warmth has to do with God's attributes and work. He is love that burns with commitment. Like the burning bush in the wilderness God's fire will never consume that which He has ordained. For the downtrodden soul, His mercy sends a fresh wind of relief, His grace soothes the soul, and His compassion serves as a balm to those who have been battered by the elements around them.

Even though I have brought this up in the past there are three main spirits in operation. There is the spirit of the world, which is Satan, the natural spirit of the "old man," and the Holy Spirit. The spirit that we walk in will determine whether we are a dark candle with no light, a smoldering candle with no fire, or a lit candle that gives off light because the Holy Spirit is the breath within us who causes the fire of devotion to take hold in our hearts.

We are told that the candle of our life is what the Lord uses to search the inward parts of our soul to expose our character. The light points to the truth of His Word, which circumcises anything that would defile us. It will also take away the blinders hindering our sight, open the ears to hear, and prepare us to walk through the prison doors that have been opened by hope.

What does your light say about your life when it comes to the matters of heaven?

Prayer: Lord Your light is what graces the life of Your people. Your light exposes all that is not of You or that would not be beneficial in our walk with You. Lord, the lights of the world will always grow dim and eventually not be seen at all, but Your light is forever and thank You for gracing my life with the gift of Your life. Amen.

December 24

"Saying, Where is he that is born King of the Jews? For we have seen his star in the east, and are come to worship him" (Matthew 2:2). What are you seeking? We know the story of the three wise men, also known as the Magi who sought out a King. They were learned men who knew how to read the signs in the sky. Guided by one star, and a sincere conviction to honor this new king, they traveled with an entourage at least 1,000 miles to find this new king.

Keep in mind they did not have planes, but traveled by some beast, mainly camels. We know that their journey to find Him was a long one. What was their goal: to worship this new King and honor Him with gifts.

Just as the star guided them, a heavenly host appeared to the shepherds in the field. Clearly, the Magi was not the first to worship Him. Those who come first to seek out the Savior are like the shepherds, who are considered the outcast, the insignificant of society.

This new king was taken to the temple so that Simeon, who had the promise from God that he would see the consolation of Israel, their Promised King and Messiah, would be there at His dedication. We must not forget Anna, a prophetess who had fasted and prayed for decades in the temple, and after seeing Jesus, was one of the first to go out and tell those of Israel that redemption had come to Israel.

For the most part many missed the great activity of God coming in humanity to walk among us, even though there are also many who testified that He had indeed come. Sadly, few believed and responded. There are many that may hear about Him, but few seek

Him. There are even those who have a brush with Him, but do not see what consolation He can bring to their sin-laden souls.

At this time, we have much ado going in religion and the world that will amount to nothing in value or significance. Like so many years ago, there are those who are missing the signs of the times, failing to take heed to the declarations, and believe the testimony of the Promised One dying on the cross. They remain lost, blind, and miserable.

Are you seeking something because nothing makes sense in this world? My affirmation is that in my search over four decades ago, I was found by Him. The key is that you must be seeking Him with your whole heart.

Prayer: Lord, we have so many priceless examples of what it means to find You, but there are many that have no concern for their soul, no urgency when it comes to the times, and unaware of the storms on the horizon. Oh Lord, how foolish we are, how blind we are, and how we are like the sheep ever being led to some slaughtering pen of the world. Amen.

December 25

"But when the fulness of the time was come, God sent forth his Son, made of a woman, made under the law" (Galatians 4:4). What is in a day? How much credence does God put on a day? I try to consider time in light of God and His timing. We are subject to time, and it plays an important part in us trying to keep track of certain events but when it comes to God, He is not subject to it.

Eternity is not marked by time; therefore, events are not really subject to a certain day; rather the environment of the times will determine the intervention of eternity into the matters of earth. It is for this reason we are reminded of the request in what we refer to as the Lord's Prayer, *"Thy kingdom come, Thy will be done in earth, as it is in heaven" (Matthew 6:10)*

For example, in the fullness of time God sent His Son. This meant everything was in place for Jesus to be inserted into history as a child to be revealed as the only begotten Son sent by God to redeem us according to the law. There are times the Creator inserted Himself into history to address certain matters. We refer to such days as the day of His visitation.

We know about the day of the Lord when great trouble will befall Israel, which will affect the whole world. We also know that the first Pentecost was to serve as a sign we were entering into the last days. We have been made aware that God set different days apart for people to celebrate certain events such as the feasts, as well as rest from labors in order to consider Him and what He has done for them as in the case of Sabbaths.

As believers we must choose what we settle for when it comes to our life in Christ. Do we settle for the scraps at the table or for the bread and meat of heaven? Do we settle for shadows or the revelation from heaven? Do we fight over bones that may have a bit of marrow of truth, doctrine, or facts, or do we want to partake of the full meal deal of God's complete counsel? Do we want to get as much as we can out of broken cisterns of man's best, or do we desire what is better and excellent, and like Paul ever press towards it.

We have a choice as to what we pursue and ultimately settle for. I have settled for the scraps, the shadows, and the bones while missing the full meal deal. There is a bit of nourishment in the scraps, little consolation in the shadows, and disappointment when left with the bones. However, when I let go of what I thought I had, and by faith sat up at the table of His Word to allow the rivers of Living Water, the Holy Spirit to impart, direct, and feed me, I left edified, satisfied, and full.

Prayer: Lord, we often chase after what proves to be least while missing what has substance. I must admit in the past I have become weary with the least, and as a result had to come to terms with what it means to be filled daily with Your Spirit who will fill me to overflowing with Your life. Amen

December 26

"And the LORD said unto Moses, and rehearse it in the ears of Joshua for I will utterly put out the remembrance of Amalek from under heaven. And Moses built an altar, and called the name of it Jehovah-nissi" (Exodus 17:14-15). It is important for us to remember the feasts and Sabbaths were mere shadows that pointed to Christ. The spring feasts pointed to Jesus' great work of redemption and the fall feasts remind us He is coming back to complete all matters concerning heaven and earth. Sabbath pointed to Him being our true Sabbath.

Since we are creatures of time, it is natural for us to try to mark events with time. We want to make sure we are on time, hit the target and are not late or left behind. As I considered these matters, I realized that man also inserted into history certain markers such as in the case of Hanukah for the Jewish people. In some cases, the Bible refers to them as memorials. One of the greatest examples of a memorial in churches is the ordinance of Communion. In fact, Mary's preparation of Jesus for His burial serves as our memorial today.

There are other examples of memorials. For example, at the first victory of the children of Israel in the wilderness, Moses marked it with an altar that also served as a visible memorial of what would prove to be prophetically true. In *Joshua 22:10-34*, the tribes of Reuben, Manasseh, and Gad erected an altar called "Ed" which means "witness", to remind them and the other tribes on the other side of the Jordan they were part of Israel.

At this time, we have marked this particular season to remind us that Christ came into the world as a baby, clothed in humanity, a Son that was ordained by His Father to become a Passover Lamb. For the most part our memorial begins with a cross that points us backward to God becoming incarnate and forward to Him coming back as the Great light in the darkness of grave evil to establish His kingdom and set all things right as King and Judge.

As John stated in *Revelation 22:20* after Jesus stated He will come quickly, my heart once again responds, *"Amen, Even so come, Lord Jesus."*

Prayer: Lord, may the altars of our heart be cleansed by consecration, our lives a reflection of You, our heart aflame with love for You, our cries and supplications incense that pleases You, and our ways a testimony of Your abiding greatness. Amen.

December 27

"And the children of Reuben and the children of God called the altar Ed: for it shall be a witness between us that the LORD is God" (Joshua 22:34). We have been talking about memorials. They are erected to cause us to pause and remember the sacrifice, price, or situation that they are marking with their presence. The problem with man is he can get caught up with the technicality of a matter and fail to see the memorial that has been established by another person.

The tribes on the other side of the Jordan were ready to go to war with the three tribes that had erected the witness until they found out what the altar stood for. It is easy to do because man often perverts what is of God to give his activities credibility, exploit them by calling them religious, use them to justify traditions of the world and abuse them for his own self-serving purpose to promote personal agendas. It can be all so confusing for those who are trying to get it right in their own mind.

The question is how can man keep a matter straight in his own walk before the Lord? To me the key comes down to establishing a personal memorial. God is not caught up with the time but the purity in which an event or happening is approached. If a believer wants to insert a memorial to remind themselves of something that is sweet and very personal to them as to their life and walk with the Lord, it is not up to others to discourage and judge it as being wrong and insignificant.

I have erected such memorials, and every time a certain time of the year comes along, I pause at it, remember what event occurred and appreciate the great significance of it, especially if it has to do with God's intervention in my life or His insertion into history to bring forth His glorious plan of salvation in my life.

Prayer: Lord, we have been told about Your intervention in history on behalf of man but how many of us have erected our own memorials to remember what You have done on our behalf? Lord, You have marked my life with much and I can't begin to mark them all with some memorial, but I have them in my life because You have established many such events that have become memorials to me. Thank You. Amen.

December 28

"When I was a child, I spake as a child, I understood as a child, I though as a child: but when I became a man, I put aways childish things" (1 Corinthians 13:11). Who do you naturally look to when you are in trouble? Even though both of my parents are gone I still tend to want to run home to them for solutions when life becomes overwhelming. I grew up knowing that if I was in over my head, I could seek their advice or help, even though they were limited in what they could do.

As you have surmised, I am no longer a child. I had to grow up. Growing up is not determined by age or intelligence; rather it is based on how one learns to face responsibilities in life. I remember when a man told me his parents wanted him to get married and have a family so he would "grow up." Apparently, even in his mid-twenties, he was still young and foolish.

To many, life is a theme park and not a serious exercise that requires them to face life head on, recognizing that regardless of age or status, life will eventually challenge their level of maturity. To maneuver the road ahead requires moral preparation to face the curves of uncertainty, the crises of losses, the disillusionment of disappointments, the anguish of betrayals, and etc.

Sadly, there are those who never "grow up." They console themselves that since they are old enough to be an adult, they must be one. As long as life goes their way, they are alright but when life begins to challenge their comfort zones, they begin to look around for someone to ride in on a white horse and save them from having to walk through it. Whether they are looking to family, friends, government, and etc., they avoid making the choice to grow up while bitterly resenting walking through any deep valley that challenges their character. And if they are Christians, test their faith.

I knew that I needed to grow up regardless of how others may have wanted to protect me from my foolishness. I made terrible decisions, but they were mine and I knew I had to face them if I was ever going to grow up and take my part in life, society, and the Church.

Prayer: Lord, none of us grow up graciously. We often resist wise advice, fight against what challenges us to come higher, and end up missing the mark in the end. How foolish we often prove to be towards You. Amen.

December 29

"Give us help from trouble: for vain is the help of man" (Psalm 108:12). In our tendency to avoid deep valleys and pits, we tend to look to others to save us. As believers, we should never be looking to mankind in one form or another to step in to spare us of having to become mature in our Christian life. We must face and walk through the valleys regardless of how dark and long they prove to be.

Spiritual maturity buds and blooms when faith towards God is activated to face life for what it is. As we choose to trust the Lord in every deep, dark valley and canyon, we learn to turn to Him quickly and put our dependency on Him.

As a child it was natural to look to my parents and as a teenager my parents made it easy for me to seek them out for guidance. However, I knew as an adult if I was to mature in my attitude, thoughts and ways, I had to face the fruits of my decisions. I knew if I was ever to grow up, I needed to learn to stand on my own as I faced life for what it was.

Now I am a believer and in order to learn dependency on the Lord, I first had to become child-like in my faith, and before I could grow up in the Lord, I had to recognize the foolishness of my flesh and the vanity of the world. As I matured in my Christian walk, I had to remember as a child of God I am weak. As one who desires to grow, I must leave foolishness behind and become wise enough to recognize my great need for the presence of the Lord in my life. When it comes to coming to full age in my Christian walk, I had to develop more grace, love, and kindness by relying totally on His faithfulness to meet me and His goodness to ensure the quality of my life.

Prayer: Lord, we like starting out as babes seeking nourishment in Your doctrine as we develop the strength to walk by learning Your Word. However, when it comes to standing in battle, running in a marathon, and enduring the storms of life, we like to skip it, and yet it is at such times we learn You are faithful and will never leave nor forsake us. Amen.

December 30

"Be still and know that I am God: I will be exalted among the heathen, I will be exalted in the earth" (Psalm 46:10). Many of us know this verse. It is important to put it in the right perspective. The reason we are spiritually still is to know in our spirit that God is God, and that we are not God. Part of meditation is learning to be still before the Lord so that He alone is exalted above all that is happening in our lives. When He is exalted the sacrifice of praise will take flight, the attitude of worship will usher us into His presence, and the sweet joy of communion will be the fruit that comes forth, greatly benefitting our lives and bringing glory to God.

What does it mean to be still? To be still is to be quiet before the Lord. You are waiting in this quietness of soul until God reveals Himself to your spirit in greater ways that will produce godly results.

Isaiah 32:17 states, *"And the work of righteousness shall be peace; and the effect of righteousness quietness and assurance forever."* Perhaps the revelation that comes out of quietness will cause greater appreciation for who God is, or it might bring necessary instruction to you concerning a matter. At such a time your mind is very attuned to hear what the Spirit has to say to you, knowing that He is establishing you on what is true and eternal.

To hear from God in meditation is not a supernatural experience but a significant event. The reason I say this is because for many they are seeking an experience in their time of meditation and not seeking God to know Him. The wrong meditation often causes one to worship their experience instead of coming out with a greater sense of awe towards God.

When you meditate on God, it will greatly impact how You perceive Him. You might gain clarity as to the principle or truth He is trying to convey to you. This clarity can bring assurance to the way you must walk to be in line with His will and purpose for your life.

Keep in mind the Bible is clear that we are to test all spirits. This means when we perceive that the Holy Spirit is revealing something to us, we still must avoid assuming it is Him; rather, we must test our attitude and what is being revealed to us with God's Word to confirm if it is the Holy Spirit. The Spirit of God will never step outside of His Word, will never steer us wrong about who God is, will not lead us astray from the truth of Christ, and will not leave us flying high in some false reality about our Creator.

To me the most wonderful part of being still before the Lord is the peace that comes with it. To be still means I am looking for a secure place that I can land on, while the quietness of soul means I have landed, and the peace I sense means I am now secure in the true place of refuge and communion to hear what the Spirit is saying.

Prayer: Lord, we seek peace but miss it because we want to fly above this world and not learn to walk by faith through it. We want supernatural experiences, but it does not make us spiritual people who properly discern what is truly of You. Lord, I just want You. Amen.

December 31

If you live in America and decide to start reading the tags and labels of your clothes, shoes, kitchen items, appliances, and "what have you" that you own, you just might begin to feel like the whole country has been invaded and subtlety taken over while you weren't looking. Not only are almost of the products that Americans buy made in some foreign country that most of us couldn't find on a map, but there is a definite decline in quality ranging from vehicles clear on down to toothpicks.

I'm old enough to remember the days when such things as houses, cars, appliances, shoes, cookware, and clothing were made in America and were designed to last for years—and some for a lifetime! Sadly, those days are long gone, and today the world that children grow up in is mostly all "plastic."

Anyone who uses a computer knows that they will end up paying for upgrades or will need to purchase a new computer because, as our tech friend told us recently, "It all has 'planned obsolescence' built into it." As maddening as that is, my instant thought was, you could say that about the entire human race. And, not only humans, but every living thing on this planet has a beginning and an end, at least as it pertains to life on this earth.

Everyone knows that their "expiration date" is an established fact, so either consciously or unconsciously knowing this causes people to make decisions about their own existence and how they want to live their life. Even if they manage to amass a fortune in gold in order to escape a shabby existence comparable to cheap plastic, there is still an expiration date in the end.

Everyone who owns a Bible, and reads it, doesn't need to guess which decisions people make that succeed and which ones don't. After all, the Holy Bible is a record of all the different decisions people made from Adam down through the ages and even into the future, and it faithfully records the end results of those decisions. Nevertheless, in spite of all the warnings in Scripture concerning the dangers of "serving two masters" or the destruction of the "broad way," or the fact that there is no profit in selling your soul to gain the whole world, people still decide to ignore all the warnings and, in agreement with Frank Sinatra sing, "I did it my way."

The Apostle John wrote, *"And the world passes away, and the lust thereof: but he that doeth the will of God abides for ever" (1 John 2:17). "Heaven and earth shall pass away, but my words shall not pass away" (Matthew 24:35).* And Jesus said, *"And, behold, I come quickly; and my reward is with me, to give every man according as his work shall be" (Revelation 22:12).* – J. Haley

Prayer: Lord, just like the end of this year and the beginning of a new year, we know that time on the earth speaks of that which is temporary and passing. All things in this age will expire, but those who believe upon You will simply leave their bodies behind and enter eternal bliss. Thanks for the promises in light of the expiration dates of this world. Amen.

Other books by Rayola Kelley:

Hidden Manna (Original)
Battle for the Soul
Stories of the Heart
Transforming Love & Beyond
The Great Debate
The Journey of a Lifetime (Author's Autobiography)
Post to Post: (1) Establishing the Way
Post to Post: (2) Walking in the Way
Post to Post: (3) Meditations Along the Way
Post to Post: (4) Inspirations Along the Way

Volume One: Establishing Our Life in Christ

My Words are Spirit and Life
The Anatomy of Sin
The Principles of the Abundant Life
The Place of Covenant
*Unmasking the Cult Mentality

Volume Two: Putting on the Life of Christ

He Actually Thought It Not Robbery
Revelation of the Cross
*In Search of Real Faith
Think on These Things
Follow the Pattern

Volume Three: Developing a Godly Environment

Godly Discipline
Prayer and Worship
Don't Touch That Dial
Face of Thankfulness
ABC's of Christianity

Volume Four: Issues of the Heart

*Hidden Manna (Revised)
*Bring Down the Sacred Cows
The Manual for the Single Christian Life
Parents are People Too

Volume Five: Challenging the Cristian Life

The Issues of Life
Presentation of the Gospel
*For the Purpose of Edification
*Whatever Happened to the Church?
*Women's Place in the Kingdom of God

Volume Six: Developing Our Christian Life

The Many Faces of Christianity
*Possessing Our Souls
Experiencing the Christian Life
The Power of Our Testimonies
*The Victorious Journey

Devotions

Devotions of the Heart: Books One and Two
Daily Food for the Soul: Books One and Two

Gentle Shepherd Ministries Devotion Series:

Being a Child of God
Disciplining the Strength of our Youth
Coming to Full Age

Nugget Books:

Nuggets From Heaven
More Nuggets From Heaven
Heavenly Gems
More Heavenly Gems
Heavenly Treasures
More Heavenly Treasures

Gentle Shepherd Ministries Series:

The Christian Life Series

What Matter Is This?
The Challenge of It
The Reality of It

The Leadership Series
Overcoming
A Matter of Authority and Power
The Dynamics of True Leadership

Books By:
Jeannette Haley

Books co-authored with Rayola Kelley:
Hidden Manna (original)
The Many Faces of Christianity (Volume 6)
Post to Post 3: Meditations Along the Way
Post to Post 4: Inspirations Along the Way
Post to Post 5: Collecting Gems Along the Way

Other Books:
Rose of Light, Thorn of Darkness
Interview In Hell} (Volume 7)
Interview On Earth} (Volume 7)
(Both Interview Books are now in one book
Angelus Assignments)
The Pig and I
Reflections of Wonder (Devotional)

Children's Books:
Little Stories for Little People
Traveler's Tales
The Adventures of Zack and Mira
The Adventures of Paul and Dana
(A House on the Beach)
The Monster of Mystery Valley

*Books that have been separated from the volumes and are now available under their own titles.

www.ingramcontent.com/pod-product-compliance
Lightning Source LLC
LaVergne TN
LVHW020646110826
845149LV00012B/1930